EPIGRAPHS IN THE ENGLISH NOVEL 1750–1850

For Mum and Dad, with my love

EPIGRAPHS IN THE ENGLISH NOVEL 1750–1850

Seducing the Reader

Corrina Readioff

EDINBURGH
University Press

Edinburgh University Press is one of the leading university presses in the UK. We publish academic books and journals in our selected subject areas across the humanities and social sciences, combining cutting-edge scholarship with high editorial and production values to produce academic works of lasting importance. For more information visit our website: edinburghuniversitypress.com

This book is freely available on a Creative Commons CC-BY-NC-ND licence thanks to the kind sponsorship of the libraries participating in the Jisc Open Access Community Framework OpenUP initiative.

© Corrina Readioff 2023, under a Creative Commons Attribution-NonCommercial-NonDerivative licence

Edinburgh University Press Ltd, The Tun – Holyrood Road, 12(2f) Jackson's Entry, Edinburgh EH8 8PJ

Typeset in 10/12.5 Adobe Sabon by
IDSUK (DataConnection) Ltd

A CIP record for this book is available from the British Library

ISBN 978 1 3995 1604 4 (hardback)
ISBN 978 1 3995 1606 8 (webready PDF)
ISBN 978 1 3995 1607 5 (epub)

The right of Corrina Readioff to be identified as the author of this work has been asserted in accordance with the Copyright, Designs and Patents Act 1988, and the Copyright and Related Rights Regulations 2003 (SI No. 2498).

CONTENTS

Acknowledgements	vii
Introduction: The Importance of Reading Epigraphs	1
1 Epigraphs in Mid-Eighteenth-Century Didactic Fiction: William Chaigneau, Sarah Fielding, and Jane Collier	14
2 Transcending Boundaries with Epigraphs: Ann Radcliffe	33
3 From Innovative Paratext to Satirical Stereotype: Charlotte Smith, Matthew Lewis, and Eaton Stannard Barrett	64
4 Mottos, Masks, and the Historical Novel: Sir Walter Scott	90
5 From Romance to Realism: Catherine Gore and Elizabeth Gaskell	116
Conclusion: A New Understanding of Epigraphs	153
Appendix	157
Notes	172
Bibliography	203
Index	225

ACKNOWLEDGEMENTS

And every praise so much your due,
Flows genuine from her heart.

Mary Robinson, 'An Epistle to a Friend' (1775), ll. 5–6

The research upon which this book was based could never have been completed without the generous financial support of the University of Liverpool and the Arts and Humanities Research Council North West Consortium Doctoral Training Partnership. Their assistance enabled me to concentrate all my energies upon my research during my doctoral studies, and the award of an Honorary Fellowship from the University of Liverpool following my graduation afforded me the opportunity to complete my dissertation's transformation into this book. I am most sincerely grateful to both institutions for enabling me to pursue my passion, and for allowing my work to reach deeper and further than would otherwise have been possible.

My warmest gratitude is for my two excellent doctoral supervisors, Greg Lynall and Matthew Bradley. Their advice and encouragement during my time as an undergraduate at Liverpool helped give me the confidence to believe that this was an interesting and worthwhile area of investigation, and it was a privilege to be able to complete my thesis under their expert guidance. I am tremendously indebted to them for their wisdom, enthusiasm, and continuing support of my work and career. My most grateful thanks also go to Marcus Walsh, a tutor, mentor, colleague, and friend, who is largely responsible for turning me into a researcher in the first place, and whose wisdom and guidance are always invaluable. In one of the first undergrad lectures I attended he recommended the class to 'read, read, read', advice that I have been sedulously following ever since.

I have received so many insights and suggestions, and so much generous assistance from colleagues throughout the field of literary studies that listing any risks accidental omissions, but I should like to express particular thanks to Paul Baines, Jennie Batchelor, Elaine Chalus, Emma Clery, Daniel Cook, Val

Derbyshire, Christine Gerrard, Matthew Grenby, Joseph Hone, Karen McAulay, Andrew McInnes, Hannah Moss, Lynda Mugglestone, Nazan Osman, Manushag Powell, Adam Rounce, Ruth Scobie, Mark Towsey, and Hazel Wilkinson. I am likewise sincerely grateful to the editorial team at Edinburgh University Press and their two anonymous readers, whose thoughtful suggestions and attention to detail have helped so much with the final stages of the writing process, and to my superb copyeditor, Eliza Wright, whose careful attention to detail has been invaluable.

The data survey that backgrounds much of this work could never have been so extensive or so rigorous without the kind assistance of many librarians and archivists around the world, including: Anne Causey (Albert & Shirley Small Special Collections Library, University of Virginia); Anthony Tedeschi (Alexander Turnbull Library); Lorna K. Kirwan (Bancroft Library, Berkeley Library, University of California); Naomi Saito (Beinecke Library); Krzysztof Soliński (Biblioteka Narodowa); Jeanne André (Bibliothèque nationale de France); Jo Maddocks, and all the staff at the Bodleian Library; Jay Moschella (Boston Public Library); Wallace Kwong (British Library); Kim Jones (Bruce Peel Special Collections, University of Alberta); Vicky Clubb (Cadbury Research Library, Birmingham); Emma Yandle (Chawton House Library); Natasha Lyandres and Holly Welch (Hesburgh Libraries, University of Notre Dame); John Overholt (Houghton Library); Stephen Tabor (Huntington Library); Julie Ramwell (John Rylands Research Institute and Library); Amy Kimball (Johns Hopkins University Library); Lynne Farrington (Kislak Center for Special Collections, Penn Libraries, University of Pennsylvania); Maureen Damiano (Myrin Library, Ursinus College); Jill Gage (Newberry Library); Elizabeth Denlinger, Timothy Gress, Kyle R. Triplett, and the General Research Division Team (New York Public Library); Barbara Bieck (New York Society Library, Special Collections); Amanda Watson and Charlotte Priddle (New York University Library Special Collections); Willa Anderson (Redwood Library and Athenaeum); Kristen Nyitray (Stony Brook University Special Collections); Emma Sillett (Trinity College Library, Oxford); Maxwell Zupke (UCLA Library Special Collections); Emerald Brampton-Greene (University of Bristol Arts and Social Sciences Library); Francesca Baseby, Daryl Green, and Stephen Willis (University of Edinburgh Library and University Collections); Nicola Howorth, née Kerr (formerly University of Liverpool Sydney Jones Library); Mary Sackett (University of Sheffield Special Collections); and Hannes Schwarzendorfer (Universitätsbibliothek Augsburg).

I am especially grateful for the friendship and support of my academic siblings and fellow early career researchers Anna Burton, Rita Dashwood, Alice Monter, and Ann-Marie Richardson. Their support, enthusiasm, good advice, and positivity have been an enormous help and encouragement in so many ways. My warmest thanks also go to the wonderful friends whose kindness,

ACKNOWLEDGEMENTS

thoughtfulness, and true friendship brighten and enrich my world so much, in particular Cara, Esther, Grace, Jessi, Katie, and Shalina, and my amazing brother Nathan.

Finally, my greatest thanks and love are for my incredible Mum and Dad, who have supported and encouraged me for so long and in so many ways. I am truly blessed in their love and support, and if I have achieved anything at all it is their unwavering faith in me that has made it possible.

INTRODUCTION: THE IMPORTANCE OF READING EPIGRAPHS

> I have tagged with rhyme and blank verse the subdivisions of this important narrative, in order to seduce your continued attention by powers of composition of stronger attraction than my own.
>
> Walter Scott, *Rob Roy*[1]

Written from the perspective of the hapless and poetically inclined hero Frank Osbaldistone, Walter Scott's classic Scottish epic *Rob Roy* (1818) is anything but dull. In a novel loaded with political intrigue, disguise, deception, imprisonment, and family conflict, the implication that the reader may require additional stimulus seems surprising to say the least. But what may seem false modesty from Scott, who had in any case composed around a fifth of the epigraphs in *Rob Roy* himself, only enhances the authenticity of the characterisation of the artistically disappointed Frank (whose passion-project translation of Ariosto's *Orlando Furioso* is both unfinished and long since abandoned at the end of the book). Conscious of his own literary limitations and afraid of losing his reader's attention, narrator Frank promises his audience the consolation of occasional nuggets of exemplary verse. It is therefore not a little ironic that such epigraphs are very often skimmed or skipped altogether by modern-day readers. The reasons for this vary from impatient enthusiasm to find out what happens next in the prose narrative to a simple lack of understanding of the context or significance of a given quotation. Even when scholarly editors include a note identifying the source of a quotation, the interpretative value of the text in its epigraphic location is rarely glossed.

The first time I remember encountering epigraphs in literature was as an eleven-year-old reading Elizabeth Gaskell's *North and South* (1854), and these short quotations puzzled me precisely because I was not sure how I was supposed to read or interpret them. Included just below each chapter title, the epigraphs appeared to occupy a strange transitional function: did they belong to the title or to the text, or were they something else altogether? Unaware of the context of many of these quotations' sources and eager to discover if the heroine Margaret Hale would ever realise what a nice fellow self-made Lancashire mill owner Mr Thornton actually was, I hurried on with the story. But my fascination with the purpose of these quotations remained and I began what turned out to be a long and difficult search to find out what this intriguing device was even called. When I finally discovered the term 'epigraph' buried in the introduction to an Oxford World's Classics edition of Ann Radcliffe's *The Mysteries of Udolpho*,[2] the next inevitable questions were: when did writers first begin to use epigraphs? And what is the function of an epigraph? Do quoted epigraphs always rely upon the context of their original source? And how does this affect the reader's experience of the text? Perhaps still more importantly, why does an author include an epigraph at all? This book is my attempt to answer these questions.

So far the most important scholarship upon the range of possible functions for epigraphic quotation is contained in Gérard Genette's landmark study of paratextual material, *Paratext: Thresholds of Interpretation*. Here Genette writes:

> The most powerful oblique effect of the epigraph is perhaps due simply to its presence, whatever the epigraph itself may be: this is the epigraph-effect. The presence or absence of an epigraph in itself marks [. . .] the period, the genre, or the tenor of a piece of writing. [. . .] The epigraph in itself is a signal (intended as a *sign*) of culture, a password of intellectuality. [. . .] With it, [the author] chooses his peers and thus his place in the pantheon.[3]

Genette identifies just three possible functions for the pre-chapter epigraph: (1) to comment upon the ensuing prose or a preceding title, (2) to modify or be modified by a title, or (3) to reference a specific author by quoting them. Yet this definition forms only a small part of a much wider investigation into the collective purpose of paratext, and Genette is himself quick to identify some of the limitations of his assessment, for example his focus upon French literature.[4] Nonetheless, Genette's survey of epigraphic paratext has become the touchstone for all subsequent references to epigraphic purpose in English literary research. In particular, emphasis is usually placed upon his concluding judgement that the ultimate function of epigraphs is as a 'password of intellectuality'. Specific analysis of epigraphs has typically, and perhaps in some ways appropriately, occurred around the edges of other investigations. Whilst exploring the relationship between epigraphs and narrative voice in George Eliot's *Middlemarch* (1871–72), for example, Michael Peled Ginsburg reaches just a little beyond Genette's definition to suggest that '[t]he use of epigraphs establishes a relation between the text and a past tradition'.[5] In a rare piece positioning epigraphs within a wider Romantic fascination with mottos and quotation, Rainier Grutman even suggests that '[m]ottoes brought particular literary works into circulation, and as such were good publicity for their authors, who could return the favour by quoting the writers that had previously quoted them', although specific examples of this in practice are not provided.[6] In a later article on a similar theme, Grutman adopts a more nuanced approach and notes that epigraphs may constitute 'a form of commentary', with the potential to even 'lead us astray, much like unreliable narrators'.[7] Like Genette, Grutman attempts to categorise epigraphic functionality, yet the very many possibilities offered by this form of paratext – as numerous and varied as the creative possibilities of the texts which they preface – defy easy summary.

So far the most detailed analyses of epigraphic quotation have typically occurred within examinations of Gothic and Romantic fiction. Gary Kelly identifies the pre-chapter quotation as 'an outside border for the narrative and all that it contains', describing it as a means through which the prose text may be 'hedged, framed, or marked off with bits of "serious literature"'.[8] Writing specifically of Ann Radcliffe's epigraphs, Edward Jacobs notes her use of 'pointedly canonical texts', suggesting once again an iconographic rather than an interpretative function.[9] However, there has been a growing shift towards appreciating the textual and contextual nuances of epigraphic texts, with Leah Price suggesting that these fragmentary verse interruptions 'force readers to pause and withdraw from the action at regular intervals' and even that the plot itself becomes demoted 'to a filler for the instices between verse epigraphs, snatches of oral lore, and excerpts from antiquarian documents'.[10] Kate Rumbold's study of the relationship between Shakespeare and the eighteenth-century novel likewise identifies the potential of '[n]arratorial epigraphs' in Gothic fiction to 'create suspense and atmosphere', whilst simultaneously inviting narrative comparisons with the plots of texts quoted (in particular the Shakespearean texts upon which Rumbold's study focuses).[11] Yet the necessarily limited focus of these investigations likewise limits their usefulness as a means of understanding the broader purpose of the pre-chapter epigraph.

In these analyses we see only how the Romantic epigraph functions at a static point; to appreciate the significance of the epigraph as a literary device, it is essential to examine its development over time and to explore its functionality within different genres of literature. My study aims to consolidate our understanding of the function of the epigraph, building upon these previous definitions to construct a more detailed comprehension of the epigraph as a textual rather than a primarily decorative, visual feature. Here, the epigraph will be approached with the presumption that it is a piece of text which is expected to be read, and that possesses the same potential for interpretative value as the prose to which it is prefixed. This will be supported via an examination of broad historical trends in the gradual development of the device, from its emergence as a paratextual feature of the novel in the eighteenth through to the mid-nineteenth centuries.

Various terms have been used to refer to paratext that occurs at the start of a chapter and which is neither a chapter title nor a pragmatic summary of the ensuing chapter. Writers of the eighteenth and nineteenth centuries, such as Walter Scott and Elizabeth Gaskell, typically refer to them as 'mottoes', whilst early twentieth-century critics such as Tom Haber and Matthew Whiting Rosa favour the appellation of 'chapter-tags' or simply 'tags'.[12] More recently, Genette refers to them as 'epigraphs', and this is the term that I have chosen to adopt here, since it encompasses a broader range of interpretive possibilities than the term 'mottos' and provides the distinction from chapter titles which the term 'chapter-tags' lacks. Here, the term 'motto' will typically only be used when referring to text presented on the title page and that is not in itself a part of the book's title or publishing information; when referring to quotations prefacing individual issues of early modern journals; or when quoting directly from contemporary references to epigraphs.

Somewhat confusingly, Genette conflates both title-page mottos and pre-chapter quotations within the term 'epigraph', a practice that has been replicated by numerous subsequent scholars. Exploring the literary context for Eliot's use of epigraphs, Eike Kronshage refers to Ann Radcliffe's *The Mysteries of Udolpho* (1794) as a text that 'contains not only a book epigraph, but continuous chapter epigraphs'. Janine Barchas's monograph exploring paratext and the material book follows the implication of Genette's survey to claim that '[t]he epigraph [. . .] disappears from the mature novel's title page' before it 'moves [. . .] predominantly into the central text of the gothic and historical novel'.[13] As examples of this trend, Barchas lists Radcliffe's *Udolpho*, Matthew Lewis's *The Monk* (1796), 'and the many novels of Sir Walter Scott';[14] yet in fact both Radcliffe's and Lewis's novels, together with the majority of Scott's prose fiction, feature title-page mottos as well as pre-chapter epigraphs. It is thus certainly not true that the pre-chapter epigraph was a re-emergence of the title-page motto, since the two frequently appear simultaneously; title-page mottos also appear in English fiction considerably earlier than the pre-chapter epigraph. Despite superficial similarities, the two devices do not appear to be developmentally interdependent, and consequently they merit separate investigation. The term 'pre-chapter quotation' is similarly fraught with complexity. Victorianist Sudha Shastri describes the epigraph as 'originat[ing] from an author and text different from the one in which it officiates as an epigraph', presenting the act of quotation as an integral characteristic of a pre-chapter epigraph.[15] Yet this definition does not take into account instances where chapters are prefaced with self-authored paratext, many of which occur in the works of authors most strongly associated with the device (for example, Radcliffe, Scott, and, later in the Victorian era, Eliot). For the purposes of the present

INTRODUCTION

investigation therefore, a chapter title has been defined as a short appellation prefixed to a section of prose text, whilst extended summaries of a chapter's content have been considered to be chapter descriptions (a related but not identical category). All other forms of pre-chapter paratext, whether quoted or not, in verse or in prose, have been considered to be epigraphs.

Whilst various estimates have been made concerning the origins of the epigraphic quotation in the English novel, most Romanticists typically credit Radcliffe with being the first canonical writer to use the device; when discussing Charlotte Smith's use of the epigraph, Stuart Curran offers the more cautious suggestion that '[a]t some point late in the century it became fashionable to ornament the chapters of fiction with verse'.[16] Since library catalogues and bibliographies do not record this kind of paratextual information, no substantial body of data has existed upon which to rest a more precise judgement.

Traditionally, pre-chapter epigraphs have also been identified as a comparatively short-lived phenomenon of Romantic fiction, with Edward Jacobs suggesting that 'after the Romantic period [. . .] chapter epigraphs became relatively rare, with most novels instead bearing chapter titles or tags'.[17] There has been a scholarly tendency to assume that the epigraph disappeared from use after the Romantic era, something that Kronshage identifies as a stylistic indicator that 'mark[s] the difference between romantic fiction and [. . .] realist writing', citing as examples of realist writers 'Austen, Balzac, Dickens, the Brontë sisters, Thackeray, Trollope, Flaubert, and Zola'.[18] My study will challenge this presumption that the epigraph died with Walter Scott, demonstrating that the epigraph continued to flourish throughout the Romantic and early Victorian periods. To support this claim I have assembled a survey of the pre-chapter paratext of as many works of English prose fiction published from 1740 to 1850 as it was possible to gain access to. The statistical results are represented in the Appendix, and the case studies presented in each chapter have been selected primarily based upon trends indicated by this analysis. The foundation for this survey has been derived chiefly from four main bibliographic sources: Andrew Block's *The English Novel, 1740–1850*; Peter Garside, James Raven, and Rainer Schöwerling's *The English Novel 1770–1829*; a digitally published additional supplement to Garside, Raven, and Schöwerling's bibliography covering the period 1830–36; and Troy J. Bassett's digitally published work-in-progress *At the Circulating Library: A Database of Victorian Fiction, 1837–1850* <http://victorianresearch.org/atcl/index.php>.[19]

Garside, Raven, and Schöwerling's survey (together with the supplement) has been used as the primary source for the years 1770–1836, whilst titles listed in Block's bibliography have provided the basis of the analysis from the years 1740–69, and 1837–50; titles from this last fourteen-year period were cross-checked for accuracy with Bassett's database. Works listed in the appendices of *The English Novel* have not been included, since Garside, Raven, and

5

Schöwerling had classified these works as only 'representative examples' of various types of publication deemed 'not to represent novels in the sense required for entry in the main listings' contained within the bibliography. These typically incorporate subgenres of fiction, such as tales written specifically for children, as well as 'reissues of earlier publications or translations later than the first English translation'.[20] As the purpose of my investigation was to construct a broad sense of the use of epigraphic quotation in general prose fiction rather than to provide a definitive catalogue of all works published with epigraphs, I felt it would be appropriate to keep these forms of prose fiction outside the parameters of my analysis. Novels that appeared twice in the same year under different publishers' names (and that are typically listed under the same number by Garside, Raven, and Schöwerling, separated into tabulated sub-records) were counted only once, to limit the risk of skewing the data model unduly; however, this kind of situation occurs only rarely. In accordance with Garside, Raven, and Schöwerling's approach, anthologies of stories have been incorporated within the definition of novels; this is largely because omitting such anthologies would have likewise necessitated the removal of publications in which two stories are presented within one published work, such as Walter Scott's *Tales of My Landlord* series. This might then have risked unfairly skewing the data model by excluding shorter narratives that have since been accredited the status of individual novels (for example, Scott's *The Bride of Lammermoor*, originally published as one of two stories in *Tales of My Landlord*, Third Series, 1819). However, where anthologies of short stories feature a prefatory quotation to each story but not elsewhere in the text, this has not been counted as a use of epigraphic quotation. Anthologies were included in the survey only where one or more of the stories feature a clear division of the narrative into sections (usually but not always given the appellation of chapters) and where some or all of these sections have been headed with a quotation or lines of verse or prose not readily identifiable as a chapter title or description. In the vast majority of cases, first editions have been consulted (i.e. the first published version of a text), or in a very few instances contemporary facsimile or scholarly editions derived from first editions.[21] In some cases this may not be the definitive version of a text – for example, there are some very minor variations between individual epigraphs in first editions of Scott's novels and later reprints, including the *Edinburgh Edition of the Waverley Novels* (which tends to prioritise authorial intention from the manuscripts over published text) – but since this survey was intended to establish a baseline for comprehending the spread of epigraphic usage, it was essential to adhere to a constant point of comparison.

This survey identified 6984 novels known to have been first-published between 1750 and 1850, of which 5939 were assessed for their paratextual content. The remaining 1045 could not be accessed, either because no copy is known to survive

INTRODUCTION

or because the only surviving copies are held at libraries that I was not able to access at the present time. Statisticians have established that a quantitative survey does not have to be exhaustive in order to offer a representation of a greater whole; it merely needs to be both large and random. Since my study has considered approximately 85% of novels known to have been published in this period, and since the selection of novels I was able to access was necessarily random, I believe both these statistical requirements have been satisfied. I was able to consult individual books myself via collections including the Bodleian Library, British Library, Eighteenth Century Collections Online, and Nineteenth-Century Collections Online: Corvey Collections; I am also extremely grateful to the many librarians around the world who have given so generously of their time and assistance to make this survey as complete as it could be within the timeframe of publication.

Of the 5939 novels that I was able to check, 1622 were found to contain epigraphic quotation in their first edition. A full chronological bibliography of all 1622 titles accompanies the present volume as an open access digital resource on the Edinburgh University Press website: the 'Chronology of Novels with Pre-chapter Epigraphs 1750–1850', available at https://edinburghuniversitypress.com/book-epigraphs-in-the-english-novel-1750-1850.html. Given the sheer quantity of novels that feature epigraphs, it has been necessary to focus upon only a few writers whose use of pre-chapter epigraphic quotation was particularly influential and/or experimental. Both Ian Campbell Ross and Steven Moore identify the first novel written in English to feature pre-chapter epigraphic quotation as William Chaigneau's *The History of Jack Connor* (1752).[22] Since a survey of 108 out of 122 novels known to have been published between the years 1740 and 1751 has discovered no rivals to this distinction, Chaigneau's work has been adopted as the literary starting point of epigraphic quotation in the English novel.

In a recent short investigation of epigraphs through literary history, Rachel Sagner Buurma identifies three possible influences for the 'literary epigraph', namely 'the armorial motto', the 'epigraph-like texts [that] appear primarily in sermons to introduce biblical texts for explication', and the quotations that sometimes feature at the head of periodical issues.[23] As Grutman points out, '[e]pigraphs can and do serve as "suggestive quotations" upon which the text itself expands' in a manner similar to that in which 'Bible verses provide preachers with a starting point for their sermons'.[24]

From the seventeenth to the eighteenth centuries, sermons – whether proclaimed from a pulpit or collected together in volumes – were, as Louis Locke notes, 'invested [. . .] with the interest and importance of a political discussion'. Indeed, Locke points out that before the arrival of the periodical journal, the sermon was the single point of contact that the general public had with literature.[25] Theological oratory was an artform in its own right, and from the late seventeenth into the early eighteenth centuries sermons increasingly found

7

their way into print. William Fraser Mitchell credits the Anglican Archbishop of Canterbury John Tillotson with transforming the sermon from a speech to be performed into an 'essay'; it is certainly telling that the prolific essayist and journalist Richard Steele described Tillotson as an 'Author' rather than by any clerical title when describing him as '[t]he most eminent and useful Author of the Age'.[26] From this perspective, it is also perhaps unsurprising that the prefatory quotation was to become a significant stylistic attribute of Steele and Joseph Addison's periodical journals the *Tatler* (1709–11) and the *Spectator* (1711–14). Through the visual similarity of the prefatory motto, the periodical essay format Steele and Addison pioneered appropriates a style which to contemporary audiences would have been readily identifiable with theological discourse.[27] This similarity theoretically remains a possibility throughout the epigraph's development across the eighteenth and nineteenth centuries, during which time sermons and other such ecclesiastical and theological writings persisted in popularity. Indeed, it may be for this reason that biblical quotations hardly ever appear within the epigraphic selections of novelists: the appropriation of religious texts for the purpose of popular entertainment in a literary form already regarded as morally dubious could only have exacerbated what Ana Vogrinčič describes as the 'moral panic' about young people reading novels on their own.[28]

Yet Grutman's claim that both sermons and periodicals used prefatory quotation to achieve the same effect, that is to 'shed light on the text they accompany', is not strictly accurate.[29] For a sermon is typically designed to provide accessible scriptural exegesis, and so the initial biblical quotation is always the starting point that provides the textual material upon which the ensuing discussion will focus. Direct reference to this quotation will often be made within the sermon itself, such as the claim in the expositional phase of one of Tillotson's sermons to discuss the sermon's topic of forgiveness 'from the *Words* which I have recited to you'.[30] In periodicals such as the *Tatler* and the *Spectator*, where the quotation is usually derived from classical texts composed in Latin or Greek, the case is reversed and the quotation is an afterthought rather than a preliminary. Addison confirms this when, on one of the rare occasions when direct allusion to the technique of prefatory quotation is made within the *Spectator* itself, he remarks that '[w]hen I have finished any of my Speculations, it is my Method to consider which of the Antient [*sic*] Authors have touched upon the Subject that I treat of'.[31] Even taking into account the possibility that the pseudonymous persona of 'Mr Spectator' is not necessarily the most reliable witness, the claim that the quotation is added last gains credence by the overwhelming absence of any discussion of the individual prefatory mottos throughout the vast majority of the publication itself. The issue that contained the Addison quotation featured above (issue 221) actually comprises the single longest discussion of the device ever provided within the journal. Here it is decisively stated that the selection of the quotation occurs after the prose text has been written, with Latin text being chosen to provide 'some Similitude for the Illustration of [the] subject'.[32]

Adding still more emphasis to this aesthetic difference, the biblical quotations used to preface sermons were usually listed at the beginning of sermon anthologies as 'The Texts of each Sermon'.[33] Although not initially called a contents page, this function is implied by the inclusion of appropriate page numbers for each entry. For the 1695 edition of Tillotson's Sermons the shortened sectional title repeated in the header is given as 'The Contents', further confirming the purpose of this paratextual space.[34] Thus the scriptural text assumes the distinction of a chapter title, even taking priority over other means of identifying the text, such as the details of the occasion upon which the sermon was originally preached (typically included before the commencement of each new text). Conversely, editions of the *Tatler* and the *Spectator* published throughout the eighteenth century never include any sort of contents list like this, with the prefatory quotation instead remaining resolutely fixed to the head of the individual issue: neither a title suitable for identifying the essay within an anthology, nor exactly a part of the main text.

The most probable explanation for this difference of paratextual function is as a consequence of a difference in the initial purpose of the journal mottos. The *Tatler*'s prefatory quotation remained unchanged for the first 40 issues of its life, thus furnishing the line with the character of a heraldic motto or statement of intent for the whole publication. That the quotation ever changed at all was due to the appearance of a rival journal, the *Female Tatler*, that attempted to claim kinship via both its title and its publication on alternate days to the *Tatler* (which was published three days a week). A change of motto was part of the *Tatler*'s oblique response to the new paper, initiating a brief but ferocious print war in which the prefatory quotation became a key battleground. The *Female Tatler* eventually returned to its original motto, 'sum canna vocalis' (I am the singing reed), as a guarantee of authenticity when a change of publisher prompted the original printer to produce a rival *Female Tatler* and a means of distinguishing the 'genuine' journal became necessary. The *Tatler* settled into a sometimes erratic system of quotation, with some prefatory mottos adorning short sequences of issues rather than only one issue.[35] A precedent had been set, and Steele and Addison were evidently attracted by the device's unique possibilities: after concluding the *Tatler*, their next journal, the *Spectator*, featured a different prefatory motto for every issue. By adopting what is at least visually a broadly theological format, Steele and Addison retained the moral authority of a religious work and used it to furnish their own text with an implicit confidence and strength based upon extensive knowledge of classical authorities.

The issue-specific motto was imitated by a plethora of other small journals with various levels of success; but of more importance for the history of pre-chapter epigraphs were the multi-volume *Spectator* anthologies that would form a staple of popular English literature for at least the next hundred years. The *Spectator* was no longer a serialised journal but had instead become a repository of pedagogical guidance upon a range of areas including manners, the arts, economics, and British nationhood. Presented in this way, as collections of essays prefaced with quotations, the *Spectator* visually established the concept of using mottos or epigraphs to preface sections of a text that unite to form a cohesive whole.[36] The mottos thus appeared as short didactic chapter heads, little nuggets of wisdom presented in a style ripe for imitation by authors eager to align their works with the *Spectator*'s success and thus claim some of the journal's intellectual capital. The scene was set for the emergence of the pre-chapter epigraph.

In his study investigating the relationship between classical languages and English literature, Kenneth Haynes suggests that novels with epigraphs 'do not form a coherent class of books at all'.[37] My study will attempt to reverse this supposition by assessing the epigraph's generic and functional qualities via the novels that include it. This means that many of the novels typically selected as influential and canonical within traditional narratives of the development of the English novel during the early eighteenth century will not be referred to here, since the majority of these do not feature any form of pre-chapter epigraph. Works such as Daniel Defoe's *Moll Flanders* (1721) and *Roxana* (1724) did not include chapter divisions at all, whilst the realism cultivated by Samuel Richardson's epistolary format in *Pamela* (1740) and *Clarissa* (1748) neither incorporates nor is suited to the practice of prefatory epigraphs (I have found only one epistolary novel that features epigraphs so far, *The Missionary*, Edinburgh, 1825). Even Henry Fielding, arguably the early canonical English novelist who experiments most with pre-chapter paratext, never uses epigraphic quotation and instead favours lengthy descriptive chapter titles larded with Cervantine humour. It does seem coincidental that the second English novel to feature pre-chapter epigraphs, *The Cry: A New Dramatic Fable* (1754), was jointly authored by his sister Sarah Fielding with her friend Jane Collier, and this may indicate some fascination with chapter-based paratext within the Fielding household. However, as there is no evidence to suggest that Sarah Fielding's decision to start using epigraphs was influenced by her brother, the first chapter instead pairs an analysis of *The Cry* with an investigation of the first novel in English known to have featured pre-chapter epigraphs, William Chaigneau's *The History of Jack Connor* (1752). In both novels, a morally didactic and instructive focus renders it still more likely that the influence for their use of epigraphic quotation came from sources such as the *Spectator*, a text that was already becoming established as a key educational resource by the mid-eighteenth century. A range of influences are examined, in particular the importance of Edmund Spenser's *The Faerie Queene* (1590–96) as an

INTRODUCTION

inspiration for various elements of Fielding and Collier's work, including their interpretation of the paratextual space of the pre-chapter epigraph. *The Cry* receives particular attention as an educational text aimed primarily at young women, with the range of languages represented in the novel's epigraphs thus constituting an implicit challenge to mid-eighteenth-century gender-based presumptions of linguistic knowledge.

Although Ann Radcliffe was thus not the first novelist to use pre-chapter epigraphic quotation (as has often been suggested), statistical data regarding the quantity of novels first-published with epigraphs during the eighteenth century does offer strong indications of the importance of Radcliffe's influence in catalysing interest in the device. Only 20 novels featuring pre-chapter epigraphs are known to have been first-published between 1750 and 1790, the year before Radcliffe's first novel with epigraphs appeared; although there is a slight rise in the number of novels with epigraphs first-published in the early 1790s, the number rises dramatically after 1794. In 1795, the year after the publication of Radcliffe's most famous novel *The Mysteries of Udolpho* (1794), a total of 8 novels are known to have first appeared with pre-chapter epigraphs, whilst in 1796 this leaps up to 15. The wave of enthusiasm Radcliffe instigated only continues as the 1790s progress, as there are at least 22 novels with epigraphs published each year in 1798 and 1799 (see Appendix, Table 1 and Figure 1). Consequently, Chapter 2 provides an examination of the development of the epigraph during Radcliffe's career as a Gothic novelist. Particular attention is given to her use of the device as a means of transitioning between chapters, and as a way of inducting her reader into the text. The posthumously published *Gaston de Blondeville* (1826) is also considered alongside Radcliffe's more popular novels of the 1790s, facilitating an assessment of the incorporation of self-authored epigraphs in Radcliffe's fiction as a steady process of evolution.

Analysis of bibliographic trends does confirm that the epigraph became strongly associated with the Gothic and Romantic genres following the publication of what was (at least epigraphically speaking) Radcliffe's most influential novel, *The Mysteries of Udolpho* (1794). Despite her contemporaneity with Radcliffe, however, Charlotte Smith must have already made her decision to use epigraphs in her novel *The Banished Man* (1794) before *Udolpho*'s actual publication. Smith's use of the epigraph is of particular interest since she later includes the device as an accompaniment to narratives of a more stereotypically Gothic nature, thus becoming a case study through which the rapid transition of the epigraph from experimental paratext to Gothic stereotype may be explored. Chapter 3 examines this evolutionary shift, beginning with an extrapolation of Smith's use of the epigraph. This is then complemented with an analysis of the role played by Matthew Lewis's *The Monk* (1796) in solidifying the association between epigraphic quotation and the Gothic genre. The perpetuation of these ideas through later satirical references and allusions to epigraphs in Eaton

Stannard Barrett's *The Heroine, or Adventures of a Fair Romance Reader* (1813) and Jane Austen's *Northanger Abbey* (1818) is also considered.

Analysis of Figure 1 in the Appendix indicated that the presence of epigraphs in English fiction remained strong well into the nineteenth century. Although a steep rise in the number of first-published novels with epigraphs around 1817 remains roughly proportionate to the number of books first-published, the actual percentage of new novels with epigraphs does climb steeply from about 1819/20. This peaks at 52% in 1820 and 53% in 1827, with the total yearly percentage only once dipping below 40% in this decade (see Appendix, Table 1). The explanation for this phenomenon is readily identifiable as Sir Walter Scott's Waverley novels that were published from 1814 to 1832, the majority of which feature some form of pre-chapter epigraphic quotation. Consequently, Chapter 4 investigates Scott's contribution towards the device's persistence in popularity, examining his enthusiasm for mottos in general as a way of understanding his fascination with literary epigraphs. His development of the epigraph as a means through which to promote the construction of a narratorial persona is then also explored. His initial experimentation with quotation-based chapter titles in *Waverley* (1814) is examined, alongside his more determined pattern of epigraphic quotation in later works such as *Rob Roy* (1818).

The final chapter moves beyond Scott to investigate the popularity of epigraphs during the early to mid-nineteenth century, a time in literary history when it has traditionally been assumed that the epigraph virtually disappeared. The survey provided in the Appendix indicates that epigraphic usage remained strong long after Scott's death (see especially Table 2 and Figure 2), and further investigation reveals that many of the novels in which the epigraph appears during this time are now broadly categorised within the then very popular genre of fashionable novels. The most prolific of these novelists is without question Catherine Grace Frances Gore, whose many novels published throughout a career spanning three decades almost invariably feature some form of pre-chapter epigraphic paratext. This chapter therefore tracks the initial absorption of the epigraph into the fashionable genre through works such as Edward Bulwer-Lytton's *Pelham* (1828), before focusing upon Gore's various uses of the device. In particular, attention is given to the capacity of Gore's fiction to incorporate elements traditionally associated with either the Romantic or realist genres. This study then concludes with an examination of Elizabeth Gaskell's similar use of such elements alongside pre-chapter epigraphs in *Mary Barton* (1848) and *North and South* (1854–55). Gaskell's inclination towards fictional realism makes her an especially helpful and interesting endpoint for this investigation, since it reflects a broader thematic tendency in English prose fiction at this time. Like Gore, Gaskell blends romance-based plots with a setting and perspective more strongly aligned with realism than previous novels that featured epigraphs. Through Gaskell, therefore, can be seen the moment when epigraphs transition from a stereotypically Gothic or Romantic textual feature to a device with sufficient generic fluidity to later become a key component of more iconically realist novels such as George Eliot's *Middlemarch*. By adhering to a strict chronological framework, this analysis aims to track the development of epigraphic function through the steady evolution of the literary landscape over time.

This study will demonstrate that the use of the epigraph is much more than a simple means through which to reference popular or acclaimed authors, but is in fact part of a wider process of reading and responding to previous generations of writers. As authors competed to reinvent and keep fresh the tropes and plotlines of romantic fiction, the epigraph became a key focus for experimentation with self-reflexive and sometimes self-critical narrative voices. By investigating the chronological development of the epigraph, this study will demonstrate the extent to which the history of the novel is actually non-linear, as writers continually cross literary genres to retrieve inspiration, paratextual function, and of course quoted text.

I

EPIGRAPHS IN MID-EIGHTEENTH-CENTURY DIDACTIC FICTION: WILLIAM CHAIGNEAU, SARAH FIELDING, AND JANE COLLIER

> While our former flames remain within,
> Repentance is but want of power to sin.
> DRYDEN.[1]

The above quotation appears as one of many pre-chapter epigraphs included in the anonymously authored 1760 novel *The Histories of Some of the Penitents in the Magdalen House.* The narrative explores sexual promiscuity and morality via the life stories of penitent former mistresses or prostitutes, designed to endorse a theologically Christian code of behaviour that permits forgiveness for perceived transgressions only through sincere repentance. Didactic in style, the novel's epigraphs provide a space in which to underscore a rigid moral compass. The epigraph presented here prefaces a chapter in which the young heroine is rejected by her father following her escape from domestic imprisonment inflicted by her elderly husband and his vengeful former mistress; following this rejection she finally agrees to live unmarried with the lover who has aided her flight. The quotation is a slight adaptation of a couplet from John Dryden's 'Palamon and Arcite',[2] a narrative poem based upon Chaucer's 'Knight's Tale', in which two imprisoned brothers fall in love with the same woman through the window of their prison cell. Like Arcite, the original speaker of the lines, the unnamed heroine of the tale from *The Histories* is unable to act upon her desires whilst imprisoned, but readily succumbs upon release. The epigraph therefore serves to remind the reader that true repentance requires self-denial when possession of the desired object is actually a possibility; resignation to the inaccessibility of something whilst the 'former flames [of desire] remain within' is not the same thing.

One of only 7 novels to be published with pre-chapter epigraphs between 1750 and 1760, *The Histories* is nonetheless far from being the only specimen of didactic fiction to feature the device. Most notably this genre also includes the first known example of pre-chapter epigraphs in English prose fiction, William Chaigneau's *The History of Jack Connor* (1752), a novel described by Ian Campbell Ross as 'among the best examples of eighteenth-century Irish fiction'.[3] Chaigneau's narrative follows the childhood and youth of the eponymous Irishman Jack Connor, detailing his many employments and sexual adventures as he improves his social condition from illegitimate peasant to gentleman. Numerous scholars have pointed out similarities between this novel and the picaresque prose fiction of Henry Fielding, and Steven Moore notes in his landmark global history of the novel that, like *Tom Jones* (1749), *Jack Connor* 'demonstrates that a novel can have a serious moral purpose and still indulge in sexual/textual fun and games'.[4] Indeed, it is Chaigneau's more 'serious' motivation here that links the text with other early adopters of the pre-chapter quotation, in particular Sarah Fielding and Jane Collier's *The Cry: A New Dramatic Fable* (1754).

When Fielding and Collier published *The Cry*, it was not exactly a success. Clark Lawlor writes that 'its contemporaries [found] it too allegorical, too experimental, and too concerned with abstract theories for their tastes',[5] and it never achieved a second edition, although it was reprinted in a two-volume Dublin edition by George Faulkner in the same year. It was advertised as a work '[i]n which the interesting Adventures of several Persons are related to a mixed Audience: with the Sentiments and Emotions of the said Audience on the Facts and Opinions as they occurred in the Relation'.[6] The basic narrative remains somewhat conventionally centred upon a young heroine's journey from mature adolescence through to eventual nuptial bliss; what distinguishes the text is the means through which this story is conveyed, together with the moral didacticism that its format both constructs and promotes. The majority of the plot is narrated by its heroine, Portia, under the auspices of Una (the personification of truth), and the eponymous 'Cry' (a metonymic representation of society and social comment). Portia relates her actions, thoughts, and attitudes with legalistic exactitude, and the morality of each is then rigorously debated by all parties. Although Lawlor is not alone in describing *The Cry* as a 'novel', Timothy Dykstal points out that this work actually 'mimics the structure of a Greek tragedy as it displays the essential selfishness of romantic love and the fatuous yearnings of audiences who read for it'; it is not simply an oversight that Portia 'spends more time asserting the right of women to book learning' than she does cooing over her beloved.[7]

Indeed, the extent of the text's philosophical approach is most keenly manifested through the logical dissection and rationalisation of emotion, for example when the heroine Portia claims that if she loved a man who chose to love another woman instead, 'I might indeed be grieved for the disappointment of my love, but I could not be angry.'[8] In *The Cry*, the educational and moral sentiments of the text are complemented and enhanced by the quotations that preface every 'scene' and which, it is clearly asserted in the preface, are intended to 'give a sanction to our own sentiments by those of the most approved authors' (*The Cry*, p. 43). Incorporating influences from a range of literary antecedents, such as the *Tatler* (1709–11) and the *Spectator* (1711–14), and Edmund Spenser's *The Faerie Queene* (1590–96), Fielding and Collier's use of the epigraph to emphasise a moral or educational message is nonetheless highly innovative. Together, Chaigneau's *Jack Connor* and Fielding and Collier's *The Cry* initiate the development of the pre-chapter epigraph as a technique of English prose fiction, establishing it as an essentially experimental element of morally informative discourse.

ARGUMENTS AND EPIGRAPHS

Divided into two volumes, *Jack Connor* contains 46 chapters with a single epigraphic quotation prefacing each. These are typically printed in an italic font, unlike later works that feature epigraphs, for example Ann Radcliffe's *The Romance of the Forest* (1791) and *The Mysteries of Udolpho* (1794), in which epigraphic quotations are usually presented in an upright (non-italic) font style similar to the main prose text. The use of italics in Chaigneau's novel may have been influenced by the fact that this was also the font style in which Latin quotations generally appeared at the commencement of issues of the *Tatler* and the *Spectator*, and (more contemporaneously) at the head of each issue of Samuel Johnson's *Rambler* (1750–52). However, unlike the majority of mottos used in this form of print culture, Chaigneau's epigraphs are always presented in English rather than Latin or Greek. Many are derived, as Moore points out, 'from the Scriblerians (Pope, Swift, Gay)',[9] and only 6 are direct English translations from a classical source (either Homer or Juvenal). Although Chaigneau's epigraphs are drawn from a range of approximately 17 different writers, 12 out of the total 46 are believed to have been composed by Chaigneau himself despite many of these bearing the attribution 'ANONIMOUS [*sic*]' (see Appendix, Figure 3). This supposition of authorship is supported by the fact that at least one of these verse epigraphs received a minor adjustment when the novel was reprinted as a revised edition in 1753.[10]

Paratextual experimentation was by no means unusual in the mid-eighteenth century, and Chaigneau's most obvious antecedent, Henry Fielding, had likewise explored the potential of pre-chapter paratext in his Cervantine chapter titles and descriptors. As the form of the English novel evolved, the division and framing of lengthy narratives was clearly becoming a key concern. Paratextual spaces offered the potential to comment upon a narrative from a space that was neither inside nor completely outside it, providing a unique means through which an author can attempt to influence how their work is read and interpreted. However, there are various characteristics of Chaigneau's self-authored epigraphs that distinguish them from Fielding's chapter descriptors. Most obviously, Fielding's descriptors are written in prose and typically refer directly to the events of the ensuing chapter, for example '[a] short Chapter, containing a short Dialogue between Squire Western and his Sister'.[11] All of Chaigneau's epigraphs are written in verse and allude only obliquely to the main text. No specific reference is ever made to characters within the actual narrative, and the relevance of the paratext to the main prose is typically oblique rather than directly informative:

> *The Rise, the Progress, of the human Heart,*
> *The real Honour, the Disguise of Art;*
> *The Wise, the Good, the Vicious;—all I sing,*
> *Oh Thou! from whom our ev'ry Actions spring,*
> *Not the poor Author, but the World inspire,*
> *If not the Stile,—the Moral to admire.*
> *Learn from the Child, he places in your Sight,*
> *To act with Justice, and to judge aright.*
> ANONIMOUS.
>
> (*Jack Connor*, p. 41)

In this epigraph to the novel's first chapter, various elements and influences combine to construct a reflection of the narrative's ultimate aims and trajectory. The three-line list of narrative elements and moral absolutes at the start of the epigraph finishes with the phrase 'I sing', a sentiment and structural arrangement that directly imitates the famous opening of Virgil's *Aeneid*: 'Arma virumque cano' ('Arms and the man I sing').[12] The sheer quantity of topics which Chaigneau claims to represent offers an amusing contrast with Virgil's much more concise focus. Further humour is generated by the subsequent revision of the epic tradition of invoking the muse, with Chaigneau instead calling upon '*Thou! from whom our ev'ry Actions spring*' (i.e. God) to '*inspire*' the novel's anticipated readership rather than its author. Together, these allusions might seem to suggest a bathetically humorous mock-epic narrative, and in many ways this is indeed what Chaigneau provides: the only quest with which his anti-hero is engaged is a personal journey of gradual moral and social improvement, during which he is preoccupied with satisfying earthly desires for food, money, and sexual companionship. However, the comedic intention is undercut by the final couplet of the epigraph, lines which the novel's editor Campbell Ross suggests are reminiscent of Proverbs 20:11: 'Even a child is known by his doings, whether his work *be* pure, and whether *it be* right' (King James Version). For all his bathetic bluster, Chaigneau's true intention here is to assist his reader to '*Learn [. . .] / To act with Justice, and to judge aright*' (*Jack Connor*, p. 240 n.).

The *Monthly Review* reported that the novel 'may be considered, upon the whole, as a truly moral tale', and the more recent reviewer Catherine Skeen suggests that '[t]he projects of *Jack Connor* include projects of social, civic, and national improvement'.[13] Campbell Ross addresses still more directly the union of burlesque humour and moral sentiment in *Jack Connor*, arguing convincingly that 'the fusion of the picaresque vision of instability with a Christian resignation makes the reader aware of something better awaiting the hero if Jack can only accomplish his envisaged moral regeneration'.[14]

Discussions of educational methods dominate much of the first volume, not only via the delineation of Jack Connor's youth, but also through lengthy passages describing the parental ethos of his patrons, Lord and Lady Truegood, with their sons. Aileen Douglas points out that Chaigneau even 'breaks the frame of the novel by having the schools Truegood establishes on his estate serve as models for those which were in fact established by the Incorporated Society for Protestant Schools in Ireland'.[15] The Truegoods' own pedagogical philosophy rejects education attained via 'the common Means of *Obligation* and *Duty*', instead promoting a system of male education in which good behaviour is rewarded with permission to '*learn* as much as they please', whilst the 'highest' punishment for misconduct involves the offender 'being depriv'd of their Book' (*Jack Connor*, pp. 63, 64). This prioritisation of literary knowledge as the ultimate benefit and means of moral improvement is likewise evident through the fact that it is Jack Connor's possession of, and familiarity with, the Protestant devotional work *The Whole Duty of Man* (1658) that provokes the 'Tenderness of the *good Man*' Mr Kindly who subsequently adopts him (*Jack Connor*, p. 54).

A similar emphasis upon the importance of the written word as a means of promoting social mores is likewise evident in Chaigneau's epigraphic choices throughout the novel, since in the majority of cases these epigraphs comment abstractedly upon issues that are exemplified within the ensuing prose narrative. The epigraph to chapter 5 is a good example of this:

> *There is a Lust in Man no Charm can tame,*
> *Of loudly publishing his Neighbour's Shame:*
> *On Eagles Wings immortal Scandals fly,*
> *While virtuous Actions are but born and die.*
>
> HARVEY'S JUVENAL.
>
> (Jack Connor, p. 56)

The concept presented here is then immediately developed further in the chapter's opening paragraph, as the knowledge of a '*Secret*' is likened to a contagion that 'is not of long Continuance' or widespread distribution when it 'takes its Rise from *Charity, Good-nature, Friendship, Benevolence*, or other remarkable Virtues' (*Jack Connor*, p. 56). Conversely, if a secret is of a defamatory nature then this 'Disorder increases its Force, nor does it stop, till it encounters some *new Frenzy* or *Secret*' (*Jack Connor*, p. 56). In the narrative which follows, Lady Truegood's maid confides to her the gossip arising from Mr Kindly's adoption of the young Jack Connor, and that has misidentified Mr Kindly's simple altruism as evidence of a secret, illegitimate paternal connection with the child. The epigraph thus represents an abstract truth which the narrative develops in the scenario that follows, effectively providing a prefatory moral to the new chapter. The fact that all the quotations are presented in English ensures that none of the novel's readers will be linguistically excluded from accessing this condensation of moral knowledge.

A similar approach to epigraphic quotation is adopted in Fielding and Collier's *The Cry*, an intellectually demanding text that includes epigraphs drawn from a range of around 21 different writers (see Appendix, Figure 4), and which also references a vast breadth of literary texts within the main narrative. When *The Cry* was published, Sarah Fielding was already an experienced writer and the author of 'the first children's school story exclusively about and for young girls',[16] *The Governess, or, the little female academy* (1749). Although *The Governess* was in some ways less experimental than *The Cry*, in his study of eighteenth-century children's literature Patrick Fleming identifies this text's importance as a representative of 'a new form of narrative: the moral tale', a genre distinct from other forms of extended prose narrative grouped within the broad definition of the eighteenth-century novel.[17] Repeatedly marketed as a work 'calculated for the Entertainment and Instruction of Young Ladies in their Education',[18] *The Governess* focuses upon good behaviour and moral virtue through the interaction and debates of characters in a manner that presages *The Cry*. Even the books' titles enhance the idea of a similarity of purpose, since they reflect a presumption that it is the business of young girls to mind their behaviour to avoid the reproof of their governess, while the aim of older, teenage girls should be to martial their actions against incurring the censure of society's 'Cry'. Where *The Governess* is concerned with fundamental behavioural issues of selfishness and temper, *The Cry* focuses upon the mature issues of feminine propriety in matters of love and marriage, thus assuming the character of a conduct manual for a young lady about to enter society and the marriage market. The inclusion of epigraphic quotation before each new 'scene' enhances this impression, since it presupposes a reader who is nearing or who has reached the end of their formal education, and who would therefore be able to understand, and perhaps recognise the source of, the epigraphic texts included.

In the introduction to *The Cry*, Fielding and Collier write that '[i]n an epic poem the proem generally informs you of the poet's intention in his work. He tells you either what he designs to do, or what he intreats some superior power to do for him' (*The Cry*, p. 40). In classical literature this means that a proem may be simply 'the opening of an epic poem',[19] with no decisive separation from the main body of the text; it is this form of proem that is indicated through Fielding's inclusion of the opening lines of the most famous epics of Virgil, Homer, and Milton to exemplify the device. Yet although Fielding and Collier appear to identify this type of prefatory material as the model for the 'plain prose' of their 'Introduction', the subsequent remark that this 'same method is observed by *Spenser* in his *Fairy Queen*' complicates the issue. The 'proem' in Spenser's work is typically defined as referring to any of the several stanzas of Spenserian nine-line verse included before each of the six completed books of which *The Faerie Queene* is comprised. As a structural technique, this appears to be reflected in *The Cry* by the short prose 'Prologue[s]' that precede each of the five 'Part[s]' into which the text is grouped (and which are then further subdivided into 'Scene[s]'). Continuing this pattern of structural reflection, the epigraphic quotations with which Fielding and Collier preface each new 'Scene' thus parallel the four-line verse 'arguments' with which Spenser commences each new canto of his epic.

Although A. C. Hamilton notes in his edition of *The Faerie Queene* that the proem is 'a device for which [Spenser] lacked any precedent in classical or Italian epic', he writes that '[i]n ballad metre or the common measure of the hymn-book, [the argument] serves as a mnemonic device in its synopsis of the canto'; furthermore, he links Spenser's implementation of this technique with 'the *Argomento* in Ariosto, and "The Argument" to each book in the Geneva Bible'.[20] Bible historian Femke Molekamp points out that this feature of the Geneva Bible was one of the 'interpretative paratexts' replicated in the authorised King James Version of the Bible, noting how '[i]n both Bibles the summaries are a hermeneutic mode of annotation, clarifying the scriptures for readers, and mediating interpretation'.[21] Similarly, this purpose of theological clarification and interpretation is evident in Spenser's work since, as Kenneth Boris and Meredith Donaldson Clark observe, '[b]y using four-line common meter arguments in *The Faerie Queene*, Spenser evokes English psalmic discourse and sacred song, fundamental for an Elizabethan Protestant poetics'. Although Boris and Clark acknowledge that 'most sixteenth-century editions of Italian romantic epics supplied an argument prefacing each canto', they argue convincingly that the simplistic form of Spenser's prefatory verse arguments are designed rather to 'evoke popular ballads as well as Psalmic hymns', thus 'constitut[ing] a unique poetic innovation'.[22] A similar technique appears in John Milton's *Paradise Lost* (1667), when the publisher requested Milton included a prose 'Argument' to summarise the text at the beginning of the work; yet the sense of this as an instance of pre-sectional paratextual experimentation is diminished by the fact that it was not until the 1674 version of the text that this Argument was broken up into smaller sections of prose prefacing each of the twelve books that comprise the work.[23] Yet whilst the general influence of Milton upon the development of English writing is undeniable, there is no evidence here to suggest that Fielding and Collier were consciously attempting to imitate the paratextual format of *Paradise Lost*. There are, however, numerous indications of a direct influence from Spenser's *Faerie Queene*, a major new edition of which had appeared in 1751, only three years before publication of *The Cry*. The most striking of these is the wholesale imitation of Spenser's character Una, originally the 'louely Ladie' who accompanies the Redcrosse Knight in the first tale of *The Faerie Queene* (p. 32, I.i.4) and a figure long identified as an allegoric embodiment of 'the true church' (in this context, the Protestant church).[24] Fielding and Collier acknowledge in their prologue that this central narrative figure is 'borrowed, we confess, from our master *Spenser*, for this very good reason, that we could not possibly find any other name half so adequate to express our meaning' (*The Cry*, p. 44). This also adds strength to the possibility of more abstract borrowing from Spenser's general approach to epigraphic paratext.

An understanding of the way in which Spenser's arguments are used in the construction of interpretive nuance can easily be gained through an examination of the oft-quoted quatrain that prefaces the first canto of the first book of his epic poem. To begin with, it reads very much like a chapter synopsis:

> *The patron of true Holinesse*
> *Foul Errour doth defeate;*
> *Hypocrisie, him to entrape,*
> *Doth to his home entreate.*
>
> (*Faerie Queene*, p. 31, I.i, argument)

Crucially the book's primary protagonist, the Redcrosse Knight, is here referred to not via his warrior status, but through his allegorical definition as '*The patron of true Holinesse*'. Thus the interpretive emphasis is placed squarely upon the qualifying clause in the book's title, in which it is stated that this is 'The Legende of the Knight of the Red Crosse, or of Holinesse' (*Faerie Queene*, p. 29, I). Still more importantly, this stanza reveals the allegorical function of other characters whom the knight will encounter in the ensuing text, such as the 'vgly monster' (*Faerie Queene*, p. 35, I.i.14) of '*Foul Errour*' and the Archimage who represents '*Hypocrisie*'. Of these, the latter is perhaps the most interesting, because although Una warns the knight that the 'wandring wood' they have approached is in fact '*Errour's den*' (*Faerie Queene*, p. 34, I.i.13), the evil tendencies of the hermit are rather less obvious. Initially appearing as a hospitable 'aged Sire, in long blacke weedes yclad' (*Faerie Queene*, p. 38, I.i.29), it is only the argument's identification of this figure as the personification of '*Hypocrisie*' that alerts the reader to the danger to which the protagonists are succumbing when they accept his invitation. Examining the function of the proems in Spenser's epic, Lesley Brill notes that '[t]hey speak neither from fully within the fiction of Faerie nor from wholly outside it', and that '[i]n all the Proems [. . .] he remains to a degree detached from the narratives that follow'.[25] As a way of interpreting Spenser's prefatory paratext, this remains relevant when extended to encompass the arguments, for here too Spenser maintains sufficient distance from the ensuing narrative for his remarks to appear as comprehensive summaries through which he points the reader's attention towards what he considers to be the most important elements of the succeeding text.

Thus it is still more significant that the arguments often feature abstract nouns in place of characters' names, such as '*Truth*' and '*falshood*' (*Faerie Queene*, p. 44, I.ii, argument). For although the concept of truth is almost invariably associated with Una, the use of the capitalised term '*Truth*' as a synonym for Una's name appears only three times in the course of the Redcrosse Knight's narrative. Of these, two instances occur in the arguments and only one in the main text. This third occurrence takes place relatively late in the text, when the narrator writes:

> Ay me, how many perils doe enfold
> The righteous man, to make him daily fall?
> Were not, that heauenly Grace doth him vphold,
> And stedfast truth acquite him out of all!
> Her loue is firme, her care continuall.
>
> (*Faerie Queene*, p. 103, I.viii.1)

Even here, it is only the female pronoun in the line following the allusion to 'truth' that confirms Una as the direct personification of the concept. The strongest indication of this personification thus appears in the arguments, when it is stated that '*The guilefull great Enchaunter parts / The Redcrosse Knight from Truth*', and when Spenser writes that '*Forsaken Truth long seekes her loue*' (*Faerie Queene*, p. 44, I.ii, argument; p. 54, I.iii, argument). In Spenser's epic, therefore, the argument becomes a space in which to underscore the complexity of the text's allegorical network, whereby characters exist both as subjects of fictional narrative and as allegorical personifications.

Significantly, it is as the manifestation of '*Truth*' that Fielding and Collier borrow Una from Spenser's epic to become the 'radiant form' antithetically opposed to the derisive '*CRY*' (*The Cry*, p. 44): a decisive indication that Fielding and Collier must have not only read, but also paid close interpretive attention to Spenser's prefatory 'arguments'. Just as Spenser's proems serve to pinpoint key allegorical, moral, and theological aspects of the ensuing text, so too do the epigraphic quotations included in *The Cry* function primarily as a way of emphasising each chapter's morally instructive purpose. The quotation that prefaces *The Cry*'s first scene is an excellent example of this:

> *And oft though Wisdom wake, Suspicion sleeps*
> *At Wisdom's gate, and to Simplicity*
> *Resigns her charge, while Goodness thinks no ill*
> *Where no ill seems—*
> — MILTON.
>
> (*The Cry*, p. 45)[26]

Taken from the third book of *Paradise Lost*, these lines describe the naivety of the angel Uriel as he proceeds to reveal the location of Earth and the Garden of Eden to a disguised Satan. Whilst the quotation is a complete statement in itself, the added knowledge that these words characterise a representative of heaven in an exchange with the personification of theological evil reflects the discursive dichotomy of *The Cry*. Here, the aim of informing the reader through debate between moral truth (represented by Una and upheld by Portia) and immoral hypocrisy (signified by the eponymous 'Cry' of society) is underscored by Milton's more overt instance of an interaction between the forces of good and evil. Given the disastrous consequences of Uriel's misplaced confidence in Satan, this quotation also carries proleptic resonance in *The Cry* through the suggestion of future trouble and treachery. These ideas are most fully explored later in the text, when Portia's beloved Ferdinand is revealed to have been the victim of the 'forgery and contrivance' of his brother Oliver's schemes to disrupt the attachment (*The Cry*, p. 324), although the retrospective nature of the narrative means that Portia is able to hint at the deception that will eventually unfold. Yet rather than using this quotation as an example of misplaced trust, Fielding and Collier actually include it as a complement to the ensuing chapter's delineation of the importance of not assuming a cynical or suspicious attitude. As Portia explains:

> how do I pity those who assuming the name of friends, surround themselves with maxims, importing the wisdom of doubt and suspicion, till they impose on themselves that very hard task of labouring through life, without ever knowing a human creature to whom they can make the proper use of language. (*The Cry*, p. 50)

Whilst this might seem a somewhat ironic observation for a novel in which dislocated quotations preface almost every section of text, in fact this assertion highlights the distinction between indiscriminate parroting of learned texts and the authors' own inclusion of quotations as a way of summarising the moral precepts which their prose then exemplifies. The most obvious reading of the epigraphic quotation from Milton would be as an indictment against naivety, given the outcome of Uriel's unsuspecting admission to Satan of the location of the Garden of Eden. Yet the similar guilelessness demonstrated by Portia actually aligns her with the moral righteousness of Milton's angel, thus supporting the chapter's endorsement of an open and unsuspicious demeanour and so reinforcing the sense that a moral compass should exist without compromise. G. A. Starr notes that 'the central subject of the book is not its events but what, in retrospect, the narrators make of them',[27] and it is this discursive, analytic nature of the text that is enhanced through the inclusion of epigraphic quotations. As isolated fragments of text, these epigraphs serve as a summary of the principle which the characters then debate throughout the ensuing chapter; the narrative of *The Cry* simply provides practical examples of the principle in action, and, where an epigraph is taken from a narrative work such as *Paradise Lost*, the quotation's original context also frequently provides a further exemplary scenario.

The tendency of the epigraphic quotation to summarise a principle or precept discussed and exemplified more fully in the ensuing chapter continues throughout the work. The epigraph to Scene III is taken from Horace and reads 'Nam qui cupiet, metuet quoque' ('for he who covets will also have fears').[28] The chapter's thematic topic is the ill-consequence of a young woman's craving for masculine attention, beginning with 'the bigger miss [who] seats herself in public at a ball, expecting every moment to be chosen by some man for a partner for that evening' (*The Cry*, p. 58). This same 'expectation of being chosen', Portia claims, is 'a very good account for the peevishness of old maids' (*The Cry*, pp. 58, 59). Read in conjunction with the epigraph, this 'peevishness' correlates to Horace's 'metuet' or 'metuere', meaning 'to fear, be apprehensive'.[29] Similarly, a woman wooed into matrimony through 'flattering speeches' with which 'the weather-glass of the lady's vanity is swell'd to the top', is also the victim of a self-absorbed longing for 'the adulation of her worshipper' which ultimately causes her to 'grow sour and morose' within a loveless marriage (*The Cry*, pp. 60–61). Despite the apparent difference between the two scenarios, the epigraph identifies a similarity of initial cause and subsequent effect, thus distilling the chapter's moral guidance into a fundamental principle. In each situation, the original error is the vanity of longing ('cupiet'): the consequence of this error is a life in which some form of fear or 'metus' predominates, whether it is the old maid's fear of neglect, or the anxious dread through which 'every thing in her husband's house will become hateful to her sight' (*The Cry*, p. 61). Just as the prefatory arguments in Spenser's *Faerie Queene* distil the author's primary focus in each textual section, so too do Fielding and Collier's epigraphs consistently reiterate the ethical point that they are trying to convey, thus constituting a kind of prefatory moral that (as a quotation) also carries with it the added benefit of literary authority.

Exploring the classical contexts for Fielding's work, Dykstal writes that 'the romance plot is not all, or even most, of the "narrative" of *The Cry*', a text which instead prioritises 'staged dialogue on both abstract philosophical, and concrete ethical, questions'.[30] In promoting this form of sophisticated intellectual approach to narrative, the epigraphic quotations become a way of focusing attention upon the most pertinent and most essential concepts that are to be discussed in the ensuing prose. That this is indeed the true purpose of *The Cry*'s epigraphs is further supported by the fact that they are only used to preface those chapters or scenes of the text in which is related some moral or ethical debate between Portia and the Cry. The first volume of the work concludes with an eighty-page long section of incident-driven narrative detailing the progression of the relationship between the philosophically immoral Cylinda and the hero's father, Nicanor, together with its financially disastrous consequences. Here, the text reverts to a more traditional form of storytelling, in which a third-person omniscient narrator relates a sequence of events with little or no explicit moral commentary. Starr comments that '[f]or a more conventional novelist, the drama of *The Cry* would lie in such material as the criminal conversation between Cylinda and Amanda's husband Eustace' (another of Cylinda's lovers); even in the aforementioned narrative section there is a strong sense of its inclusion being a necessity rather than a textual focal point. In the prologue preceding this section, Fielding and Collier write that

> in order to relate such matters as are necessary to be known [. . .] it appears in our judgment by no means impertinent to offer to our reader's view a retrospect of the family, with which our principal person is so intimately connected. (*The Cry*, p. 105)

A similar attitude is assumed for the novel's epilogue, also presented without any prefacing epigraph and included 'only to inform our reader what became of the principal characters introduced in our story' (*The Cry*, p. 350), thus providing a sense of narrative conclusion to the work.

SANCTIONING SENTIMENTS AND APPROVING AUTHORS

Yet while Fielding and Collier would seem to have borrowed the essential function of their prefatory epigraphs from Spenser, other influences become apparent through the fact that they begin each narrative section not with words of their own composition, but with the 'sentiments [. . .] of the most approved authors' (*The Cry*, p. 18). Epigraphs were unusual enough and anthology volumes of the *Spectator* popular enough in the mid-eighteenth century for there to be considerable likelihood that Fielding and Collier derived epigraphic inspiration from this source. Further evidence of influence appears in the form of five individual references to either Addison or the *Spectator* contained within the text of the second volume of *The Cry*. Although no such allusions occur in either the first or third volumes (something which might be a consequence of different sections of the text having been written by two authors), these five references are sufficient to reveal a considerable awareness of both the *Spectator* and Addison's work more generally. Of the three instances in which Addison's name is mentioned, two of these are accompanied by quotations from his writing (*The Cry*, pp. 189, 199, 239). Both allusions to the *Spectator* feature obscure references to characters from the periodical, for example a character is likened to 'the poor man in the *Spectator*', whilst members of the eponymous '*Cry*' are referred to as 'having read the story of *Arria* and *Petus* in the *Spectators*' (*The Cry*, pp. 202, 212). Although the identification of the Cry as readers of the *Spectator* has the potential to denigrate the intellectual value of the periodical through association, this suggestion is deftly undercut by the book's integral precept that awareness of knowledge is not the same as understanding and assimilating knowledge. It is the Cry who are at fault for having only 'read the story', and then overlooked its moral principles as they interpret Portia's identification with the character of Arria as a demonstration of her own 'immense vanity and presumption' (*The Cry*, p. 212). This not only suggests that *The Cry*'s authors were extremely well acquainted with Addison's writing, and with the *Spectator* in particular, but it also implies an expectation that the reader will possess a similarly close knowledge of this periodical, to the extent that explanations of the background of individual characters becomes superfluous. In her examination of the authorship of *The Cry*, Carolyn Woodward identifies its essential similarity to other works by Sarah Fielding through various stylistic features, and not least of these is 'its presentation of Addisonian characters'.[31] More specifically, Mika Suzuki has examined the direct influence of the *Spectator* in Fielding's writing in her *Familiar Letters*, noting in particular that 'one of the gentlemen is endowed with the congenial characteristics *The Spectator* demanded of those wishing to follow Horace'.[32] Thus Suzuki identifies a three-way link between Fielding, the *Spectator*, and the ideals and precepts of classical writers that is most particularly relevant when encountering *The Cry*, and which becomes crystallised through the epigraphic quotations that preface almost every new section, or 'scene', of Fielding and Collier's narrative.

The *Spectator* had asserted that its aim was to 'br[ing] Philosophy out of Closets and Libraries, Schools and Colleges, to dwell in Clubs and Assemblies, at Tea-Tables, and in Coffee-Houses',[33] implying a fairly gender-neutral attitude towards this dissemination of knowledge. In her study of women and eighteenth-century consumerism, Elizabeth Kowaleski-Wallace points out that the domestic tea table was perceived as 'a gendered site, a "feminine" locus where the civilizing process could occur'.[34] Yet when Addison claims in issue 370 of the *Spectator* that '[m]any of my fair readers [. . .] are extremely perplexed at the Latin Sentences at the Head of my Speculations', he is also obliquely perpetuating the idea that this is as it should be, and that rather than giving these 'fair readers' a classical education, 'Translations of each of [the epigraphs]' would be the only correct solution to this problem.[35] The assumption that women could not be expected to understand the Latin and Greek epigraphs thus signals the periodical's retention of traditional gender stereotypes in which women are presumed to possess a knowledge base markedly different to that of men. Writing of the 'canonical' status which the *Spectator* rapidly assumed in the eighteenth century, George Justice observes how it was used to provide 'a practical reading [. . .] for moral inculcation' as well as to assist with the attainment of 'the skill of a particular model of English composition'.[36] It would therefore have been able to make an ample contribution to the perpetuation of a belief that gender discrimination in education was to be encouraged.

Fielding and Collier would seem to present an alternative attitude, however. In the *Spectator*, extracts from the writings of Horace provided material for around a third of the prefatory quotations, making this the most frequently referenced epigraphic source. Similarly, Horace is also the most commonly quoted writer in the epigraphs of *The Cry*, with quotations from his works appearing 8 times in the text's 42 pre-chapter epigraphs (see Appendix, Figure 4). As Dan Hooley states in his study on the reception of classical literature in eighteenth-century England, Horace is one of those poets whose work 'appear[s] with unprecedented frequency in English literature, not only satirical, from 1660 on through to the 1780s'.[37] Stretching back far into the seventeenth century, aspiring male scholars had 'perfected their Latin with Horace, Lucan, Martial, Persius, and Seneca'.[38] The selection of Horace as an epigraphic source in *The Cry* thus simultaneously evokes both the *Spectator*'s somewhat superficial claims of disseminating knowledge and also the Latin education that Merry Wiesner notes was intended to 'prepare [boys] for later attendance at a university and an eventual career'. That a work by two women writers should attempt this at a time when academic study for women 'was viewed as at best impractical and at worst dangerous' only strengthens the symbolic aspects of the gesture.[39] By incorporating so many quotations from Horace within *The Cry*, Fielding and Collier are effectively and implicitly refuting the attitude that women should neither possess nor demonstrate knowledge of such a stereotypically male area as the Latin writings of a Roman poet. For, unlike most anthology editions of the *Spectator* published after 1744,[40] no translations are provided of non-English epigraphs.

Unlike the *Spectator*, in which epigraphic quotations are selected as a non-essential reflection of succeeding prose, *The Cry* relies upon the reader understanding the prefatory quotations if they are to access the full complexity of the Spenserian relationship between epigraph and text. The possibility that the presence of the quotations is more important than audience comprehension is raised by Fielding and Collier's initial claim of using the quotations 'to give a sanction to our own sentiments by those of the most approved authors' (*The Cry*, p. 43). Yet the 'sanction' bestowed would only really be evident to a readership able to understand these quotations, and who would therefore have to be familiar with four different languages. In fact, of the 42 epigraphs included across the three volumes of the work, only 23 are in English. That 15 of the remaining 19 epigraphs are presented in Latin is most especially significant given the probable gender bias of the text's original readership (see Appendix, Figure 5). For although the preface refers to the hypothetical 'reader' with only the male pronouns 'he' and 'his' (*The Cry*, p. 41), these terms seem to be intended to convey gender neutrality rather than the expectation that the text would enjoy a primarily male readership. Indeed, although the earliest advertisements for *The Cry* avoided gender-specific marketing, by December 1754 (some eight or nine months after the first publicity appeared) it was being described as a work 'designed to shew to the Ladies in particular, the superior Beauty and Excellence of Truth and Simplicity in their behaviour'.[41] Possibly the publisher had originally hoped for a broader readership but ultimately concluded that, since the book itself appealed most especially to female readers, a more targeted marketing strategy might boost sales. Certainly, the text's moral didacticism appears aimed most especially at a primarily female readership.

Through this implicit assumption of a gender-biased audience, therefore, the linguistic variety of the epigraphic quotations becomes a practical means of asserting educational equality for women. Although Fielding's biographer Linda Bree allows that Fielding and Collier do advocate women's education, she believes that they demonstrate only 'cautious support for women's rights', since the immorality of 'the most learned lady in the book', Cylinda, is portrayed as a consequence of too much time spent studying abstract concepts and too little devoted to 'a distinctly nonclassical Christian virtue, without which the logic and philosophy of the classical writers is shown to be worthless'.[42] Brought up by her father and educated with her male cousin, Cylinda states that by the age of sixteen she was 'an exceeding good *latin* scholar, and was pretty far advanced in *greek*' (*The Cry*, p. 218). Her subsequent sexual promiscuity is presented as a direct consequence of her having 'prided [her]self more in remembering a verse of *Homer, Virgil* or *Horace*, or a sentiment in *Plato*, than in knowing the whole doctrine of the old and new testament' (*The Cry*, p. 282). It is the limited focus of Cylinda's education that Fielding and Collier are criticising here, and ultimately it is more rather than less study that is advocated.

In this sense, Cylinda serves as the moral foil to the consistent perfection of Portia's behaviour and attitude. These attributes are accredited to a more balanced education that has encompassed classical knowledge as a means through which Portia may 'employ [her] own mind agreeably' (*The Cry*, p. 286), yet which has bestowed still more emphasis upon the cultivation of religious sensibility. As Portia herself states, '[m]y home was to be the christian faith into which I was baptized; and all my trust was to be placed in the revelation of God' (*The Cry*, p. 286). That the propriety and worth of women's education is being promoted is further indicated through the fact that it is the eponymous 'Cry', the manifestation of society within the text as the antithesis of moral virtue, who denigrate it by bestowing upon its advocate, Portia, 'their whole collection of ironical taunts, by talking of *wits, women of sense, pretenders to penetration,* &c.' (*The Cry*, pp. 89–90). Since it is the business of the text to demonstrate that everything else which the Cry support is either erroneous or morally corruptive, their lack of support for such an educational programme may be inferred as an authorial endorsement of its morality. However, Bree's belief that Fielding and Collier's support for women's rights more generally is only 'cautious' retains credence, since the motivation behind Portia's education is to gain a form of marital advantage. Portia herself notes that her father 'not only designed [her] learning as a means of being a companion to a man of *real* understanding, but to prevent [her] being sought after by any other' (*The Cry*, p. 286).

Nonetheless, the benefits of such a broad education are also continually exemplified through Portia's use of classical and philosophical logic, and of polemical structure in her defence of moral virtue against the disruptive influence of the Cry. Indeed, the very structure of the text is so obviously derived from the Greek dramatic dialogues of Socrates and Plato that it would be somewhat hypocritical to suggest that knowledge of this form of literature might not be useful and enlightening. By including epigraphs, a stylistic device which at that point in time would have been most readily identifiable with the prefatory mottos of the *Spectator*, Fielding and Collier are thus cultivating an association between their narrative and the periodical that would subliminally convey an impression of refined taste and educational merit. In the *Spectator*, one of the functions of the epigraphs had been to emphasise the intellectual authority of the author. In Fielding and Collier's work, the epigraph does not just serve as the device through which they attempt to convince the reader that a classical education should be regarded as both desirable and expected in a woman, but it also functions as a focal point through which to demonstrate the intellectual knowledge that provides the authors with the authority to speak with conviction upon such a subject. For despite Bree's identification of Cylinda as 'the most learned lady in the book',[43] that distinction should in fact be jointly awarded to the authors themselves, as their knowledge is revealed by the breadth and variety of texts from which they draw both quotations and inspiration. Epigraphic quotations alone are drawn from a range of around 21 different sources, with the most frequently featured writers including (in order of frequency) Horace, Edward Young, Shakespeare, and Milton. Two epigraphic quotations each are also included from Ben Jonson, Samuel Garth, Montaigne, and Virgil, but only 1 quotation each is included from each of the remaining 13 epigraphic sources (a list which includes Beaumont and Fletcher, William Whitehead, and Rochefoucauld alongside Lucretius, Homer, and the Bible). Clearly Fielding and Collier considered it important not just to demonstrate a degree of literary allegiance with major Latin and English writers such as Horace and Shakespeare, but also to convey a solid breadth of literary knowledge (see Appendix, Figure 4).

At the time *The Cry* was written, the extraction of quotations from longer works for memorisation had long been a common educational device. In his influential study of commonplace books and authorship in early modern England, Adam Smyth discusses the popular practice of commonplacing and creating notebooks in which 'aphorisms, plucked from reading or conversation, were arranged under thematic headings to provide the compiler with a storehouse of pieces of eloquence'. Furthermore, Smyth writes that during 'the early modern period [. . .] the commonplace book flourished as a crucial component in the humanist educational system'.[44] It continued to do so throughout the eighteenth century, although as Lucia Dacome points out even one of the greatest exponents of the format, John Locke, 'had cautioned against the memorization of arguments and sentences'. Parroting authors in this simplistic way was identified with 'images of pedantry personified by the bore, the impolite, and the pedant'.[45] Indeed, references to commonplace books in early eighteenth-century texts often exploit this potential for a negative image. In John Oldmixon's *A Complete History of Addresses* (1710), a hypothetical lawyer's speech is identified as 'in neither *Cook* nor *Littleton*, nor *Bracton*, but it might be in Sir *T. Montgomery*, or Sir *B. Shower's* Commonplace Book'.[46] Jonathan Swift is still more abrasive in his comment that 'the Taylor's Hell is the Type of a Critick's *Common-Place-Book*', a remark elucidated by Marcus Walsh as meaning that '[t]he critic's collection of apothegms is put together by the same process of "cabbaging" by which tailors screwed up offcuts and hid them under the shop-board for their own use'.[47]

When used as part of a broader educational strategy and not as a shortcut to superficial intellectualism, however, keeping a commonplace book is generally regarded as a useful custom. John Boswell, an author and clergyman who had worked as a private tutor before taking his degree at Oxford, staunchly defends the use of a commonplace book in his *A Method of Study* (1738–43), asserting that the practice 'has been recommended by most Gentlemen, that have writ of Education, and if the Book be well contriv'd, if the Passages taken from Authors are dispos'd in a regular Manner, the Expedient must necessarily be of Service to the Student'.[48] In 1745, John Mason's *Self-Knowledge* offered a compromise, advising those wishing to improve their knowledge to

[r]ecur to the Help of a *Common Place-Book*, according to *Mr. Locke's* Method. And review it once a Year. But take care that by confiding to your Minutes or memorial Aids, you do not excuse the Labour of the Memory; which is one Disadvantage attending this Method.[49]

The widespread popularity and influence of Mason's work may be inferred from its having remained almost continuously in print until the end of the century, by which time, Dacome notes, 'versions of the Lockean method started to circulate in print and prospective Lockean compilers could purchase commonplace books with a pre-stamped version of the Lockean index'.[50]

Through Fielding and Collier's incorporation of prefatory quotation in *The Cry*, therefore, they not only borrow the epigraphic concept from the *Spectator* and moral intertextuality from Spenser; they are also harnessing a contemporary belief in the informative and edifying potential of dislocated text. Boswell had written that commonplace books were useful 'if the Book be well contriv'd' and arranged 'in a regular Manner',[51] and certainly *The Cry's* consistent pattern of quotations followed by discussion and exemplification could hardly be more structured. The concept of a professionally produced rather than a personally compiled commonplace book was by no means new. Stephen Bernard has explored how Edward Bysshe made 'the transition into print of a commonplace book *in English*' with *The Art of English Poetry* (1702), the majority of which consisted of a 'dictionary of quotations'.[52] This was sorted thematically, so that readers may easily identify an appropriate text when they 'are at a loss [. . .] for proper Epithets or Synonymes [*sic*]'.[53] The editor of the *Oxford Dictionary of Quotations*, Elizabeth Knowles, actually credits Bysshe's efforts here with establishing the 'principle of identifying the author of a selected passage'.[54] Bysshe's later sequel, *The British Parnassus* (1714), further emphasised the commonplace tradition in its subtitle, 'A Compleat *Common-Place-Book* OF ENGLISH POETRY'; inside, it claimed to be '*a Repository, where may be seen at one View the Gold and Jewels of our Poets, without raking in the Filth and Rubbish*'.[55] Although *The Cry* transcends any simplistic structural or generic definition, incorporating a miscellany of stylistic elements from philosophical discourse, moral and educational treatises, essay writing, and conventional romantic fiction, its inclusion of such a broad range of quotation correlates remarkably well with the fundamental concept of the commonplace book. For in *The Cry*, as in commonplace books, the intention is to use short, and therefore more readily memorable, quotations to provide the reader with both literary knowledge and moral education. As in *Jack Connor*, a major motivation for the inclusion of epigraphic quotation is to provide an educational subtext to the prose narrative; however, whilst Chaigneau prioritises linguistic accessibility, Fielding and Collier attempt to harness the presumed intellectual abilities of the readership to cultivate moral and ethical comprehension.

This blend of morality with romance narrative effectively channels concerns regarding the function and usefulness of novels that remained relevant throughout the eighteenth century. The author Anna Maria Mackenzie would later identify Miguel de Cervantes as the originator of this 'new source of amusement', an umbrella term for romantic fiction which in her definition encompasses Henry Fielding and Samuel Richardson as well as 'their numerous copyists'. Significantly, Mackenzie praises the former of these for having contributed literary entertainment 'without violating the dictates of reason and good sense': imitations designed merely to '[inflame] the passions' are considered unworthy by comparison.[56] This sense of purpose is implicitly present in both novels discussed here, as each cultivates a balance between moral improvement and Romantic adventure. Chaigneau's narrative imposes an educational framework upon the risqué picaresque of Henry Fielding, whilst Fielding and Collier draw upon the chivalric and Romantic ideals as well as the theological and moral purpose of Spenser; even the anonymous *Histories of Some of the Penitents*, quoted at the beginning of this chapter, inverts tropes of romance and adventure to fulfil a didactic purpose. It is a characteristic that would remain relevant as the epigraph became absorbed by the fiction trend that would come to dominate the literary market at the end of the eighteenth century, the Gothic Romance.

2

TRANSCENDING BOUNDARIES WITH EPIGRAPHS: ANN RADCLIFFE

—— Is it not dead midnight?
Cold fearful drops stand on my trembling flesh,
What do I fear?

SHAKESPEARE[1]

The scene is an Inquisition dungeon, the novel Ann Radcliffe's *The Italian* (1797). Accused of abducting a nun from her convent, the hero Vivaldi is undergoing an unsettling interrogation that has come to focus upon his experiences with the scheming monk Schedoni. Numerous narrative possibilities arise when Vivaldi's almost supernatural encounter with a mysterious, anonymous monk is immediately followed by the deployment of an epigraph in which Shakespeare's Richard III attempts to explain a possibly imagined encounter with the ghosts of his victims. Teasing the reader with narrative comparison, Radcliffe provokes speculation: is the mysterious stranger a ghost or a real person? Can he be trusted to help Vivaldi, or does he have a darker purpose? Is there a reason why the emotions of the so far heroic Vivaldi are being ventriloquised through the words of the murderous Richard III? For some readers, this text would also be readily identifiable with David Garrick's iconic performance of the play's title role, immortalised in oils by William Hogarth and reproduced in countless small engravings.[2] Invoking a drama of fear in the pause between one chapter and the next, between the nocturnal visit of one night and the interrogation of the next, Radcliffe's epigraph here eloquently demonstrates her unique mastery of the device.

Indeed, so closely has Radcliffe become identified with the epigraph that it has long been commonplace to label her as its originator; Edward Jacobs's analysis of Radcliffe's relationship with print culture and Romantic-era intertextuality even goes so far as to credit her alone with having 'invented' the technique.[3] Stuart Curran is more cautious, suggesting instead that Radcliffe only popularised the device and identifying a novel with epigraphic quotation that predates Radcliffe's work, namely the fourth edition of Elizabeth Helme's *Louisa; or, The Cottage on the Moor* (1787; fourth edition advertised November 1787).[4]

Including Chaigneau's *Jack Connor* and Fielding and Collier's *The Cry*, this study has established that at least 21 novels with some form of pre-chapter epigraphs were published between the years 1750 and 1790, all of which precede Radcliffe's experimentation with the device in *The Romance of the Forest* (1791).[5] So far it has only been possible to check the paratext of 985 out of 1158 novels first-published during this period (approximately 85%), therefore some further instances of pre-chapter epigraphs may yet remain to be discovered;[6] but of the 21 novels that I identified during my survey, 11 appeared within the four-year period 1787–90.[7] The majority of these 11 received distinctly disparaging reviews,[8] and only 4 appear to have achieved more than one edition: Elizabeth Helme's *Louisa*, Anna Maria Makenzie's *Retribution* (1788) and *Calista* (1789), and John Moore's *Zeluco* (1789). Whilst Mackenzie's only claim to this distinction lies in French editions of her two novels published in 1788 and 1798 respectively, both *Louisa* and *Zeluco* feature on a list of just 67 novels that passed through more than five editions in Britain in the years between 1770 and 1829. Other writers whose work appears on the list include Ann Radcliffe, Matthew Lewis, Frances Burney, William Godwin, Elizabeth Inchbald, and Charlotte Smith. Helme's novel in fact achieved 38 editions between 1770 and 1829, a figure almost four times the number of editions that Frances Burney's *Evelina* (1778) attained over the same period; Moore's *Zeluco* stands at an even higher 54 editions.[9] However, in terms of literary influence upon epigraphs exerted after immediate publication, the effect of both *Louisa* and *Zeluco* seems to have been limited. So far I have found that fewer than 5 novels featuring pre-chapter epigraphs were published per year in any of the four years preceding 1791 when Radcliffe's *The Romance of the Forest* appeared (see Appendix, Table 1 and Figure 1). Likewise, Radcliffe's work is currently one of only 3 novels with epigraphic paratext known to have been first-published in 1791, a year in which at least 74 new novels appeared (and of which 68 have been checked for epigraphic material).[10]

Although *Zeluco* appeared with epigraphs from its first edition onwards, Helme's *Louisa* is a more interesting case. Originally published around May 1787 as a continuous prose narrative without chapters of any kind, it progressed rapidly through three editions in the following months. The novel's fourth edition appeared in late November 1787 with a notice on the title page stating that this version is '*corrected, with* ADDITIONS *and ornamented with Frontispieces, neatly engraved*'. There is also a further notice following the preface which proclaims that '[t]*his edition is divided into chapters, mottos added to each, and the whole carefully revised*'.[11] As well as chapter divisions and epigraphs, chapter titles have also been added so that each new section of text is now presented with an unusual abundance of prefatory paratext. Chapter titles appear to have enjoyed a comparatively muted popularity at this time, featuring in only 14 of the 51 novels known to have been published in 1787 (of which 48 have been checked for epigraphic material), and 7 of these were the production of just one publisher, William Lane.[12] Such chapter titles seem to occur only where the novel is presented through continuous prose rather than in an epistolary format, but the use of the device in the work of multiple writers who published their books with Lane promotes the possibility that this kind of paratext was included at the publisher's instigation rather than the writers'. A further indication of publishers' influence in paratextual decisions may be that Helme's publisher George Kearsley is also responsible for producing *The Adventures of a Watch!* (1788), one of only three novels with epigraphs first-published the year after *Louisa* appeared. More evidence appears in the somewhat restricted range of the epigraphs added to the fourth edition of *Louisa*: there are only 24 epigraphs in all, allowing only 1 for every chapter, and these are selected from a range of only 6 different writers. Of the total 24, there are 14 derived from James Thomson's *The Seasons* (1726–30), with 8 of these being taken from the same section of his poem, 'Spring' (see Appendix, Figure 6). This limited scope makes the epigraphs seem like hasty additions, intended not so much to contribute towards textual interpretation, but rather as a form of ornamentation akin to the also newly added engravings. It is not difficult to perceive the marketing advantage of constructing a more attractive edition of an already popular text, and whether or not these alterations were made at the instigation of Helme or Kearsley, it seems unlikely that they were made for any other reason than to exploit the novel's runaway success.

A further instance of epigraphic usage in 1787 that would also point to this being a formative time for the pre-chapter epigraph is the publication of a major economic study, John St. John's *Observations on the Land Revenue of the Crown* (1787). Whilst a detailed examination of pre-chapter paratext in non-fiction is outside the scope of the current investigation, it is worth noting that the *European Magazine* review of this work concluded with the declaration that '[i]t is almost ludicrous to mention it, but we confess ourselves to have been much struck by the curious felicity of the quotations prefixed to each chapter'.[13] All 6 of the work's pre-chapter epigraphs are then provided in the Latin in which they were originally written and presented in St. John's treatise. No English translations are given in either the review or the printed volume. It is difficult to be certain quite why the reviewer felt it was 'ludicrous to mention' the quotations; possible explanations might be that it was unusual to use epigraphs in this specific genre, or that the inclusion of pre-chapter epigraphs was in itself remarkable, or even simply that it seemed such an insignificant aspect of such a major work as to scarcely justify a reviewer's comment. Certainly, the ensuing transcription of every one of the epigraphs points towards the possibility that this use of quotation was so remarkable and innovative as to have provoked a kind of fascination on the part of the reviewer.

Yet while it is not true that Radcliffe invented the pre-chapter epigraph, she is nonetheless the writer whose work did more to popularise the device than any previous novelist. Indeed, many of her predecessors in the Gothic genre had chosen not to include any sort of chapter division at all, with notable examples including Jacque Cazotte's *The Devil in Love* (1772), Clara Reeve's *The Old English Baron* (1778), and William Beckford's *Vathek* (1786). Gothic works in which the prose narrative is divided into sections are typically arranged either in an epistolary format, for example Sophia Lee's *The Recess* (1783), or in sections headed with the word 'chapter' followed by the appropriate Roman numeral, for example Horace Walpole's *The Castle of Otranto* (1764). It is this latter form of narrative division that Radcliffe also employs in her earliest fiction, *The Castles of Athlin and Dunbayne* (1789) and *A Sicilian Romance* (1790). Later, in still more influential novels such as *The Romance of the Forest* (1791), *The Mysteries of Udolpho* (1794), and *The Italian* (1797), Radcliffe's decision to incorporate pre-chapter epigraphs constitutes an experimental expansion and development of textual divisions within her work that represents a conscious attempt to cultivate her own unique form of narrative style.

Analysing Radcliffe's use of terror across her oeuvre, Kim Ian Michasiw describes Radcliffe's final work, *Gaston de Blondeville* (published posthumously 1826), as 'a markedly experimental novel',[14] but the incorporation of epigraphic paratext throughout her prose fiction suggests a more accurate assertion would be that Radcliffe was a markedly experimental writer. Indeed, the scarcity of pre-chapter epigraphic quotation before Radcliffe means that from the moment she first includes the device in *The Romance of the Forest* she has entered – whether she is aware of it or not – the same realm of paratextual experimentation occupied by Fielding and Collier's *The Cry*. This chapter will provide a fresh framing of Radcliffe's oeuvre from *The Romance of the Forest* to *Gaston de Blondeville*, highlighting a developmental arc in her creative career that aligns with, and is illuminated by, her continual experimentation with pre-chapter paratext. Expanding upon the long-standing assumption that the transgression of boundaries is a fundamental characteristic of Gothic fiction,[15] I will demonstrate that it is not just the aesthetic boundaries of imagination and gender which Radcliffe redefines within her work. In two of her most influential novels, *The Romance of the Forest* and *The Mysteries of Udolpho*, her use of epigraphic quotation enables the transcendence of another, more pragmatic boundary: that which exists between successive chapters.

Furthermore, I shall establish that Radcliffe's epigraphs indicate that she is not content merely to entertain her reader: though not so overtly didactic as Fielding and Collier's work, Radcliffe's *Udolpho* features a pattern of pre-chapter quotation that becomes an essential element in her strategy to obliquely instruct her readers. David Punter's history of Gothic fiction identifies Radcliffe's indebtedness to 'Richardson, Prévost, and the sentimental novel', noting in particular that her writing shares many of the same elements, for example 'sublimity, melancholy, tragic aspiration and downfall'.[16] These influences are reflected in the endurance and essential purity of her heroines and, less directly, in the preservation of a strict sense of morality within the text. This chapter will explore how these didactic nuances find expression through Radcliffe's use of epigraphic paratext to emphasise key narrative concepts and to explore and transcend the boundaries that exist not just between chapters, but also between the conscious and the unconscious mind, and ultimately between the reader's reality and the imagined realm of the text.

An Epigraphic Beginning

In both *The Romance of the Forest* and *Udolpho* there is an eagerness to promote the novels' genre-crossing qualities. The title pages of both describe the ensuing text as being '*Interspersed with some pieces of poetry*', something that has often been assumed to refer to both Radcliffe's own poetry located within the text, and the epigraphic quotations.[17] Writing on the development of the novel during the Romantic period, Gary Kelly categorises both epigraphs and in-text poetry as simply variants of the way in which verse is used to '[articulate] meaning and form in several ways that Radcliffe made her own'.[18] However, when one of the earliest reviewers of *The Romance of the Forest* alludes to these '*Pieces of Poetry*', it is only 'the original verses interspersed through the work' to which he is referring and from which he proceeds to quote.[19] Later, reviews of *Udolpho* perpetuated this definition by identifying 'the poetical productions interspersed in these volumes' as 'ample proof of [Radcliffe's] poetical talents'.[20] Even when the *British Critic*'s reviewer notes that '[t]he verses which are interspersed [and] are announced in the title-page' are part of a growing 'fashion' for 'the introduction of verses in publications', the ensuing assertion that 'Mrs. Radcliffe's poetical abilities are of the superior kind' confirms that it is only those poems inserted into the main text which are under consideration.[21] This interpretation of the phrase is further confirmed by the use of the similar phrase '*interspersed with some poetical pieces*' on the title page of Helen Maria Williams's *Julia, A Novel* (1790), a work which does not feature any form of pre-chapter epigraphs.[22] As Jacobs has rightly argued, these are in fact 'two different ways of introjecting poetry into novels'.[23]

The inclusion of poetry within the main text is generally used as a way in which to nudge some of Radcliffe's own verse into the novel under the transparent cover of being the composition of one of her characters. In-text quotations sourced from other writers are somewhat rare in all of Radcliffe's novels, with only 13 in *The Romance of the Forest* and 28 in *Udolpho*: an increase consistent with the greater length of *Udolpho* which may be roughly approximated through the quantity of chapters rising from 26 in *The Romance of the Forest* to 57 in *Udolpho*. These in-text quotations rarely extend beyond 3 lines in length (often with the first or last line clipped accordingly). Indeed, of the 13 in-text quotations in *The Romance of the Forest* a total of 10 are 3 lines long or less; of the 26 in-text quotations in *Udolpho* a total of 19 are 3 lines long or less. Although in-text quotations are generally presented as indented text and spaced away from the main prose, there are 3 instances in *The Romance of the Forest* and 8 in *Udolpho* in which the quoted text is incorporated into Radcliffe's narrative. In such situations the insertion appears as a hybrid between a quotation and an idiomatic description. A good example of this is the phrase 'softened into silence' quoted when describing how 'a strain of music stole on the calm' (*Udolpho*, p. 209), a previously unidentified quotation that is in fact a variant of Nicholas Rowe's 'softens into silence' in *The Tragedy of Jane Shore* (1714).[24] Here, as with other in-text quotations in Radcliffe's work, the function of such inclusions does not appear to extend beyond the superficially descriptive qualities of the text selected. This is also true even of some of the longest in-text quotations, for example the inclusion in *The Romance of the Forest* of two quatrains of 'Cynthia, An Elegiac Poem' published in Dodsley's *A Collection of Poems* (1758).[25] In this instance the lines are introduced into the text almost as if the hero has been reminded of them by the sight of his beloved, as Radcliffe states that '[h]er charms appeared to him like those since so finely described by an English poet' (*The Romance of the Forest*, p. 172). A similar descriptive function is evident in *Udolpho*, where longer quotations typically become a form of descriptive short-hand, as when a lengthy quotation from Thomson's *Seasons* is used to convey an impression of the surrounding scenery whilst the heroine and her father picnic:

> by breezy murmurs cool'd,
> Broad o'er *their* heads the verdant cedars wave,
> And high palmetos lift their graceful shade.
> ————————————*they* draw
> Ethereal soul, their drink reviving gales
> Profusely breathing from the piney groves,
> And vales of fragrance; there at distance hear
> The roaring floods, and cataracts.

(*Udolpho*, p. 54)[26]

Much effort is made to assert the quoted nature of this text: the use of elliptical hyphenation, the italicisation of plural pronouns where they have replaced the original singular forms, and a conspicuous footnote at the bottom of the page identifying Thomson as the author. In content, however, this quotation is typical of Radcliffe's in-text quotations with its descriptive focus upon 'roaring floods, and cataracts', and in its relevance to a limited, immediate scenario. Considered alongside the usually much shorter length of in-text quotations compared with pre-chapter quotations, this also suggests an inherent difference between the intended effects of these two forms of quotation.

Various theories have so far been advanced to explain Radcliffe's inclusion of pre-chapter quotations. In his study of the relationship between Romantic-era poetry and prose, John Claiborne Isbell identifies a range of possible functions for the epigraph including as 'fetish authenticity for a narrative, a marker for historical continuity, [and/or] a tuning-fork setting for what follows'.[27] JoEllen DeLucia focuses more specifically upon Radcliffe's relationship with the Scottish Enlightenment, arguing that her extensive quotation from Scottish writers 'create[s] a temporal disruption or unevenness that invites readers to leave the main narrative and enter a distant Scottish past': specifically, the romanticised past that had been popularised earlier in the century by Scottish poets such as James Thomson, James Macpherson, and James Beattie. DeLucia later reaffirms this connection, suggesting that her 'paratextual apparatus' associates her with authors who, 'like Radcliffe, found inspiration in the Celtic periphery', including Thomas Gray and William Collins alongside Thomson, Macpherson, and Beattie.[28] However, it should be noted that Macpherson is never quoted by Radcliffe in any of her pre-chapter epigraphs, whilst Gray's work is epigraphically included only four times throughout all of Radcliffe's fiction (see Appendix, Figure 10). Examining Radcliffe's Shakespearean sources, Rictor Norton prioritises her fascination with canonical writers, noting in particular her enthusiasm for quoting Shakespeare and suggesting that this facilitated and promoted her publisher's strategy of 'market[ing] her as a Shakespearean property'.[29] Yet although Shakespeare is certainly the most frequently quoted epigraphic source in Radcliffe's novels, his works provide material for only 42 out of a total of 118 epigraphs across the three novels that feature pre-chapter epigraphs, *The Romance of the Forest*, *Udolpho*, and *The Italian* (1797). As a percentage, this amounts to only 35.5% of the total number (see Appendix, Figure 10), a proportion that is also broadly correct for each of these three novels individually (see Appendix, Figures 7, 8, and 9). Thus while a Shakespearean presence is clearly strong within Radcliffe's paratext, the sense that she is simply seeking 'to align her work with high culture' is somewhat diminished.[30] Indeed, the quantity and range of the writers from whom only one or two quotations have been selected for inclusion as an epigraph does suggest that Radcliffe was making her selections based more upon content than canonical status (see Appendix, Figures 7, 8, and 9).

In her study of the significance of poetry and music in *Udolpho*, Joanna Kokot states simply that each epigraph 'comment[s] upon the events presented there, as well as on the general tone and atmosphere', while Leah Price's investigation of the development of the novel suggests that these quotations 'force readers to pause and withdraw from the action at regular intervals'.[31] Investigating the relationship between Gothic prose and drama, Francesca Saggini argues that Radcliffe's quotations 'work on two interconnected levels: whilst expressing both the author's and the character's feeling [. . .] they also claim a higher generic and cultural status for the novel'.[32] Kelly identifies the pre-chapter quotation as 'an outside border for the narrative and all that it contains'; for him, it is a means through which the Gothic prose 'is hedged, framed, or marked off with bits of "serious literature"'.[33] More recently, Jacobs has expanded upon this, assimilating Radcliffe's epigraphs with other forms of pre-chapter paratext by linking them to the growing popularity of '[c]hapter breaks in novels [. . .] accompanied by a variety of paratexts'. This connection is then strengthened as he writes:

> [Henry] Fielding's recognition that the paratexts appended to chapter breaks gave authors the chance rhetorically to frame readers' approach to a chapter's narrative foregrounds how the chapter epigraphs that Radcliffe invented used that framing opportunity to 'canonise' the novel conventions she authored.[34]

To some extent, this interpretation of the epigraph as a form of substitute for a chapter title is obliquely supported by the commencement of volume 1 chapter 5 in Radcliffe's *The Romance of the Forest*. Here, instead of the usual epigraphic quotation, a form of fragmented, descriptive title is used to preface the chapter: '*A Surprize – An Adventure – A Mystery*' (*The Romance of the Forest*, p. 59). This is the only chapter to be titled in this way out of a total of 26, and its narrative content is in no way startlingly out of character with the rest of the text: a suspicious 'stranger' is introduced and his identity revealed, after which he investigates 'the ruins of a small building' in the forest whilst the heroine Adeline is bewildered by the growing 'unkindness' of her protector Madame La Motte (*The Romance of the Forest*, pp. 66, 73, 74). The descriptive aspect of this chapter heading invites comparison with the pre-chapter titles of such influential novels as Henry Fielding's *Tom Jones* (1749) and Oliver Goldsmith's *The Vicar of Wakefield* (1766). Derived from the lengthy comedic descriptions with which Miguel de Cervantes prefaces chapters of *Don Quixote* (1605), Fielding's chapter titles generally take the form of lengthy proleptic sentences, for example '[t]he reader's neck brought into danger by a description, his escape, and the great condescension of Miss Bridget Allworthy'.[35] Examining self-reflective commentary within narrative, Ansgar Nunning points out that in Fielding's novels 'the synoptic chapter headings not only have a metanarrative character, but also contribute considerably to directing the way these novels are received'.[36]

Radcliffe's much briefer, one-off prose chapter title appears significantly less sophisticated by comparison. Yet the simple combination of a particle with a noun is extremely reminiscent of chapter headings, such as those in Goldsmith's *The Vicar of Wakefield*, in which such a phrase is often combined with a longer, more descriptive sentence, for example '*A migration. The fortunate circumstances of our lives are generally found at last to be of our own procuring.*'[37] Without delving too far into the speculative, it is perhaps plausible to suppose that Radcliffe's one variation from the epigraph format may have been simply the result of an inability to discover a suitable quotation. In such a situation, the inclusion of some text, even a succession of brief epithets, might have seemed preferable to a blank heading.

Jacobs also argues that '[w]hereas chapter titles or tags framed readers' expectations through titles or summaries written by the text's author, Radcliffe's epigraphs framed those expectations by putting her chapters [. . .] in the context of other, pointedly canonical texts and voices'.[38] Yet this only reinforces Kelly's assertion that Radcliffe uses poetry in her novels in a way that 'marks the outer and innermost borders of narrative',[39] and thus overlooks the integral paradox of Radcliffean epigraphs. For while the inclusion of a quotation may superficially appear to reinforce an established boundary, the textual content of such epigraphs enjoys a much closer relationship with the prose narrative on both sides of the chapter division. Exploiting the transitional quality of the space, Radcliffe's epigraphs are therefore not so much a frame for the text as a bridge between two narrative sections. In *The Romance of the Forest*, this bridging effect is perhaps best exemplified by the epigraph that prefaces the first chapter. Although the prose text exists on only one side of the chapter heading here, this epigraph nonetheless achieves more than simply highlighting the commencement of the novel. Rather, it becomes a means through which to induct the reader into the imagined world of the text.

The epigraph in question is adapted from the words of one of the murderers Macbeth hires to assassinate Banquo in Shakespeare's *Macbeth*:

> I am a man,
> So weary with disasters, tugg'd with fortune,
> That I would set my life on any chance,
> To mend it, or be rid on't.
>
> (*The Romance of the Forest*, p. 1)[40]

The only deviation from the original text of the play is that the first line actually reads 'And I another', with the conjunctive enhancing the stichomythic balancing of one full line of iambic pentameter between the two assassins (*Macbeth*, III.i.111). Previous to Radcliffe's use of the line, this text had been adapted for inclusion in *Modern characters for 1778. By Shakespear* (1778) as a description of the character of the Duke of St. Albans, though on this occasion the phrase 'I am one' had been substituted for the opening line of the speech in a neat appropriation of the words of Shakespeare's other murderer.[41] Though there is nothing to indicate whether Radcliffe may have been influenced by this, her own adaptation of the line demonstrates a sense of poetic rhythm keen to preserve the iambic metre even when this means incorporating words and phrases not lifted directly from Shakespeare's text. It is also worth noting that this omission of attribution occurs only in the first London edition, and in the Dublin editions of the text; the second and subsequent editions of *The Romance of the Forest* printed by Radcliffe's London publishers Hookham and Carpenter attribute this quotation to *King John*. Since editions of the complete works of Shakespeare seem to have frequently placed *King John* in the same volume as *Macbeth*, this is perhaps an easy mistake to make and, together with the slight variation from the original line, may indicate that Radcliffe transcribed the epigraph from memory. However the error crept in, Radcliffe's Dublin publishers would seem to have noticed something odd about the citation, as contemporaneous Irish editions omit an attribution of any kind for this one quotation.

Writing on Radcliffe's use of Shakespearean quotation throughout her novels, Kate Rumbold argues that Radcliffe's 'character-inflected epigraphs dramatise and amplify the unspoken anxieties of individuals in the text', effectively 'reveal[ing] the thoughts, wishes, and sometimes delusions of her characters'.[42] In this instance the epigraph does provide a direct, succinct summary of the character and attitude of the bankrupt protagonist Pierre La Motte as he flees into the night to escape prosecution from his creditors in Paris. That the ensuing chapter is focalised through the consciousness of La Motte only underscores this connection, as the dramatic immediacy of the epigraph's first-person narration complements the main narrative. More obliquely, the original context of the quotation might also be intended as a proleptic suggestion that, despite his prominence in the book's expositional phase, La Motte is only a subsidiary character whose crimes, like those of Macbeth's murderers, are often only the transferred crimes of others. When he eventually agrees to murder Adeline, for example, it is against his inclination and only so as to avoid 'the destruction that threatened him from the vengeance of the Marquis' (*The Romance of the Forest*, p. 227), the primary villain of the novel who has the power to inform La Motte's creditors of his hiding place.

What prevents this epigraph from becoming a simplistic framing device, however, is the visual appearance of the text upon the page, and the way in which this complements the ensuing prose. Given no attribution and marked off with inverted commas on every line, the epigraph is thus structurally almost indistinguishable from the novel's opening paragraph, since this begins with a few sentences of prose reportedly spoken by La Motte's legal friend the Advocate Nemours. Like the epigraphic quotation, this direct speech features the eighteenth-century practice of including double inverted commas at the commencement of every line of a quotation. Thus it is not until the reader arrives at the end of this paragraph that its status as direct speech rather than quotation becomes apparent. Indeed, even then the identification of the prose as speech rather than quotation is diminished through the inclusion of an oblique attribution at the start of a new paragraph: 'Such were the words of the Advocate Nemours to Pierre de la Motte' (*The Romance of the Forest*, p. 1). Neither a quotation, therefore, nor conventional direct speech, the paragraph becomes a unique transitional space through which the reader is conducted into the midst of the narrative before it has even apparently started, thus allowing the reader to encounter a narrative that not only begins *in medias res* but which crucially also provides a tangible sensation of doing so.

Following this advice from Nemours, it is said that La Motte 'thanked him for this last instance of his kindness; the assistance he had given him in escape' (*The Romance of the Forest*, p. 1); the qualifying clause is important here, identifying La Motte's gratitude as a response to practical 'assistance' rather than to Nemours's apparent declaration. Concluding with the hope that '[t]he time may come my friend, when death shall dissolve the sinews of avarice, and justice be permitted to resume her rights' (*The Romance of the Forest*, p. 1), Nemours's declaration would thus hardly be the most comforting words with which to console a bankrupt friend fleeing the just claims of his defrauded creditors. Although the reader is assured that Nemours has said this to La Motte 'as the latter stept [*sic*] at midnight into the carriage which was to bear him far from Paris' (*The Romance of the Forest*, p. 1), the attribution of the statement in a new paragraph, rather than immediately following the text, suggests that like the epigraphic quotation preceding it, Nemours's philosophy exists for the reader's benefit rather than La Motte's. David Durant argues that Radcliffe was 'philosophically traditional' and essentially conservative in her endorsement of moral integrity, epitomised for her in a domestically centred 'life of seclusion',[43] and it is this quality of her approach to the Gothic novel that is important here. For rather than prefacing her narrative only with the darkly supernatural framing offered by paratext selected from *Macbeth*, she in fact uses Nemours's speech to defuse this atmosphere of foreboding by countering it with the morality and logic that are the usual means through which her narratives are typically resolved. By identifying 'sordid interest' as 'an enemy alike to virtue and to taste' (*The Romance of the Forest*, p. 1), Radcliffe is alerting her reader to her novel's abstract worth as a book not just with a story to tell, but with a *moral* story to tell. The only difference to her epigraphic antecedents *Jack Connor* and *The Cry* is that here the moral epithet is not actually contained in the epigraph, but in the text of the narrative that follows. Rejecting a reliance upon the words of previous writers to furnish her text with moral authority, Radcliffe instead uses the epigraph to attune her reader to the emotional state of the chapter's main protagonist.

For crucially, Radcliffe's implementation of epigraphs effectively exploits and blurs the boundaries between prose and blank verse, between the reader's world and the imagined realm of the text. At least in the first and in all Dublin editions, the absence of an attribution for the epigraph combines with its first-person perspective to allow for the possibility that the Shakespearean quotation represents the words of La Motte before Nemours starts speaking. Radcliffe thus establishes these apostrophised sections of text as simultaneously both quotation and direct speech, and through this ambiguity conducts her reader seamlessly from their own everyday world (in which literary quotations from Shakespeare are quite literally a commonplace) into the imagined realm of the narrative where the dramatic emotions experienced and demonstrated by Shakespeare's characters constitute reality.

Although the dynamic innovation of the epigraph to the first chapter is never replicated elsewhere in the novel, there are nonetheless indications that Radcliffe was very much in the process of experimenting with ways in which to integrate epigraphic quotation within her work. At the end of the first chapter, for example, the La Mottes and Adeline are travelling towards the 'dark towers' which they have seen in the distance. The last sentence describes La Motte peering through a gap in the trees to gain 'a nearer, though imperfect, view of the edifice' (*The Romance of the Forest*, p. 14). The epigraph to the following chapter might almost be a description of what La Motte thinks and feels as he surveys the distant prospect:

> How these antique towers and vacant courts
> Chill the suspended soul! Till expectation
> Wears the face of fear: and fear, half ready
> To become devotion, mutters a kind
> Of mental orison, it knows not wherefore.
> What a kind of being is circumstance!
>   HORACE WALPOLE.
>   (*The Romance of the Forest*, p. 15)[44]

Although this epigraph is attributed, the sense that this is an extract from another writer's longer work diminishes given the relevance of the actual quotation to the narrative on both sides of the chapter division. Indeed, the narrative of the second chapter continues as if no such division existed, opening with the pronoun 'He' that implicitly assumes the reader will have progressed immediately from the first chapter. Indeed, even if this is not the case, the pronoun would guide the reader back to the end of the first chapter to confirm the identity of the person alluded to before they can progress on to the second chapter.

Although this does not guarantee that the epigraph will actually be read as part of this process, it does mean that the reader's eye would have to travel over the quotation before they could resume their reading at the commencement of the second chapter. Thus Radcliffe is consciously and deliberately guiding her audience to incorporate the poetry within their interpretation of her narrative. Rather than simply prefacing the ensuing prose, this epigraph is an example of a quotation that bridges the gap between two chapters, splicing them together as two parts of a narrative continuum. The chapter boundary here thus functions not so much as an interruption to the story, but rather as a space in which to focus attention upon Radcliffe's inclusion of the high-register description afforded by the epigraph.

A possible influence upon Radcliffe's development of this technique may be perceived via a previously unidentified epigraph with which she prefaces chapter 13 of *The Romance of the Forest*. This is in fact taken from Francis Quarles's *Emblemes* (1635):

> Nor sea, nor shade, nor shield, nor rock, nor cave,
> Nor silent desarts, nor the sullen grave,
> Where flame-ey'd Fury means to frown – can save.
>
> (*The Romance of the Forest*, p. 199)[45]

Within Radcliffe's work, this text fulfils the same function identified above: of bridging a transition or boundary in the narrative. The previous chapter details Adeline's journey as she flees the captivity of the Marquis's house with the hero Theodore, and his ensuing swordfight with the vengeful Marquis; the new chapter begins as both men nurse their injuries, while Adeline is escorted back to the doubtful safety of La Motte's guardianship. With its anaphorically repetitious syntax emphasising the relentless impossibility of attaining safety anywhere from 'flame-ey'd Fury', the quotation thus expresses Adeline's inability to escape the Marquis's persecution conveyed at the end of chapter 12 rather than reflecting the incapacitated condition of both men detailed in chapter 13. More relevant to the present argument, however, is the structure of the quotation's original source.

Divided first into books and then into smaller sub-sections marked with Roman numerals, Quarles's *Emblemes* also features biblical quotations at the commencement of each of these shorter sections of poetic narrative. The transitional character of these quotations is succinctly exemplified by the quotation used to preface the second such section, from the biblical Epistle of James:

> *Then when lust hath conceived, it bringeth forth sin; and sin, when it is finished, bringeth forth death.*
>
> (*Emblemes*, p. 9, I.ii)[46]

The previous section of Quarles's poetic dialogue had detailed the Serpent's temptation of Eve in the Garden of Eden, concluding with Eve's finally succumbing with the acknowledgement that 'Fruit's made for food: / I'll pull, and taste, and tempt my *Adam* too / To know the secrets of this dainty' (*Emblemes*, p. 6, I.i.54–56). Following the epigraph, the new section begins with the exclamatory 'Lament, lament; look, look, what thou hast done: / [. . .] / Lament thy fall, lament thy change of state' (*Emblemes*, p. 9, I.ii.1, 4). Although the biblical quotation is neither from Genesis nor directly referring to the temptation of Eve, the ideas it contains of *'lust . . . bring[ing] forth sin'* function as a way of transitioning between the temptation and its consequences. The juxtaposition of a poetic retelling of the Genesis narrative with a text taken from a New Testament section of the Bible thus fashions each as an interpretation of the other. For Quarles, the quotation becomes a way not merely of emphasising the theological authority of his work, but also of creating a continuum of cause and effect within the narrative. Such a sophisticated use of epigraphic quotation, in particular of epigraphs fulfilling a transitional function within a text that incorporates narrative elements (albeit poetry rather than prose), may therefore have provided a potentially quite influential source of inspiration for Radcliffe's later employment of a similar device.

However, the absence of any attribution for the Quarles quotation complicates the issue. Despite some indications of this Renaissance poet receiving more attention towards the close of the eighteenth century, the prevailing attitude of general disparagement towards his poetry may provide one explanation for Radcliffe's reluctance to actually name him within her novel. Although a certain amount of reverence for the poet may be implied in Paul Miner's recent suggestion that 'William Blake frequently turned to Francis Quarles's *Emblemes*, 1635, for graphic and textual inspiration',[47] late eighteenth-century commentators on Quarles were generally less than complimentary. On one of the rare occasions when his name is mentioned in the *Gentleman's Magazine*, it is in a letter bemoaning the fact that '[p]oor sleeping Quarles is at length disturbed' by critics such as William Jackson, who had discussed the poet's work favourably in his *Thirty Letters on various subjects*.[48] Indeed, even when praising Jackson for so doing, the enthusiasm of a contemporary reviewer remained somewhat lukewarm, stating that he had 'extracted a considerable portion of precious metal from the dross of that fantastical and unequal poet [Quarles]'.[49] It is by no means impossible, therefore, that the absence of an attribution on the Quarles epigraph in *The Romance of the Forest* was a conscious decision on Radcliffe's part not to associate her work with the doubtful merit of Quarles's oeuvre.

However, Radcliffe's commitment to providing attributions seems decidedly evident in the fact that there are only 5 out of 27 (or, in the London version from the second edition onwards, 4 out of 27) epigraphic quotations non-attributed in *The Romance of the Forest*. Of the remaining three non-attributed quotations from this work, the longest is a three-line quotation from Thomson's *The Seasons*:

> Drag forth the legal monster into light,
> Wrench from his hands Oppression's iron rod,
> And bid the cruel feel the pains they give.
>
> (The Romance of the Forest, p. 332)[50]

The only difference from the original is that here the plural 'legal monsters' (i.e. those individuals with the power to abuse laws for their own gain and security) are rendered into the singular 'legal monster', thus directing the quotation more specifically at the Marquis as his murderous crimes are finally exposed in the ensuing chapter. The two other non-attributed quotations are both extremely short, each only about a line in length. The first of these, taken from Shakespeare's *Macbeth*, reads 'Present ills / Are less than horrible imaginings',[51] which Chloe Chard notes is 'a misquotation of "Present fears . . ."' (*The Romance of the Forest*, pp. 97, 376n.). Since little material difference is made to the text whether the word used is 'ills' or 'fears', both this inconsistency and the lack of attribution would most adequately be explained by the quotation having been transcribed from memory rather than copied from an open volume. Similarly, the third of these unidentified quotations is a single line taken from Thomson's *Seasons* – 'While anxious doubt distracts the tortur'd heart' (*The Romance of the Forest*, p. 345)[52] – a quotation so short that subsequent editors of the work have likewise been unable to discover its origin (only located now through the use of computer searches). Crucially, this means that the absence of attribution for these three quotations is most probably not owing to deliberate omission or carelessness, but rather is a natural consequence of the difficulty of identifying a single line of blank verse transcribed from memory.

Elsewhere in *The Romance of the Forest* paratextual experimentation becomes rarer. In general, epigraphs are selected to reflect the ensuing narrative whilst preserving an invisible division between quotation and prose. In chapter 4, for example, there are two epigraphs, only one of which uses a first-person pronoun:

> ————My May of life
> Is fall'n into the sear, the yellow leaf.
> MACBETH
> Full oft, unknowing and unknown,
> He wore his endless noons alone,
>   Amid th' autumnal wood:
> Oft was he wont in hasty fit,
> Abrupt the social board to quit.
> WHARTON.
>
> (The Romance of the Forest, p. 44)[53]

The prose of the chapter begins with a description of how 'La Motte had now passed above a month' in hiding at the ruined castle (*The Romance of the Forest*, p. 44). The name tells the reader this is who the epigraphs are referring to; however, distance from the text is preserved here through the longer quotation's use of the third-person 'he' and 'his', and through the inclusion of attributions to the quotations. It prefaces the chapter, suggesting the action that is to follow and highlighting the predominant theme, that of a lonely, middle-aged man wandering by himself in the forest. This sense of distance is further enhanced in moments such as chapter 9, when a prefatory quotation taken from Thomas Warton's 'The Suicide' (1777) features a male pronoun even though the character in Radcliffe's narrative whom it has been appropriated to refer to is Adeline: 'Full many a melancholy night / He watched the slow return of light' (*The Romance of the Forest*, p. 127).[54] Yet although this epigraph resists absorption into the narrative in this way, it nonetheless demonstrates a more progressive use of prefatory quotation in its connection with the conclusion of the preceding chapter. In the last sentence, Radcliffe describes how 'Adeline passed the evening in melancholy thoughts, and retired, as soon as possible, to her chamber, eager to seek in sleep a refuge from sorrow' (*The Romance of the Forest*, p. 127). By Radcliffe's selection of a quotation for the following chapter that continues with a description of just such 'a melancholy night', in which the subject similarly '[seeks] the powers of sleep; / To spread a momentary calm', the poem gains significance not only as a reflection of the narrative, but also as an expression of the atmospheric tenor of the piece.

From the brief experimentation with the potential of the epigraphic device displayed in *The Romance of the Forest*, it is possible to see the groundwork for the more sophisticated use of epigraphs that would feature in Radcliffe's next and arguably most influential novel, *The Mysteries of Udolpho*.

EPIGRAPHS, SUBLIMITY, AND SLEEP

Although there are always exceptions, the epigraphs in *Udolpho* generally do not simply preface a chapter, but rather they develop the idea of the epigraph as a way of bridging the gap between two chapters through the incorporation of the quoted text as a way of accessing or provoking meaning within the imaginative space that this gap represents. A good example of this bridging effect is the epigraph used to preface volume 2 chapter 5 of *Udolpho*:

> Dark power! with shudd'ring, meek submitted thought
> Be mine to read the visions old
> Which thy awak'ning bards have told,
> And, lest they meet my blasted view,
> Hold each strange tale devoutly true.
> COLLINS' ODE TO FEAR
> (*Udolpho*, p. 222)[55]

The previous chapter had concluded with Emily 'retir[ing] to her bed, not to sleep [. . .] but to try, at least, to quiet her disturbed fancy' (*Udolpho*, p. 221). Following the usual chapter heading and epigraph, the new prose then begins with the words 'Emily was recalled from a kind of slumber' (*Udolpho*, p. 222). When read continuously, the gap between chapters thus becomes representative of the nocturnal time and space within which the heroine sleeps or attempts to sleep. At this moment in the narrative, Emily fears she is to be married the next morning to a man she detests, Count Morano. The selection of an epigraph from a poem dedicated to an exploration of fear thus becomes immediately appropriate not just to the ensuing chapter, but also to the crisis in the heroine's narrative that exists upon both sides of the chapter boundary. The quotation is appropriated as a representation of Emily's subconscious emotional spectrum as she enters a 'kind of slumber' that refracts her fears into a heightened state of nightmarish activity. Rumbold suggests that 'the epigraphs in Radcliffe's mature fiction [. . .] are not removed from the characters, but amplify their feelings and their voices'.[56] Indeed, when the specific narrative context of the epigraph is considered, this device becomes not just a means of 'amplify[ing] their feelings', but also of describing and expressing the subtlety of those feelings and emotions in a suitably nuanced and sophisticated manner.

Examination of narrative events surrounding such chapter boundaries reveals that using epigraphic quotation to cover the passage of night is far from being unique within the text. In fact, of the 56 divisions between chapters in *Udolpho*, around 36 occur at a moment of transition from evening or night-time to the beginning of a new day in the following chapter, of which 23 specifically refer to a character retiring to bed (if not actually to sleep). Another 4 chapter transitions occur at moments when a character has just died. Furthermore, the majority of these transitions occur in the early and middle phases of the narrative, in particular during Emily's persecution by her aunt and Montoni in Venice, and at the castle of Udolpho. Such a preoccupation with sleep is perhaps unsurprising given the genre in which Radcliffe is writing. *Udolpho* was advertised on its title page as 'A Romance', and Marshall Brown's overview of Romanticism identifies 'dreaming or daydreaming in dark grottoes' as part of the kind of 'Romantic nature feeling' that was 'widespread in the writing of the second half of the eighteenth century'.[57] Describing popular eighteenth-century perceptions of sleep and dreaming, Kenneth Winkler notes that the 'standard view' followed the belief expressed by David Hartley in his *Observations on Man* (1749) that '[d]reams are to be explained [. . .] by the impressions and ideas lately received (in particular, those of the previous day); by the state of the body, especially the stomach and brain; and by association'.[58] The continual disruption of the narrative of *Udolpho* at nightfall – generally after Emily has suffered an exhausting day of terrified oppression – thus means that in the continuum of the plot the dislocated text of the epigraph occupies the space of Emily's unconscious thoughts. Essentially, it is akin to a dream, with the fragmentary nature of the quotation only enhancing the sense of semi-lucidity associated with dreaming. Indeed, regarded from this perspective it becomes possible to extend Robert Miles's observation that in Radcliffe's fiction 'one encounters the creation of inner space' that consists of 'the blurring of the boundaries between subject and object, dream and the rational'.[59] For this is quite literally achieved via the epigraphic quotations, with the heightened register and metrical structure of poetic verse dissolved within the narrative scenario of a slumbering consciousness.

A good example of this is the epigraph that occurs after Emily perceives 'something like a human form' walking upon the castle ramparts (*Udolpho*, p. 356), but before she discovers there is no truth to her suspicions that Montoni has murdered her aunt, Madame Montoni:

> Such are those thick and gloomy shadows damp,
> Oft seen in charnel-vaults and sepulchres,
> Lingering, and sitting, by a new-made grave.
> MILTON
>
> (*Udolpho*, p. 357)[60]

The suggested shade or ghost described here evokes 'the mysterious form' whilst the 'new-made grave' recalls the imagined death of Madame Montoni. In the prose narrative, Emily's initial sense 'that she had witnessed a supernatural appearance' is quickly replaced with the more rational possibility of a much more human intruder (*Udolpho*, p. 356). The nocturnal scene concludes with the end of the chapter, by which point Emily is attempting to subdue her fears with the resolution to watch for and possibly speak to the figure on the following night. But the ensuing epigraph returns the reader with Emily to the nightmarish realm of suspicion and fear, underscoring existing anxieties and blurring the boundary between the real and the imagined.

Much has already been written on the influence of philosophical writers upon Radcliffe's construction of the Gothic: Kristin Girten points out that '[s]cholars typically read Radcliffe's aesthetics in line with Burke's or Kant's' before responding with the more probable suggestion that Radcliffe was actually influenced by both.[61] It is worth revisiting these connections here, since it is through these two philosophers' ideas regarding poetry and the sublime that it is possible to explain Radcliffe's tendency to combine chapter breaks with epigraphic quotation and moments of sleep. In particular, it is Radcliffe's definition and construction of terror as a sublime experience that has typically been considered to owe much to the ideas of Edmund Burke: as Coral Ann Howells summarises, 'Burke analysed sublimity in his treatise and Mrs Radcliffe dramatized her analysis in her fiction, adding narrative interest to aesthetic speculation.'[62] Offering a more nuanced interpretation, Girten argues that Radcliffe deviates from Burkean and Kantian philosophy in a key point, since their belief that 'the sublime is contingent on the observer's physical safety' seems contradicted by a tendency in her novels to allow 'characters [to] regularly experience the delights of sublimity while immersed within threatening situations'.[63]

A further complication is presented by the inclusion and narrative positioning of the epigraphic quotations. As Andrew Smith's study of Radcliffe's aesthetics rightly remarks, it is a 'commonplace to note that Radcliffe's writings privilege Burkean obscurity over an aesthetics of Horror';[64] but less commonly referred to is Burke's identification of this same obscurity as one of the most characteristically sublime elements of poetry. Writing in his *Philosophical Enquiry into the Sublime and Beautiful* (1757), Burke quotes Milton's depiction of Satan in *Paradise Lost* (1667) in which it is stated that Satan appears:

> [. . .] *as when the sun new ris'n*
> *Looks through the horizontal misty air*
> *Shorn of his beams; or from behind the moon*
> *In dim eclipse disastrous twilight sheds*
> *On half the nations; and with fear of change*
> *Perplexes monarchs.*[65]

It is, Burke claims, an exemplary instance of 'sublime description', and he uses it to illustrate his claim that '[t]he images raised by poetry are always of this obscure kind'.[66] Later, Burke continues with his delineation of the relationship between words and emotion, claiming that 'we find by experience that eloquence and poetry are as capable, nay indeed much more capable of making deep and lively impressions than any other arts, and even than nature itself in very many cases'.[67] As Smith interprets, it is '[t]he obscurity within the poetic discourse [. . .] which moves us and stimulates the imagination'.[68] By including poetic quotations at every chapter break, Radcliffe is thus harnessing a form of discourse that accesses thoughts and emotions in a much less pragmatic way than the prose of her narrative. There, Emily's physical terror is easily expressed, as when she 'screamed in despair' (*Udolpho*, p. 261) in response to Morano's invasion of her bedroom, or when she peered behind the black veil and 'dropped senseless on the floor' (*Udolpho*, p. 249). During her persecution at the castle of Udolpho, Emily only has an opportunity to sleep (or at least to retire to her chamber for the night) when enjoying a temporary respite from immediate danger. Indeed, in a rare moment where Emily's sleep is disturbed by the sexual danger posed by Count Morano's intrusion into her chamber, there is no chapter break and therefore no poetic epigraph. Anne Williams writes that '[t]he power of Radcliffe's strategy lies in her "expanding" the reader's

51

imaginative powers in suspense and speculation';[69] this 'suspense and speculation' aligns with the fears – or more appropriately *terrors* – of the persecuted heroine, whose only opportunity for processing the emotion of terrified anticipation comes when she enjoys the temporary security and privacy of her own chamber. Under this philosophy, the epigraphic quotation represents a sublime emotion conveyed within a sublime form of textual discourse.

Furthermore, a deeper dimension may be regarded through Kant's assertion that 'it is the attunement of the spirit evoked by a particular representation engaging the attention of reflective judgement, and not the object, that is to be called sublime'.[70] Most importantly, as Terrence Des Pres explains, it is Kant's belief that 'terror becomes the mind's opportunity to transcend its ordinary limits and thereby recognize its own sublime dominion over even the worst threats'.[71] As a concept, this correlates very well with Radcliffe's distinctive motif of prioritising the rational over the supernatural, of reason triumphing over the inexplicable. Similarly, when Emily retires to sleep it is not generally to indulge in the experience of terror but, as when she is faced with the prospect of a forced marriage to Morano, 'to collect strength of spirits sufficient to bear her through the scene of the approaching morning' (*Udolpho*, p. 221). Later, when staying at Udolpho, sleep often only comes to Emily once her rational mind has asserted itself in some way that counteracts abstract fears, for example when she 'listened till all was still again' outside her room (*Udolpho*, p. 310), and again when she uses (albeit doubtful) empirical reasoning to convince herself that if the strange musical sounds she has heard 'were human [. . .] I shall probably hear them again' (*Udolpho*, p. 331). The epigraph which immediately follows amplifies this rationalisation process yet does so only by simultaneously reinforcing the sense that further mysteries and crimes remain to be discovered:

> Then, oh, you blessed ministers above,
> Keep me in patience; and, in ripen'd time,
> Unfold the evil which is here wrapt up
> In countenance.
>
> SHAKESPEARE
>
> (*Udolpho*, p. 331)[72]

For although the epigraphs occupy the narrative space of the unconscious mind, and despite being couched in the obscurity of poetic syntax, they nonetheless represent a comparatively formal, structured response to an experience of terror. Effectively this containment allows for safe, regulated expression of passionate feelings, before returning to Emily's broadly logical and pragmatic outlook in the new chapter, on the new day. Indeed, through this key distinguishing characteristic the epigraphs become part of Radcliffe's broader, morally instructive aim for her novel. For while Girten suggests that through

Radcliffe's fiction her readers 'learn how to identify the sublime and to appreciate the transports it makes possible',[73] Vartan Messier identifies a broader educational intention as he claims that 'Radcliffe carefully aims to gently entertain her reader by providing a moral framework, rationalizing the supernatural, and merely suggesting an idea of terror.'[74] Similarly, Markman Ellis observes that *Udolpho* 'describes how Emily achieves her innate innocence and virtue by a course of education and advice, and furthermore, it offers itself as a way of disseminating this advice and education to its own readers'.[75] Through the epigraphic quotations this morally constructive tendency is implicitly presented, since it incorporates a form of literary discourse that does not simply construct sublime emotion, but does so in a profoundly organised and regulated manner.

As Emily's oppression at Udolpho continues and her aunt's health fails, the epigraph that falls between two accounts of potentially supernatural omens once again becomes the space in which to vocalise her worst imaginings. Although in the prose narrative Emily remains 'half smiling' at the guards' fears that they have seen 'the devil' walking the castle ramparts (*Udolpho*, p. 370), the chapter concludes and the epigraph appears with her struggle to repress an inclination towards irrational fear:

> But her imagination was inflamed, while her judgment was not enlightened, and the terrors of superstition again pervaded her mind.
>
> CHAPTER IV
> There is one within,
> Besides the things, that we have heard and seen,
> Recounts most horrid sights, seen by the watch.
> JULIUS CÆSAR
> (*Udolpho*, p. 371)[76]

Radcliffe resists completing the quotation, which continues to describe how 'graves have yawned and yielded up their dead', instead choosing to prioritise the source of these anxieties and omens, namely 'the watch' or guards. Here Radcliffe likewise avoids quoting from an arguably more famous Shakespearean instance of a ghost seen by castle guards walking the ramparts at night in the first act of *Hamlet*: taken in conjunction this indicates that it is not the ghost itself upon which Radcliffe wants her readers to focus. In the play from which she does quote the omens are simply abstract expressions and amplifications of more pragmatic threats: the fevered excuses of Caesar's wife as she tries to deter him from attending the forum on the day he is killed by an all-too-human collection of murderers. As an expression of Emily's subconscious musings the epigraph thus highlights the struggle between the rational and the imagined, in which perceived omens become a reflection of real dangers.

The 'figure' that haunts Udolpho will turn out to be only the imprisoned Monsieur Du Pont, who later becomes Emily's means of liberation from the castle; Emily's supernatural fears here are only an expression of the much more tangible threat Montoni poses to her life and her aunt's. The epigraph is immediately followed with a thoroughly practical assessment of Madame Montoni's physical state: 'she had slept little, and that little had not refreshed her; she smiled on her niece, and seemed cheered by her presence, but spoke only a few words' (*Udolpho*, p. 371). The epigraph is once again a transitional space that expresses and envisions the process by which Emily's subconscious reorders her thoughts to focus upon her real anxieties. Radcliffe is thus not simply indulging her readers with a formulaic repetition of 'a single scene of disorientation or fear' as Joseph Crawford suggests.[77] Rather, she is providing her reader with that experience of fear or terror, and then pragmatically demonstrating a way in which to rationalise such emotions through a consistent narrative pattern of sleep – epigraphic poetry – awakening.

FRAME NARRATIVES AND EPIGRAPHS

In her final two novels, Radcliffe demonstrates once again a creativity and originality that resists succumbing to the formulaic. The introduction of pre-chapter epigraphs in *The Romance of the Forest* and *Udolpho* had constituted a pronounced shift away from the plain prose style of her earliest novels, *The Castles of Athlin and Dunbayne* (1789) and *A Sicilian Romance* (1790), and a key element of the development of her aesthetic of terror. In her remaining novels, *The Italian* (1797) and *Gaston de Blondeville* (published posthumously in 1826 but believed to have been mostly completed by 1802–03),[78] it is a gradual drift away from the use of quotations in epigraphic paratext that is most noticeable. For while every pre-chapter epigraph in *The Romance of the Forest* and *Udolpho* has now finally been accounted for, the same cannot be said for *The Italian*. Of the 34 epigraphs included in this novel, 7 of those given no attribution by Radcliffe continue to be unidentifiable within any other text of earlier or contemporary date. There is still a possibility that these epigraphs are translations of extracts from Continental literature, yet there remains no evidence in support of this. If they were translations then the most probable explanation for their apparent non-appearance in other contemporaneous English texts would be that Radcliffe had translated them herself; however, if this had been the case, she should surely also have been able to provide an attribution for the original source material. Her comparative scrupulousness in identifying quotations from the work of others within her earlier novels (discussed above) thus greatly diminishes the likelihood of her having deliberately quoted or translated without attribution in this instance.

The probability that she composed these epigraphs herself is then further increased when *The Italian* is considered alongside her final novel, *Gaston de*

Blondeville, a work that replaces the pre-chapter quotation with something Jacobs describes as 'ekphrastic epigraphs'.[79] This new style of epigraphic paratext consists of prose written by Radcliffe to describe what an entirely imagined facing image would have depicted in the ancient 'manuscript [. . .] written on vellum, and richly illuminated' (*Gaston*, p. 18) from which the main narrative claims to be derived, for example:

> *At the head of this chapter was a drawing, of the King and Queen, with their train, passing under the towers of Kenilworth. Near the King rode a young knight of a very spirited air; in one hand he held his cap, bending towards the King, who seemed to be speaking to him, and with the other he reined in his fiery courser.*
>
> (*Gaston*, p. 28)

Previous commentary upon *The Italian* has tended to consider it largely as a response to Lewis's notorious Gothic novel *The Monk* (1796), with Syndy Conger even going so far as to argue that it was the 'first significant literary protest against *The Monk*'.[80] Similarly, Andrew Smith argues that Radcliffe's *The Italian* 'moves beyond the type of aestheticism developed in *Udolpho* because her various Gothic devices were turned by Lewis into a self-parodying rhetoric', identifying the 'poetic omissions' of *The Italian* (compared with Radcliffe's earlier work) as a symptom of Lewis's influence.[81] Yet while it is true that the main prose of *The Italian* does not feature the extensive verse compositions that populate the pages of *Udolpho*, Radcliffe's inclusion of her own blank verse in the paratextual space of the epigraph in this later work suggests a gradual shift rather than an abrupt revision of her creative approach. Indeed, when considered alongside the entirely self-composed epigraphic paratext of *Gaston de Blondeville*, this difference in style between *The Italian* and its predecessors appears more as a stage in a continually evolving process of literary experimentation. The chronological distance between the composition of her novels, and the fact that Radcliffe wrote 'for pleasure rather than for profit',[82] only further promotes this perception of Radcliffe as a writer whose first aim was always to create something innovative and to avoid the repetition of ideas and literary effects.

This originality is further evidenced in both *The Italian* and *Gaston de Blondeville* through Radcliffe's experimentation with frame narratives. Constituting a distinct move away from the kind of direct interiority offered in *The Romance of the Forest* and *Udolpho*, this device not only enables Radcliffe to provide her last novels with greater contemporary relevance, but also allows her to explore the way in which epigraphic paratext can be used to exaggerate and emphasise this difference between a recognisably conventional reality and the Gothic fantasy of the text. The exact geographical location of this fantasy is something that Radcliffe's earlier novels tend to remain rather vague about: *The Romance of the Forest* uses the most obviously French of cities, Paris, as the place from which La Motte is fleeing, just as *Udolpho* would later identify cities such as Paris, Venice, and Toulouse as three similarly vice-infested metropoles. Other locations, such as the castle of Udolpho, La Vallée, and (in *The Romance of the Forest*) the Abbey of St Clair, are described in terms of their aesthetic rather than their precise cartographic situation. In *The Italian*, however, Radcliffe appears more than usually keen to identify the text with a very specific place and time. A succession of clear identifying facts loads the first sentence:

> About the year 1764, some English travellers in Italy, during one of their excursions in the environs of Naples, happened to stop before the portico of the *Santa Maria del Pianto*, a church belonging to a very ancient convent of the order of the *Black Penitents*. (*The Italian*, p. 3)

Unlike the typically anonymous monasteries or imaginary castles of Radcliffe's earlier writing, this is a genuine Italian church built in 1657 'outside the walls of seventeenth-century Naples in the district of Poggio Reale'. Situated over the Grotta degli Sportiglioni, one of the mass graves for Neapolitan victims of the 1656 plague epidemic, it was intended as a 'memorial chapel to the unnumbered plague dead who lay beneath it'.[83] Although there appears to be no evidence directly connecting the church with a monastic order such as the Black Penitents to whom Radcliffe refers, the church itself is mentioned briefly in Henry Swinburne's *Travels in the Two Sicilies* (1783–85), together with a sentence explaining its history and the reason for its construction.[84] An uncharacteristically pragmatic introduction to a Gothic novel, Radcliffe's opening sentence might itself almost be a line from a travelogue, and as such would have resonated strongly with those for whom European travel was somewhere between a realistic possibility and an educational necessity. Diego Saglia suggests that this 'prologue provides a useful insight into Radcliffe's interweaving of the Grand Tour approach with the circular quest structure of the romance', reflecting the characters' later 'Grand Tour-like travels across Italy'.[85] More immediately, this would have enabled Radcliffe's readers (or at least those from the middle and upper classes) to slide easily into her textual world, their own curiosity ventriloquised through that of the Englishman. The anonymisation of these 'English travellers' (*The Italian*, p. 3), together with the absence of chapter numeration or title for this section, only enhances the effect. Similarly, and most importantly, this frame narrative is allowed no prefatory epigraph.

The main plot is introduced through the conceit of being a genuine occurrence connected with 'some very extraordinary circumstances' that took place at the confessional box at Santa Maria del Pianto. The text itself has purportedly been 'written by a student of Padua, who [. . .] was so much struck with the facts [. . .] he committed them to paper' (*The Italian*, p. 6). The frame text ends when this account is delivered to the English traveller, of whom it is then stated that '[h]e read as follows:' (*The Italian*, p. 6). The concluding colon is followed only by the paratextual material associated with the first chapter:

> VOLUME 1
> > CHAPTER 1
> > > What is this secret sin; this untold tale,
> > > > That art cannot extract, nor penance cleanse?
> > > MYSTERIOUS MOTHER
> > > > (*The Italian*, p. 7)[86]

By implication, the epigraphic quotation is an element of the manuscript created by the 'student of Padua', thus subtly distancing it from the direct authorial influence of Radcliffe. Admittedly, the prominent identification of Radcliffe as the novel's author on the book's title page would have made it extremely unlikely that her readers would have ever believed the frame text to be anything but an artistic flourish. Yet this delayed introduction of epigraphic paratext does serve to locate it very strongly within the fictional realm of the plot, rather than the Englishman's more pragmatic world where questions generally receive immediate, uncomplicated answers (for example, '"Do your altars, then, protect the murderer?" said the Englishman. "He could find shelter no where else"', *The Italian*, p. 4). There have already been prominent indications that the plot of this novel will focus upon the content of 'the confession' to which the nameless Italian refers in the introductory section (*The Italian*, p. 5), and now the epigraphic quotation reinforces the idea with its questioning '[w]hat is this secret sin[?]' (*The Italian*, p. 7). Reflecting the multiple layers of text and paratext at the opening of *The Romance of the Forest*, this expositional structure in *The Italian* allows for a similar transportation from the reader's world to the fictional realm of the plot. There is an important difference in textual construction here, however, and it is this that preserves the element of surprise as, once again, the reader is plunged unexpectedly into the narrative. Having first created a realistic Grand-Tourist scenario, *The Italian* then undercuts this conventionality through the identification of the sightseers' destination as the focal point of a convoluted tale of which only glimpses are given. Unlike in *The Romance of the Forest*, it is the frame text that here constitutes the textual borderland where Gothic mystery connects with the everyday, while the epigraphic quotation is demoted to the means of signalling the completion of this transition to the fantasy world.

Yet as a textual signpost the epigraph is granted a new significance. Whilst its content perpetuates the sense of uncertainty and secrecy cultivated in the frame narrative, the quotation also immediately introduces implications of sexual deviancy via the notorious text from which it derives and to which it is carefully attributed: Walpole's drama of illegitimacy and incest, *The Mysterious Mother* (fifty copies of which were printed at Strawberry Hill in 1768 but not made widely available to a public readership until 1791).[87] Regarding the relevancy of this quotation, Robert Miles notes that '[t]he reader is halfway through *The Italian* before a possible application emerges', identifying its function as a reflection of the initially unknown (albeit ultimately non-existent) filial relationship between the heroine Ellena Rosalba and the sinister monk Schedoni.[88] However, as Caroline Gonda's study of eighteenth-century women's fiction points out, '[t]here is no explicit mention of incest', and despite Gonda's suggestion of sexual undertones in Schedoni's observation of the sleeping Ellena before his abortive attempt at murder,[89] it is difficult to perceive serious erotic interest in Radcliffe's brief description of Ellena 'in deep and peaceful slumber' (*The Italian*, p. 223). Throughout the scene, Schedoni's interest in her appears entirely murderous, and the adjustment he finds it necessary to make to Ellena's clothing so that it does not 'interrupt the blow' (*The Italian*, p. 223) of the dagger serves more to suggest his ineptitude as an assassin and to facilitate the discovery of his presumed paternity via the miniature Ellena wears. Furthermore, this incident in itself has little to do with the actual confession referred to in the frame narrative immediately preceding the introduction of the quotation. For when the content of this confession is finally revealed, it involves Schedoni's lust for the wife of his brother rather than for a direct blood-relation and the crimes this occasioned, which include (in order of occurrence) murder, abduction, rape, and attempted murder (*The Italian*, pp. 322–23). The obvious difference between this and the immorality of *The Mysterious Mother* is that in Radcliffe's novel the concealed crimes are all violent and only fuelled by sexual desire, whereas in Walpole's play it is the nature and object of that desire that renders it criminal. The relevance of the quotation Radcliffe attaches to the first chapter of her novel would therefore seem more likely to rest upon its immediate situation within the text. Indeed, this implication is further enhanced by the fact that in Walpole's play these lines are spoken in a church by a friar enquiring after the secret reason for the guilty grief of the eponymous '*Mother*', which does not appear to be allayed by her religious observances: the parallels with the assassin and confessional box in Radcliffe's frame narrative are readily apparent.

David Salter suggests that, as well as frequently 'evoking a sense of mystery and dread', the epigraphs in *The Italian* 'provide a commentary on the text designed to steer or guide the reader to a particular interpretation of events'.[90] As an example of this, he cites an epigraph from the novel's first volume that consists of two lines from Shakespeare's *Romeo and Juliet*: 'What if it be a poison, which the friar / Subtly hath ministered?' (*The Italian*, p. 53).[91] At this point in the novel, Ellena's guardian Signora Bianchi has been unexpectedly discovered dead, and Vivaldi is secretly investigating his fears that the lady may have been murdered (perhaps via poison) by the shadowy priest who has been stalking him near Ellena's home. Salter suggests that the 'use of this particular Shakespearean quotation is obviously designed to act as a hint to the reader that the friar is indeed guilty as suspected';[92] yet in fact this is only one of various possibilities introduced into the narrative here by the invocation of this moment in Shakespeare's play. For in *Romeo and Juliet*, it is crucially *not* poison that the friar has given to Juliet, it is only a sleeping draught designed to imitate death. Nor is Shakespeare's well-intentioned (if not always well-advised) Friar Lawrence in any way analogous with the description of the priest stalking the Rosalbas' house as 'looking like some supernatural messenger of evil' (*The Italian*, p. 49). Rather than supporting Vivaldi's fears, the quotation in fact challenges them: if Juliet's potion was only a sleeping draught, is the death of Ellena's guardian also a clever imposition? And if so, is the mysterious priest responsible or did she take it herself? In a genre where it is not uncommon for the presumed-dead to return to life (as Ellena's own mother effectively does in the novel's denouement), these questions are by no means idle. Yet as with the epigraph to the first chapter, the implications prompted by the quotation are ultimately proved to all be false: when Schedoni's crimes are eventually acknowledged, Vivaldi is finally 'convinced that [Bianca's] death was in consequence of some incident of natural decay' (*The Italian*, p. 379), while the shadowy figure whom he had suspected to be involved in the crime is proved to be an accomplice of Schedoni rather than the priest himself. Thus it appears it is not the similarities between her novel and the narratives of others that Radcliffe wishes to suggest, but the differences; her epigraphs here are not clues, but literary red-herrings, designed to distract her readers with false possibilities and thus prevent the premature deduction of the tale's real secrets.

Numerous other instances of epigraphic text being used in this way occur throughout the narrative, though the extent to which the original context of the quotation diverges from the ultimate trajectory of Radcliffe's novel does vary widely. The epigraph to volume 1 chapter 7 is taken from Shakespeare's *Hamlet* and is the line immediately preceding the first appearance of the ghost of Hamlet's father: 'The bell then beating one!' (*The Italian*, p. 68).[93] Within Radcliffe's narrative, this prefaces Vivaldi's eerie night-time encounter with the 'thrilling accents of the monk' who informs him of Signora Bianchi's death (*The Italian*, p. 70). Ultimately, however, this encounter transpires to have been in no way supernatural, since the monk is proved to be simply an accomplice of Schedoni and not a ghost, while the death of which he speaks is not a murder (unlike the death of Hamlet's father). Similarly, the epigraph prefacing the chapter in which Schedoni makes his aborted attempt upon Ellena's life is taken from *Macbeth*, and is in fact the last thing Macbeth says before the offstage murder of Duncan: 'I am settled, and bend up / Each corporal agent to this terrible feat' (*The Italian*, p. 214).[94] The quotation is still further blended into the text when Macbeth's hesitations prior to murder are paralleled by the doubts of Schedoni in the chapter preceding the epigraph, when 'even he could not now look upon the innocent [. . .] Ellena, without yielding to the momentary weakness [. . .] of compassion' (*The Italian*, p. 213). Since all of Radcliffe's previous novels followed narratives that always close with the heroine happily married to her hero of choice, the retention of a mood of serious threat must have proved increasingly challenging. Anticipating her readers' expectations, however, Radcliffe's inclusion of this particular quotation from *Macbeth* greatly assists in preserving the sense of serious peril, effectively preventing the reader from becoming too comfortable in the assumption that Radcliffe will not allow the murder of her heroine. Noting the importance of 'authors and authority, reading and readers, plotting and plotters' in *The Italian*, Andrew Warren writes that 'even if readers were familiar with Radcliffe's narrative strategies – which, judging from contemporary reviews, they undoubtedly were – they could not judge with certainty *when* or even *if* supernatural claims would be retracted or corrected'.[95] This sense of fathomless mystery is an important element of Radcliffe's success as a writer, and the doubtful reliability of the epigraphic quotations as an indication of narrative direction is a significant if subtle means of promoting this effect.

Conversely, not all the epigraphs in *The Italian* are derived from a work possessing a strong and immediately relevant narrative dimension: aside from the seven quotations that have already been established as most probably Radcliffe's own composition, there are quotations from short poetic works by writers such as Milton and Collins. The chapter in which the arrival of officials, ostensibly from the Inquisition, results in the abandonment of Ellena and Vivaldi's wedding is prefaced with a quotation from Milton's 'On the Morning of Christ's Nativity' (1645). The lines in question describe the anticipated atmosphere of the Day of Judgement, and their inclusion here represents a prioritisation of aesthetic rather than narrative relevance at this point. Yet the idea of retribution for sin that the quotation thus introduces does provide a point of thematic contact between the two chapters, linking the 'mournful music' of the requiem that twinges the conscience of the Marchesa (Vivaldi's mother) as she contemplates the murder of Ellena (*The Italian*, p. 169) with the calling to account of Vivaldi for having seemed to have 'stolen a nun from her convent' (*The Italian*, p. 180). The quotation establishes a connection between the otherwise disparate ideas of both chapters, in a manner not dissimilar to the transitional qualities provided by epigraphs in Radcliffe's previous novels. The only difference is that here it is the conscious fears of two separate characters that are vocalised, rather than the subconscious terrors of a sleeping heroine. Unlike *Udolpho*, Radcliffe's *The Italian* possesses a plot that requires multiple character perspectives, which means that chapter breaks are typically an opportunity to move from one character or character-grouping to another. Yet by linking both groupings thematically via the epigraph, Radcliffe is able to maintain a similar sense of claustrophobic complexity within the narrative.

In Radcliffe's last novel, *Gaston de Blondeville*, the construction of sublimity through obscurity surfaces once again as the descriptive nature of the text which prefaces each chapter, or 'Day', is rendered mysterious by the ambiguity of the scene presented. A contemporary reviewer described them as '"arguments"' and noted that 'they often remind one of the fanciful vignettes which are to be found in books and manuscripts of an ancient date', and this is certainly the impression that Radcliffe seems to have been endeavouring to produce.[96] For example, the 'Third Day' commences with the following text:

> *Here was a drawing of the inside of the great hall, with the King and Queen holding festival. In the back-ground was a sketch, of what seemed to be a pageant acted there; and yet the spectators appeared to be looking on, with an interest too serious for so trifling a performance. In the margin, also, was drawn, the chapel before mentioned, with a marriage ceremony at the porch.*
>
> (*Gaston*, p. 69)

Although characters are anonymised, sufficient information is conveyed in the preceding chapter to enable the reader to identify the '*marriage ceremony*' as a reference to the anticipated nuptials between the eponymous Sir Gaston de Blondeville and the woman to whom he is betrothed, Lady Barbara. However, visually the marriage itself has been relegated to '*the margin*', with precedence instead given to the royal '*festival*'. That this only '*seemed to be a pageant*' (emphasis added) enhances the sense of uncertainty concerning the nature of the scene about to be presented, whilst the fact that '*the spectators appeared to be looking on, with an interest too serious for so trifling a performance*' only heightens the tension still further. By combining disparate, symbolic elements in this way, Radcliffe tantalises the reader with the idea that the wedding itself is about to be overshadowed by something, but without revealing precisely what that thing will be. Since the new chapter begins with the wedding, it is some time before the full meaning of the epigraph is revealed in the ensuing festivities via the inclusion of a tableau akin to the 'Mousetrap' play in Shakespeare's *Hamlet*. During this scene, which concludes the pageant, a robber is depicted murdering a knight, after which the latter figure stands 'pointing with his sword to the Baron de Blondeville, who stood trance-bound [. . .], his eyes glared' (*Gaston*, p. 94). Yet it is only much later in the narrative that Gaston's guilt is definitively revealed when it is established that he had murdered his kinsman in pursuit of wealth. Once again, Radcliffe is styling her pre-chapter paratext in accordance with Burkean principles of sublimity, and preserving the terror of suspense by only slowly revealing glimpses of character and narrative to her readers. The difference here is that the character in peril from the (this time, genuinely) supernatural threat is a murderer rather than an unjustly persecuted heroine.

In his history of Gothic literature, Punter suggests that this deviation from the narrative structure of Radcliffe's previous novels was 'largely because of the growing influence of Scott and a consequent increased involvement with "real" history';[97] yet this takes no account of the fact that the majority of the book was already written by late 1803, more than ten years before Walter Scott published his first novel. Indeed, the fact that the novel was not published until 1826 (after Radcliffe's death) means that its capacity to influence literary tastes was severely overshadowed by developments in prose fiction during the intervening decades.

Although the majority of reviewers were politely complimentary, there is an inescapable sense of nostalgia as they refer to the novel as a way through which 'Radcliffe's name has again broken in upon us with the light of other years'; a disappointing consequence of this is that *Gaston de Blondeville*'s place in literary history has largely been defined by the seemingly collective judgement that it was 'on the whole, unworthy of the source from which [it] sprung'.[98] By examining *Gaston de Blondeville* within the context of the time when it was composed, and by returning it to its place in the continuum of Radcliffe's own creative development, the novel actually appears as a strikingly innovative and experimental work and a natural next stage in her constantly evolving oeuvre. Once again, Radcliffe is reacting to the changing literary field, resisting the increasingly prevalent quoted epigraphic texts that she had herself popularised just as she avoids rationalising her ghost. Like the notorious dark veil that conceals the memento mori in *Udolpho*, the epigraphs and frame narrative weave an obscuring cloud of antiquity about the tale that repositions the sublimity of the half-seen as an intrinsic quality of the text. The present-day reader has only a narrow glimpse of the past through the lines of the manuscript and so the supernatural elements may safely be permitted to frustrate attempts at rationalisation.

Although Radcliffe ceased novel-writing after the composition of *Gaston de Blondeville*, her fascination with extracting quotations from longer works did not disappear. Only one of her commonplace books is known to have survived, used by Radcliffe from May to November 1822 and recording details of her last illness before her death in February 1823. Cheryl Nixon has analysed the way in which Radcliffe's descriptions of her own illness demonstrate an attempt to rationalise it and thus 'exert control over her insecure position'.[99] But as well as including details of symptoms and doctor's prescriptions, the earliest pages of the book also include an array of quotations, carefully copied out and attributed. Unlike Radcliffe's epigraphs, these quotations are all from prose works, for example:

> "Neither have we to reproach him, that, grounded and rooted in ~~the~~ a pure Protestant creed, he was foolish enough to abandon it for the more corrupted doctrines of Rome." Walter Scott; Life of Dryden: p. 315.[100]

As Nixon points out, however, the formal regularity suggested by the textual transcriptions is not representative of the character of the notebook as a whole, and she observes that 'it appears as if, from the start, the book would not be limited to one form of writing'. On the verso side of the leaf upon which the above quotation is written, there is 'a small, simple and utterly charming drawing of stars', carefully labelled. Although there are only five pages of these quotations at the beginning of the notebook, Nixon has identified them to four different sources.[101] Whilst both literary form and subject matter differ considerably from the quotations which feature in Radcliffe's fiction, this notebook nonetheless offers the only glimpse available of the way in which Radcliffe may have approached the process of gathering extracts of text for later consultation and use. Here, the quotations are typically formal in character but also recorded without explanation and at least have the potential to be interrupted by other, presumably unconnected, notes such as the star diagram. They cease only when her own failing health intrudes, and the book becomes a record of illness rather than of significant sentences.

Radcliffe's enthusiasm for quotation, paratext, and literary experimentation constituted a critical element of the innovative originality that made her novels so wildly popular, and later so persistently imitated. She was influential both in her use of epigraphs and, more broadly, as a catalysing agent for change in the direction of Romantic fiction. Rather than simply telling her readers about her characters' adventures, Radcliffe's use of epigraphs in both *The Romance of the Forest* and *The Mysteries of Udolpho* developed this paratextual form as a means through which to vocalise the sentiments and emotions of her characters. Anticipating some of the concerns of realist fiction in her epigraphic construction of psychological interiority, Radcliffe shifted the pre-chapter quotation from a means through which an author may comment upon a text into a means of commenting from within it. In *The Italian* and *Gaston de Blondeville* she began to transcend this function, experimenting with the capacity of the narrative voice of the epigraph to lead and mislead as well as to directly illumine the inner life of characters. Both developments would have significance for the myriads of novelists and epigraphic users who came after her.

3

FROM INNOVATIVE PARATEXT TO SATIRICAL STEREOTYPE: CHARLOTTE SMITH, MATTHEW LEWIS, AND EATON STANNARD BARRETT

Sæpe caput scalpet, vivos et roderet ungues.
HOR.
(he would oft scratch his head and gnaw his nails to the quick)[1]

Published in the same year as Radcliffe's *The Mysteries of Udolpho*, the one-volume anonymous novel *Argentum: or, Adventures of a Shilling* (1794) presents the autobiography of a coin's experiences and impressions of the world as it passes from person to person. The epigraph presented above heads a chapter in which the shilling has just fallen into the hands of a scapegrace medical student who is obliged to take a job at a 'fashionable newspaper' following a disagreement with the relation upon whom he is financially dependent. The narrator drily points out:

> To such an employment the line of Horace, quoted above, is truly applicable. To such an employment I might, possibly, in the heat of resentment, wish an enemy condemned; but I trust I should have sufficient charity to remit his punishment in a short time.[2]

The joke relies upon the reader having read and understood the prefatory epigraph (sans translation), which thus functions both as a headline for the chapter's description of the new owner and as a self-reflexive joke upon the practice and profession of writing. The extent to which readers engaged with prefatory paratext might be difficult to determine, but the self-awareness of the authors who use epigraphs is readily apparent. Still more significantly, although this novel appeared after Radcliffe's *The Romance of the Forest* (1791), it is not in any way attempting to imitate her, with regard to either narrative or epigraphic content.

Although the publication of *The Romance of the Forest* and *Udolpho* undoubtedly sparked an increase in the number of novels to feature epigraphic quotation, the identification of the epigraph with the wider Gothic genre was actually quite slow to develop. So far only 3 of the 58 novels known to have had their first editions published in 1792 have been found to contain pre-chapter epigraphs out of a total of 50 surveyed. The following two years appear to demonstrate similarly limited usage, with only 4 novels featuring epigraphs currently identified for each year in 1793 and 1794. It is not until after the publication of *Udolpho* that this figure really begins to rise: I have found at least 8 novels that were published with epigraphs in 1795, and in 1796 there were at least 15. However, it should also be considered that there appears to have been a substantial increase in the number of novels known to have been published between these two years, with Garside, Raven, and Schöwerling listing only 50 published in 1795, whilst 91 appeared in 1796. Of these, it has been possible to check the epigraphic content of 49 of the novels published in 1795 and 84 of those published in 1796. This has revealed that the percentage of books with epigraphs published in each of these two years is almost identical, standing at 16% in 1795 and nearly 16.5% in 1796 (both a substantial increase on the similarly calculated 7% of novels published with epigraphs in 1794).[3] Some of these novels have since been categorised as part of the booming genre of Gothic fiction, for example the anonymously authored *Arville Castle* (1795), Anna Maria Mackenzie's *Mysteries Elucidated* (1795), and Francis Lathom's *The Castle of Ollada* (1795).[4] On the other hand, there were many other Gothic novels published at the time that did not have any form of pre-chapter epigraph. Eliza Parsons's *Castle of Wolfenbach* (1793) does not even have chapter divisions let alone epigraphs, and despite a prolific output in the ensuing decade she does not seem to begin using epigraphs until *The Valley of St. Gothard* (1799). Some novelists whose works are typically considered to be Gothic and/or Romantic in character, for example Isabella Kelly and Charlotte Dacre, never used epigraphs at all. Nor were epigraphs always solely the preserve of the Gothic genre, at least in the early 1790s. As has already been discussed, the novels which preceded Radcliffe's use of the epigraph frequently featured a moral, philosophical, or picaresque quality, and examples of this include texts such as *The Amicable Quixote* (1788)[5] and *Argentum* (mentioned above). This use of the epigraph as an educational tool resurfaces briefly in the 1790s in Margaret Mitchell's *Tales of Instruction and Amusement* (1795), in which the narrative is divided into sections of text prefaced with short, self-authored verse that highlights the moral principles about to be presented in the ensuing prose.[6]

Immediately preceding the proliferation of Gothic novels with epigraphs sparked by Radcliffe, the novelist and poet Charlotte Smith published a novel that self-consciously rejects a romance-based narrative and that uses epigraphs as part of this wider experimental theme. In *The Banished Man* (1794), Smith addresses cultural dislocation and political exile in the wake of the French Revolution, focusing upon the dispossessed son of a French aristocrat, D'Alonville. Smith's use of the epigraph is of particular interest since she later includes the device as an accompaniment to narratives of a more stereotypically Gothic nature, thus becoming a case study through which the rapid transition of the epigraph from experimental paratext to Gothic stereotype may be explored. In this chapter I will examine the introduction and evolution of epigraphs in Smith's work, using this analysis to demonstrate that, despite Smith's adoption of Gothic stereotypes in some of her prose fiction, her deployment of the epigraph began as an innovative extension of a narrative-based polemic calling for peace and humanitarian empathy within a war-torn post-revolutionary Europe. The investigation of Smith's epigraphs will then be followed by an examination of the role played by Matthew Lewis's *The Monk* (1796) in solidifying the association between epigraphs and the Gothic genre to the point where this connection later becomes a focus of satirical humour in works such as Eaton Stannard Barrett's *The Heroine, or Adventures of a Fair Romance Reader* (1813) and Jane Austen's *Northanger Abbey* (1818).

Epigraphs and Social Harmony

By the time Charlotte Smith published *The Banished Man* in 1794, she had already authored six novels. Of these, none featured pre-chapter epigraphic quotations, and only *The Old Manor House* (1793) included any sort of title-page motto. In this, her last major work before commencing *The Banished Man*, may be glimpsed the beginnings of her experimentation with paratextual quotations via the use of a different motto for each volume of *The Old Manor House*. Although a detailed survey of title-page mottos is outside the scope of this monograph, there are indications that the more usual practice at the time was to feature the same, unaltered motto on every volume of a novel.[7] Only the most experimental novels feature different title-page mottos for individual volumes of the same work, for example William Chaigneau's *The History of Jack Connor* (1752) and Laurence Sterne's *The Life and Opinions of Tristram Shandy, Gentleman* (1759–67); in Sterne's case the unusual practice of publishing further volumes of the novel at intervals of one or more years is exaggerated by the inclusion of a new motto for every new pair of volumes.

In Smith's case, the use of such innovation in *The Old Manor House* demonstrates the development of her interest in the piecemeal incorporation of others' texts within her own. Indeed, the absence of quotation-based paratextual experimentation in her work prior to this may be pragmatically accounted for by the sheer time and effort necessary for the identification of relevant texts. A single parent struggling to finance the needs of a large family, Charlotte Smith relied, if not quite wholly then at least to a very large extent, upon the income supplied by her literary career. When she first started writing novels in the late 1780s it was not unusual for books to be published without even a motto on the title page, and as Smith was financially obliged to prioritise business over art she may simply have not been able to afford to spend time on embellishments that would enhance creative quality rather than book sales. The editor of her correspondence, Judith Phillips Stanton, notes the difficulty of ascertaining whether Smith 'engaged in her tremendous literary effort only for the money, or was there an underlying seriousness about the artistic value of what she wrote?'[8] The most obvious answer to this lies in her own angry tirade against the publisher Joseph Bell, whom she indignantly believed regarded her 'as a miserable Author under the necessity of writing so many sheets a day'.[9] It was only after the conclusion of her unsatisfactory contract with Bell that she first began to use pre-chapter epigraphic quotations; the novel in question was to be one of the most innovative and acutely personal in her whole oeuvre.

As with her other writing, *The Banished Man* was composed at a time when the financial pressures upon Smith were extreme. On 9 October 1793 she wrote to her friend and business associate in Ireland, the antiquarian Revd Joseph Cooper Walker, and narrated in agonised terms her son's forced return from the war in France owing to a leg amputation. It was her concern to be able to afford for him all necessary comforts that had, she says, 'set me to work again on a Novel, which as fast as I write I get my daughters to copy'.[10] Yet what she produced was not the predictable Gothic Romance potboiler that might have been expected in such circumstances. Instead, the narrative follows the adventures of the French émigré D'Alonville as he travels through Europe to escape persecution in war-torn France, and suffers continual and humiliating suspicion and rejection. Even though D'Alonville's adventures do eventually include his meeting, courting, and marrying the Englishwoman Angelina Denzil, this romance remains very much a subplot to the novel's main aim of presenting and exploring ideas of cultural dislocation and exile inflicted by civil conflict. Smith even underscores the experimental nature of her work by taking the unusual step of prefacing the work's second volume with a section entitled 'Avis Au Lecteur' (or 'Advice to the Reader'), in which she acknowledges her avoidance of a conventional romance narrative by stating that she believed 'the situation of [her] hero was of itself interesting enough to enable [her] to carry him on for sometime, without making him violently in love'.[11] As Jillian Heydt-Stevenson and Charlotte Sussman point out in their study of Romantic-era ethical experiments in literature, *The Banished Man* is an excellent example of the way in which 'the Romantic-era novel was engaged with rewriting the narrative conventions inherited from previous generations'.[12]

The title of the novel would seem to contradict this, since Stuart Curran notes that it was taken from a poem by Matthew Prior in which a man asks his lover if she will join her life with his or leave him 'Condemn'd in lonely / Woods a banish'd Man to rove'.[13] Yet the romantic elements of Smith's narrative remain very much a subplot, and there is no real happy-ever-after for D'Alonville and Angelina: both become exiled from their homelands as their only option to establish a stable domestic life is ultimately to move to Verona. As Antje Blank notes in her study of the Gothic elements of some of Smith's politically focused literature, 'D'Alonville [. . .] is by no means the only persecuted "banished man"' in the novel.[14] In fact numerous and varied instances of banishment and socio-political exile occur throughout the book, prompting a note of surprise from Heydt-Stevenson and Sussman as they suggest 'Smith's narrative might be more accurately described as a novel of mass experience' that thus 'challenges the convention that novels tell the story of individuals'.[15] As a way of describing the extreme loneliness and lack of belonging experienced by those displaced by the conflict, however, Smith's title is a subtle way of succinctly expressing the nature of this 'mass experience' in terms of its personal impact.

The inspiration for the novel's hero D'Alonville has long been identified as Smith's own son-in-law, le chevalier Alexandre Mark Constant de Foville of Notre Dame Alikermont. Acknowledging the possibility that others might infer a connection here, Smith notes in her preface that D'Alonville 'resembles in nothing but merit, the emigrant gentleman who now makes part of [her] family' (*The Banished Man*, p. 109). Despite this disclaimer, however, A. A. Markley considers this connection to be the key to much of Smith's success in conveying D'Alonville's 'thoughts, desires and motivations throughout the novel'.[16] Certainly de Foville's marriage in 1793 to Smith's beloved daughter Anna Augusta would have added an acutely personal impetus for her to convey the horror and political complexities of the French Revolution, especially from the perspective of those individuals who became inadvertently embroiled in it. One of the most popular scholarly assertions about this book is, as Dani Napton and Stephanie Russo phrase it in their investigation of place and narrative, that 'it can neither be considered a counterrevolutionary novel nor an uncomplicated acceptance of conservative maxims'.[17] Rather, it is a statement of the terrible hardships (both physical and emotional) inflicted by civil conflict, and an identification of the source of such hardships within the individual selfishness and greed of those in power, whether such be aristocrats or revolutionaries. Napton and Russo write that in *The Banished Man* '[t]he most positive social and cultural changes emanate not from those who are in control of revolutionary France but from within the family unit and the domestic space'.[18] More specifically, it is Smith's fervent belief in the significance of individual fortitude and moral character which is demonstrated here. Through the castle of Vaudrecour, with its 'instruments of torture' and the 'dark gulph' of the oubliette into which the condemned would be thrown (*The Banished Man*, p. 325), Napton and Russo note that Smith 'demonstrates the potential for revolutionary idealists to become effectively those very tyrants whom they have fought so hard to vanquish'.[19] Yet D'Alonville's bravery and chivalric sense of natural justice set him apart from this form of tyrannical aristocracy: he is himself disgusted with the dungeon and frees the man trapped in the oubliette without thought to political allegiance and with only 'the humane hope of rescuing a fellow creature from a death so deplorable' (*The Banished Man*, p. 326). Similarly, it is the individual vanity and greed of those such as the self-interested Heurthofen who are identified as the real culprits for derailing the originally worthy aims of the French Revolution.

That it is the choices, behaviour, and attitudes of individuals who shape socio-political developments is further underscored by the friendship of the English and French aristocrats Ellesmere and D'Alonville with the Polish revolutionary Carlowitz. This friendship is made possible only through their shared aims of achieving freedom and justice, and through the acknowledgement that the means of accomplishing these aims may be shaped by perspective, a concept summarised through D'Alonville's admission that if their situations had been switched, 'I might have thought and have acted as you have done' (*The Banished Man*, p. 214). The nuance here is important, since it suggests that, far from being simply a rapidly written bread-winning novel, *The Banished Man* is in fact a carefully crafted extrapolation of Smith's political and moral sentiments. It is thus extremely significant that this is also the first of Smith's novels to include pre-chapter epigraphic quotations, and the text has much to reveal with regard to the importance of epigraphs both within Smith's writing and more widely throughout the prose genre.

Suggestions of a connection of literary influence between Smith and Radcliffe are not unusual: Blank describes Radcliffe as Smith's 'literary rival', while Stanton writes that '[Smith] and Ann Radcliffe read each other's novels and influenced several of each other's works'.[20] Whilst Melissa Sodeman considers Smith's epigraphic quotations through an anthological context, she too believes that Smith 'borrows not so much from the anthology as from Radcliffe'.[21] However, at the time Smith was writing *The Banished Man*, Radcliffe had only published one novel that included pre-chapter quotations (*The Romance of the Forest*, 1791). Although *The Mysteries of Udolpho* had been published on 8 May 1794 (some months previous to *The Banished Man*, which appeared in August 1794), it is most unlikely that the epigraphs in Radcliffe's novel could have had any influence on Smith, who was about to 'send up the 3rd & part of the 4th Volume' of her novel to the publisher on 4 May 1794.[22] There is a printer's error in the first edition in which the third chapter of the third volume was prefaced by both its own epigraph and that of the following chapter, an error most easily explained if the quotations were listed separately to the main manuscript in the form of a numbered chapter list. However, as none of Smith's manuscripts are known to have survived, there is sadly no evidence to support this, beyond the unlikelihood of the printer having transposed the entire quotation in the wrong place from a chapter heading that would have come some distance later in the manuscript. In either case, a letter to Thomas Cadell dated 22 June clarifies that the first three volumes of the novel had already been set by this point, making it extremely implausible that there would have been any opportunity for adding epigraphic quotations to the text block at this time. It is therefore more probable that the quotations were included with the original manuscripts despatched to the publisher at the outset. The fact that Smith makes no mention of the decision to include epigraphs in her correspondence may serve as an indication of a growing acceptance of the device (though the survival of only part of Smith's epistolary archive renders this supposition uncertain).

While Smith's inclusion of epigraphs might still have been influenced by Radcliffe's *The Romance of the Forest*, a simple comparison makes it rapidly apparent that the approach of both novelists to this paratextual device is markedly different. Throughout the four volumes of Smith's *The Banished Man* there are a total of 45 pre-chapter epigraphic quotations, with typically only 1 quotation attached to each new chapter. The only exception to this is the presumed printer's error in the first edition (mentioned above), in which the third chapter of the third volume was prefaced by both its own epigraph and that of the following chapter (*The Banished Man*, p. 513 n. 298a). These 45 epigraphs are derived from a range of at least 29 different writers, and 1 further unidentified source (see Appendix, Figure 11). Of these 29 writers, only 6 are responsible for more than 1 of the 45 quotations: Shakespeare, Cowper, Guarini, Voltaire, Horace, and Milton. Appearing in 8 epigraphs throughout the novel, Shakespeare is undeniably the most frequently quoted epigraphic source, to some extent reflecting his similar prevalence within Radcliffe's epigraphs. However, these 8 quotations represent just under 18% of the total epigraphs in Smith's novel; in fact, more than half of the epigraphs in *The Banished Man* (i.e. 23 in total) are taken from sources that occur only once within Smith's pre-chapter paratext. This list of writers includes individuals as various as La Fontaine, Samuel Johnson, Petrarch, Alexander Pope, Matthew Prior, 'Le-Roi de Prusse' (the King of Prussia), Jean-Jacques Rousseau, Sophocles, and Lady Elizabeth Wardlaw; overall, the effect is one of a diverse tapestry of literary referencing that suggests a considerable breadth of reading on Smith's part (see Appendix, Figure 11). Smith's daughters did assist in preparing her manuscripts for presentation to publishers, but there is no evidence to determine whether or not their involvement may have extended further than simply copying their mother's finished text.[23] Importantly, this breadth of quotation also differs greatly from Radcliffe's more focused epigraphic strategy: although *The Romance of the Forest* is only three volumes in length compared with *The Banished Man*'s four volumes, the 27 epigraphs it includes are derived from a range of only 11 different writers, with more than half of these quotations originating in the work of just 3 of these authors (Shakespeare, Collins, and Beattie). This specificity would become even more pronounced in Radcliffe's only four-volume novel, *Udolpho*, in which there is a range of only 12 writers across 57 epigraphic quotations (see Appendix, Figures 7 and 8). Furthermore, whilst Radcliffe's epigraphs remain firmly within the scope of English literature (or occasionally English translations), 14 out of Smith's 45 epigraphs are written in either French, Italian, or Latin (see Appendix, Figure 12).

Smith was, of course, not the first writer to incorporate pre-chapter or pre-section quotations in languages other than English: as has been mentioned previously, Fielding and Collier had included epigraphs in the same four languages in *The Cry* (1754), and more contemporaneous to the Gothic movement, the anonymous author of *The Amicable Quixote* (1788) also featured pre-chapter quotations derived from French and English sources. In the latter novel, there is a scene in which 'applause' is bestowed upon a character for the 'epigrammatic application' of a few lines of Italian poetry which he adds to a drawing,[24] thus providing a useful perspective through which to interpret other dislocated quotations within both the text and its accompanying paratext. That the anonymous author adds the qualifier that only 'those who understood [the lines]' were 'forcibly struck' by them establishes this form of witty quotation as an entertaining pastime reserved for the linguistically adept.[25] Yet whilst Smith apparently demands similar breadth of knowledge in her readership if they are to appreciate all aspects of her novel, the narrative of *The Banished Man* lends a more striking relevance to the use of epigraphs sourced from a variety of languages. The whole purpose of this novel is to explore the concept of cultural dislocation: as Stephanie Russo notes, '[t]he sheer cosmopolitan breadth of this novel demonstrates that the effects of the revolution have not simply been felt in France'.[26] Smith's biographer Loraine Fletcher observes that with *The Banished Man*, '[Smith] is attempting action on an epic scale, [. . .] drawing in the political situations of Germany, Austria, Poland and England as well as France.'[27] Of course, the narrative itself does include Polish, German, and Austrian characters, yet neither German nor Polish features in the epigraphs. The reason for this is debatable: even if Smith was unlikely to have personal competency in these languages (given her early marriage and lack of educational opportunities), access to suitable quotations via the networks of refugees she helped would not have been outside the realms of possibility. More probably the selection of languages was a deliberate choice based upon what her readership would be most likely to understand. The identical match between the epigraphic languages used by Smith and those used by Fielding and

Collier in *The Cry* (1754) reaffirms that these four languages (English, French, Italian, and Latin) were the standard range with which a well-educated reader might reasonably be expected to be familiar. Thus Smith is essentially providing a comprehensive sample of '[t]he confusion of tongue' created by the refugees in her own drawing room,[28] whilst not rendering the actual meaning of her epigraphs too inaccessible to her target audience.

Indeed, Sodeman argues that 'Smith's interest in exile and wandering [is] inseparable from form', although the connection she identifies is one of literary rather than of cultural exile. In particular, Sodeman cites the frequent errors and misquotations in Smith's epigraphic quotations as evidence that this paratext should be interpreted as a way of 'registering a literary exile that requires [Smith] to make meaningful that process's need to borrow from other sources'. However, although Sodeman states that misquotations are 'more typical than aberrant', in actuality only 17 out of 43 identifiably quoted epigraphs appear to feature such mistakes.[29] Many of these are also very minor alterations: for example, in the epigraph from Shakespeare's *Hamlet* that prefaces volume 3 chapter 12, the word 'hath' appears to have been substituted with 'has' (*The Banished Man*, p. 368).[30] Furthermore, Sodeman also claims that '[m]any of [Smith's] quotations are inexact or paraphrastic, to the extent that editors tasked with tracking down these passages are occasionally forced to acknowledge that the source cannot be found'.[31] Yet this is actually more accurate for Smith's later novels, *Marchmont* (1796) and *The Young Philosopher* (1798), which feature 9 and 13 unidentified epigraphic quotations respectively (see Appendix, Figures 13 and 14). Only one epigraphic quotation in *The Banished Man* remains unidentified, although the novel's most recent editor Matthew Grenby notes that this epigraph's allusion to a 'sad historian' is probably a reference to Oliver Goldsmith's *Deserted Village* (*The Banished Man*, p. 488 n. 37).

Whilst Sodeman's theory is one way of retrospectively interpreting Smith's epigraphs, it nonetheless leaves unanswered questions regarding the original motivation for including them. If anything, Smith seems to have been actually rather scrupulous in her attention to detail, writing indignantly to her publisher Thomas Cadell, Jr that she had 'observe[d] with extreme vexation such numerous errors of the press as [she] never observed before in any work'. She then proceeds to note that 'as to the French, Italian, and Latin sentences, they are sadly incorrect, & of that perhaps the discredit will fall on me', the concluding concern here pointing to Smith's pride in her professional attitude towards, and presentation of, her work.[32] Rather than conveying a sense of literary exile or abandonment through her epigraphic quotations, Smith originally seems to have aimed at a more orderly and precise presentation of paratextual material in *The Banished Man*. Indeed, by incorporating such a comparatively broad range of authors, texts, and languages, Smith establishes the epigraphs as a textual parallel of the cross-national friendships and social cohesion attained within the narrative. The paratext becomes a space in which to establish, or perhaps rather to highlight, a communal cultural identity shaped through literature, thus underscoring the book's aim of pointing the way towards social harmony through justice, tolerance, mutual respect, and the avoidance of prejudicial stereotyping. This concept of a universal literary canon is further supported by the fact that, despite the frequent move of geographical location within the novel, the languages of the epigraphs do not appear to have been chosen with any sort of geolinguistic correlation in mind. For example, the chapter in which D'Alonville returns to his native France from exile in Britain (volume 3 chapter 4) is prefaced with a quotation from Shakespeare's *Henry V*, a seemingly incongruous juxtaposition of French nationhood with one of the most quintessentially English plays by one of the most emblematic of English writers.

Yet while the disjunction here might have been intentional, with this form of transnational quoting possibly intended to reflect themes of cultural dislocation within the text, there is no consistent pattern of this throughout the rest of the novel. Elsewhere, epigraphs are simply included where the meaning of the text is relevant to the narrative, and in this instance the quotation itself is taken from a description of the state of France just after the Battle of Agincourt and at the close of the war with England:

> Her vine, the merry chearer of the heart,
> Unpruned lies; her hedges even pleach'd,
> Like prisoners wildly overgrown with hair,
> Put forth disorder'd twigs: her fallow lees
> The darnel, hemlock, and rank fumitory
> Doth root upon.
>
> SHAKESPEARE.
> (The Banished Man, p. 306)[33]

It appears most likely, therefore, that this epigraph has been chosen based upon the quotation's content rather than upon its cultural significance, thus also implicitly suggesting that the truth of a statement exists irrespective of nationality or socio-political allegiance. Once again, this only reinforces the idea that, whilst Smith is keen to demonstrate the plight of exiles and the culturally dispossessed, she is still more interested in pointing out ways of achieving social unity, cohesion, and reintegration. In this way, *The Banished Man* is also more than a little didactic in tone, as Smith uses both the narrative's plot and its structure to present ways of achieving socio-political harmony.

Also unlike Radcliffe, the applicability of Smith's epigraphs is generally confined to the chapter which they preface, effectively headlining the ensuing prose. A good example of this proleptic function is the epigraph prefacing volume 1 chapter 6, a slight misquotation from Voltaire's *Amélie ou le Duc de Foix* (1752):

> Il n'est point de peril, que je n'ose affronter,
> Je hazarderai tout.—
>
> > VOLTAIRE.
>
> (There is no danger that I dare not face.
> I will hazard all.)
>
> > (*The Banished Man*, p. 149)[34]

The previous chapter concludes with the '[r]age and hatred' of Heurthofen's private musings as he determines to seek out 'more ardently than ever for occasions to raise himself' (*The Banished Man*, p. 148). The silent subterfuge with which he schemes finds little similarity in the bold daring of the following epigraph, which instead prefigures D'Alonville's determination to retrieve the abandoned deeds and papers upon which depends much of his benefactresses' property 'at whatever risk' to himself (*The Banished Man*, p. 151). Other events also occur in the new chapter: there is the discovery of the absence of the required deeds, the interrogation of Heurthofen upon the subject, then D'Alonville has a minor disagreement with Heurthofen before arranging to meet in secret with the lady's maid of one of the women so as to discover the precise location of the lost deeds. The epigraphic quotation focuses upon only one element of the prose narrative, and crucially an abstract rather than a pragmatic element as it directs attention to D'Alonville's sense of chivalry and justice. Smith is therefore using the epigraph to guide her reader to the aspect of the ensuing chapter upon which she wishes them to focus. A further clear example of this occurs in the epigraph to chapter 4. Here, the quotation from Matthew Prior's *Solomon* (misattributed to Pope's *Odyssey* in the first edition) conveys a powerful sense of emotional turmoil during a moment of transition:

> On either side my thoughts incessant turn
> Forward I dread, and looking back I mourn.
>
> > POPE'S ODYSSEY.
> >
> > (*The Banished Man*, p. 134)[35]

There is little in the quotation to connect it with the most dramatic, and therefore memorable, occurrence of chapter 4, which is the moment when the family of Madame de Rosenheim and Madame D'Alberg are nearly drowned crossing a river. Yet the reason that they are crossing the river in the first place is because of the family's forced abandonment of their home due to the approaching conflict caused by the Revolution. It is to this sense of geographical and socio-political displacement that the quotation refers, and to which Smith is attempting to draw her reader's attention.

There are, however, some notable exceptions to the forward-looking nature of Smith's epigraphs. The quotation prefacing volume 2 chapter 10 is derived from Euripides though presented only in English:

> Exiles, the proverb says, subsist on hope;
> Delusive hope still points to distant good,
> To good that marks approach.
>
> EURIPIDES.
>
> (The Banished Man, p. 265)[36]

Here the concept of hope in exile has direct application to the conclusion of the preceding chapter in which the exiled Madame de Touranges, living in England and separated from the husband whose fate she does not know, temporarily 'look[s] forward from amidst the depression of exile' and enjoys the hope 'of seeing the house of De Touranges restored to its original splendour' (*The Banished Man*, p. 264). In the chapter which the epigraph actually prefaces, the hope presented is less overt, instead consisting of D'Alonville's budding love for Angelina Denzil. Her acquaintance lifts D'Alonville from the 'depression of exile' by proving to him 'that there was in the world one being for whom it was worth while to wish to live' (*The Banished Man*, p. 267).

Similarly, the first volume's second chapter concludes with the image of D'Alonville 'retir[ing] to the mattress that was prepared near the bed of his father, who remained nearly in the same state of hopeless depression' (*The Banished Man*, p. 128). The third chapter continues with this image of the man and his dying father refracted through the opposing perspectives of the self-interested Heurthofen and the more charitable hostess Madame D'Alberg. The facetious mockery of Heurthofen's sneer that D'Alonville, 'it seems, is quite a modern Æneas' (*The Banished Man*, p. 129) is effectively countered by the solemnity of the pre-chapter epigraph printed just above it. Although the quotation is unattributed in the first edition, it derives from Pope's *Iliad*, and is taken from the words of King Priam as he watches his son Hector awaiting Achilles by the gates of Troy:

> Sad spectacle of pain,
> The bitter dregs of fortune's cup to drain:
> To fill with scenes of death these closing eyes.
>
> POPE'S ODYSSEY.
>
> (The Banished Man, p. 129)[37]

The poetry crystallises the emotional tenor of the narrative at this point, providing a smooth transition from the scene itself to the way in which it is regarded by exterior observers. That it is this immediate image provoked by the dislocated text that is important, rather than the invocation of the original source material, is further supported by the incompatibility of the context of the lines and their situation in Smith's narrative. Although it is his own 'closing eyes' to which Priam is referring here, it is in fact his son Hector who is about to die whilst battling Achilles.

However, there are occasions when the context of the quotation appears to have been granted far greater importance in epigraphic function. The quotation from Milton's *Paradise Lost* that prefaces volume 1 chapter 5 is an excellent example:

> Long were to tell
> What I have done; what suffer'd – with what pain
> Voyaged the vast unbounded deep!–
> But I,
> Toil'd out my uncouth passage, forced to ride
> Th' untractable abyss.
>
> MILTON.
> (*The Banished Man*, p. 142)[38]

Originally spoken by Milton's Satan upon his return to Hell following his successful contrivance of humanity's Fall from Grace, these lines here preface a chapter in which Heurthofen delivers an embellished narration of how he escaped the death he was presumed to have suffered. In the immediate context of the narrative, the obvious parallel of Heurthofen with Satan strikes an almost comedic note, since at this point the pompous pride of the former seems to have limited scope for malevolence. A darker proleptic nuance to this connection becomes apparent when Heurthofen later appears as one of the 'malignant' judges of the turbulent French Republic (*The Banished Man*, p. 337), and thus also the man by whose agency D'Alonville's brother is condemned to execution (*The Banished Man*, p. 367). Although the descriptive element of the quotation is eminently relevant to the ensuing prose, the full appropriateness of the quotation becomes apparent only if its source is known to the reader. Heurthofen has already been portrayed in the narrative with sufficient negativity to identify him as a thoroughly dislikeable character; yet the added invocation of Satan provides a valuable early signpost of the likely way in which his pride and self-interest will develop. Individuals who appear merely self-interested and venal in times of plenty, Smith implicitly warns, are also those who will become satanic tyrants when opportunity allows. More than a simple commentary, the epigraph thus becomes central in provoking critical thought regarding personal morality: here the falsehood of a tall story is not simply an excusable sample of exaggeration, but an indication of cowardice and deception on a level with that of Satan.

To some extent, therefore, Smith appears inconstant in her use of the original context of epigraphs; yet these two approaches can be reconciled if she is considered to be invoking not so much literal as aesthetic context. The epigraph to volume 1 chapter 3 is, after all, aesthetically concerned with the imminent loss of one half of a paternal relationship within a military conflict. Similarly, the Milton quotation harnesses the insidious impositions of a self-interested deceiver. Further examples of an aesthetic contextual relevance are present throughout the novel, for instance the epigraph that prefaces the chapter in which the execution of King Louis XVI of France is announced:

> After life's fitful fever, he sleeps well.
> Treason has done his worst: nor steel nor poison,
> Malice domestic, foreign levy, nothing
> Can touch him farther.
> > SHAKESPEAR.
> > > *(The Banished Man*, p. 244)[39]

These lines are taken from a moment in Shakespeare's *Macbeth* when the eponymous villain soliloquises about the murdered King Duncan. Once again Smith is using the quoted text to draw attention to the moment in this chapter that she most wants her readers to notice and absorb: the unlawful murder of a king by one or more of his own subjects. Although in pragmatic terms King Louis's execution is only reported within the plot and has little direct impact upon the characters of the novel, save to render any safe return to France for the émigrés still more improbable, the psychological effect is considerable. Through the careful deployment of paratext, Smith creates an aesthetic tone for the ensuing chapter that poignantly reflects and conveys a communal emotional experience.

Nowhere else in Smith's canon does she ever achieve such innovative originality with her epigraphs. Her next novel, *Montalbert* (1795), features no epigraphs at all, an omission that Curran considers strange given the incorporation of the device in her subsequent (final two) novels.[40] A possible explanation might be that this novel is, as Fletcher notes, 'imaginatively and cleverly structured', in particular with regard to its avoidance of conventional romantic tropes such as the rescue of the heroine by none but the narrative's hero.[41] If epigraphs were regarded as integral to Gothic fiction at this time, Smith's avoidance of them here might therefore fit into this somewhat anti-Gothic pattern. However, the number of novels published with epigraphs had remained proportionately low until 1795, a year in which only 8 novels are known to have featured some form of pre-chapter epigraphic paratext; the previous year there were only 4 (see Appendix, Table 1 and Figures 1 and 2). Too early to be a silent critique of the epigraph, the lack of epigraphs in *Montalbert* is thus more probably a consequence of the speed with which Smith was obliged to complete the book. In the preface to her next novel, *Marchmont* (1796), she writes a form of apology for the faults of *Montalbert* in which she attributes such failings to the emotional and financial struggles that confronted her following the long illness and eventual death of one of her daughters, at which point she states that it became 'absolutely necessary for [her] to sit down to finish a novel for which [she] had received money'.[42] The reason for the absence of such a comparatively non-essential embellishment as pre-chapter epigraphs is abundantly clear.

Similarly, the renewed incorporation of epigraphs in Smith's final two novels, *Marchmont* (1796) and *The Young Philosopher* (1798), may be considered less a consequence of a renewed interest in paratextual experimentation than a shrewd manoeuvre to identify her work with the exponentially fashionable genre of Gothic Romance. Although *Marchmont* lacks much of the sense of serious threat contained in the more exemplary Gothic novels of, for example, Radcliffe, there are nonetheless numerous tropes and motifs throughout the narrative that mimic staples of Gothic fiction. There is a beautiful heroine subjected to patriarchal oppression and the machinations of an unsympathetic stepmother, an attempt (albeit non-aggressive) at a forced marriage, a ruined house which ghosts are rumoured to inhabit, and even a debt-collector appropriately named 'Vampyre'.[43] Whilst it would be inaccurate to suggest that all such novels included pre-chapter epigraphic quotations, the majority of novels published with epigraphs around this time do self-identify as '*A Romance*', '*An Historical Romance*', or similar.[44] Smith was, above all, a businesswoman, and if epigraphs were becoming fashionable then she was not going to inhibit the potential for sales of her novel by not including them, even if this meant sacrificing some of her preference for precision and presentation. In 1794, Smith had written of her frustration at not being able to identify a specific quotation required for *Rural Walks* (1795). Excusing her delay in posting the 'seven and twenty Pages that remain to compleat the Volume', she writes to her publisher:

> I had the prose & original part of what I now send finish'd the middle of last Week, but it is as strange as true, that, having occasion to quote those lines of Pope's which begin "Where is the North?" I could not procure at Mr Bull's or Mr Barratt's, the Volume of Pope in which they are &, after losing some days, was under the necessity of altering the sentence and omitting the lines. The last Chapter is in exactly the same predicament.[45]

By the time she was writing *Marchmont*, the lack of attribution had evidently become secondary to the need to include a quotation, in itself a useful indicator of the importance the device had gained by this point. Addressing the failure to provide attributions for any of the epigraphs in this novel, she states in the preface that:

> From my few books also I have been absent, and the libraries of bathing towns rarely contain such as I have had occasion to refer to: the mottoes and quotations I have used have, therefore, been either copied from memory or a common-place book; and as neither the one nor the other always furnished me with the name of the poet or essayist whose words I borrowed, I have omitted the names of all. (*Marchmont*, p. 4)

Since the partial inclusion of epigraph attributions was not unusual at this point (Radcliffe's novels are a particularly high-profile example of this practice), Smith's determination to credit none if she cannot credit all of her epigraphs may seem strange. The explanation she offers suggests editorial consistency, and perhaps also a sense of not wishing to appear to prioritise those authors whose works may be identified not because of any thematic seniority implied by the inclusion of a name, but simply owing to the haphazard nature of her notetaking. A further possibility is raised by Smith's tendency to incorporate representations of herself within her work, whether abstractly via representation of exile and abandonment, or more pragmatically through the inclusion of characters who must earn their living from their writing such as Charlotte Denzil in *The Banished Man* and the eponymous hero of *Marchmont*.[46] By identifying the absence of epigraph attributions with her status as an unfairly impoverished gentlewoman, Smith does to some extent transform the epigraphs into a performative space through which she can continually remind the reader (with every new chapter's non-attributed epigraph) both of her limited financial resources and of her own substantial intellectual capabilities. The interconnected paratext would thus become a strategy of self-marketing likely to succeed with the readers of sentimental novels in which vicarious suffering is the chief form of entertainment. However, this judgement should be balanced with the fact that there is nothing untrue in what Smith writes here: she seems to have moved around between at least three different towns during the year between the publication of *Montalbert* and the appearance of *Marchmont* in 1796, and so probably was genuinely working from memory or from some form of notebook.[47] Her scrupulousness as an editor is attested by numerous references in her letters to publishers complaining about mistakes they have introduced; she even goes so far as to include with a letter to Thomas Cadell, Jr a note addressed specifically '[t]o the Printer employed by M[r] Cadell & Davies to Print "Rural Walks"' in which she 'entreats that, if the Printer sees any word which he cannot read, that He w[d] write to M[rs] S. for an explanation'.[48] Whilst marketing strategy does provide a very plausible explanation, it would be unfair to Smith to totally discount her perfectionist longing for the clearest, most professionally presented text possible: the omission might say as much about the importance of aesthetic consistency on the page as it does about Smith's tendency towards self-representation.

Epigraphic quotations in *The Young Philosopher* pass similarly unattributed, perhaps for similar reasons. However, unlike *Marchmont*, no explanation is given, something which suggests either that the elicitation of sympathy was not actually the main motivation for the decision not to include sources, or perhaps that the incorporation of unattributed epigraphs was becoming so common as to require no justification. That the range of writers from which these quotations are sourced only drops to 22 in *Marchmont* and around 20 in *The Young Philosopher* from *The Banished Man*'s 29 surely says much for Smith's ability to remember and to identify relevant quotations. Since the function of the epigraph in both these novels does not progress beyond the scope of Smith's initial experimentation with the device in *The Banished Man*, analysis of equal depth has been omitted here to avoid repetition. A point that is worth noting, however, is that despite the use of different title-page mottos for each volume of some of her earlier works, including *The Banished Man*, Smith published *The Young Philosopher* with one constant motto adorning each new volume. Whilst more research would be required to determine whether this effect extends more broadly across literature of this time period (cursory examination does suggest much variation in the consistency of title-page mottos between volumes of the same novel), it does indicate that for Smith, the parameters and functions of paratext were sharpening into a clear structural pattern. Title pages have been confirmed as a place of certainty and consistency, whilst epigraphs allow scope for variety and reflection upon the ensuing text. It is not a coincidence that it is in *The Young Philosopher* that Smith's epigraphs gain stronger clarity of direction, their relevance typically pointing the way forward in the narrative rather than linking back to the preceding prose. To give just one brief example, volume 2 chapter 6 of the novel begins at a moment when the heroine of the sub-narrative, Mrs. Glenmorris, is afraid that the in-law in whose house she has been forced to reside is already plotting the death of her as-yet unborn son. The accompanying epigraph describes a new baby that 'Stretch'd its stiff limbs, and on thy lap expired',[49] thus forming a proleptic reflection of the ensuing narrative in which the baby is both born and dies. Yet the quotation only goes so far as to confirm the reader's pre-existing fears for the heroine's unborn child; there is no indication of whether or not the death will prove to have been murder. Here, Smith demonstrates growing awareness of the potential for the epigraph to tease the reader with suspense, leaving clues as to what direction the narrative might take next.

THE GOTHIC EPIGRAPH AFTER RADCLIFFE

The confirmation of the epigraph's stereotypical association with the Gothic genre was solidified in 1796 by the publication of Matthew Lewis's notorious novel *The Monk*; here too is a more striking instance of an epigraph proleptically suggesting narrative direction. The main plot focuses upon the progressive descent of the eponymous monk Ambrosio into increasingly heinous forms of criminal behaviour. A strict theologian ultimately corrupted by vanity and self-interest, Ambrosio finds a suitable parallel in the epigraph to the first chapter, taken from the description of the similarly hypocritical Lord Angelo in Shakespeare's *Measure for Measure*:

> —Lord Angelo is precise;
> Stands at a guard with envy; Scarce confesses
> That his blood flows, or that his appetite
> Is more to bread than stone.
> *Measure for Measure.*[50]

For those readers who were aware of the quotation's context, the epigraph provides a substantial clue to the ensuing narrative; Coral Ann Howells even goes so far as to suggest that, through this quotation, 'Lewis actually reveals the secret of *The Monk*.'[51] The quotation prepares the attentive reader to expect the introduction of an apparently perfect model of morality, and the presentation of Ambrosio as 'a Man of noble port and commanding presence' who is 'surnamed, "The Man of Holiness"' amply fits the description (*The Monk*, p. 15). However, at this point he is regarded only through the eyes of other characters; Lewis's narratorial perspective does not shift to Ambrosio himself until the commencement of the second chapter. At the beginning of the novel, there is little indication of Ambrosio's centrality to the narrative, and no indication of his impending decline into deceit and vice save for the clue provided by the original context of the epigraph. If Lewis was truly intending to '[reveal] the secret of *The Monk*', he has chosen a strange place to do it, since any quotation relative to the narrative as a whole might more appropriately have been placed on the title page. Yet the motto he selects for this purpose is much less precise, simply listing the numerous supernatural elements that appear throughout every strand of the narrative: '*Dreams, magic terrors, spells of mighty power, / Witches, and ghosts who rove at midnight hour*' (*The Monk*, p. 1). The epigraph to the first chapter is instead only one small instalment in the pre-chapter paratextual pattern that extends throughout the novel. Like Smith's epigraphs in *The Banished Man*, Lewis seems to be using the quotation to point out the moments that he most wants his reader to pay attention to, even when (or perhaps especially when) the importance of such moments is not directly indicated within the main prose. Furthermore, if the epigraph is considered in this thematic sense as a means of preparing the reader for instances of moral hypocrisy, its inclusion becomes still more explicable as a means of highlighting the (albeit often unacknowledged) hypocrisy of many of the other characters: Don Christoval distracts Dame Leonella with thoroughly insincere flirtation so his friend can court Antonia, Don Lorenzo's motives in offering to assist Antonia in securing her inheritance are extremely doubtful given his ill-concealed enthusiasm for her beauty, and even the apparently innocent Antonia betrays an almost sexual interest in the acclaimed monk Ambrosio, as his appearance creates 'a pleasure fluttering in her bosom which till then had been unknown to her' (*The Monk*, p. 15). More than just a clever revelation of the novel's trajectory, the epigraph is thus also a way of signposting Lewis's presentation of the universality and inevitability of human frailty, even in the hero and heroine of a novel.

This is, however, the only epigraph in the novel to possess such a complex and multivalent relationship with the following prose. Elsewhere, the quotations chosen to preface chapters typically possess only the most superficial relevance to the text, and their connection to the plot on either side of the chapter boundary is limited. A good example of this is the epigraph that prefaces volume 2 chapter 4:

> ————Ah! how dark
> These long-extended realms and rueful wastes;
> Where nought but silence reigns, and night, dark night,
> Dark as was Chaos ere the Infant Sun
> Was rolled together, or had tried its beams
> Athwart the gloom profound! The sickly Taper
> By glimmering through thy low-browed misty vaults,
> Furred round with mouldy damps, and ropy slime,
> Lets fall a supernumerary horror,
> And only serves to make Thy night more irksome!
>
> *Blair.*
>
> (*The Monk*, p. 197)

The original source of these lines is near the beginning of Robert Blair's landmark graveyard poem *The Grave*, in a section that details the poet's descent into the gloomy supernatural realm of tombs and graves.[52] In Lewis's novel, the verse prefaces the chapter in which Ambrosio is finally convinced by his diabolical lover Matilda to form a pact with the devil, a procedure that involves sorcery in a crypt below his monastery (*The Monk*, pp. 197–215). Whilst Blair's lines do to some extent reflect this, there is no specific clue here as to the direction the narrative is about to take. Rather, they provide a background of primarily descriptive dislocated text, enhancing the sense of a collage of supernatural elements promised by the title page's motto but without close relation to the specific details of Lewis's plot.

Rare instances of greater epigraphic relevance do occur in the novel but never to the same level of intertextual complexity as the initial epigraph. For example, the quotation from *Macbeth* used to preface volume 2 chapter 1 consists of lines that would have been instantly recognisable as the moment when Macbeth sees the ghost of the murdered Banquo:

> Avaunt! and quit my sight! Let the Earth hide thee!
> Thy bones are marrowless; thy blood is cold;
> Thou hast no speculation in those eyes
> Which Thou dost glare with! Hence, horrible shadow!
> Unreal mockery hence!
>
> *Macbeth.*
> (*The Monk*, p. 101)[53]

In her study of the relationship between Shakespeare and the eighteenth-century novel, Kate Rumbold suggests that Lewis's use of this quotation 'dramatises the distress of key characters' since it 'expresses not just fearful anticipation, but also physical revulsion at a hideous sight'.[54] However, even here the direct application to the ensuing narrative is limited. Shakespeare's lines are the horrified proclamation of someone directly involved in the ghost's death. Although Lewis uses the text to alert the reader to the imminent arrival of a ghost within his narrative, the character who actually sees the ghost, Don Raymond, was not personally involved in the death of the bloody nun who haunts him. Don Raymond's romance with the beautiful Agnes and his attempt to liberate her from her domineering relations clearly casts him in the role of the heroic lover, making it unlikely that Lewis is deliberately attempting to confuse his reader with different potential plot trajectories as Radcliffe does in *The Italian*. More probably, Lewis is simply using this quotation as a kind of aesthetic shorthand, evoking a sense of fear of the paranormal via the readily accessible medium of popular drama.

Although Lewis's approach to epigraphs is thus rather less nuanced than Radcliffe's, it is nonetheless extremely probable that he took his paratextual inspiration directly from her work. In a letter to his mother dated 18 May 1794, Lewis wrote that he had recommenced work on the 'romance' he was writing, having been 'induced to go on with it by reading the "Mysteries of Udolpho," which is, in my opinion, one of the most interesting books that has ever been published'.[55] This 'romance' may or may not have been a draft of *The Monk*; either way, Lewis's biographer David Lorne Macdonald writes that he 'seems to have made a new beginning under the influence of Radcliffe'.[56] In writing *The Monk*, Lewis appropriated not only the pre-chapter epigraphs that Radcliffe had popularised, but also many of the same tropes of persecuted maidens and haunted castles that invariably recur in her prose fiction. Here, however, the similarities end. More gratuitously sexual and violent than any of Radcliffe's works, and far more ready to literalise the supernatural, Lewis's novel was in the words of one of its earliest reviewers, 'a romance, which if a parent saw in the hands of a son or daughter, he might reasonably turn pale'.[57]

Further differences are also immediately apparent in the structural approaches of the two authors. Most obviously, there are only 12 chapters in *The Monk*, and therefore only 12 epigraphic quotations throughout the entire novel. This forms a stark contrast to the 57 chapters and associated quotations included in *Udolpho* or even the 26 chapters in *The Romance of the Forest*, a novel that is similar in length to *The Monk*. Unlike in *Udolpho*, where a clear pattern is discernible in Radcliffe's habit of ending a chapter with a character retiring to sleep, chapter breaks in *The Monk* typically occur at moments when the narrative shifts from one character or group of characters to another. Thus narrative divisions appear to be suited to the exigencies of the plot rather than positioned due to any underlying aesthetic strategy, such as the connection between epigraphs and the unconscious mind cultivated by Radcliffe in *Udolpho*. Similarly, the division of the text into so few sections means that more narrative is covered in each section, thus reducing the immediacy of effect of epigraphic paratext. A further consequence of this small quantity of chapters is that it necessarily produces a less extensive range of epigraphic sources than appears in a Radcliffe novel, since there are fewer opportunities for quoting. Thus even though, like Radcliffe, Lewis takes only a third of his epigraphs from Shakespeare, this proportion corresponds to a much smaller numerical value. Rather than the 8 Shakespearean epigraphs that feature in *The Romance of the Forest*, for example, only 4 chapters are prefaced with the words of Shakespeare in *The Monk* (see Appendix, Figure 15). Indeed, the small number of chapters in this work means that the only writer other than Shakespeare to feature more than once in a pre-chapter quotation is Blair, thus in reality providing a much stronger sense of Shakespearean influence than is present in the epigraphs of any of Radcliffe's works.

When the whole spectrum of writers quoted in Lewis's epigraphs is examined more closely, still more differences become apparent. In a list of the seven most quoted writers in the pre-chapter quotations of *The Romance of the Forest* and *Udolpho*, the names of Shakespeare, Thomson, Beattie, Collins, Milton, Mason, and Gray would all appear (see Appendix, Figures 7 and 8). As Gary Kelly points out, Radcliffe's selection of epigraphic sources 'constitutes very much a late eighteenth-century lady's bookshelf of recognized "classics" along with "modern" poets of moral feeling'.[58] Despite claiming influence from Radcliffe, Lewis features only two of these seven writers in his own pre-chapter quotations: Shakespeare and Thomson. Aside from these two, the epigraphs in *The Monk* are taken from the writings of Blair, Cowper, Lee, Pope, Prior, and Tasso (see Appendix, Figure 15). Of these writers, only Cowper was active during the late eighteenth century and was still alive at the time of the novel's publication; the majority of the others were most active during the early to mid-eighteenth century, or even earlier in case of Shakespeare and Tasso. Whilst the strong emphasis upon Shakespearean texts might be regarded as a concession to fashionable literature, the other epigraphic selections point towards a highly individualistic approach. Lewis may have borrowed the device from Radcliffe, but the way in which he uses it is entirely his own.

John Claiborne Isbell's analysis of the relationship between Romantic prose and verse identifies the Gothic novel, and in particular the work of Radcliffe and Lewis, as the means through which epigraphs are introduced into prose fiction. He suggests that 'Gothic irony and wit rely on a divided self', positioning the epigraph as a paratextual reflection of this division; epigraphs, he argues, had been 'broadly unknown in the European novel until then'.[59] Although the existence of novels such as Chaigneau's *Jack Connor*, Fielding and Collier's *The Cry*, and Smith's *The Banished Man* contradicts this, it is nonetheless obliquely evident that the use of epigraphs by Radcliffe and Lewis popularised the device to such an extent that it became deeply associated with the genre of Gothic and/ or Romantic fiction in which they were both working. Nor has this association been noticed only in retrospect.

The connection between epigraphs and Gothic prose was subject to contemporary satiric commentary, for example by Eaton Stannard Barrett in his three-volume Gothic parody *The Heroine, or Adventures of a Fair Romance Reader* (1813). The novel relates the exploits of a farmer's daughter called Cherry who, to escape the dullness of life as the heiress of a modest fortune engaged to a kindly cousin, imagines herself the sole survivor of a noble family and disowns her father to pursue her fictitious claim. Disrupting the harmonious domesticity of others and unwittingly making herself the dupe of those who exploit her weakness for romantic fiction, Cherry is eventually rescued from her own folly by her devoted cousin, whom she then finally marries. In her analysis of the novel's strong patriarchal subtext, Jessamyn Jackson describes it as 'an energetic burlesque of the sentimental and gothic novels so popular – and so strongly associated with women writers and readers – in the late eighteenth and early nineteenth centuries'.[60] The majority of *The Heroine* is written in epistolary format, something Kelly observes was 'conventionally the form used in the eighteenth century for psychological realism and immediacy'.[61] This sense of realism is further promoted via the contrast with a shorter 'novel' included within the second volume and supposedly authored by the woman Cherry has been tricked into believing is her mother. Despite a length of only 29 pages, 'Il Castello di Grimgothico, or Memoir of Lady Hysterica Belamour. A Novel' possesses an elaborate title page and is divided into seven chapters. Of these, two chapters are prefaced with three quotations each, a further two chapters feature two epigraphs each, and the remaining three chapters each have only one epigraph. In each case, the prefatory quotation is then followed by an extensive list of descriptive phrases, linked only with hyphens, that describe the ensuing action. The fact that none of the chapters is longer than a few pages only adds to the absurdity created by such an abundance of prefatory paratext. Although all the quotations featured in the epigraphs are genuine, they have been carefully selected so as to contribute little to the ensuing text. The first chapter begins thus:

> Blow, blow, thou wintry wind.
> SHAKESPEARE.
> Blow, breezes, blow.
> MOORE.
>
> (*The Heroine*, p. 170)[62]

The superfluous extravagance of using two or more almost identical quotations to make the same point is a recurring theme of Barrett's epigraphs here, and mocks the tendency of some novelists to incorporate multiple epigraphs at the commencement of their chapters. As previously discussed, writers such as Radcliffe, Lewis, and Smith generally featured only one quotation per chapter, but this is not always true of less well-known writers.[63] Even discounting the multiplicity of epigraphs, the quotations are both so short as to be almost unrecognisable as lines of verse: it is a direct and highly effective jibe at a perceived reliance upon the quoted work of others to create expositional atmosphere. The following chapter carries the joke even further by quoting simply:

> "Oh!"
> MILTON.
> "Ah!"
> POPE.
>
> (*The Heroine*, p. 174)[64]

Here it is the perceived purpose of epigraphic quotations in Gothic and Romantic novels that is critiqued, since both 'quotations' are terms typically used to convey inarticulate emotion. To some extent, Barrett thus mimics Radcliffe's tendency to vocalise characters' emotions through epigraphic verse. However, the fact that the names of the writers quoted from are longer than the epigraphs themselves aims directly at the conventional assumption – since perpetuated within paratextual scholarship – that epigraphic quotations exist primarily so that aspirational authors can identify their prose with the works of more famous canonical poets.

As Barrett's satire progresses, however, the focus of the critique shifts from the epigraphs themselves and he actually begins to use the quotations as part of the wider satirical project. Typically, chapters that feature more than one quotation do so to mock epigraphs, while those with only one quotation use the space to interact with the surrounding prose. The epigraph to chapter 4 is a useful example here:

> Sure such a pair were never seen,
> So justly formed to meet by nature,
> SHERIDAN.
>
> *(The Heroine*, p. 185)[65]

Like so many of Radcliffe's epigraphs, this quotation eases the transition between the two chapters, since the lovers in this narrative have just been reunited at the end of the preceding chapter but do not engage in prolonged conversation until the commencement of the next. The lines themselves come from Richard Brinsley Sheridan's *The Duenna* (1775), originating in a song to accompany the courtship between the anti-Semitic stereotype Isaac Mendoza and the ageing Duenna who has disguised herself as the heroine so as to secure a wealthy husband. Rather than the pleasant image of romantic harmony cultivated by the lines themselves, Barrett is paralleling the two lovers here with a comedic rather than a romantic couple. By using the device in this way, Barrett reveals that it is not actually the epigraph itself that he is criticising, but rather the failure to incorporate epigraphs that genuinely contribute towards or have a connection with the narrative in which they are placed. Indeed, this is confirmed by the fact that Barrett had already used pre-chapter epigraphs in his earlier prose satire *The Miss-led General; A Serio-comic, Satiric, Mock-Heroic Romance* (1808), described by Kelly as an attack 'directed against the inglorious military career of the Prince of Wales's brother Frederic, Duke of York, and the scandalous sale of army commissions through the Duke's mistress, Mary Anne Clarke'.[66]

Nor was this the only example of the satirising of quotations in Gothic and Romantic prose. Although the manuscript of the novel that would later become *Northanger Abbey* (1818) predated Barrett's *The Heroine*, Katherine Sobba Green argues that the latter work 'was almost certainly in Jane Austen's mind when she revised' the tale into its final form.[67] Austen herself described it as a 'delightful burlesque, particularly on the Radcliffe style'.[68] Near the beginning of *Northanger Abbey*, a description of the heroine Catherine Morland includes a summary of her education, which has included 'all such works as heroines must read to supply their memories with those quotations which are so serviceable and so soothing in the vicissitudes of their eventful lives'.[69] This is then followed by what Leah Price describes as 'a parodic catalogue of quotations', included '[a]s if to get a novel's worth of epigraphs over with at once'.[70] Despite the slight exaggeration here – since only 6 quotations are provided, whilst a novel such as Radcliffe's *The Romance of the Forest* features 27 epigraphs – there is much truth in Price's appraisal. It is debatable whether Austen is critiquing epigraphs specifically or simply the incorporation of any kind of quotation within Romantic prose; certainly the range of writers included here is consistent with the sources typically used in Gothic and Romantic epigraphs, with the four poets quoted including Pope, Gray, Thomson, and Shakespeare. Rachel Sagner Buurma's brief overview of the epigraphic form suggests that Austen uses this to '[remind] us that in Radcliffe's novels, the epigraph [. . .] may be [. . .] evidence of the possible expression of a heroine's thoughts'; however, further investigation suggests Price's more satirical interpretation is probably closer to the truth.[71] The content of the lines is typically descriptive of the heroine's situation rather than introspective, whilst the fact that three of the quotations listed are Shakespearean obliquely parodies the frequency with which Gothic writers reference his many works. Notoriously, Austen also misquotes from Gray's 'Elegy Written in a Country Churchyard', which she gives as:

> Many a flower is born to blush unseen,
> And waste its fragrance on the desert air.
>
> *(Northanger Abbey*, p. 7)

The original line gives 'sweetness' instead of 'fragrance', a comparatively trivial difference that does not materially adjust the meaning of the verse, but which finds deeper resonance here as a potentially deliberate reflection of the tendency of some novelists, such as Charlotte Smith, to quote – or rather misquote – from memory. Austen scholar Bharat Tandon points out that this same line is misquoted in an identical manner in Austen's *Emma* (1815), this time uttered by the pretentious and irritating Mrs Elton, the eponymous heroine's social antagonist. Here, Tandon suggests, the error becomes a 'splendidly wicked' way of making 'comedy at Mrs Elton's expense', and there is therefore the possibility that the misquotation was deliberate.[72]

Admittedly, Austen is not infallible, and something as simple as an erroneous transcription in a commonplace book could easily be to blame for the similarity of the mistake; yet the subtlety of Austen's satire renders plausible the possibility that the misquotation was, in both cases, absolutely intentional. Like Barrett, Austen parodies the perceived superficiality of appropriated text, and of epigraphic quotations in particular. Yet it is worth remembering that these parodies are not necessarily focused upon pre-chapter paratext itself, but upon the conventions of Gothic literature, and that both therefore target the epigraph only as a popular characteristic of that genre. Indeed, Rumbold's identification of Austen's catalogue of quotations in *Northanger Abbey* as a means of critiquing 'rote-learning' suggests that what Austen is really challenging here is not the existence of pre-chapter epigraphs, but rather their misuse as decoratively imitative rather than interpretative spaces.

The ingenious and imaginative function of epigraphs in some of the earliest novels which they adorn, such as Radcliffe's *Udolpho* and Smith's

The Banished Man, only underscores the device's experimental status. Unlike some paratexts, for example titles and publisher information, epigraphs are never compulsory and thus always represent a conscious decision on an author's part to exert control over the critical textual border between the words on the page and the meaning in the reader's mind. Even in novels such as *Marchmont* or *The Young Philosopher*, where the epigraphic function is much simpler and less socio-politically didactic than in Smith's earlier and more experimental *The Banished Man*, there is nonetheless a deliberate effort to frame the reader's perception and interpretation of the text. Of course, even within an individual novel the extent to which this effort is successful can vary considerably. At the start of the decade some novelists had avoided this problem by not prefacing every chapter with an epigraph, for example *Zeluco* (1789), which features a prefatory quotation in only 68 out of 100 chapters and which typically includes chapter titles for those sections that are without an epigraph. By the late 1790s there is a growing sense of the need for a uniform approach that sometimes produces inconsistency of application, for example in Lewis's *The Monk* where one or two intertextually complex epigraphs are complemented by some that are simply perfunctorily descriptive. Yet throughout the 1790s and early nineteenth century the connection between prefatory epigraphs and didactic literature remains strong. Even when Austen satirises the device in *Northanger Abbey* it is as a means of imparting education and not as a descriptive embellishment that the epigraph is critiqued. More than just a means of attempting to legitimise romantic literature through a simple association, epigraphs had gained and were maintaining status as a means through which to impose a didactic authorial commentary or, more subtly, to stimulate reflection and critical thought upon the texts within which they were included; the only limitation was the skill and ingenuity of the authors who selected or composed them.

4

MOTTOS, MASKS, AND THE HISTORICAL NOVEL: SIR WALTER SCOTT

And we—behind the Chieftain's shield,
No more shall we in safety dwell,
None lead the people to the field,
And we the loud lament must swell,
Och hone a righ, Och hone a righ,
The pride of ALBIN'S line is o'er.
                                    SCOTT.[1]

Taken from the final two stanzas of Sir Walter Scott's poem 'Glenfinlas, or Lord Ronald's Coronach' (1801), this epigraph prefaced the fifth chapter of Christian Isobel Johnstone's four-volume Scottish epic, *Clan-Albin: A National Tale* (1815). In the ensuing narrative the elderly 'oracle of a genuine Highland hamlet' (*Clan-Albin*, I, 14), Old Moome, recounts a vision she witnessed in her youth in which a mysterious green-clad woman had prophesied the decline of the novel's eponymous clan. The incident mirrors the narrative of Scott's poem, in which the arrival of two supernatural women dressed 'in vest of green'[2] is associated with the death of clan chief Lord Roland, whose last fatal adventure the ballad depicts. Originally published in Matthew Lewis's collection *Tales of Wonder* (1801), Scott's 'Glenfinlas' is itself prefaced by a quotation, five suitably ethereal lines of verse taken from William Collins's 'An Ode on the Popular Superstitions of the Highlands of Scotland, Considered as the Subject of Poetry' (written c. 1749–50, published 1788).[3] Although the use of prefatory quotations in poetry is not the focus of the present study (the subject would be vast enough to merit separate investigation), this is nonetheless a striking example of Scott's enthusiasm for quoted text more than a decade before he began the novel-writing phase of his career.

From Johnstone's novel to Scott's poem, quotation nests within quotation like a series of nesting dolls, creating a pattern of thematically aligned intertextual connection and bardic mythologising that aims to construct a sense of

Scottish folkloric heritage, even if it does not in fact stretch very far chronologically into Scottish literary history. Significantly, Johnstone has chosen a quotation that features the only Gaelic phrase to appear in Scott's poem, the lament 'och hone a righ' (roughly equivalent to 'alas for the king'); Scott possessed only limited knowledge of Gaelic, which may also account for Johnstone's silent alteration to the spelling of this phrase that appears in 'Glenfinlas' as 'O hone a rie'.[4] Linguistic accuracy is clearly important to her, but the phrase itself is explained in the context of the verse it adorns and this combines with the newness of that verse to confirm that the intention is to create a sense of history rather than to provide authentically antique or Gaelic verse. As with Chaigneau, Fielding and Collier, Radcliffe, and Smith, the overarching aim is to construct an additional perspective for narrative voice; in Johnstone's novel this is achieved by providing a space in which she can corroborate or confirm the authenticity of the text. It is probably only coincidence that Scott's own verse should be quoted as an epigraph in the same year as the publication of his first novel to feature an epigraph before every chapter, *Guy Mannering* (1815); yet it does reflect a significant and continuing interest in pre-chapter paratext within the literary industry.

By the first decade of the nineteenth century, pre-chapter epigraphs had been formalised into a narrative device that was used in prose fiction about as frequently as chapter titles, though not generally at the same time as a chapter title. For the first decade of the nineteenth century (1801–10), the percentage of novels with epigraphs averages at between 23% and 26%, depending on whether the figure is calculated as a proportion of all first-published novels or only those that have been checked for epigraphs; however there is considerable deviation between the lowest and highest percentages in the range. In 1804, 1807, and 1808, the percentages of new novels with epigraphs are all below 20%, while at the other end of the spectrum the years 1802, 1809, and 1810 all have percentages over 30%.[5] As the previous chapter demonstrated, however, the incorporation of epigraphic quotation was itself becoming increasingly associated with the lurid genre fiction that writers such as Eaton Stannard Barrett and Jane Austen took delight in satirising. When Scott's first novel, *Waverley* (1814), was published anonymously the year after Barrett's *The Heroine* (1813), it had at first seemed that nothing would change. In *Waverley*'s introductory chapter, Scott deliberately dissociates the work from the contemporary field of genre fiction. Later, in his introduction to Ballantyne's 1824 edition of Radcliffe's works, Scott would praise her with the now famous appellation of 'the first poetess of romantic fiction';[6] yet perhaps unsurprisingly, at the start of his novel-writing career he appears keen to claim generic difference from the work of a literary antecedent still popular enough to be a plausible competitor. He writes:

> Had I, for example, announced in my frontispiece, "Waverley, a Tale of other Days," must not every novel-reader have anticipated a castle

scarce less than that of Udolpho, of which the eastern wing had been long uninhabited, and the keys either lost or consigned to the care of some aged butler or housekeeper, whose trembling steps, about the middle of the second volume, were doomed to guide the hero, or heroine, to the ruinous precincts?[7]

Whilst there is no explicit criticism of Radcliffe's or any other writer's work, Scott nonetheless projects the persona of a writer who is both keenly aware of generic conventions and confident in avoiding them. Unsurprisingly, no direct mention is made here of pre-chapter paratext, but that does not mean it is any less a part of Scott's broader dissociation of himself from the genre. Throughout the first two volumes of *Waverley* there are no epigraphs, only short titles at the beginning of each chapter. Yet the fact that brief quotations appear instead of these titles in a handful of chapters toward the end of the book's third volume suggests that, just as Barrett's *The Heroine* eventually succumbs to making serious use of the device it had initially parodied, so too does Scott ultimately become drawn in by the creative possibilities of epigraphic quotation.

The fluidity with which Scott switches between quotation and prose title in *Waverley* is quite unusual, since at the time the majority of texts that feature chapter titles do so without any form of epigraphic quotation, and vice versa. There are a few exceptions to this: for example, Isaac D'Israeli's comic novel *Flim-Flams! Or, the Life and Errors of My Uncle, and the Amours of my Aunt!* (1805) includes both epigraphs and lengthy prose descriptions of the ensuing narrative at the commencement of each chapter. D'Israeli's text is not entirely typical of prose fiction, however, since it features an array of paratextual material that could rival Swift for sheer quantity, including prefaces, advertisements, dedications, and an 'Explanation of the Plates'.[8] A more conventionally narrative-based work that adopts this format, without any additional and unusual quantity of paratext elsewhere in the work, is *The Assassin of St. Glenroy; or, The Axis of Life* (1810) by Anthony Frederick Holstein (pseud.), which includes both a title and an epigraph for each chapter (a style which Holstein continued to use in the majority of the many novels he published over the next few years).[9] Generally, however, epigraphs appear only in books that do not have additional paratext (such as chapter titles) prefacing the chapter; there are also some rare instances predating Scott's *Waverley* that feature chapters prefaced with *either* a title *or* an epigraph but not usually both together. Two examples have been found from this latter category. The first is Henry Kett's *Emily, A Moral Tale* (1809/11), in which the majority of chapters feature epigraphs, but there are occasional instances where a title will have been provided instead.[10] Similarly, the anonymously authored *The Citizen's Daughter; or What Might Be* (1804) typically features epigraphic quotation at the start of each chapter but does occasionally incorporate chapter descriptions instead.[11] In both cases, this is possibly owing to an inability to discover a suitable quotation, or at least to discover one in time for printing.

This almost universal preference for using either epigraphs or chapter titles but very seldom both together indicates a strong perception of synonymy and thus interchangeability between these two forms of paratext. Writing of French literature in the period, Rainier Grutman identifies Victor Hugo's move from epigraphs to chapter descriptions as his career progressed as indicative 'that mottoes and titles competed for the same "peritextual" space'.[12] A still more unusual instance of this specific synonymic functionality in anglophonic literature is provided by two early nineteenth-century novels, John Davis's *The Post-Captain* (1806), and Sarah Green's *The Private History of the Court of England* (1808). Both list their pre-chapter epigraphs alongside chapter numbers and pagination in their contents pages in exactly the same way that chapter titles might be listed. Rather unusually, Davis also attributes any epigraphic quotations that are his own composition to '*Author*' instead of the more conventional absence of attribution typically used when a writer composes their own epigraph.[13] This might also suggest a growing concern for uniformity of presentation at this time. Later, Scott too had a tendency to provide some form of attribution for the majority of his epigraphic quotations, frequently concealing his authorial influence behind a vague epithet such as '*Old Play*' or '*Old Ballad*' (although there are some interesting exceptions to this, which will be examined later).

A more determinate strategy of alternation between epigraphs and chapter descriptions appears in Robert Charles Dallas's *The Knights: Tales Illustrative of the Marvellous* (1808). Anticipating Scott's *Tales of My Landlord* series, this work is divided into two shorter novellas, 'The Knight of Tours' and 'The Knights Errant', of which only the first features pre-chapter quotation. Chapters in 'The Knights Errant' are uniformly prefaced by short descriptions of the ensuing narrative. All chapter divisions are listed in a 'Contents' section at the commencement of each volume; yet whilst the prefatory descriptions provided in 'The Knights Errant' are transcribed alongside numeration and page number in this 'Contents', the epigraphs used in 'The Knight of Tours' are not and no mention of the quotation is made. Although the two devices occupy similar paratextual space within the narrative, the implicit suggestion here is that there is no direct equivalence between them, and that either the author or the publisher (or both) considered the epigraphs to be part of the main text rather than a structural feature.[14]

Already a poet, a voracious reader, and a reviewer at the time when he began publishing his prose fiction, Scott would have been keenly aware of such paratextual variations. As has been noted above, his own poetry was already being appropriated as epigraphic paratext, both in *Clan-Albin* (already discussed) and in the anonymously authored *St. Clyde; A Novel* (1816), although there is no way of ascertaining whether Scott knew his work was being used in this way.[15] Indeed, the anonymity under which Scott composed his novels would probably have meant those appropriating his poetry for paratextual purposes (at least during the earliest stages of his novel-writing career) would not have been aware that the writer whom they were quoting was himself an enthusiastic user of pre-chapter epigraphs in prose fiction. In this chapter I will examine Scott's fascination with epigraphic quotation and his use of the transitional space of the epigraph as an opportunity for self-reflexive narrative commentary, sometimes for comedic purposes and always as a way to direct how his readers would interpret the narrative presented. Integral to this is Scott's use of self-authored epigraphs, and his prolific contribution to the development of the invented quotation will also be explored here in detail.

'DECORAMENTS' OR COMMENTARY?

Writing in his private journal on 24 March 1826, Walter Scott noted that '[i]t is foolish to encourage people to expect mottoes and such like Decoraments [*sic*]. You have no credit for success in finding them and there is a disgrace in wanting them.'[16] Although this comment was prompted by a request from his publisher for a title-page motto for the novel *Woodstock* (1826), it has also been identified as evidence of Scott's growing indifference towards and even frustration with the incorporation of all forms of mottos and epigraphic texts within his novels.[17] Despite the antipathy this assertion suggests, however, nearly all of Scott's 23 published works of prose fiction incorporate some form of pre-chapter epigraphic quotation.[18] The only exceptions are his first novel, *Waverley* (1814) – in which chapters are headed with titles, or very occasionally in the third volume with short quotations masquerading as chapter titles – and his seventeenth novel, *Redgauntlet* (1824), which does not feature chapter divisions at all. His next work, *Tales of the Crusaders* (1825), was published with 7 out of the 60 chapters featuring no form of prefatory quotation, and was the first since *Waverley* to appear with only partial epigraphic quotation (though, unlike *Waverley*, without any paratextual equivalent attached to the chapters not bearing quotations). Strikingly, despite Scott's private grumbling about Ballantyne's request for a title-page motto for *Woodstock*, the novel itself features an epigraphic quotation at the start of all but 1 of its 38 chapters. Whatever might have been Scott's real views concerning title-page mottos, the evidence of the novels themselves implies that he regarded pre-chapter quotation as much less dispensable.

Pursuing the idea that Scott's reading public 'expect[ed] mottoes', J. H. Alexander's analysis of epigraphic quotation in the Waverley novels also cites an early review of *Tales of My Landlord* (First Series, 1816) written anonymously

MOTTOS, MASKS, AND THE HISTORICAL NOVEL

by Thomas McCrie and published in the *Edinburgh Christian Instructor*.[19] McCrie quotes the assertion of 'a friend' that Scott's pre-chapter epigraphs 'have contributed as much as anything to the popularity of the Tales', and that 'the uniform practice of purchasers, on taking up the book, is to look at the title page and beginning of the chapters, and upon perceiving the poetical impress on these, they at once draw the conclusion and throw down the money'.[20] Aesthetic considerations are monetised and, rather than enhancing literary quality, the epigraphic function is reduced to a means of promoting sales amongst a novel-reading public whose only aim is 'to kill time'.[21] Yet the authority of this observation is rendered doubtful by this same 'friend' then identifying the use of epigraphic quotation itself as a means for concluding that the *Tales* 'were written by the author of Waverly [*sic*] and Guy Mannering'. The presumption of Scott's innovation is made more explicit by McCrie's declaration that '[t]he author of the Tales [has] struck out a new species of fictitious writing, [. . .] has given it a distinctive mark, by prefixing to each chapter a select piece of English poetry'.[22] In the year of the *Tales*' publication alone, 28 novels were published with some form of pre-chapter paratextual feature out of a total of 59 novels known to have been first-published (and of which 54 have been surveyed). Of these 28, there are 18 which feature epigraphic paratext. From the years 1800 to 1815 inclusive, at least 283 novels had been published with some form of epigraphic quotation, rendering Scott's use of the device by no means unique or unusual to anyone familiar with the world of publishing. Furthermore, McCrie's assessment of the *Tales* is significantly biased by his belief in Scott's prejudicial portrayal of the Scottish Presbyterians, in particular the Covenanters who fought for religious freedom in Scotland in the late seventeenth century. Referring to the review in a letter to his friend Lady Louisa Stuart, Scott described it as 'a most energetic attack, upon the score that the old Covenanters are not treated with decorum', although he claimed that he had not actually read the review 'and certainly never shall'.[23] Despite this mild dismissal, Scott immediately published an anonymous review of his own novel in the *Quarterly Review*. Nicholas Mason points out that he does 'take himself to task at certain points', but ultimately Scott cannot resist the opportunity to align McCrie's religious scrupulousness with that of Shakespeare's notorious puritan Malvolio.[24] In some ways it is quite a mild riposte for such a lengthy and antagonistic attack: although McCrie promises in his review to indicate the 'beauties' of Scott's work as well as its faults, he never seems to find space in which to do so during the course of an article that extends across three successive issues of the *Edinburgh Christian Instructor*, and that ultimately totals around 106 pages. The first instalment of the review begins with a dismissive diatribe against 'habitual readers of novels', whom McCrie claims have 'vacant' minds and 'dread [. . .] being left to serious reflection'.[25] The discussion of epigraphs occurs at the commencement of the second instalment, which is itself prefaced with a quotation that McCrie has ostensibly included in response to the perceived popularity of 'prefixing a few lines of poetry' to prose publications.[26] But the deployment of this prefatory verse quickly assumes a character of imitative mockery when McCrie sneeringly continues that 'the practice appeared to us to savour very strongly of affectation and puerility'.[27]

But even if McCrie's judgement and motives are questionable, the identification of epigraphs with superficiality is something that still resonates in the popular consciousness even today. Written nearly a decade after the review debacle, Scott's own description of epigraphs as 'Decoraments' suggests that he saw them as a non-essential, though highly desirable, adornment or complement to the main text. His own fascination with epithets, epigraphs, and mottos is certainly evident through the various occasions upon which he acted as a consultant for the selection of appropriate mottos for inscription upon objects, and through the very careful attention which he gives to such matters. In 1810 he sought the assistance of his friend Miss Clephane to provide a short phrase of Scottish Gaelic to engrave upon a small harp intended as a present. However, not content to leave the choice of words entirely up to her, his letter to her includes two suggested epithets before he finally transfers to her the responsibility of the actual selection (and this only because of her superior knowledge of Gaelic): 'it should not exceed two or three words as "The Harp of Albin" or "Let me be heard again" or in short anything you please that can be twind concisely into Gaelic'.[28] Later, when advising the Duke of Buccleuch on the design of a ceremonial cup, he makes an apparently unprovoked suggestion 'for a mottoe [*sic*] being taken from an ancient Scottish Canzonette'.[29] Scott also seems to have been keenly aware of the significance of relevant and appropriate epithets: when advising on the inscription for a St Andrew's Cross to be presented to the Hanoverian King George IV in 1822, he tactfully suggests replacing '"Righ Albainn gu brath," that is, "Long Life to the King of Scotland"' with '"Righ gu brath"' [. . .] "The king for ever"'.[30] The reason given is that the latter 'would make a good motto for a button', but there is, of course, the added advantage of the implied unity of Britain by removing the individual reference to Scotland. A similar attention to detail is also evident when he advises John Richardson on a coat of arms in 1819, and recommends the addition of two words to a motto because he believes the phrase '[f]or the truth is rather a common motto. I should prefer "for the truth of God" as bringing old Rowlands [*sic*] principles more fully out'.[31]

This fascination with heraldic mottos is also evident within Scott's literary output, for example in *Ivanhoe*, when detailed descriptions of heraldic devices are often provided, frequently with appropriate mottos.[32] When attempting to discover the identity of the mysterious Black Knight, Ivanhoe (unable to reach the window himself) asks Rebecca if she can see the motto on the Knight's shield as well as the emblem she has also described as '[s]omething resembling

MOTTOS, MASKS, AND THE HISTORICAL NOVEL

a bar of iron, and a padlock painted blue on the black shield'.[33] That this points towards a fascination with quotation rather than just heraldic antiquarianism becomes evident through other references in Scott's letters. In 1824 he remarks that 'I have got a-joug which I intend to put up at the gate with the mottoe [sic] Serva jugum. It will serve to hang a bridle upon.'[34] Later the same year, he writes proudly of owning 'a dirk with the mottoe [sic] "Better kind fremit as fremit kind" – it has a good deal of sense in it'.[35] The concluding 'it has a good deal of sense in it' points to a delight in mottos and epithets not just for their own sake, but for the sake of the wit and appropriateness of a quotation in situ. In both cases, it is the meaning of the phrase and its appropriateness to the situation that is important rather than its source.

An assumption of synonymy between epithets on objects and at the heads of chapters is indicated by the fact that Scott refers to both using the same term: 'mottoes'.[36] As such, his fascination with and observations upon the use of inscriptions on objects provides valuable insight into his broader attitude towards epigraphs within fiction. Like the motto for a bridle on his gate, or the motto for the Duke of Buccleuch's cup, pre-chapter epigraphs are apparently a form of 'Decorament': a non-essential but nonetheless desirable attribute. But like all decorative embellishments, their value upon an object or within the text comes from the performative artistry with which they are deployed within the creative work as a whole. As Alexander reports, on one occasion when Scott's amanuensis George Huntly Gordon 'was rash enough to suggest a motto to fill a gap at the beginning of Chapter 31 of *The Fortunes of Nigel*', Scott's publisher John Ballantyne noted that the selection was 'applicable, but surely reads common-place'.[37] That Scott readily provided an 'almost defiantly oblique'[38] composition of his own to replace the 'common-place' Shakespeare his secretary had suggested demonstrates not just deference to his publisher, but also a very clear and determined envisioning of the function of epigraphs as a space in which to challenge and provoke intertextual dialogue with the narrative, rather than simply to reflect or describe.

It is perhaps because of this prioritisation of meaning and appositeness that of the 879 pre-chapter epigraphs which occur in the first editions of Scott's novels, 248 appear to have been entirely his own composition (equivalent to approximately 28% of all his epigraphs). As Alexander notes, the attribution of 'Old Play' was '[Scott's] favourite method of designating original mottoes', although only by a very narrow margin; for while there are 91 instances of as-yet unidentified epigraphs attributed to 'Old Play', there are also 87 unidentified pre-chapter quotations that are attributed to a presumably invented source title. Only 2 unidentified epigraphs are attributed to 'Old Ballad', not including 1 attributed to 'Old Scotch Ballad', and another to 'Ancient Scottish Ballad'; a further 3 are attributed to 'Old Song', and 1 each to 'Old Poem' and 'Song'.[39] With regard to both this latter group and those quotations attributed

97

to 'Old Play', it seems to have been a fairly open secret that these were primarily the work of the author: a writer for the *Edinburgh Review* notes that '[w]e take it for granted, that the charming extracts from "Old Plays," that are occasionally given as mottos to the chapters of this and some of his other works, are original compositions of the author whose prose they garnish'.[40] Tom Haber's early survey of Scott's 'chapter-tags' took the optimistic view that errors in Scott's transcriptions of attributed quotations elsewhere in the novels may be an indication that 'a more careful scrutiny of the "anonymous" chapter-tags might result in tracing the source of some others to forgotten poetic miscellanies, of which Scott's brain was so full'.[41] Whilst this always remains a possibility, the considerable scrutiny of the *Edinburgh Edition of the Waverley Novels* makes this increasingly unlikely. In my own investigation of Scott's epigraphs, I was able to trace the source of only one of the previously unidentified quotations in Scott's novels, an epigraph in *The Fair Maid of Perth* that is attributed simply to '*Taming of a Shrew*' but which is in fact transcribed from David Garrick's adaptation of Shakespeare's play, *Catherine and Petruchio* (1754).[42]

Scott's biographer John Gibson Lockhart provides a short anecdote regarding the commencement of Scott's authorship of his own epigraphic verse when writing of the composition of *The Antiquary*:

> It may be worth noting, that it was in correcting the proof-sheets of this novel that Scott first took to equipping his chapters with mottoes of his own fabrication. On one occasion he happened to ask John Ballantyne, who was sitting by him, to hunt for a particular passage in Beaumont and Fletcher. John did as he was bid, but did not succeed in discovering the lines. "Hang it, Johnnie," cried Scott, "I believe I can make a motto sooner than you will find one." He did so accordingly; and from that hour, whenever memory failed to suggest an appropriate epigraph, he had recourse to the inexhaustible mines of "*old play*" or "*old ballad*," to which we owe some of the most exquisite verses that ever flowed from his pen.[43]

The Antiquary was not in fact the first occasion when Scott composed an epigraphic quotation, since he already seems to have done so the previous year for chapter 17 of *Guy Mannering*.[44] Yet what this story does demonstrate is an attitude towards identifying quotations that is paradoxically quite informal but also acutely precise with regard to meaning and interpretation. Just as Radcliffe eventually succumbed to the composition of her own epigraphic paratexts, so too does Scott ultimately prioritise the narrative appropriateness of the epigraph over its status as a quotation from another's work. A further solution when epigraphic inspiration waned may have been to choose multiple

MOTTOS, MASKS, AND THE HISTORICAL NOVEL

quotations from the same text. Alexander notes that '[f]rom time to time sets of two or more mottoes work in sequence', offering as an example a series of four epigraphs in *The Heart of Midlothian* (1818) which preface chapters in close proximity, though not in immediate succession. Alexander's further observation that three of these were 'supplied at proof stage' might suggest that Scott had simply run out of time for seeking relevant epigraphs in other texts, and even possibly for writing his own.[45] Instead, the connection between epigraph and text becomes centred in narrative or thematic similarities between his own novel and the quotation's source text (for example, in this instance the concept, shared by both *The Heart of Midlothian* and Shakespeare's *Measure for Measure*, of criminality incurred through sexual deviance from social mores and of sibling saviours).

The most public statement Scott made regarding his approach towards epigraph selection occurred comparatively late in his career, when he finally acknowledged the open secret of his authorship of the Waverley novels in the Introduction to *Chronicles of the Canongate* (First Series, 1827):

> The scraps of poetry which have been in most cases tacked to the beginning of chapters in these Novels, are sometimes quoted either from reading or from memory, but, in the general case, are pure invention. I found it too troublesome to turn to the collection of the British Poets to discover apposite mottos, and, in the situation of the theatrical mechanist, who, when the white paper which represented his shower of snow was exhausted, continued the storm by snowing brown, I drew on my memory as long as I could, and, when that failed, eked it out with invention. I believe that, in some cases, where actual names are affixed to the supposed quotations, it would be to little purpose to seek them in the works of the authors referred to. (*Chronicles of the Canongate*, p. 9)

The impression Scott creates of himself here is of a slothful intellectual: slothful because he 'found it too troublesome' to research for quotations, but also an intellectual since he was actually able to quote 'from reading or from memory' (albeit often imperfectly). The extent to which this is intended as literary showmanship is debatable, but the sincerity of his claim is supported by a letter to his publisher Archibald Constable in which he writes rather meekly that '[i]t is odd to say but nevertheless it is quite certain that I do not know whether some of the things are original or not'. He continues that he had '[found] it inconvenient to toss over books for a motto [and] generally made one without much scrupling whether it was positively & absolutely his own or botchd up out of pieces & fragments of poetry floating in his memory'.[46] His reference to himself here in the third person as 'The author

99

of Waverley' distances him from the position of authorial agency and thus also from this haphazard manner of choosing epigraphs, perhaps indicating a certain amount of guilt or shame for having not approached the selection of epigraphs in a more organised manner.

Yet this imprecision does seem to have developed over time, as Scott continued to use epigraphic paratext, with later novels typically incorporating far more self-composed epigraphs than his earlier works. Before 1820, the largest number of invented epigraphs in any one novel is 14 in *The Antiquary* (1816), with the majority of Scott's other novels around this time featuring only occasional original epigraphs. In 1820 – the year when Scott published *Ivanhoe*, *The Monastery*, and *The Abbot* – the quantity of self-composed epigraphs soars, and then continues high for much of Scott's remaining career (see Appendix, Figure 16). Around seven years before his observation to Constable, Scott had written to Ballantyne during the publication of *Guy Mannering* to note that there is 'a good mottoe [*sic*]' for the third chapter of the book 'in Byroms [*sic*] poems which are in the Chalmers collection of British poets'. He continues with a request to Ballantyne to 'get me sight of thi[s] volume', establishing not only that he did at least intend to verify the quotation with a definitive printed text, but also that (like Charlotte Smith) he was reliant upon his publisher for access to books from which to obtain or confirm epigraphic quotation.[47] Whether Ballantyne obliged upon this occasion is uncertain though, since the third chapter was ultimately prefaced with a quotation from Samuel Butler's *Hudibras* instead (*Guy Mannering*, p. 13). What is certain is that Scott did eventually possess his own copy of Chalmers's *The Works of the English Poets*, as it is listed in the catalogue of books at Abbotsford.[48] Many competing editions of British and English poetry were published at this time, but if Scott's slip in his letter to Ballantyne is indicative of a habit of referring to Chalmers's anthology as the 'British Poets', then it would not be unreasonable to suppose this is also what he is referring to in the Introduction to *Chronicles of the Canongate*. The only other possible contender based on the contents of Scott's library would be Thomas Campbell's seven-volume *Specimens of the British Poets; with biographical and critical Notices, and an Essay on English Poetry* (1819).[49]

The terminological distinction between 'British' or 'English' poetry is important because, following in the tradition of writers like Ann Radcliffe rather than Charlotte Smith, Scott restricts himself to a spectrum of almost entirely monolingual epigraphs. There are only four exceptions to this: *A Legend of Montrose*, published as part of *Tales of My Landlord* (Third Series, 1819), features a Gaelic verse accompanied by an English translation at the start of chapter 18; *The Abbot* (1820) uses an '*Ancient Roman Epitaph*' in Latin as one of two epigraphs to the first chapter; *St Ronan's Well* (1824) includes a Latin quotation from Virgil as one of two epigraphs to the second chapter; and

MOTTOS, MASKS, AND THE HISTORICAL NOVEL

Chronicles of the Canongate (First Series, 1827) incorporates a brief Latin quotation as the epigraph to its first chapter.[50] Although works by writers in other languages are occasionally featured, such as Tasso, Schiller, and Homer, these are invariably presented in translation, usually by a noted British author such as Alexander Pope. Whether or not it refers to a specific anthology, the preference for the term 'British Poets' rather than 'English' is a subtle promotion of unionisation that points further towards the national inclusivity of the literary patriotism that Scott is endorsing. The persona Scott creates is not English or Scottish, but always determinedly and implicitly British.

Scott's most lucid visualisation of this authorial persona in the Introduction to *Chronicles of the Canongate* begins with a lengthy anecdote through which Scott compares his own anonymous authorship to the masked antics of the Harlequin-type figure of early Italian theatre, Arlechino 'whose mouth [. . .] is filled [. . .] with quips, and cranks, and witty devices, very often delivered extempore'. In particular, Scott emphasises that 'the mask was essential to the performance of the character', thus initiating a discourse of theatrical imagery that is continued later in the Introduction through the analogy of the 'theatrical mechanist' to describe his approach to epigraphic paratext.[51] The significance of this image is profound, since it encapsulates Scott's habitual cultivation of an authorial or narrative persona within his fiction.

In *Waverley*, this takes the form of an ironic narrator whose presence within the narrative remains constant though not always obvious. The first and most prominent appearance of this narrative persona occurs before the commencement of the actual plot, in the aforementioned introductory chapter. It is a moment of paratextual experimentation which Margret Fetzer notes 'formally belongs to the body of the novel, thus tricking most of us into reading it'.[52] Here Scott sets out his creative vision for the book, primarily through a series of negatives: as Angela Wright points out in her study of the Scottish Gothic, '*Waverley* becomes defined by what it is not.'[53] Whilst Wright continues by associating this negativity with 'the mourning for a lost nation [that] lies at the heart of this tale',[54] Michael Gamer posits a more pragmatic suggestion that Scott is effectively 'clear[ing] the stage of competitors before Edward Waverley's entrance'.[55] The narrative persona appears as someone keenly aware of contemporary literary fiction, and who is anticipating a similarly knowledgeable audience. This is especially noticeable when this persona uses a series of rhetorical questions to include the reader in the reasoning behind some of his own creative decisions:

> had my title borne, "Waverley, a Romance from the German," what head so obtuse as not to image forth a profligate abbot, an oppressive duke, a secret and mysterious association of Rosycrucians and illuminati, [. . .]? Or if I had rather chosen to call my work a "Sentimental Tale," would it

not have been a sufficient presage of a heroine with a profusion of auburn hair, and a harp, the soft solace of her solitary hours [. . .]? (*Waverley*, p. 4)

The discourse thus initiated continues throughout the novel, albeit in subtler ways. Of the 72 chapters that comprise *Waverley*, only 6 commence with a quotation; the number rises to 7 if the chapter title 'DULCE DOMUM' is included (*Waverley*, p. 351), a phrase which editor Claire Lamont identifies not so much as a quotation but rather as the 'title of a song said to have been written by a scholar at Winchester in the seventeenth century'.[56] The song features in *The Psalms, Hymns, Prayers, Graces, and Dulce Domum, Used by the Scholars of Winchester College* (1760); yet whilst the title within the volume is given as simply 'Domum', the phrase 'Dulce Domum' recurs multiple times in the song's chorus.[57] An English translation of this Latin text may be found in Helen Maria Williams's *Poems on Various Subjects* (1823), in which the title is given and explained as 'Dulce Domum, / An Old Latin Ode. / Sung Annually by the Winchester Boys Upon Leaving College at the Vacation'.[58] In either case, all 7 such quotation-based titles appear in the third volume of the work; the remaining 65 chapters are prefaced with, usually quite short, chapter titles. Alexander draws a distinction between the first of these quotation-based titles, suggesting that it is a chapter that 'has for its title a quotation', whilst in the later chapters 'a motto appears in place of, rather than as, a title'.[59] The distinction appears to be primarily typographic, since the only real difference between the two situations is that the first quotation-based title is surrounded by inverted commas and not attributed to Shakespeare, whereas later quotations are generally attributed and do not feature quotation marks. Previous historical fiction had not typically featured this form of paratext: in a study of the genre during this period, Anne Stevens identifies 85 historical novels published between 1760 and 1813, of which only two appear to have chapter titles throughout. A further three novels feature a limited form of chapter titling, whilst four are divided into sections or chapters with descriptions of the ensuing prose. The most popular form of chapter paratext in this kind of fiction was without question the epigraph, with 20 out of Stevens's 85 novels featuring pre-chapter quotations.[60] By choosing to use chapter titles, Scott is subtly ensuring a stylistic difference between the majority of previous historical fiction, including both the 20 published with epigraphs and at least 50 others published with no form of chapter paratext at all.

Observing that Scott's chapter titles in *Waverley* are 'generally routine', Alexander also points out that the title to chapter 30 'has a distinctly Fielding-esque ring to it'[61] as it states that the ensuing prose 'SHOWS THAT THE LOSS OF A HORSE'S SHOE MAY BE A SERIOUS INCONVENIENCE' (*Waverley*, p. 158). This faintly facetious tone is a proleptic indication of further intrusions of Scott's narrative persona still to come, most prominently in the third volume.

Here, chapter 50 (the volume's third chapter) commences with the disparaging title 'RATHER UNIMPORTANT' (*Waverley*, p. 252), whilst chapter 62 issues the imperative 'WHAT'S TO BE DONE NEXT?' (*Waverley*, p. 305). This transition towards a light-hearted tone is especially significant since this is also the section of the book in which the hero's military and romantic endeavours are in the most doubt and danger. The first quotation-based title features a line from a song in Shakespeare's *Much Ado About Nothing*: 'TO ONE THING CONSTANT NEVER' (*Waverley*, p. 270).[62] It prefaces a chapter in which Waverley, having become aware that his amorous aspirations towards the politically passionate Flora MacIvor are totally hopeless, has also realised the transfer of his affections to the more domestically inclined Rose Bradwardine. Whilst Edward and Rose read passages from Shakespeare's *Romeo and Juliet*, Flora discreetly signals her approval of Waverley's shift in affections through a parallel with Romeo's switch of allegiance from Rosalind to Juliet, stating that 'it was impossible that Romeo's love, supposing him a reasonable being, could continue without hope' (*Waverley*, p. 272). Key to this sentence is the idea of the hero as 'a reasonable being' since it underscores Scott's deliberate avoidance of generic conventions of romantic loyalty. Lamont's annotations to the novel point out that the astute reader will have already suspected this outcome via the narrator's delicacy in asserting that Rose 'deserves better [. . .] than to be introduced at the end of a chapter' (*Waverley*, p. 43): a conscious parallel of Fielding's *Tom Jones*, which states that 'it is by no means proper' that the 'intended heroine [. . .] should make her appearance at the end of a book'.[63] This early narratorial intrusion is compounded by the quotation from *Much Ado About Nothing* that prefaces the later chapter, for whilst the characters themselves are mediating their love-lives through quotations from the tragedy of *Romeo and Juliet*, the means through which Scott comments upon the narrative is from a popular and recognisable comedy. Unlike Radcliffe, for whom epigraphs were a way of enhancing emotional interiority, Scott remains firmly in the role of external narrator and maintains a subtle but persistent distinction between the experiences of the characters and his own views upon those experiences. Through the chapter title's invocation of *Much Ado*'s bright refrain, he encourages his reader to do likewise and enjoy the amusement afforded by the earnest solemnity of those who believe themselves to be in love, a pleasure entertaining only to those who are on the outside of that emotional nucleus. Unlike the epigraphs used by Radcliffe and her imitators, which experimented with the vocalisation of the emotional register of characters within the text, Scott here appears more akin to Chaigneau or Fielding and Collier as the epigraph becomes a critical extension of the novel's omniscient narrator. The purpose of Scott's tale is not so much to live vicariously through the adventures of a hero or heroine, as it had so often been in Gothic fiction, but to be entertained by them.

This aesthetic alliance between the narrator and reader is further emphasised through the distance Scott places between them and the narrative itself during the novel's denouement, with chapters 66–71 featuring a near continuous pattern of quotation-based titles. The primary narrative ends with the conclusion of chapter 72, and the only chapter to follow this succession is entitled 'A POSTSCRIPT, WHICH SHOULD HAVE BEEN A PREFACE' (*Waverley*, p. 362), a paratextual demarcation that separates it still further from the preceding prose. A good example of the use Scott makes of these quotation-based titles may be found in the title to chapter 68: 'To-morrow? O that's sudden!—Spare him, spare him' (*Waverley*, p. 340).[64] The line originates in *Measure for Measure*, and vocalises the horror of a sister at the news of her brother's imminent execution. Here, the chapter which it prefaces details Waverley's attendance at the sentencing of the Jacobite leader Fergus, and his subsequent meeting with Fergus's sister Flora MacIvor following the inevitable pronouncement of capital punishment. Joan Garden Cooper suggests that Scott does not depict the whole trial so as to demonstrate 'that Fergus's ominous fate is a preordained event',[65] yet a more powerful motivation may be perceived in the avoidance of narratorial partisanship elsewhere in the novel. As Juliet Feibel notes in her analysis of second sight in Jacobite histories, '*Waverley* is remarkable for its celebration of Jacobite sentiment and loyalty while depicting the Hanoverian triumph as a victory for common sense and historical progress.'[66] Indeed, it is the 'wavering loyalties' of Scott's protagonist that Alan Freeman's study of nationalism in Scottish fiction claims 'enable[s] sympathetic portrayal of both sides of the conflict'.[67] By not including Fergus's trial, Scott limits the opportunities for introducing political discourse into his text and instead prioritises the emotional tenor of the narrative. Even during the sentencing, the majority of narrative attention is given to Evan Dhu Maccombich's gallant offer of himself and 'ony six o' the very best of [Fergus's] clan' in exchange for the life of their chief (*Waverley*, p. 342). The chapter's prefatory quotation promotes this focus upon heroism and self-sacrifice not just through the anticipation of Flora's sorrow for her brother's fate, but also to some extent through its encapsulation of Waverley's grief. As Margaret Bruzelius points out in her history of adventure fiction, Waverley is 'the foremost example' of the 'aimless young man who gets involved in an adventure by accident and is rescued from the toils of others by good luck', while Isabelle Bour goes even further by suggesting that this inactivity places him 'incontrovertibly in a feminine position'.[68] Waverley had once sought a familial relationship with Fergus via marriage to his sister Flora, thus the quotation 'Spare him, spare him' both conveys his emotions whilst also aligning him with the generic passivity of female characters in contemporary romantic fiction. Beyond the superficial similarities of situation, however, the contextual relevance of the quotation ends, for whilst Shakespeare's Isabella takes an active role in saving her brother's life, there is never any possibility of a reprieve for Fergus through the agency of either Flora or Waverley.

The execution itself is prefaced with lines from Campbell's 'Lochiel's Warning':

————————A darker departure is near,
The death-drum is muffled, and sable the bier.
CAMPBELL
(*Waverley*, p. 346)[69]

By ventriloquising the scene through the words of another poet, Scott effectively distances the action from his own authorial influence. Cathrine Frank suggests that Fergus's refusal to allow Waverley to attend his execution 'places a sentimental wedge between Edward's revolutionary "past" [. . .] and the peaceful future that awaits his union with Rose'.[70] More dynamically, it also prevents the sympathy for Fergus and the Jacobite cause from becoming too inflammatory because too unpleasantly pragmatic. Michael Gamer has linked Waverley's 'state of unheroic passivity' with Scott's own enthusiasm for object narratives, in which the reader's gaze is always limited to what the object itself can perceive.[71] By restricting Waverley's, and thus also the reader's, gaze in this chapter, Scott ensures Fergus's final appearance is coloured by his recollection of the supernatural tale of the Bodach Glas. Apparently the ghost of a fallen ancestor who appears to senior members of Fergus's clan 'when any great disaster was impending, but especially before approaching death', this spirit was seen by Fergus the day before his capture and then again, standing in a 'slip of moonshine', the night before his execution (*Waverley*, pp. 294, 347). Fergus thus exits the narrative entwined with legend and superstition, a depiction that is only enhanced by the paratextual lens of Campbell's poetry. The flexibility of Scott's narrative persona (allowed through a primarily paratextual construction) enables a seamless shift from sage commentator to dispassionate antiquarian. Events are recorded and their poetry and pathos savoured, but without actually committing to a political judgement.

'[T]O SEDUCE YOUR CONTINUED ATTENTION'

Scott's next novel, *Guy Mannering*, represents a significant paratextual shift since it is the first of his prose works to feature pre-chapter epigraphic quotation throughout. Prior to the work's publication, he wrote to Ballantyne that he 'intend[ed] the new novel to operate as something more permanent than a mere accommodation'. He subsequently details a strategy of initial self-publication to establish the work's popularity and thus secure the highest price possible for it before selling to a major publishing house.[72] The composition of *Guy Mannering* in 1814–15 coincided with one of the several temporary declines in usage which the practice of epigraphic quotation seems to have suffered in the first two decades of the nineteenth century: at least 24 novels were first-published with epigraphic quotations in 1814 (constituting just over 39% of the total first-published that year), but this number drops sharply to 16 novels the following year (just over 29% of the total first-published that year). The percentage of novels first-published with epigraphs lingers around 29% over the next few years (see Appendix, Table 1 and Figures 1 and 2); yet the fact that someone as familiar with the business of publishing as Scott chose to incorporate pre-chapter quotations in a novel he intended to have lasting durability says much about the kind of status and importance epigraphs were attaining. Through his paratextual selections in *Guy Mannering*, Scott uses his epigraphs as a space in which to further develop the technique – already experimented with in *Waverley* – of seeming to separate his own authorial influence from the actions of his characters.

Although Alexander notes that 'the first three [mottos . . .] were added after the initial composition' of *Guy Mannering*,[73] there are nonetheless numerous indications after this point that Scott is keen to emphasise the connection between text and paratext. Chapter 11 is prefaced by a quotation from the chorus in Shakespeare's *The Winter's Tale*:

> *Enter Time, as Chorus.*
> I—that please some, try all; both joy and terror
> Of good and bad; that make and unfold error—
> Now take upon me, in the name of Time,
> To use my wings. Impute it not a crime
> To me, or my swift passage, that I slide
> O'er sixteen years, and leave the growth untried
> Of that wide gap.————————
>
> *Winter's Tale*
> (*Guy Mannering*, p. 59)[74]

By including not only the lines themselves but also the stage directions, '*Enter Time, as Chorus*', Scott appropriates the whole theatrical framework of the play. Taken in conjunction with this, the ensuing chapter's expositional and rather ordinary use of a collective pronoun in the declaration that '[o]ur narrative is now about to make a large stride' (*Guy Mannering*, p. 59) also becomes a means through which to further emphasise Scott's alignment with the reader, and thus as an external spectator rather than an internal authority. The relevance of the *Winter's Tale* quotation to the text is also reinforced by the closeness of the chronological match: whilst Shakespeare's play 'slide[s] / O'er sixteen years', Scott similarly 'omits a space of nearly seventeen years', i.e. sixteen full years (*Guy Mannering*, p. 59). Rather than a compositional afterthought, the epigraph here has been dove-tailed very precisely into the text.

MOTTOS, MASKS, AND THE HISTORICAL NOVEL

Later, an even closer relationship between text and paratext appears when chapter 15 begins with two stanzas from the ballad 'The Heir of Linne':

> My gold is gone, my money is spent,
>   My land now take it unto thee.
> Give me the gold, good John o' the Scales,
>   And thine for aye my land shall be.
>
> Then John he did him to record draw,
>   And John he caste him a gods pennie;
> But for every pounde that John agreed,
>   The land, I wis, was well worth three.
>
> (*Guy Mannering*, p. 82)[75]

A parallel for the poem's 'John o' the Scales' is readily available in the character of Gilbert Glossin, the purchaser and thus usurper of the ancestral property of the Bertram family. Indeed, rather than leave the reader to identify the connection for themselves, Scott underscores the connection by referring to Glossin in the chapter's first sentence via this exact analogy: 'The Galwegian John o' the Scales was a more clever fellow than his prototype. He contrived to make himself heir of Linne without the disagreeable ceremony of "telling down the good red gold"' (*Guy Mannering*, p. 82). Although not present in the epigraph itself, the allusion to 'telling down the good red gold' is likewise taken from 'The Heir of Linne', thus further cementing the connection and its importance in the text. Figured as a character in a traditional ballad, Glossin becomes a usurper not just of land, but of the cultural heritage represented by the ballad quoted. Since Glossin's actual name is never mentioned in this chapter, Scott is also ensuring that the epigraph must be read before the chapter itself can be comprehended. Even if the reader had initially bypassed the quotation, they would eventually find their way back to it in attempting to unravel the euphemistic title 'John o' the Scales'. More than simply reinforcing the connection, Scott is forcefully directing his reader to pay attention to paratextual details.

A further, albeit less integral, allusion to an epigraph appears in chapter 26, when a returning fishing party are indirectly associated with 'Johnnie Armstrong and his merry-men' (*Guy Mannering*, p. 138), characters who are also referenced in a similar context in the chapter's prefatory quotation:

> The Elliots and Armstrongs did convene,
>   They were a gallant company!
>   *Ballad of Johnnie Armstrong*
>   (*Guy Mannering*, p. 136)[76]

EPIGRAPHS IN THE ENGLISH NOVEL 1750–1850

Although this kind of intertextual referencing is comparatively rare within this novel, its persistent recurrence steadily promotes Scott's self-identification as an external commentator upon his own work. This becomes particularly important towards the end of the novel, via the epigraph used to preface the chapter in which the text's hero Vanbeest Brown is revealed to be the long-lost Harry Bertram and heir to the wealthy estate of Ellangowan:

> *Justice*. This does indeed confirm each circumstance
> The gypsey told!————————
> No orphan, nor without a friend art thou—
> *I* am thy father, *here's* thy mother, *there*
> Thy uncle—This thy first cousin, and these
> Are all thy near relations!
>
>

 The Critic

 (*Guy Mannering*, p. 303)[77]

Taken from Richard Brinsley Sheridan's satirical play *The Critic* (1779), this quotation parodies the conventional Romantic trope of sudden, implausible reunion between long-lost family members. Wright notes that the improbable discovery of true identities and familial relationships in *Guy Mannering* 'demonstrates Scott's indebtedness to the classic Gothic plot motif',[78] but the epigraph complicates this. Rather than hurry past the familiar trope in his novel, Scott draws attention to it in a way that allows his readers to perceive its approach and find humour in its conventionality. Scott had avoided narrating Harry Bertram's kidnapping at the start of the novel because to do so, Robert Irvine argues in his analysis of this tale, would have been 'to admit outright that astrology, in this case, had actually and remarkably succeeded in predicting the future'.[79] Scott again uses a quality of narrative structure (in this case the paratext) to parry or distract attention away from potential accusations of implausibility before they even arrive. In the Sheridan epigraph, as with the quotation from *The Winter's Tale*, Scott retains the italicised theatrical apparatus (for example, '*Justice*') in a manner that, though not entirely unusual in epigraphic paratext, once again reiterates the sense of the novel itself as a fictional construct. The fact that Brown's true identity has already been both implied and then explicitly stated before this chapter's public revelation further facilitates Scott's use of the epigraph as a means to position author and reader as narrative spectators, rather than as opposite components of the literary relationship. As in *Waverley*, Scott uses chapter paratext in *Guy Mannering* to establish just enough distance between the narrative and his own authorial persona to distract from any weaknesses or implausibilities in the text. Just as the quotation from *Much Ado* invited the reader to find humour in *Waverley's* sudden transition of affections from Flora to Rose, so too does the prominent

MOTTOS, MASKS, AND THE HISTORICAL NOVEL

self-commentary provided via the epigraph from Sheridan's *Critic* distract from the potential disappointment of encountering such a familiar trope.

This kind of distancing effect is still more apparent in Scott's later novel *Rob Roy* (1818), where his own authorial presence is cloaked behind multiple narratorial personas. An 'Advertisement to the First Edition' offers a 'discovered manuscript' premise for the novel akin to that of Henry Mackenzie's *The Man of Feeling* (1771), or Radcliffe's *The Italian* (1797) and *Gaston de Blondeville* (1826). The 'Author' had, Scott claims, 'received a parcel of Papers, containing the Outlines of this narrative, with a permission [. . .] that they might be given to the Public with such alterations as should be found suitable' (*Rob Roy*, p. 3). Amongst these alterations are the 'mottoes' or pre-chapter epigraphs:

> Several anachronisms have probably crept in during the course of these changes; and the mottoes for the Chapters have been selected without any reference to the supposed date of the incidents. For these, of course, the Editor is responsible. (*Rob Roy*, p. 3)

Fetzer records an ambiguity here, since the first-person narrator of the main narrative, Frank Osbaldistone, later claims that he is in fact the person responsible for having 'tagged with rhyme and blank verse the subdivisions of this important narrative' (*Rob Roy*, p. 22). This confusion, Fetzer writes, compounds with the 'openly anachronistic' nature of some of the quotations to draw attention to 'the artificiality of the novel's set-up'.[80] Yet it is possible to reconcile the two statements if the responsibility of Scott's 'Editor' is considered to refer primarily to the 'anachronisms' alluded to in the first clause of the preceding sentence, thus serving as an acceptance of historical inaccuracies within both the text and the epigraphic paratext. Nor was this the first time that Scott's enthusiasm for historical accuracy had come into conflict with his poetic knowledge and taste: following a descriptive (in-text) quotation from a poem by Anna Seward in *Waverley*, he had included a parenthetical qualifier about 'these beautiful lines (which however were not then written)' (*Waverley*, p. 222). Since *Rob Roy* is premised as the composition of an aged Frank addressing his friend Will Tresham, quotations from works not written until after the tale's 1715 setting (such as Daniel Defoe's *Robinson Crusoe*, 1719) remain for the most part entirely plausible. That Scott felt further explanation was required only underscores the importance of historical accuracy for him. Once again, Scott is subverting his own creative agency by concealing it behind the fictional agency of a narrative persona, in this case first Frank and then the fictional 'Editor' responsible for the most modern authors quoted (such as Joanna Baillie and William Wordsworth).

The motivation which narrator-Frank claims for including epigraphs is 'to seduce your continued attention' (*Rob Roy*, p. 22), a claim which Fetzer identifies as evidence that 'Frank considers personal involvement an artistic weakness' and which she regards as an indication that the epigraphs are meant as 'distancing devices' through which Frank relinquishes agency over the text.[81] Certainly, the unobtrusiveness of the frame narrative upon the plot itself introduces the potential for narrator-Frank's statement about epigraphs to be not just a communication from Frank to Tresham, but also from Scott to the reader. Although the novel's presumed narrator is in line with the type of mature persona adopted by Scott in previous novels, Andrew Lincoln's analysis of this text points out that instead of 'a clearly defined difference between youth and age, we find continuity'.[82] Although Lincoln allows this may be a symptom of the 'confessional nature' of a tale in which narrator-Frank is preoccupied with 'self-justification',[83] Deborah Rogers's examination of gender and limitations on female creative agency in *Rob Roy* likewise observes narrator-Frank's lack of 'analytical elaboration' upon the events of his youth. Like Lincoln, she cites this as evidence that '[his] experience leaves him unchanged' and just as 'unperceptive' as his youthful equivalent.[84] In this sense, narrator-Frank appears as nothing more than a rather inadequate camouflage for the real author. But the situation is further complicated when the 8 non-attributable epigraphs that feature in the novel are also considered. For if Scott has attempted to mask his identity behind that of Frank, to whom should the epigraphs be attributed within the fictional conceit of the narrative?

A resolution to this dilemma, and a complication to Frank's apparent self-distancing from the events of his youth, is offered by the epigraph to chapter 22. Despite a convincingly precise attribution including act and scene numbers, the quotation itself remains unidentified:

> Look round thee, young Astolpho—here's the place
> Which men (for being poor) are sent to starve in,—
> Rude remedy, I trow, for sore disease.
> Within these walls, stifled by damp and stench,
> Doth Hope's fair torch expire—and at the snuff,
> Ere yet 'tis quite extinct, rude, wild, and wayward,
> The desperate revelries of wild despair,
> Kindling their hell-born cressets, light to deeds,
> That the poor captive would have died ere practised,
> Till bondage sunk his soul to his condition.
> *The Prison*, Scene III. Act I
> (*Rob Roy*, p. 173)

The ensuing chapter details Frank's meeting with the as-yet unidentified Rob Roy, who leads him to the prison cell in which his father's head clerk Owen has been interred. David Hewitt notes that '[n]o play called *The Prison* has been traced, but the lines imitate Coleridge's 'The Dungeon', also pointing out that 'Astolpho was one of Alcina's prisoners in Ariosto's *Orlando Furioso*' (*Rob Roy*, p. 528 n. 173). This latter observation gains significance when juxtaposed with the young Frank's literary aspirations, since it is upon his translation of *Orlando Furioso* that his poetic ambitions largely depend. Although not necessarily a direct attempt at translation from *Orlando*, the reference to Astolpho invokes the character of Ariosto's heroic, and magically talented, English knight. In this context it parallels the young Frank's romantic self-image and his rejection of worldly business. Since Scott squarely identifies the pre-chapter quotations as primarily the work of narrator-Frank, the epigraph thus constitutes a paratextual space in which the protagonist assumes a function of commentator upon his own life and actions, and upon the events which unfold around him. It is an effective continuation of Scott's typical earlier narrative strategies in which the narrator is usually a mature, amused, and ironic omniscient deity.

Furthermore, this quotation also offers a valuable example of Scott's tendency to invent sources for some of the epigraphs he self-authored. Here the title, '*The Prison*', serves to explain the place only obliquely described within the stanza itself. Although the references to 'walls, stifled by damp and stench', 'wild despair', and 'the poor captive' offer hints as to the verse's subject, the directness of the appellation '*The Prison*' provides an immediate and accessible context for a text that (since it is invented by Scott for the purpose) would have no other point of reference within literature. Scott's success in establishing a context for his lone stanza is evidenced by its subsequent appearance in Isaac Gomez's *Selections of a father for the use of his children* (1820), together with the same attribution to scene and act number, and later inclusion in John Addington's *Poetical Quotations* (1829) under a section of poetry on the subject of prisons.[85] Since the quotation itself has so far not been identified in any extant text, and as no further attribution has been provided than that given by Scott in *Rob Roy*, it seems likely that this is evidence of the enduring influence of epigraphs that were not simply visual 'decoraments' but texts that would be read, remembered, and replicated.

Nor was this the only occasion when Scott concealed a self-composed epigraph with an invented title. As noted above, approximately 87 of the 248 unidentified epigraphs in Scott's novels appear to follow this pattern, making the technique second only to the attribution of '*Old Play*' in terms of frequency. Although Alexander labels such attributions 'imaginary and arbitrary',[86] a more consistent pattern appears indicated by the fact that some works repeat the same source title in multiple unidentified pre-chapter quotations throughout the work. For example, *The Abbot* features 4 epigraphs apparently from '*Spanish Father*' (or '*The Spanish Father*'), *The Monastery* has 2 attributed to '*Reformation*' (or '*The Reformation*'), *The Fortunes of Nigel* (1822) ascribes

EPIGRAPHS IN THE ENGLISH NOVEL 1750–1850

3 to 'The Chamberlain', and Peveril of the Peak (1822) gives 2 non-sequential epigraphs the source title of 'The Chieftain'.[87] Haber writes that 'the same ballad [. . .] is sometimes cited in the mottoes for two or more chapters';[88] but just as Alexander suggests that the attribution to 'Old Play' is a way of 'reflecting the predominant old drama style',[89] so too do these, usually blank verse, quotations frequently appear more closely akin to extracts from dramatic works. Although the precision of the reference to 'The Prison, Scene III. Act I' in Rob Roy is strikingly rare within Scott's oeuvre, titles such as the aforementioned 'The Chamberlain' will occasionally feature a generically dramatic subtitle, for example 'The Chamberlain – A Comedy'. There is also the occasional use of apparently invented sources in more than one novel: for example, a quotation in Kenilworth (1821) features the same title ('The Woodsman') as two of the similarly untraced quotations in The Abbot,[90] something which might strengthen the possibility of this yet proving to be a genuine rather than a purely invented source. Likewise, The Fortunes of Nigel features one epigraph attributed to 'The Reformation', which (as noted above) features twice in the epigraphs of The Monastery (although, in this case, differences between both the subject matter and the verse structure make it unlikely that these could ever have been supposed to be from the same text).[91] Yet this kind of duplication is rare, with these apparently invented titles more typically functioning, like 'The Prison' in Rob Roy, to establish a secure context for the epigraph and a point of connection with the ensuing narrative.

In Kenilworth, for example, the epigraph to chapter 25 appears to be Scott's composition despite an attribution to the apparently non-existent work 'The Glass Slipper':

> Hark, the bells summon, and the bugle calls,
> But she the fairest answers not—the tide
> Of nobles and of ladies throngs the halls,
> But she the loveliest must in secret hide.
> What eyes were thine, proud Prince, which in the gleam
> Of yon gay meteors lost that better sense,
> That o'er the glow-worm doth the star esteem,
> And merit's modest blush o'er courtly insolence?
> The Glass Slipper
> (Kenilworth, p. 249)

At this point in the narrative, the secretly married Amy Robsart has disguised herself as a peasant to travel to her husband's castle, where he is busy organising a grand entertainment for Queen Elizabeth I. The parallel established in the verse is easily accessible since it states that 'she the loveliest must in secret hide'. The reference to the 'proud Prince' who has 'lost that better sense, / That o'er

112

the glow-worm doth the star esteem' is likewise unquestionably an allusion to her husband, the Earl of Leicester, whose fidelity to his secret wife is strained by the opportunity of power presented by the Queen's growing affection for him. Still more strikingly, the epigraph's attributed source immediately associates the text with the popular fairy tale of Cinderella, which in the eighteenth century frequently passed under the name of 'Cinderella, or the Little Glass Slipper'.[92] Here, of course, the conventional narrative of the fairy tale is rearranged, as the epigraph conveys the sense that the Prince is distracted by the 'gay meteors' and 'courtly insolence' of his surroundings and thus blinded to the true worth of 'the loveliest'. Similarly, there is no possibility for a happy ending in Scott's novel: although the question of whether Amy Robsart was murdered remains unresolved, she did nonetheless die as Scott's heroine does, from a fall within her home.[93] The epigraph thus offers a point of aesthetic contrast for the informed or returning reader, whilst potentially misdirecting the unsuspecting reader by leading them to believe that a happy outcome might be possible. When Scott invents titles for epigraphs elsewhere in his novels, any attributions will typically operate in a similarly obvious manner, thus further emphasising the importance of epigraphic paratext as a rapidly accessible form of commentary which is increasingly imitating the descriptive function of a chapter title.

Despite this evident interest in initiating paratextual dialogue, however, Scott's enthusiasm for epigraphs generally seems to have waned in the latter half of his prose fiction career. Haber provides one possible explanation for this, noting that Scott only omits to include epigraphic paratext 'in novels written under stress of ill health or financial worries'.[94] Certainly at first there is a noticeable increase in his tendency to self-author epigraphs rather than leave blank the commencement of a new chapter; but when he published *Tales of the Crusaders* in 1825 there were 7 chapters out of a total of 61 that were without any form of prefatory paratext. Prompted by a query from Ballantyne, Scott remarked that '[t]here is no absolute reason for having mottoes to each chapter'.[95] But alongside this growing apathy towards epigraphic quotation, a distinct lack of originality was developing within Scott's own writing. He grumbled in his journal about Ballantyne's criticisms of the manuscript of *Woodstock* (1826), writing that:

> J. B. is severely critical on what he calls imitations of Mrs. Radcliffe in *Woodstock* [. . .] yet I am of opinion he is quite wrong [. . .]. In the first place I am to look on the mere fact of another author having treated a subject happily as a bird looks on a potatoe bogle which scares it away from a field otherwise as free to its depredations as any one's else.[96]

Though the critique is primarily levelled at Scott's use of the Radcliffean trope of offering a rational explanation for a supernatural occurrence, Ballantyne is also tacitly pointing out that Scott has, ironically, succumbed to the very generic identification he had so strongly resisted in *Waverley*. The subtitles of *Ivanhoe* and *Kenilworth* had both identified these novels as part of the 'Romance' genre, and even without this paratextual guidance a reviewer of *Tales of the Crusaders* proclaims one of the work's heroines as 'the most heavenly Peri that ever flitted through the pages of Romance'.[97] Likewise, as Scott's fiction drifted back towards the styles and tropes of his literary antecedents in Romantic and Gothic fiction, so too was the epigraph reaffirmed in its identification with these forms of literature. The epigraphic experimentation of Scott's earlier prose fiction largely disappears as his pre-chapter paratext assumes a broadly descriptive character.

Despite this eventual decline, however, Scott had become and would remain a powerful influence upon the incorporation and development of epigraphs. Admittedly, the quantity per year of first-published novels with epigraphs had already risen to just under 40% in 1813 (before Scott's epigraphic influence could possibly be held responsible), yet such occasional anomalies are not unusual in the preceding decade (for example, 1810 sees a sudden peak of 31%). Scott's importance can be discerned in the persistent increase in the use of epigraphs: throughout the 1820s, the quantity of novels with epigraphs never drops below 30%, and frequently exceeds 40% of the number of novels first-published within a year.[98] Since the number of novels first-published each year also rises steeply during this period, this represents a significant leap in the number of novels with epigraphs appearing each year, from between 12 and 20 in the first decade of the nineteenth century to between 33 and 48 per year in the 1820s. That this increase was largely down to Scott's influence is indicated by the many other paratextual tributes to him in fiction of this time. For example, David Carey's *A Legend of Argyle* (1821) imitates *Waverley* with a subtitle proclaiming that *''Tis a Hundred Years Since'*, whilst the anonymous author of *Nice Distinctions* (1820) includes a dedication to Scott's pseudonym of Jedediah Cleishbotham.[99] Both works also feature pre-chapter epigraphic quotation throughout. Later, when Scott's authorship of the Waverley novels had become much more of an open secret, some epigraphic users begin to dedicate novels to Scott by name, for instance Matthew Weld Hartstonge in his novel *The Eve of All-Hallows* (1825).[100] The vastness of Scott's literary influence is encapsulated by Alexander Sutherland (also a user of epigraphs) when he writes that his own dedication to Scott in *Tales of a Pilgrim* (1827) has been made 'with no permission, / but that which his genius has conferred / on admiring millions'.[101]

Through experimentation and innovation, particularly in his earliest novels, Scott broadened the paratextual possibilities of the epigraph. Having initially followed in the footsteps of Chaigneau, and Fielding and Collier to use the epigraph's potential as a space for self-reflexive narrative commentary (for example, in *Guy Mannering*), Scott's approach to prefatory paratext later developed

Radcliffe's understanding of the epigraph as a means through which to convey characters' emotion from within the text (for example in *Rob Roy*, where a first-person retrospective narrative allows for the roles of main character and commentator to be combined). In Scott's work, the epigraph becomes an extension of narrative voice, intended to develop and enhance the authorial persona he had striven so hard to create. Scott was also more influential than any other author in promoting the concept of the invented epigraph that pretends to be a quotation from something else. Rather than simply omitting an attribution, as Radcliffe had done for her self-authored epigraphs, and instead of including either a vague attribution such as Chaigneau's 'ANONIMOUS [*sic*]' or the bluntly honest 'AUTHOR' that accompanies this kind of prefatory verse in works such as John Davies's *The Post-Captain* (1806),[102] Scott allows his self-authored epigraphs to masquerade as samples of a longer, external work. By so doing, he prioritises the epigraph's capacity to constitute an extension of the fictional text, finally confirming that the usefulness of an epigraph is very far from being defined solely by the contemporary popularity or canonical status of the author quoted.

5

FROM ROMANCE TO REALISM: CATHERINE GORE AND ELIZABETH GASKELL

If any hopes thy bosom share
But those which Love has planted there,
Or any cares but his thy breast enthral;
Thou never yet his power hast known,
Love sits on a despotic throne,
And reigns a tyrant if he reigns at all.
                              MRS. BARBAULD.[1]

The murder by poison of the Warwickshire baronet Sir Theodosius Broughton by his brother-in-law Captain Donellan at their family home of Lawford Hall on 30 August 1780 provoked 'incredible [. . .] curiosity' throughout the county.[2] Newspaper reports tracked the progress of the case in exhaustive detail, from the initial death and coroner's inquest through to Donellan's trial and execution.[3] Sixty years later, historic accounts of the incident formed the inspiration for a fictionalisation of the crime in Katherine Thomson's fifth novel, *Widows and Widowers* (1842). The main narrative follows the romantic fortunes of Adeline Meadows, whose marriage to the dissipated scoundrel whom she loves, Stanhope Floyer, causes her to be staying at the same house in which her husband's friend Mr Lawson poisons his brother-in-law Sir Horace Wentworth with laurel-water. A short preface allows Thomson to justify the novel's subtitle, 'A Romance of Real Life', with the explanation that 'one of the main incidents [the murder] is founded [. . .] on fact' (*Widows and Widowers*, p. v). Indeed it is this foundation of truth that holds in check any sense of gratuitous sensationalism, lending authority and realism to a narrative that elsewhere features an almost Austenian depiction of the relationships and social struggles of supporting characters. Pre-chapter epigraphs appear throughout, with the

116

example included above interacting with both sides of a narrative break just as Radcliffe's epigraphs had done. In the chapter immediately preceding this epigraph's appearance, the hero Eustace Floyer has settled the ruined financial affairs of his feckless cousin Stanhope to enable the latter's marriage to Adeline even though Eustace is himself in love with her; the new chapter begins with the triumphant arrival of Stanhope to claim his bride. Derived from a poem that claims to 'teach thee what it is to love, / And by what marks true passion may be found',[4] the epigraph thus highlights the sincerity of Eustace's selfless devotion and invites the reader to compare this with the often neglectful behaviour of Stanhope. Yet for paratextual history, the most significant aspect here is perhaps the fact that this mid-nineteenth-century novel included epigraphs at all.

There has long been a tendency within paratextual scholarship to assume that the use of pre-chapter epigraphic quotation virtually disappears in the nineteenth century after the death of Walter Scott in 1832, to suddenly reappear more than thirty years later in George Eliot's *Felix Holt* (1866), *Middlemarch* (1871–72), and *Daniel Deronda* (1876).[5] In fact, out of 2324 novels known to have been first-published between 1837 and 1850 a range of 1744 have been surveyed and 551 proved to contain some form of pre-chapter epigraphic quotation. This means that the percentage of novels with epigraphs as a proportion of the total number of novels first-published is around 24% (or 32% of novels actually surveyed). Statistical analyses of epigraphic usage presented in earlier chapters were compiled from the more recent bibliography edited by Garside, Raven, and Schöwerling to cover the period 1770–1829, and a comparison assessment of the year 1836 indicated minor numerical differences between each reference work (for example, due to minor discrepancies between recorded publication years). Because of this, a year-by-year comparison of earlier years covered by Garside, Raven, and Schöwerling with later years covered separately by both Block and Bassett would be impractical and unhelpful. However, a broad comparison was achieved by calculating an average percentage for a similar fourteen-year period immediately preceding the later time span only covered by Block and Bassett, and based upon the Garside, Raven, and Schöwerling data. This suggests that in the period 1823–36, at least 1212 novels were published, of which 1144 have been assessed. Of this number, 494 novels featured some form of epigraphic content, representing approximately 41% of novels first-published during this period (or 43% of novels actually surveyed). Despite the necessarily incomplete nature of these figures, it is nonetheless clear that, notwithstanding a partial decline in the use of epigraphs, the popularity of the device persists as an overall trend. Indeed, the annual percentage of novels with epigraphs as a proportion of novels surveyed during 1837–50 never falls below 25% (see Appendix, Tables 1 and 2, and Figures 1 and 2).

If the epigraph has appeared to fall out of use during and after the 1830s, then it is most probably because the works in which it occurs have typically been deemed unworthy of much (or any) academic investigation. For example, when Edward Jacobs's study of Radcliffe's epigraphic paratext suggests that during this later period 'most novels instead [bear] chapter titles or tags',[6] the generalisation is based on a consideration of canonical writers such as Dickens, Thackeray, and the Brontës. Only when the works of writers outside the traditional canon are included does it become apparent that this was actually a time of much experimentation with chapter-based paratext. Throughout the 1840s in particular there is a modest but clear increase in the use of combinations of epigraphs with either chapter titles or chapter descriptions. As has been previously discussed, pre-chapter epigraphic quotation before the 1830s typically appeared instead of, rather than as well as, other forms of chapter paratext such as a title or description. But of the 551 novels known to have been published with epigraphs between 1837 and 1850, there are 137 that feature epigraphic quotation alongside an additional form of paratext (for example, a chapter title or description). The most extreme example of this form of paratextual layering occurs in Frederick Chamier's *Ben Bradshawe; The Man without a Head* (1843), in which chapters typically commence with a title, a short description of the content, and finally a quotation.[7] A less unusual variation in chapter paratext at this time is the juxtaposition of a chapter title with an epigraph, with the title usually (though not always) appearing first on the page, followed by one or more quotations.[8] Yet the majority of writers who used epigraphs in the early to mid-nineteenth century still favoured the more traditional stand-alone quotation format, with the most frequent users of this style including Hannah D. Burdon, Edward Bulwer-Lytton, Lady Charlotte Susan Maria Bury, Catherine Grace Frances Gore, Horatio Smith, and Katherine Thomson. Although many of these writers are comparatively obscure today, they were all highly successful and well-known novelists within their own lifetimes, meaning that during this period the epigraph would have been a much more prominent feature on the landscape of nineteenth-century prose fiction than literary criticism has retrospectively made it appear.

Of the many novelists whose published works incorporated pre-chapter epigraphs during this period, the most prolific was undoubtedly Catherine Grace Frances Gore. In the course of a career that spanned more than three decades, Gore authored around 42 novels, of which 29 feature some form of pre-chapter epigraphic quotation. She also wrote 18 anthologies of shorter fiction, of which at least 7 feature a minimum of one story that incorporates chapter divisions with epigraphic quotations.[9] Gore wrote 12 novels that feature no form of epigraphic quotation, and for the most part these fall at the end of her career. Statistically, Gore was thus the single most prolific user of pre-chapter epigraphs during the 1830s and 1840s, and her potential for influencing the development of the device in the nineteenth century was further enhanced by the fact that she was also one of the most successful and well known. As Molly Engelhardt points out in her analysis of Gore's literary impact, during this time she 'achieved more visibility and sold more books than any other writer in the popular market-place'.[10] Scholarship has typically classified Gore as working within the tradition of 'silver-fork' novels, a term that derives from William Hazlitt's scathing attack upon Theodore Hook's *Sayings and Doings* (published in three series in 1824, 1825, and 1828) and Benjamin Disraeli's *Vivian Grey* (1826/27). Critiquing the 'servility, egotism, and upstart pretensions' of contemporary writers in general, Hazlitt finally focuses his critique upon Hook's apparent preoccupation with pragmatic details of life amongst 'the quality', such as the fact that they 'eat fish with silver forks'.[11] Unsurprisingly, no specific mention is made of Gore's fiction, since by the time that Hazlitt was writing in 1827 Gore had published only two narrative poems (*The Two Broken Hearts*, 1823; *The Bond, A Dramatic Poem*, 1824) as well as a few novellas and anthologies of shorter fiction; yet this chronological discrepancy has not prevented Hazlitt's criticism being repeated in virtually every scholarly appraisal of Gore's work.

Indeed, Cheryl Wilson points out that the genre of the fashionable novel constitutes an 'important transitory space' as literature moved from 'the eighteenth-century Gothic novel and novel of manners to the Victorian realist novel'.[12] Attempts to further differentiate the genre of 'silver-fork' fiction have typically resulted in the identification of two distinct categories. Muireann O'Cinneide explains that one of these 'recounts the progress of a young man in fashionable society', whilst the other 'depicts the introduction of an innocent young woman to high society, often through marriage, and her gradual temptation, corruption, and either redemption or fall'.[13] Pioneering Gore scholar April Kendra likewise supports this gender-based division of silver-fork novels, defining these categories more succinctly as male 'dandy' and female 'society' fiction.[14] Gore described her own longer works as 'fashionable novels', identifying this as the genre in which previous writers such as Samuel Richardson and Maria Edgeworth had been working.[15] More recently, critics have generally agreed that the society novel does indeed derive from what is now termed 'the novel of manners', with Ella Dzelzainis taking this further in her analysis of the relationship between Gothic fiction and the fashionable novel by pointing out that the 'female silver-fork novel [is] a transitional form between the novel of manners as practised by Jane Austen and the emergence of the Victorian realist novel' represented by writers such as Elizabeth Gaskell and George Eliot.[16] It is because of this that Gore is such an important figure in the development of pre-chapter epigraphic quotations, since her persistent use of the device throughout her career establishes her work as a valuable case study of the moment when the epigraph also makes the transition from Gothic and Romantic to realist prose fiction. The majority of this chapter will therefore be dedicated to examining how Gore's use of epigraphic quotation was influenced by shifting currents of the literary market, and to exploring the development of a more comedic dynamic for the epigraph that aligned with the witticisms and *bons mots* of contemporary salon culture. I shall also demonstrate the evolving functionality of Gore's epigraphs as they move from supernatural scene setting to constructing a narratorial persona to rebuffing misogynistic reviewers. This chapter will then conclude with an analysis of both the practical and interpretive functions of epigraphs within the fictional realism of the only two of Gaskell's novels to feature the device, *Mary Barton* (1848) and *North and South* (1854–55). By placing together the works of both novelists, Gore and Gaskell, I shall trace the epigraph's journey from stereotypical association with Gothic and Romantic literature through to its slow adoption by the realist genre.

Elegance and Epigraphs

An oft-quoted criticism of Gore's work is Thackeray's parody of various fashionable novelists in his short series *Punch's Prize Novelists* (1847), which targets her alongside other silver-fork novelists including Bulwer-Lytton and Disraeli. As Kendra explains, the series consisted of 'short pieces [. . .] presented as excerpts from longer novels and written in the style of well-known popular authors'.[17] The 'excerpt' parodying Gore's fiction is given the title '"Lords and Liveries," by the Authoress of "Dukes and Dejeuners," "Hearts and Diamonds," "Marchionesses and Milliners," etc. etc.', with the parallel syntax and alliteration of the parodic titles suggesting that the content of these additional works will be similarly repetitive.[18] Academic critique of Gore has historically perpetuated this presumption of her writing's inferior quality and repetitiveness, with the author of the first major survey of the 'silver-fork' school Matthew Whiting Rosa proclaiming that whilst Gore 'merit[s] considerable attention' it would nonetheless be 'inappropriate' to compare her 'with the great masters of English fiction'.[19] However, April Kendra's more recent efforts to restore recognition of Gore's achievements argue convincingly that Thackeray's attack is not a fair representation either of Gore's work or of Thackeray's attitude towards it: as Kendra points out, in Thackeray's more serious works he 'imitates' Gore just as much as he 'spoofs' her here, and he later privately admitted to Gore that his earlier criticism of her work had probably been motivated by 'a secret envy & black malignity of disposition'.[20]

Far from being simplistic 'formula stories',[21] Gore's range of work in fact suggests considerable acumen with regard to detecting and exploiting popular trends in fiction. One of Gore's earliest novels was the one-volume *Theresa Marchmont; or, The Maid of Honour* (1824). After Gore's death in 1861, an obituary in *The London Review* stated that this was 'her first work [. . .] which was followed, after an interval, by other tales of fashionable life'.[22] But the implicit categorisation of *Theresa Marchmont* as a narrative of 'fashionable life' is strikingly inaccurate. The tale itself centres upon the young Lady Helen Greville, who resolves to live apart from her husband once she discovers that he is already married to a mentally unstable woman who had once been betrothed to Helen's now-deceased brother. Whiting Rosa aligns *Theresa Marchmont* with two other works of shorter fiction by Gore, classifying them all as 'historical romances'.[23] But Cheryl Wilson presents a more accurate assessment in her history of the silver-fork genre, in which she notes that '[a] number of silver fork novels [. . .] borrow from the Gothic genre', using 'plot devices such as mistaken or disguised identities, damsels in distress, and compromised fortunes and virtues'.[24] This is especially true of *Theresa Marchmont*, where the use of Gothic and Romantic motifs is so pronounced as to suggest it does not in fact belong in the genre of 'silver-fork' fiction at all. The home of the protagonist's husband was a 'gloomy' former monastery consisting of a 'maze of useless corridors' and adorned with tapestries of 'faded hues and mouldering texture'; upon their arrival a servant spread a story of a ghostly woman 'who glides through the apartments'; and when Helen saw this figure she 'fell insensible on the floor'.[25] Radcliffe's concept of the explained supernatural haunts the novel throughout, and Gore deviates from this only by not avoiding the kind of sexually focused moral crisis which Radcliffe often hints at but never actually realises in her fiction.

Although *Theresa Marchmont* consists of only four chapters, the epigraphs that preface these chapters fulfil important functions within the text. The epigraph to the opening chapter is taken from the moment when Banquo's ghost appears at the feast in Shakespeare's *Macbeth*:

> Take any shape but that, and my firm nerves
> Shall never tremble. Hence, horrible shadow!
> Unreal mockery, hence! – MACBETH
>
> (Theresa Marchmont, p. 1)[26]

This moment from *Macbeth*, if not always this precise configuration of lines, was previously referenced epigraphically in both Radcliffe's *The Romance of the Forest* (1791) and Lewis's *The Monk* (1796). In Radcliffe's novel it prefaces a moment in which, inevitably, a potentially supernatural encounter is revealed to be pragmatically explicable, whilst in *The Monk* it heads Lewis's history of the genuinely ghostly 'Bleeding Nun'.[27] Francesca Saggini also notes that a similar line appeared in James Boaden's stage adaptation of Radcliffe's *The Romance of the Forest*, entitled *Fontainville Forest*, when the villain is haunted by a ghost of his own imagining and finally exclaims that it has 'Gone! 'tis an illusion'.[28] Saggini believes the echo functions on a 'metatextual level', referencing 'Boaden's complex relation with both Shakespeare and Shakespeare's legacy in the form of John Philip Kemble's contemporary revisions of the Bard'.[29]

In Gore's novella, the relevance of the original Shakespearean context is much less direct: although there is the rumour of a ghost, this figure transpires to be a living woman, and although Helen's husband has publicly declared his first wife to be dead, he has not actually committed murder or hired assassins as Macbeth has. But the cultural metadata associated with this dramatic moment as a text repeatedly quoted and referenced within Gothic fiction is the more important dynamic at work here. Whilst the short length of Gore's book and the variation of phrasing in the quotation give an appearance of differentiation, the inclusion of such a recognisable and memorable epigraph is nonetheless a powerful means of alerting her readers to the pseudo-supernatural genre in which she is working.

Echoes of Lewis's and Radcliffe's writing recur throughout Gore's work, albeit with varying degrees of admiration. In her early novella *The Reign of Terror* (1827), the epigraph to the first chapter is taken from one of Lewis's poems.[30] In her later work *Cecil: Or, The Adventures of a Coxcomb* (1841) – a mildly satirical novel critiquing fashionable dandyism of the 1810s and 1820s – the eponymous narrator remarks upon his enthusiasm to experience 'what the novelists call "a faint scream," a thing I had always been particularly curious to hear, from the moment of my acquaintance with the pages of Monk Lewis and Mrs. Radcliffe'.[31] Yet the fact that Cecil actually claims to have heard this sort of 'faint scream' makes plausible something which he has evidently previously considered improbable, thus ensuring that the reference remains an affectionate tribute to Lewis and Radcliffe rather than a criticism.

Elsewhere, the epigraphs in *Theresa Marchmont* tend to have a distinctly proleptic quality. The revelation that it was 'the licentious addresses' (*Theresa Marchmont*, p. 82) of King Charles II which persuaded Theresa to agree to the protection offered by marriage with Lord Greville is obliquely hinted at in an epigraph taken from Shakespeare's *Richard III* that rhetorically proclaims '[l]et not the Heavens hear these tell-tale women / Rail on the Lord's anointed' (*Theresa Marchmont*, p. 63).[32] But the effect is more pronounced in the concluding chapter's epigraph, which in the narrative appears at the climax of Lord Greville's confession to his second wife that his first is still living. The lines are taken from Shakespeare's *Anthony and Cleopatra*:

> Courteous Lord – one word –
> Sir, you and I have lov'd – but that's not it –
> Sir, you and I must part. –
> ANTONY AND CLEOPATRA.
> (*Theresa Marchmont*, p. 94)[33]

It comes at the moment when Greville attempts to provoke Helen's empathy for his situation, and to justify having falsified his first wife's death to involve the unwitting Helen in a bigamous marriage. He leaves her to await 'the result of [her] judgment' as to how they should proceed (*Theresa Marchmont*, p. 109), but the reader can already be confident that Helen will choose the most morally acceptable resolution because in a literal sense the epigraph has identified the inevitable need for the couple to separate. Once again, the Shakespearean context is only vaguely applicable: the line is spoken by Cleopatra when her lover Anthony is obliged to return to Rome and, rather than encouraging him to leave as this short extract suggests, she is actually trying to persuade him to stay. There is a small variation from the original as the phrases 'you and I have lov'd' and 'you and I must part' swap places here, thus weighting the extract's conclusion with the idea of separation. Although this could simply be the consequence of a lapse of memory in transcribing the quotation, it does also diminish the sense that Gore might be attempting to invoke the jealous frustration of Shakespeare's Cleopatra that forms the original context of the lines. Thus it is only in the conflict between love and necessary separation that the lines possess relevance, even if in Helen's case the situation is reversed, since she must insist upon the kind of separation that Shakespeare's Cleopatra is trying to avoid.

The reception of *Theresa Marchmont* seems to have been good, since it was later reproduced in Gore's anthology *Romances of Real Life* (1829), whilst Gore's authorship of the work is used as a tag-line to advertise another one-volume narrative in 1827, promoted as being by '[t]he very clever authoress of "Theresa Marchmont"'.[34] Despite this, Gore did not continue long in such an overtly Gothic vein, and her first three-volume novel *The Manners of the Day* (1830) fully embraces the genre of the fashionable novel, featuring a contemporary setting that exchanges sensational revelations for more mundane incidents of everyday life in high society. There are some aesthetic connections between the two genres, with Royce Mahawatte noting in her analysis of the connections between George Eliot's work and silver-fork novels that 'Gothic, sensation writing and fashionable fiction overlap because all three seek to link the experience of the material to the construction of meaning.'[35] Gore's first novel also incorporates the standard Gothic trope of the woman manipulated into a marriage with a man whom she does not love, yet here the melodramatic potential is neutralised by a contemporary setting and a plausible scenario of parental persuasion followed by marital miscommunication. One probable reason for the sudden shift in focus in Gore's work is indicated in her later novel *Cecil* (1841), in which the eponymous narrator declares that he 'love[s] a little mystery. So did the public, till Mrs. Radcliffe gave them a surfeit of it' (*Cecil*, p. 16). As her biographer Winifred Hughes notes, Gore was 'a shrewd businesswoman' who also 'seems to have been the chief breadwinner for her husband and children'.[36] Despite an initial reluctance to venture into lengthy fiction, she appears to have done so as a pragmatic response to the contemporary literary market: a letter to her publisher Richard Bentley shortly after the publication of *The Manners of the Day* returned a contract for a mooted anthology of short 'tales' which the novel had evidently replaced. This anthology was 'abandoned on account of the number of works bearing that shape and title which have been lately published', even though Gore notes that '[i]t would have suited me far better to write detached stories than a long novel'.[37] That she had also shifted the generic focus of her writing by this point is a further indication both of an awareness of the literary market (which the subsequent success of her career proves to have been extremely shrewd) and also of a readiness to produce what that market required.

But although Gore identifies her own third three-volume novel *Pin Money* (1831) as '[e]xhibiting an attempt to transfer the familiar narrative of Miss Austin [*sic*] to a higher sphere of society', she does not replicate Austen's preference for plain chapter numbers without title or epigraph.[38] In adopting the epigraph, she instead seems to be continuing a pre-existing pattern of pre-chapter quotation within silver-fork novels, regardless of whether they fall within the subcategories of male 'dandy' or female 'society' fiction. Influential precursors such as Thomas Lister's *Granby* (1826), Lady Charlotte Susan Maria Bury's *Flirtation* (1827), Bulwer-Lytton's *Pelham* (1828), and Lady Caroline Lucy Scott's *A Marriage in High Life* (1828) all feature epigraphically headed chapters.

However, the incorporation of the epigraph into this developing genre of fashionable fiction also seems to have generated a subtle shift in the kind of texts being used to preface chapters. During the late eighteenth and early nineteenth centuries, it was not unheard of for prose texts to be quoted as epigraphs occasionally, but the most successful and influential epigraphic users had almost invariably confined themselves to using epigraphs derived from poetry or drama. Radcliffe and Lewis only ever quoted epigraphs from poetry or drama, and out of Scott's total of 879 pre-chapter epigraphs, only around 8 are obviously attributable to prose sources. In contrast, out of the total of 1175 epigraphs that Gore used throughout her novels, at least 283 are obviously from prose works, representing around 24%.[39] The initial shift itself does not seem to have been entirely attributable to Gore, since in Lister's *Granby* 15 out of 61 epigraphs are readily attributable to prose sources and in *Pelham* there are at least 17 out of 101. Although a smaller number of prose epigraphs appear in Bury's novels, a smaller total number of epigraphs overall means that the proportion of prose quotations remains broadly the same, with 4 out of 26 prose epigraphs appearing in *Flirtation* (1827) and 3 out of 24 in *The Separation* (1830).

However, it is worth noting that even within the genre of fashionable fiction, this was not the only epigraphic model available to Gore. The 15 epigraphs in Caroline Scott's *A Marriage in High Life* are, like Walter Scott's epigraphs, almost universally sourced from poetry or drama (only one epigraph, so far untraced, retains the possibility of originating in a prose source), whilst Bury's later novel *The Divorced* (1837) also resumes a similarly rigid focus upon verse-form epigraphs. In *A Marriage in High Life* Caroline Scott uses the epigraph primarily as a proleptic or transitional reflection of the prose narrative. The plot begins as the heroine Emmeline marries the wealthy Lord Fitzhenry to whom she has been betrothed since late childhood, but who, unbeknownst to her, now loves another. At the start of the second chapter, the narrative moves back in time to explain Fitzhenry's lack of enthusiasm for his new bride, a sentiment echoed in the choice of a prefatory epigraph from a play that likewise takes parentally enforced marriage as its starting point:

> Do I entice you? do I speak you fair?
> Or rather, do I not in plainest truth
> Tell you—I do not, nor I cannot love you?
> MIDSUMMER NIGHT'S DREAM.[40]

This chapter finishes with a letter from Fitzhenry to his wife in which he confesses his devotion to his mistress and his determination to keep their marriage platonic because of this. Accordingly, the subsequent new chapter begins with a quotation that prefigures Emmeline's reaction to this unexpected news:

> My husband! no not mine—but we were wedded;
> This ring was here in hallowed nuptial placed;
> A priest did bless it.
> ELLEN.
> (*A Marriage in High Life*, I, 62)[41]

A still more concise pattern of epigraphic function occurs in Bury's *The Divorced* (1837), which portrays the struggles of a divorced woman and her second husband (now Lord and Lady Howard) to regain status within a society still scandalised by their adulterous affair. The epigraphs here become a space in which to reiterate poetic expressions of doomed love drawing to tragic conclusions, beginning with a lengthy speech from *A Midsummer Night's Dream* (1600) in which '[t]he course of true love' ends with 'jaws of darkness'.[42] Later epigraphs suggest the inevitability of imperfection – as Shakespeare's Ferdinand claims to have never found any woman '[w]ith so full soul, but some defect in her / Did quarrel with the noblest grace she ow'd'[43] – or indicate a belief in the inescapability of moral challenges since 'in this world the fondest and the best / Are the most tried' (*The Divorced*, II, 29, 119). In both *A Marriage in High Life* and *The Divorced*, the epigraphs exploit the contrast between poetry and prose, assuming a Radcliffean prioritisation of the verse epigraph as a space in which to establish an emotional pulse parallel to the main prose, and that crystallises the themes explored. Gore's decision to include more prose quotation within her epigraphs after the publication of *Theresa Marchmont* effectively rejects this concept of the epigraph as a means of creating intertextual dialogue that crosses literary forms, thus confirming her move away from a Radcliffean Gothic aesthetic.

Since Gore uses 1175 epigraphs throughout her novels, and since only one of these novels (*Cecil: Or, The Adventures of a Coxcomb*) has ever received the editorial attention of a scholarly edition, it is not yet possible to know whether all of her attributions can be relied upon. Because of this, therefore, charts detailing the sources of Gore's epigraphs have not been compiled for inclusion in the Appendix. However, a preliminary examination reveals the inclusion of epigraphs from already well-quoted poets and dramatists such as Shakespeare, Milton, Byron, Ben Jonson, and Molière alongside a range of prose sources, including the *Spectator*, Francis Bacon, the French essayist La Bruyère, travelogues by William Beckford, and, on one occasion, Elizabeth Montagu's letters. Some epigraphs are also taken from the work of other novelists, including Samuel Richardson, Oliver Goldsmith, and even her epigraph-using predecessor Walter Scott. In one instance, Gore actually attributes a lengthy epigraph to a 'WRITER IN BLACKWOOD',[44] having sourced the quotation in an anonymously authored piece of short fiction published in *Blackwood's Magazine* a little before the appearance of Gore's own novel.[45] Even without knowing whether all of Gore's attributions are accurate, the fact remains that the majority of her epigraphs do appear to be credited to an identifiable work or writer's name. There does not appear to have been any major attempt to self-author epigraphs, whether unattributed like Radcliffe's apparently self-authored epigraphs in *The Italian* or, as in Scott's novels, attributed to a spurious source such as '*Old Play*'. One plausible reason for Gore's reluctance to self-author poetic epigraphs may be a sincere belief in the inferiority of her poetic abilities. In 1832, she challenged Bulwer-Lytton, as the editor of the *New Monthly*, upon the subject of an unfavourable review which had appeared in the magazine, and in defence of her continued allegiance to the genre of fashionable fiction she promised to send him 'a volume of poems of mine now out of print to show you how very badly I *can* write when I venture off my ormolu railroad'.[46] Yet the fact that Gore included such a large percentage of prose quotations indicates that it was not simply a reluctance to expose her poetic failings to ridicule that would have deterred her from self-authoring epigraphs. In fact, she seems to have been especially keen to emphasise the quoted nature of her epigraphic texts by providing attribution wherever possible – even when she is only able to give the credit to an anonymous 'WRITER IN BLACKWOOD'.

FROM ROMANCE TO REALISM

Significantly, earlier contemporaries of Gore who were working in the fashionable genre likewise almost invariably used quoted rather than self-authored texts, and this is directly related to a modification of the epigraph's function. In Bulwer-Lytton's *Pelham*, for example, awareness of the original context of an epigraphic quotation can add an enhanced dimension of humour to an otherwise pragmatically descriptive statement. The epigraph to chapter 9 prefaces the eponymous hero's 'ardour for continental adventures'[47] with a line from Shakespeare's *Henry V*, albeit attributed to the wrong *Henry*:

> Therefore to France.
> *Henry IV.*
>
> *(Pelham*, I, 57)[48]

Taken literally, the line appears to be nothing more than proleptic description. However, in the original play, the line is spoken by the Archbishop of Canterbury as part of a long speech encouraging the young King Henry V to pursue a technical claim to certain French lands. In *Pelham*, the hero is encouraged to venture to France at the instigation of an aristocratic 'schoolfellow' (*Pelham*, I, 57). The context of the epigraph is thus appropriated for the purpose of establishing a bathetic parody, with Pelham's projected adventures promoted to an equivalence with the success of Henry V's military conquest against overwhelming odds in France. Significantly, this type of humour had already featured within the novel's main narrative, during a fashionable soirée when some of the guests are exchanging unsatisfactory accounts of staying at an inn known as 'the Crown'. One comments that he 'never shall [. . .] forget that inn, with its royal name, and its hard beds— "Uneasy sleeps a head beneath the Crown!"', a slight misquotation of a line from Shakespeare's *Henry IV Part Two* that metaphorically reflects upon the challenges and responsibilities of kingship.[49] The joke is continued when another guest adds that upon seeing 'that immense General Grant' leave the inn, he had remarked that *'that's the largest Grant I ever saw from the Crown'*. That this latter witticism is in itself a quotation is underscored by the use of italics, and by the inclusion of a footnote stating that '[i]t was from Mr. J. Smith that Lord Vincent purloined this pun' (*Pelham*, I, 24).

In the world of fashionable society, witticisms or *bons mots* were of major importance in securing status. The popularity of such *bons mots* was not a new innovation, as Antoine Lilti notes the French tradition that was based upon 'the memory of old *bons mots* pronounced by a few great figures, such as Fontenelle or Madame de Sévigné'.[50] The practice is sometimes invoked in late eighteenth-century fiction, for example the aforementioned scene in *The Amicable Quixote* (1788) in which a character receives 'applause' for bestowing a suitably witty 'epigrammatic application' to a drawing. However, in an 1833 biographical entry in the *National Portrait Gallery of Illustrious and Eminent Personages*,

William Jerdan identifies a specifically French context for this practice, noting that 'the French, esteem so much, the saying of clever things, and the uttering of pointed expressions which remain upon the memory'.[51] Lilti reports how the novelist Madame de Staël once wrote that '[b]ons mots [. . .] are the events of Paris. They are the subject of conversations for several days.'[52] Indeed, the significance of *bons mots* could extend far beyond the moment of speech. As Lilti notes, they could be '[t]ransmitted by conversation, by multiple visits, and by correspondence', with the most successful witticisms being 'published in news sheets and gazettes, and then in the *ana* (collections of witticisms and pleasantries) that supported collective memory'. More immediately, such demonstrations of wit gave status to the originator and those associated with them, 'enhanc[ing] the reputation of the host and hostess [of the salon] by spreading the image of a house in which guests amused themselves and were witty'.[53] Although this model of sociability may have originated in France, Amy Prendergest notes that 'the English salon also copied the French literary model in its shared function as a facilitator of intellectual exchange relating to prose, poetry, drama, and imaginative prose writing'.[54] Indeed, the practice of perpetuating witticisms through repetition is evident in the italicisation and attribution of the remark concerning '*the largest Grant*' in *Pelham*. By extending this form of humorous wordplay and appropriated context to his novel's epigraphic paratext, Bulwer-Lytton is directly immersing his reader within the type of discourse used by those who attended those kind of high society soirées and salons. As Wilson points out, it was essential for fashionable novelists seeking to promote the popularity, and thus saleability, of their work to project an impression of 'insider' status. If the purpose of fashionable fiction was to provide an immersive experience of life in high society then '[r]eaders [. . .] would be more likely to trust an author who positioned herself as an insider'.[55] It was for this reason that authors who were also titled members of the aristocracy typically received higher prices for their novels.[56]

During the 1830s, Gore herself became 'a Parisian *salonnière*' when she and her husband moved to France so that he could take up a diplomatic post.[57] Her Sunday afternoon salons in the Place Vendôme were attended by a teenage Coventry Patmore, who later wrote that 'her rooms were full of the best literary and political society of Paris'; sadly, he did not record who precisely attended Gore's salon, since at the time he was distracted by his own romantic obsession with Gore's daughter.[58] In Gore's sequel to *Cecil*, originally titled *Cecil, a Peer* (1841), an allusion is even made to 'the mottoes of French sugar plumbs',[59] further reiterating the connection between physical luxuries and witty epithets that existed within the highest levels of society. Kendra notes the proliferation of 'material culture' in the genre of fashionable fiction, pointing out that it was 'notorious for its wealth of information about dress, furnishings, and conspicuous consumption'.[60] Edward Copeland takes this idea still further, suggesting that 'commodities are irresistible attractions for novelists and their readers', not least because they provide a tangible, material way to 'catalogue contemporary society' for the delectation of the reader.[61] By embodying and perpetuating the concept of salon wit in epigraphic quotation, fashionable novelists such as Bulwer-Lytton and Gore continue this material construction of nineteenth-century high society in their fiction.

One epigraph in *Pelham* even takes this idea one step further, apparently quoting a catchphrase associated with a figure in British literary society even though the phrase itself does not seem to have been explicitly transcribed or published elsewhere prior to the novel's publication. The quotation itself is brief and, as with the *Henry V* epigraph, superficially descriptive in character:

> My humble abode.
> MISS SPENCE.
>
> *(Pelham*, I, 45)

The reference appears to be to Elizabeth Isabella Spence, a writer who began her career as a novelist but whose later foray into travel writing caused her to be remembered by Anna Maria Hall as 'a certain little Miss Spence, who, on the strength of having written something about the Highlands, was most decidedly BLUE'. Hall further recalls Spence inviting

> young *littérateurs* [. . .] to her "humble abode," where tea was made in the bedroom, and where it was whispered the butter was kept cool in the wash-hand-basin! There were "lots" of such-like scandals about poor Miss Spence's "humble abode"; still people liked to go.[62]

The excessive repetition of the quoted phrase 'humble abode' within Hall's account further emphasises the frequency with which Spence seems to have used it. In the chapter which this prefaces, the eponymous Pelham's concern for his friend Glanville causes him to seek out and visit Glanville's lodging, which transpires to be 'a small, wretched room, to which the damps literally clung' (*Pelham*, I, 47). If, as O'Cinneide suggests, much of the success of a fashionable novel depended upon its creation of a sense of readerly '[i]nclusion in the exclusive spaces of high society',[63] then the use of this phrase here could be a means of reinforcing the text's authority as the work of a member of the fashionable society it describes. Yet the humour the epigraph creates relies upon the reader possessing prior knowledge of the phrase's context, something that would be probable only if they were already acquainted with Elizabeth Spence and/or invited to the literary gatherings she hosted in her tiny rooms. Since the only people granted this latter privilege appear to have been established writers,[64] this greatly reduces the number of people likely to understand the epigraph as a joke rather than a simple piece of proleptic description. Superficially, the creation of humorous intertextual commentary via epigraphic quotation bears similarities to Walter Scott's use of the epigraph. Yet unlike Scott, whose paratext tended to dissolve the boundary between reader and author through the sense of a mutual external perspective upon the text, Bulwer-Lytton allows the reader a sense of inclusivity only to defeat it by then incorporating references that can be fully understood only through a knowledge of not just literature, but also literary society. In her own epigraphic selections, Gore roundly rejects such an exclusive and elitist form of humour.

One of Gore's earliest novels, *Pin Money* (1831), begins its first chapter with a quotation taken from Oliver Goldsmith's *Letters from a Citizen of the World* (1762):

> When a couple are to be married, if their goods and chattels can be brought to unite, their sympathetic souls are ever ready to guarantee the treaty. The gentleman's mortgaged lawn becomes enamoured of the lady's marriageable grove; the match is struck up, and both parties are piously in love – according to Act of Parliament.
>
> GOLDSMITH.
> (Pin Money, I, 1)[65]

The humour here is essentially contained within the quotation itself, and in the image of two people being 'piously in love' because of an agreeable compatibility between the debts of the man and the saleable property of the woman. The epigraph is immediately followed by the financially motivated enthusiasm of Lady Olivia Tadcaster for her niece Frederica's engagement to Sir Brooke Rawleigh. Whilst Frederica's mother praises Rawleigh's character as 'so steady, and so unlike the idle dashers of the day', Lady Olivia is delighted with Rawleigh's 'very pretty little estate in Warwickshire' and promptly instigates the complete organisation of all financial settlements relating to the marriage (*Pin Money*, I, 3). The betrothed couple themselves are both in love and indifferent to these material arrangements, with Frederica content simply with the offer of Rawleigh's 'hand and heart' whilst Rawleigh gives her '*carte blanche*' on the matter of settlements (*Pin Money*, I, 17, 18). This provides a stark contrast with the epigraph's emotionless marriage-of-convenience, thus establishing the pre-chapter paratext here as a sarcastic reflection upon those who, like Lady Olivia, consider marriage to be a primarily financial arrangement. Unlike Bulwer-Lytton's epigraphs, the original narrative context of the quotation is not necessary to appreciate the humour which its inclusion creates.

Later, an epigraph taken from Scott's *The Bride of Lammermoor* functions as a similarly humorous comparison with regard to both the preceding and the ensuing chapter:

> The one coach was green, – the other was blue; and not the green and blue chariots in the Circus of Rome or Constantinople excited more turmoil among the citizens, than the double apparition occasioned in the mind of the Lord Keeper.
>
> SIR WALTER SCOTT.
>
> (*Pin Money*, I, 315)[66]

The chapter previous to this epigraph concludes as Frederica finds herself obliged to superintend the presentation at the Court of St James's of the woman whom her brother is likely to marry, Leonora, and Leonora's mother, Mrs. Waddlestone. Although Leonora is an heiress, her fortune comes from the soap-boiling business inherited by her mother, whose 'vulgar familiarity' of manner receives further ridicule through the description of her in her court dress as resembling a 'globose mass of green and gold tissue' (*Pin Money*, I, 314). The reference to the colour 'green' is then almost immediately followed by an allusion to the 'blue chamber' of the royal court into which she is ushered, thus constituting a pigmentary reflection of the carriage colours in the epigraph which follows on the next page (*Pin Money*, I, 314). Significantly, in Scott's novel these two carriages are also occupied by supporters of opposing socio-political factions, thus further underscoring the class snobbishness and conflict that occurs between the nobility and the working-class Waddlestones. Proleptically, the juxtaposition of coaches creating 'turmoil' in the mind of a nervous husband such as the Lord Keeper presages the new chapter's ultimate conclusion, during which Frederica departs in a carriage just as her husband arrives in one. In Gore's narrative, Rawleigh's alarm is generated by the fear that his wife has been indulging in wanton dissipation during his lengthy absence in pursuit of a Parliamentary seat. Although the moment itself occurs at the end of the chapter, the prefatory epigraph and the developing plot serve to create a sense of inevitability regarding both the climax and the misunderstandings likely to ensue. Whilst in some ways the reliance upon elements of the epigraph's original context here is akin to Bulwer-Lytton's epigraphic approach, the cultural centrality of Scott's prose fiction during the early nineteenth century ensures that the scope of the reference's relevance remains broadly accessible to a general audience.

In fact, the specific original narrative context of an epigraph was sometimes entirely irrelevant to its capacity to create humour, something that may be exemplified by one of the pre-chapter quotations in Gore's *Mothers and Daughters* (1831):

> When Greek meets Greek – then comes the tug of war.
>
> *Shakespeare.*[67]

Within the context of the narrative, this prefaces an impending confrontation between the ambitious new brides of two brothers competing for the paternal

EPIGRAPHS IN THE ENGLISH NOVEL 1750–1850

inheritance. Bathetic humour is created solely through the implicit identification of the two sisters-in-law as akin to Greek warriors, about to engage in the 'tug of war' of domestic micro-aggression. Since the line is actually an imperfect quotation from Nathaniel Lee's play *Rival Queens* (1677), Gore's erroneous attribution to Shakespeare confirms that it is only the quoted text itself that is relevant here.

Yet Gore's epigraphic wit was not always universally accessible to anglophonic readers. Of the 1175 epigraphic quotations that occur throughout her novels, there are 363 non-English epigraphs. Of these, 263 are French, whilst the remaining 100 non-English epigraphs are (in order of diminishing frequency) Latin, Italian, Greek, German, Spanish, and Turkish. At the time, much criticism was levelled at the 'excessive introduction of French' into her fiction, even though she was by no means alone in emphasising French quotations in her epigraphs.[68] Indeed, even as the *Edinburgh Review* disparages the use of 'foreign phrases' in *Manners of the Day*, it tacitly reveals that this phenomenon is in fact a 'piebald style which has lately prevailed, of sayings and quotations, tricked out with italics and inverted commas', an acknowledgement that also establishes that the criticism is of multilingualism throughout the text and not just in the epigraphs.[69] In Bulwer-Lytton's *Pelham*, the fashionable hero's equally fashionable mother warns him to 'be careful, in returning to England, to make very little use of French phrases; no vulgarity is more unpleasing' (*Pelham*, I, 232). In a sly dig at his literary competitors, Bulwer-Lytton then allows his character to denounce the literature of the 'common people' whom the fashionable Lady Pelham declares always 'ma[k]e us talk nothing but French' (*Pelham*, I, 232). The purpose of this critique within *Pelham* is somewhat debatable, however, since there is no scarcity of French in the novel's text and many of the chapters actually conclude with a comic punchline delivered in French. For example, one chapter ends with a description of a society lady who 'had some reputation for talent, was exceedingly affected, wrote poetry in albums, ridiculed her husband, who was a fox hunter, and had a great *penchant pour les beaux arts et les beaux hommes*', with the French text concealing the risqué allusion to the woman's taste for '*les beaux hommes*' (attractive men) (*Pelham*, I, 21). In fact, Lady Pelham's critique of the use of French as a social affectation only reveals her own ignorance of the society that she pretentiously claims to occupy.

Gore's own use of French is far from being an affectation, since she had lived in France for eight years between 1832 and 1840, and her surviving correspondence frequently features French phrases incorporated into otherwise English sentences (for example, 'et pas consignent' [off the record], 'en attendant je vous fais mes adieux' [in the meanwhile I will make my adieus to you]).[70] Furthermore, three manuscripts which William Beckford noted that he had read aloud to Gore on various Sunday afternoons in 1840 and

132

1841 are also written in French, suggesting that Gore's own knowledge of the language was probably excellent.[71] Likewise, characters in fashionable novels frequently travel to and around the Continent, befriending foreign nobility to the extent that a knowledge of more languages than just English is not only plausible but necessary. In *Mothers and Daughters*, Lady Willoughby moves her daughters to France to complete their education; the eponymous hero of the *Cecil* novels roams throughout Europe. The hero of *Pelham* sojourns in France for a considerable time, whilst the divorced Lady Howard's son seeks refuge in France from the shame of his family's disgrace in Bury's *The Divorced*. Concerns regarding the possibility of unintended linguistic exclusion do seem to have influenced some fashionable writers: examining the portrayal of Paris and French culture in British literature, Elisabeth Jay notes an instance when Bury included a narratively significant letter supposedly written in French by simply telling her readers that was the case before presenting it in English.[72]

In his foundational early twentieth-century assessment of the silver-fork genre, Whiting Rosa remarks that Gore's 'most irritating characteristic' is her 'use of foreign tags' (the term 'tags' almost certainly referring to her pre-chapter epigraphs).[73] Although the paragraph references a contemporary reviewer's more general criticism of Gore's 'excessive introduction of French' throughout one of her novels, the focus is clearly upon epigraphic quotation as Whiting Rosa goes on to note that 'German is more sparingly used [. . .] Italian is still rarer'.[74] He also highlights the consternation that greeted Gore's sudden incorporation of Latin and Greek quotations in some of the novels published around the midpoint of her career in the very early 1840s (in particular her *Cecil* novels), since 'she had hitherto displayed no signs of a classical education beyond the use of a few standard quotations easily dug out of a dictionary'.[75] Certainly, when quotations from Latin writers do occur they are always presented only as English translations, for example the epigraph to volume 1 chapter 5 of *The Heir of Selwood* (1838), 'Churlishness is a spurious kind of freedom'.[76] In this instance, the exact phrasing actually features in a broadly contemporaneous edition of *The British Essayists* anthology of periodicals, where it is included alongside Tacitus's original Latin as a prefatory motto to issue 65 of the *Lounger*.[77] In its original serialised form, the *Lounger* gave only the untranslated Latin version,[78] thus confirming *The British Essayists* collection as the most probable source for the quotation. A similar situation occurs with the use of a quotation by Cornelius Nepos to preface volume 2 chapter 2 in *Stokeshill Place* (1837), which also features as a prefatory motto to one issue of the *Spectator*. As before, Gore presents the text only as an English translation: '[a]ll those must submit to be accounted tyrants who exercise perpetual power in a state that was before free'.[79] The phrasing here is quite closely akin to the translation given in *The British Essayists* – '[f]or all those are accounted and denominated tyrants, who exercise a perpetual power in that state, which was before free' – but there are some small differences.[80] The most significant of these becomes apparent when the original Latin phrase is considered: '[o]mnes autem et dicuntur et habentur tyranni, qui potestate sunt perpetua, in ea civitate quae libertate usa est'.[81] The passive mood on the verbs 'habentur' and 'dicuntur' is reflected in *The British Essayists* translation, but not in Gore's rendering of the first clause, in which the imperative declaration that '[a]ll those must submit' makes the subject active in the sentence. Possible explanations for this anomaly could be that Gore misremembered the quotation, or that she deliberately shifted the phrasing away from that of *The British Essayists* to avoid detection, or that she translated it herself with an imperfect knowledge of Latin grammar.

Whichever explanation is the correct one, what is clear is that even if Gore had no knowledge of Latin herself, she could have included these lines in their original language had she wished to by simply copying them from something like *The British Essayists* collection. That she did not do this indicates a conscious authorial decision to refrain from using Latin text in these particular novels. Likewise, her shift to using original Latin and Greek quotations as epigraphs in the *Cecil* novels is also a thoroughly deliberate stylistic decision. Both *Cecil* and its sequel, *Cecil, a Peer*, are written from the first-person perspective of the eponymous Cecil Danby and together they constitute an autobiographical portrait of the imagined author as he travels through life, frequently deluding himself into the belief that young and attractive women are in love with him. Although this love is occasionally reciprocated in the earliest stages of the first novel, by the later sections of Cecil's narrative the ladies in question generally prove to have been secretly in love with or engaged to a different man all the time, whilst on one notable occasion the unfortunate Cecil even mistakes the effects of sinus congestion for symptoms of love. The review in which the anonymously published *Cecil* was first attributed to Gore acknowledges the likelihood of her authorship only under the qualification that she must have had 'the aid of a learned friend to supply the quotations, and, perhaps, some scraps of a posthumous diary or journal to work upon'.[82] When surveying her work in 1844, R. H. Horne identified this 'learned friend' as William Beckford, writing that

> [t]he public have been often perplexed by Mrs. Gore's Greek and Latin, which, although they were never paraded so impertinently as the polygott [*sic*] pretensions of Lady Morgan, were still remote enough from the ordinary course of female accomplishments to startle the public. Where they came from on former occasions we know not; but in this instance they may be referred to Mr. Beckford, together with the still more recondite scraps of far-off tongues that are scattered through the work.[83]

However, the suggestion that Gore's coxcombical Cecil Danby was tacitly based upon Beckford is, perhaps unsurprisingly, dismissed by his early twentieth-century biographer, who asserts that simply reading the *Cecil* novels 'will satisfy those acquainted with the characteristics of Beckford that he had little or nothing in common with the absurd, highfalutin dandy'.[84] Beckford's vast colonial wealth inherited from his father together with his early marriage, bisexuality, and fascination with expensive and extravagant architecture are just a few of the most obvious points in which he differs from Gore's Cecil.

The accreditation of Beckford as the source of 'Gore's Greek and Latin' seems likewise founded upon little else than a presumption that a knowledge of classical languages is not one of the 'female accomplishments'. Beckford and Gore only seem to have become friends in 1839 after she had sent him a copy of her latest anthology of short fiction, *The Courtier of the Days of Charles the Second, and other Tales* (1839). Not yet personally acquainted with her, Beckford wrote to his bookseller around 15 August 1839 to request that he 'convey to her through the means of Mr Colburn – her present publishers' a formal, appreciative acknowledgement of the gift.[85] Following this, the manuscripts of three of Beckford's French tales feature discrete annotations that the text had been 'read to Mrs Gore' or 'r^d. to M^{rs}. G' alongside a date (all within either 1840 or 1841).[86] The dates almost invariably correspond to Sundays, making it at least plausible that it is to one of these occasions that Beckford is referring in a surviving invitation in which he writes that if she is 'disengaged next Sunday [. . .] Mr Beckford will have the honour of reading to her the chapter which, perhaps, Mrs Gore may recollect his having mentioned'.[87] Whilst it is entirely possible that Gore likewise shared with him her own writing, there is absolutely no surviving evidence to suggest that this was the case, and thus also no evidence to support Horne's claim that Gore relied heavily upon Beckford's knowledge when writing *Cecil*. Two Beckford quotations appear as epigraphs in *Cecil*, but the possibility that these were intended as a tacit expression of gratitude for linguistic assistance is diminished by the fact that the two different works in which they originate were republished in a compilation edition in 1840. Since Gore is likely to have been working on *Cecil* around this time, and as this would not be the only occasion upon which she selected a quotation from a brand new or recently reprinted source, the likelihood that she may have deliberately sought out quotations from Beckford's works is perhaps outweighed by the simple convenience of their appearance at the time she was writing.[88] Furthermore, Gore continued to publish novels featuring Latin and Greek epigraphic quotations after Beckford's death in May 1844, most notably *Self* (1845), which includes 15 Latin and 4 Greek epigraphs, and *The Story of a Royal Favourite* (1845), in which there are 11 Latin epigraphs as well as 1 in Greek. It is thus extremely unlikely that Gore was reliant upon Beckford for her knowledge of classical texts.

Similarly, Horne's allusion to 'scraps of far-off tongues' is vague and misleading since only six languages appear in the epigraphs to *Cecil*, all of which are Eurocentric and therefore by no means unusual within Victorian high society. In order of frequency, these are French, English, Latin, Greek, Italian, and German. In fact, in his metropolitan world Cecil himself soon encounters an unfamiliar language when he hears a girl with whom he is fast falling in love 'converse cheerfully with her [companion] in some unknown tongue' (*Cecil*, p. 51). He guesses correctly that the language is either Spanish or Portuguese, but no transcriptions of the conversation are included and he readily confesses to the reader that '[a]ll I knew was, that it was neither French nor English,—German nor Italian; and further, neither Eton nor Oxford enabled me to determine' (*Cecil*, p. 51). Notably, this range of languages with which Cecil is familiar also precisely matches the variety of languages used in the novel's epigraphs. Through this alignment, Gore exploits the contemporary perception (exemplified by Horne) that familiarity with classical languages was not one of the 'female accomplishments' to enhance the concept of Cecil as a distinct, male, authorial persona.

Throughout Gore's construction of the *Cecil* novels and beyond, there is a determined effort to dissolve the sense of her own authorial agency within the narrative persona of Cecil himself. The novels were published anonymously, a strategy involving publicity advantages with which Gore was evidently very familiar, having written to Bentley soon after the publication of *Manners of the Day* (1830) to reiterate that the authorship of her novel was something he 'would do well to have [. . .] in doubt'.[89] But rather than simply sparking an authorship debate, with *Cecil* she exploits the potential of the character as a separate pseudonymous identity. Gore later offered an article to Bentley for his *Miscellany* to be attributed to 'the author of Cecil' and at one point even appears to have signed a personal letter to Benjamin Disraeli as 'Cecil' rather than her usual signature of 'C.F. Gore' or 'CFG'.[90] Within the novel itself, the boundary between fiction and reality is further challenged by the inclusion of Byron as both a character and, in five separate instances, as an epigraphic source. Whilst it was not unusual for fashionable novels to draw upon real-life individuals in their fiction, such inspiration would typically be concealed behind an imagined name and fictional identity. A particularly notorious example of this genre of pseudo-memoir was Lady Caroline Lamb's *Glenarvon* (1816), described by Wilson as a 'somewhat biased attempt to rewrite the love affair between Lamb and Lord Byron'.[91]

The first appearance of Byron within *Cecil* occurs when Cecil claims to be on the point of revealing an unpublished Byronic witticism, writing, 'As my friend Byron said one night at Watier's,—but no! —had he intended the *mot* for publication he would have printed it himself' (*Cecil*, p. 163). Later, Cecil claims that '[h]e and I were always squabbling, upon paper, about the poetry of nature and the poetry of civilization' (*Cecil*, p. 187), again teasing the reader with the sense of an unpublished intimacy with an established literary figure. Despite this, however, all of the Byronic epigraphs which Gore includes are (perhaps inevitably) taken from readily accessible published works. Significantly, four out of these five quotations are prose rather than poetry and are typically derived from Byron's letters and journals, thus reinforcing the impression that it is Byron's sociability and celebrity status which Gore wants to emphasise here rather than his poetic abilities. For example, one chapter is prefaced with two quotations, the second of which is taken from one of Byron's published journals:

> Metaphysics, – mountain, – lakes, – love unextinguishable, – thoughts unutterable, – and the nightmare of my own delinquencies. –
> BYRON.
>
> (*Cecil*, p. 219)[92]

Having inadvertently contributed towards the death of his young nephew, a grief-stricken Cecil flees 'the cruel insinuations' (*Cecil*, p. 219) of his titular father (a parent in name only, since Cecil is in fact the consequence of his mother's adulterous affair with a society dandy), and returns to the Continent. Once there, he participates in the Battle of Waterloo before seeking out 'some tranquil spot in one of the Rhenish principalities' (*Cecil*, p. 220). Like Byron, therefore, Cecil is prey to 'the nightmare of [his] own delinquencies', whilst surrounded by an assortment of picturesque scenery including 'the blackened and shattered walls of Ehrenbreitstein' and 'the blue serenity of the Rhine' (*Cecil*, p. 221). Yet unlike Byron, who during the period in his own life which this quotation describes produced the poem *Childe Harolde*, Cecil becomes obsessed with a beautiful married woman living in the opposite house. Rather than provoking a creative literary response in Cecil, this incident merely prompts him to examine 'the leaves of nearly the whole edition of Goëthe and Kotzebue, for a quotation germane to the matter, and [he] found more than enough to fill half-a-dozen common-place books' (*Cecil*, p. 223). The implicit parallel between the real Byron and the imaginary Cecil further promotes the construction of Cecil as a distinct narrative and authorial persona, whilst their different responses to the same emotional crisis described in the epigraph provides a bathetically humorous point of contrast. If the range of epigraphic languages reflects Cecil's pragmatic abilities, then their substance also conveys much of how he wants to be regarded: as an intelligent, cosmopolitan traveller and a connoisseur of wit and beauty. Like Scott, therefore, Gore is using epigraphic paratext to cultivate a distinct fictional narrative persona. Yet while Scott used pre-chapter paratext to establish the persona of a commentator typically aligned with the reader as an outsider to the text, in Gore's novel the epigraphs facilitate the construction of the narrator as a complex individual whose real motives and character can only be glimpsed beneath the fashionable, self-absorbed façade Cecil has created for himself.

EPIGRAPHS IN THE ENGLISH NOVEL 1750–1850

Following the composition of the two *Cecil* novels, and a third novel (*Self*) in which Cecil is presented as the third-person narrator, Gore shifts back to using primarily English and French epigraphs in the majority of her novels, thus further supporting the idea that her epigraphic selections in these works were chiefly intended to promote the construction of Cecil's character. Despite this, however, there persisted a kind of mythology surrounding the breadth of languages quoted by Gore, with Edgar Allan Poe describing her as a writer who 'quotes all tongues from the Chaldaean to Chickasaw'.[93] This is, of course, an extreme exaggeration of the truth. A few years before the appearance of *Cecil*, a particularly vicious reviewer had declared that Gore's novels were 'too much interlarded with foreign tongues'. Caustic and misogynistic throughout, the article also describes Gore's appearance, refers to her work in the past tense when comparing it unfavourably with Scott's (even though, at this point, Gore was still very much in the middle of her literary career), takes sentences from her novels out of context to argue that they are 'immoral' or 'wicked', mocks her expression of political opinion in her books by declaring that although it is not 'well for a lady to deal too largely in politics [. . .] Mrs. Gore [. . .] would make a good member of Parliament', and then finally (after about four pages of critique) expresses 'regret' that the reviewer was 'without the space to expatiate as much upon the merits of Mrs. Gore as we freely could'.[94] Gore had already demonstrated earlier in her career that she was not the kind of person to ignore or overlook criticism. Writing to Bentley shortly after the publication of her first three-volume novel, she points out that '[t]he book has been <u>very</u> scantily advertised – <u>scarcely at all previous to the subscription</u>; and coming after the florid claptraps that have been lavished upon The Exclusives, you could scarcely expect it to have a marked success in three days'.[95] Bury's novel *The Exclusives* focused upon a fashionable society group of the same name, and even eleven years after this incident Gore indulges in a slight against the work when a remark is made to the reader in *Cecil, a Peer*, that '[p]eople are beginning to forget the Exclusives; I believe because they were written out of fashion by a remarkably bad novel' (*Cecil, a Peer*, I, 34). Diluted through the rather pompous persona of her narrator, it is unclear whether it is the fictitious author Cecil or the real author Catherine Gore who is truly making this comment, but in either case the humour is made at the expense of a work that had once been given precedence over Gore's.

During the early stages of her career, Gore also challenged an unfavourable review in the *New Monthly* by writing to its editor Bulwer-Lytton to point out the reviewer's evident dislike for the genre in which she was writing. Identifying her own work as occupying a genre of 'fashionable novels' shared with works by Samuel Richardson, Frances Burney, Maria Edgeworth, and Benjamin Disraeli, she writes that she leaves these novels 'to plead their cause, and intrench [*sic*] myself in the obstinacy of a woman's opinion that every picture of passing manners [. . .] is valuable'. She even concludes with a

138

declaration of intention to 'write another fashionable novel in order that you may abuse it and I may show how indifferent I am to criticism'.[96]

Such a defiant response renders it not outside the realms of plausibility that she might have wanted to reply in some way, however obliquely, to the persistent attempts to undermine her through criticism levelled at the multilingual character of much of her work. This response seems to appear in 1843, with the publication of the serialised novel *Modern Chivalry* in *Ainsworth's Magazine* (reprinted in two volumes by John Mortimer at the end of the same year). Like the *Cecil* novels, *Modern Chivalry* mocks the entitlement and solipsistic self-esteem of a fashionable male bachelor, who frequently misjudges the affections and aspirations of the women he meets. Although the majority of reviews considered it to be 'a fine exposure of heartless and complacent selfishness',[97] some were less impressed. One reviewer, writing at the conclusion of the work's original serialisation, summarised their critique in the simple declaration that '[t]he tale is ended—and the readers [. . .] are, we doubt not, glad it is so'.[98] Yet the novel also features a deployment of epigraphic paratext that is unique within Gore's oeuvre, since in this instance she does not merely incorporate epigraphs in languages other than English but also includes translations alongside the majority of them. Each English version is described in an accompanying attribution as a '(*Translation for the Country Gentlemen*)',[99] an epithet that immediately identifies any readers who must rely upon the translations as less metropolitan and less fashionable, as well as less knowledgeable. Individuals such as the reviewer who had derided Gore for writing in 'foreign tongues' typically give no reason why this comment should constitute negative criticism, thus prompting a supposition that they themselves are not cognisant of the languages featured and are thus effectively locked out of reading the text. The motivation for the epigraphic translation Gore offers here is to ridicule the personal bias of such attacks. The additional nuance that the translations are for '*Gentlemen*' (emphasis added) identifies this as a retaliation against the fundamental misogyny of the attacks that had been levelled at Gore's work, since it deliberately limits the range of readers likely to require linguistic assistance to a specifically masculine group. The effect of intellectual classism is further enhanced when a lengthy prose quotation by Étienne de Jouy (presented in the original French) is truncated into a comparatively tiny rhyming couplet of English:

> "Les peines de l'ame, quelque vive qu'elles puissent être, sont des situations qu'on a prévues, auxquelles l'expérience des autres a pu vous préparer, où vous finissez quelquefois par trouver un certain charme. Mais ces tribulations de toutes les heures, ces petites vexations sourdes qui s'emparent d'un homme au sortir du lit et le harcèlent tout le jour, violà ce qui rend la vie insupportable."—
>
> JOUY.

Pricking to death with pins' points, is the devil;
A tragic poniard is not half the evil.—
(Translation.)
(Modern Chivalry, I, 111)[100]

Despite the apparent helpfulness of the translation, inevitably a reader unable to comprehend the French original would be left feeling that they were missing out in some way.

Having long been accused of incorporating text in 'far-flung tongues', Gore also finally reaches beyond her Western European focus to include a quotation presented in Turkish, accompanied by a translation:

"Akibét tilkinin dérist kurktchnun dukianina ghélun."
TURKISH PROVERB.

In spite of all its cunning running past,
The furrier gets the fox's skin at last.—
(Translation for the Country Gentlemen.)
(Modern Chivalry, II, 27)

In this epigraph, the Turkish text is rendered phonetically, and in modern Turkish the same phrase would be written: 'Tilkinin dönüp dolaşacağı yer kürkçü dükkanıdır'. The translation Gore offers here is a poetic recasting of the proverb's literal translation, which may be given in English as 'No matter how far the fox runs he will still end up in the fox-fur shop.'[101] However, it is worth noting that both the phonetic transcription of the proverb and the translation are unlikely to be entirely Gore's handiwork. In 1832, an issue of the *Revue de Paris* featured an article entitled 'La Peau du Renard Vient Toujours a La Boutique Du Pelissier' (i.e. 'the skin of the fox comes always to the furrier's shop'). This title is then followed by the attribution 'proverbe Turc' (Turkish proverb) and then, after a further line drop, by an almost identical match to the Turkish text used by Gore.[102] Only two letters are different (for example, in Gore's version 'dérisi' has become 'dérist', and 'ghélur' has become 'ghélun'), variations that may reasonably be attributed to a simple transcription error. The unusual character of this epigraph, combined with the fact that this is the only one of Gore's novels in which (excepting the translations) none of the epigraphic quotations are written in English, makes it quite probable that Gore is using this opportunity to retaliate against her detractors. By finally offering a quotation that embraces the accusation of using 'far-flung tongues' in her novels, Gore also obliquely points out the previous absurdity of the statement.

Furthermore, this particular quotation also provides a possible clue to Gore's method of selecting epigraphs more generally. As has already been discussed,

Gore appears to have been something of a literary opportunist in her epigraphic choices, known to have chosen epigraphs that would have been readily available whilst she was writing. Here, it also becomes apparent that she was not averse to making use of a quotation already used as an epigraph by another writer; nor is the Turkish proverb presented in *Modern Chivalry* an isolated example. The quotation that prefaces volume 2 chapter 8 in Gore's *The Tuileries* (1831) almost exactly matches the epigraph to chapter 44 of Scott's *Guy Mannering*:

> A prison is a house of care,
>   A place where none may thrive,
> A touchstone true to try a friend,
>   A grave for one alive!
> Sometimes a place of right,
>   Sometimes a place of wrong,
> Sometimes a place of rogues and thieves,
>   And honest men among.
>   THE EDINBURGH TOLBOOTH.[103]

Whilst an identical choice of epigraph might not necessarily indicate a connection between the two, on this occasion it does seem highly probable that Gore took her quotation not from the Edinburgh Tolbooth itself (as indicated by the attribution), but from Scott's novel. The text was apparently originally inscribed upon the wall of the Old Tolbooth in Edinburgh, but the building was demolished in 1817 and few transcriptions of the poem seem to have existed.[104] A historical account printed in the *Edinburgh Literary Journal* in 1829 includes a copy of the poem with the same alternate line indentation Gore uses in her version. However, the *Journal* edition gives the phrase 'for men alive' instead of Gore's 'for one alive', and uses the word 'jades' instead of 'rogues' in the penultimate line.[105] Since the wording of Gore's text matches Scott's exactly, it is thus much more probable that she had taken the transcription from Scott's novel; that she also occasionally incorporated quotations from the main text of some of Scott's other works in her epigraphs only further strengthens this possibility. Whiting Rosa speculates that, previous to publishing the *Cecil* novels, Gore had 'displayed no signs of a classical education beyond the use of a few standard quotations easily dug out of a dictionary'.[106] Yet a far more probable explanation for the source of Gore's epigraphic breadth is simply that she copied quotations from other journals, novels, and anthologies. Whilst original text is always scrupulously credited, the works from which quotations are borrowed neither require nor are given such accreditation. This may have allowed Gore to incorporate a more varied range of epigraphs by avoiding the need to have read the source text, and, as demonstrated by the example of the Turkish proverb given above, may even have enabled her to quote in languages in which she was not personally fluent.

Although Gore continued to use epigraphs in her novels for the majority of her life, after 1853 she ceased using the device altogether. This also coincides with a change of publisher, from Henry Colburn to Hurst and Blackett, but this does not seem to be the reason for her abandonment of epigraphic paratext, since her first novel with Hurst and Blackett, *The Dean's Daughter* (1853), still features the device. A more likely explanation may be discovered in Hughes's observation that '[f]or some period before her death Gore was completely blind, although still writing'.[107] Gore would author a further six novels before her eventual death in 1861 but none of these features epigraphs, the reason doubtless being that the identification of suitable quotations must inevitably involve a considerable amount of reading and skimming through books, even if an author has already collected possible epigraphs into commonplace books. Such searching must have become more difficult if Gore was obliged to structure her work around worsening eyesight problems, or even if she was using an amanuensis. In a letter to Disraeli written in 1859, the year after following the publication of her final novel, Gore herself notes poignantly that she is writing to him 'before the failure of my last half-eye'.[108]

'I HAVE DECIDED ON MOTTOES': GASKELL'S EPIGRAPHIC AFTERTHOUGHTS

Unlike Catherine Gore, Elizabeth Gaskell included pre-chapter epigraphs in only 2 out of 6 full-length novels. Her first novel, *Mary Barton* (1848), featured at least one, and occasionally two, quotations at the start of each chapter, and no chapter titles. As has been noted, Gore was not the only novelist of the 1830s and 1840s to incorporate prose epigraphs, and also epigraphs in languages other than English (usually French); yet Gaskell's epigraphs are invariably both in verse-form and in English. That the latter was a conscious choice rather than an unavoidable default is evident through Gaskell's own multilingualism: when she was a child, her brother had 'coach[ed] her in languages and Latin'. As an adult she struggled to learn German, but nonetheless quotes 2 (possibly self-authored) English translations of poetry in German within the epigraphs of *Mary Barton*.[109] Only the dedicatory motto at the commencement of the novel is presented in the original German, a quotation believed to be an allusion to the deaths of two of Gaskell's children (*Mary Barton*, p. 4). In a short piece analysing these lines, Muriel Smith suggests that the retention of the German language in these lines might be a way of 'shield[ing] them from the mass of her readers' because of their 'very special significance for her'.[110] Yet at least some of Gaskell's readership would have been familiar enough with German to effect a translation, and a more reasonable explanation might be that she was reluctant to mar the linguistic beauty of a poem so important to her by translating it. That said, the use of only English epigraphs elsewhere in the novel does suggest an intention of rendering both novel and paratext accessible to as broad a range of anglophonic readers as possible. Since it is

FROM ROMANCE TO REALISM

a book that sets out with the intention of promoting social improvement and understanding between different levels of the social strata, this is perhaps also a sensitive avoidance of alienating readers less educationally advantaged (even if the novel itself later draws attention to the extent and high quality of self-education within some working-class communities).

The use of English verse epigraphs is also in subtle conformity with the format established by earlier canonical epigraph-users such as Radcliffe and Scott. Gaskell's biographer Jenny Uglow notes her enthusiasm for Scott, identifying him as '[t]he most popular novelist of Elizabeth's youth' and detailing how Gaskell once claimed to have got herself 'in a scrape' with another minister's wife for having used *Kenilworth* 'to illustrate the character of Queen Elizabeth' in a Sunday School lesson.[111] Exploring Gaskell's experimentation with historical settings, Marion Shaw notes that Gaskell adopted Scott's style of writing historical fiction in which 'opposing forces in times of turmoil and change are represented by "typical" characters'; Shirley Foster also points out the connections between Gaskell's shorter fiction and the earlier Gothic genre, 'especially the novels of Ann Radcliffe'.[112]

That Gaskell was familiar with Gore's fiction is evident in a letter in which she surveyed contemporary English fiction for the Parisian publisher Louis Hachette. Here, Gaskell notes that Gore's novels are 'numerous' and 'have very little plot in them, their principal interest (for those who read them,) consisting in a lively, spirited epigrammatic description of the manners of lords and ladies'.[113] The parentheses distance Gaskell herself from 'those who read them', a rather disparaging differentiation that renders it unlikely that she would have sought to emulate Gore in her own writing. This does not entirely exclude the possibility of some silent paratextual borrowing, however: it may simply be coincidence, but the title of Gaskell's last novel *Wives and Daughters* (1864) does bear noticeable similarity to that of Gore's *Mothers and Daughters*.

A further possible inspiration for Gaskell's use of epigraphs may have been the historian and novelist Katherine Thomson, whose frequent use of pre-chapter quotation produced the epigraph used to preface this chapter, and who was related to Gaskell by marriage.[114] Gaskell's faith in Thomson's good opinion is highlighted through Elizabeth Barrett Browning's assertion that 'Mary Barton was shown in MS. to Mrs Thomson & failed to please her; and in deference to her judgement certain alterations were made.' This was apparently before Gaskell had even begun to approach publishers with the manuscript, since Barrett Browning goes on to note that after this the novel 'was offered to all or nearly all the publishers in London, & rejected'.[115]

However, if Thomson's paratext influenced Gaskell at all, it could only have been by providing a distant background to her understanding of how the epigraph might be used. For unlike Scott's method of including epigraphs at various stages of the drafting and proofing process, it is clear that Gaskell added

143

the pre-chapter quotations in *Mary Barton* at a comparatively late stage of production. Writing to her publisher Edward Chapman on 21 March 1848, Gaskell reminds him that, when they had met in person early in the preceding January, he had told her 'that my work was to follow Miss Jewsbury's in the publication of your Series [of Original Works of Fiction]'.[116] Receiving no answer, she wrote to him again on 2 April, reiterating his assertion that *Mary Barton* 'would succeed Miss Jewsburys; [*sic*] and would be published in two or three months from that time'.[117] The novel by Geraldine Jewsbury to which she refers – a two-volume work entitled *The Half-Sisters* – had been advertised as '*nearly ready*' at the end of January, and then as published '[o]n the 6th instant' in a bulletin published in February 1848.[118] According to this schedule, Gaskell would have been expecting to see her novel in print by the end of April or early May, thus explaining her apparent anxiety at having heard nothing from Chapman. Indeed, in her March letter she tentatively remarks to him that '[a]s you have the MS in your hands I am trusting to you to see that it is set up so as to make the right quantity'.[119] If Gaskell was using the phrase 'set up' in a typographical sense, as seems probable, then she was clearly anticipating the publication of her novel to be at quite an advanced stage – so advanced, in fact, as to render it extremely unlikely that she was planning to request the addition of pre-chapter epigraphic quotation at this point. In neither letter is there any mention of epigraphs (or 'mottoes' as they are termed in future correspondence), only an earnest desire to see the printed book published as soon as possible. Chapman's reply to Gaskell's second letter has not yet come to light, but it evidently contained various recommendations for adjustments to the text before publication, since her subsequent reply states:

> Thank you for your suggestions; you will see that I have adopted the additional title of '*Mary Barton*', a Manchester Love Story.
> It is so difficult living in Lancashire to decide upon words likely to be unintelligible in another county; but my husband has put notes to those we believe to require them. The three verses of the Oldham Weaver are enclosed. You will see that I have decided on mottoes.[120]

As Joanne Wilkes records, Gaskell would later confide to her friend Mary Ewart that '*John Barton* was the original name' of the novel, whilst Uglow has established that the working title of 'Manchester Love Story' was Gaskell's own choice and not something she had been 'forced to consider [. . .] by her publisher'.[121] The title of '*Mary Barton*' was, she told Ewart, 'a London thought coming through the publisher'. This is important because the syntax through which she accepts Chapman's suggestion of title – 'you will see that I have adopted' – is then directly paralleled when she writes that '[y]ou will see that I have decided on mottoes'. This indicates implicitly that the pre-chapter epigraphs were likewise added as part of this later consultative phase, and that they could also quite plausibly have been one of Chapman's 'suggestions'.[122] The final decision was clearly Gaskell's, but certainly the timing and phrasing of the correspondence suggests that the idea may have been in some way prompted by Chapman, and that Gaskell most probably selected and added the quotations between the receipt of Chapman's answer to her letter (dated 2 April) and the dispatch of her subsequent reply (17 April 1848).

If Chapman was involved in suggesting the idea of using epigraphs in *Mary Barton* then a pragmatic motivation for their inclusion becomes a distinct possibility. Gaskell was also requested to supply an 'explanatory preface', and to extend some passages in the second volume during the summer of 1848.[123] That Gaskell was reluctant to alter or expand her original draft too much is evident in a letter to Chapman dated 26 May in which she writes that 'it is such a relief to find I shall not have to dilute my story so much as I feared'.[124] Since it was the publisher rather than Gaskell who must have sought these extra extensions, the most obvious reason for desiring them would be that the novel was in danger of being too short to fill the required two volumes. If Chapman had foreseen such an exigency in the preceding April, this may also explain the sudden decision to incorporate epigraphic quotation. Of the 38 chapters in *Mary Barton*, only 2 feature epigraphs that are less than 4 lines in length, and the majority are much longer. The phrasing of Gaskell's letter when she writes that she has 'decided on mottoes' affirms that the final judgement was hers rather than Chapman's, but it is not unreasonable to suppose that an influencing factor may have been a desire to reduce the risk of having to add to her prose text. Although the two-volume edition of *North and South* also features pre-chapter epigraphs, 39 out of 54 of these are 4 lines or less in length and only 2 chapters feature more than 1 epigraph. Many of the 15 epigraphs that do exceed 4 lines in length do so by only 1 or 2 lines. During the publication of *Mary Barton*, Gaskell's allusion to having also included 'three verses of the Oldham Weaver' with her letter to Chapman could lend further support to the possibility that the quotations were added for the sake of length, since the version of the 'Oldham Weaver' that was finally printed actually features a total of seven verses. If Gaskell had originally included a truncated version of the poem, then Chapman may have requested the extra verses to complete it and thus also nudge the work towards more comfortably filling two volumes.

Whilst Gaskell draws *Mary Barton*'s pre-chapter quotations from a range of at least 21 different writers, of which 15 feature only once in the novel's epigraphs, there are 11 quotations in the first edition that remain unattributed to any other source (12 in later editions, since the original Wordsworth quotation used to preface chapter 30 was replaced).[125] Editorial annotations typically assume that unidentified quotations were written either by Gaskell or by her husband William, and if this were the case then an examination of the

EPIGRAPHS IN THE ENGLISH NOVEL 1750–1850

titles given to these could prove useful in gaining further understanding of the function they were intended to fulfil. For example, a lengthy verse epigraph to chapter 23 bears the title 'THE CONSTANT WOMAN', which, if the lines were composed solely for the novel, could be an indication of Gaskell attempting to guide the reader's interpretation of her succeeding prose (*Mary Barton*, p. 212). In the narrative, the heroine Mary Barton has just come to the realisation that it is not the murdered Harry Carson whom she loves, but the childhood friend now accused of his murder, Jem Wilson. The chapter begins with her excitement at having discovered the possibility of a valuable clue to legally proving his innocence, with the selflessness of Mary's determination to pursue this information revealed through the declaration that '[s]he longed to do all herself; to be his liberator, his deliverer; [. . .] though she might never regain his lost love by her own exertions' (*Mary Barton*, p. 213). The concept of 'CONSTANT' love indicated by the epigraph's attribution cultivates the idea that Mary's sudden devotion to saving Jem is as a consequence of self-discovery, thus reducing the risk of the reader attributing it to the less admirable motive of changeability. Yet in some cases there are indications that, even if the unidentified epigraphs were written by Gaskell or her husband, they might not have been written exclusively for the novel. The epigraph to chapter 20, entitled 'THE BIRTLE TRAGEDY', features elliptical dots between the two verses presented, an editorial signal that these lines are merely extracted from a separate, longer work (*Mary Barton*, p. 189). A more subtle clue may be discerned in the use of the same attribution ('LOVE-TRUTHS') for the epigraphs to two successive chapters (*Mary Barton*, pp. 143, 152), where the verse quoted is also written in the same blank verse and loose iambic pentameter, thus also promoting the idea that they are both extracts rather than specially composed epigraphic verse.[126]

Without definitive evidence, it is difficult to say with absolute certainty that these quotations will never be identified. Given the extent of Gaskell's social network within the literary community of the mid-nineteenth century, there still remains the possibility that she may have drawn upon the works of poets who remained obscure or perhaps even unpublished. Yet the likelihood that either Gaskell or her husband authored some or all of these unidentified quotations surely becomes more likely if, as her correspondence suggests, the epigraphs were assembled during a brief two-week period in April 1848. Like Scott, Gaskell might well have found that it was sometimes quicker to pen verse herself, or to ask her husband to, than it was to seek a suitable text already in existence. The biographer of William Gaskell, Barbara Brill, has identified two epigraphs given the attribution of 'MANCHESTER SONG' (*Mary Barton*, pp. 11, 53) as the composition of Gaskell's husband,[127] a title that strongly evokes Scott's frequent use of attributions such as '*Old Play*', '*Old Ballad*', or '*Old Song*' to disguise those epigraphs which he himself had authored. Later,

146

an unidentified epigraph attributed to a 'Scotch Ballad' in the two-volume edition of *North and South* likewise seems suspiciously akin to Scott's habitual practice (*North and South*, p. 282). A review of *North and South* actually suggested that Gaskell 'seems bent on doing for Lancashire and the Lancashire dialect what Miss Edgeworth did for Ireland and Scott for the land across the border',[128] and from an epigraphic perspective Gaskell certainly exploits the potential of paratext to evoke a sense of local literary identity.

In his lengthy survey of Victorian literature, James Eli Adams considers that the eventual subtitle of the novel, '"A Tale of Manchester Life," suggests an understanding of Manchester as a distinctive social order shaped by industrial labor'.[129] Gaskell subtly extends this paratextual assertion of Northern identity through her epigraphic selections, most obviously through the two quotations from her husband's 'MANCHESTER SONG', and also via a third epigraph that references the name of a hamlet of Greater Manchester in its title, 'THE BIRTLE TRAGEDY' (*Mary Barton*, p. 189). As Uglow points out, through the selection of epigraphs Gaskell demonstrates that the working class of Lancashire 'have a rich culture of their own'. She implicitly emphasises this by also including 'radical verse' by poets such as Ebenezer Elliott.[130] Although Marcus Waithe notes that Elliott 'was not a poor man himself, but something more like a local businessman',[131] the public perception of him as a Radical political advocate for the Northern, working-class community to which he belonged makes Gaskell's inclusion of his poetry a potentially quite powerful statement. By presenting his poetry in the same paratextual space that elsewhere in the book encompasses 'Gaskell's favourite seventeenth- and eighteenth-century and Romantic poets', Gaskell asserts a level of equality between them all that reflects her intention that the novel should promote social equality and unity.[132] Referencing Elliott's popular nickname of the 'Corn Law Rhymer', Jayne Hildebrand notes in her study of his work that although his fame endured throughout the 1830s and 1840s, it was only after the publication of his *Corn Law Rhymes* (1831) that Elliott 'gained exposure to a national readership'.[133] Yet as Foster points out, Gaskell undercuts Elliott's reputation as a radical political figure by quoting not from the *Corn Law Rhymes* themselves, but 'from the milder and more literary form of his writing', for example from texts such as 'Withered Wild Flowers' (1834) and 'The Splendid Village' (1834).[134]

However, although Gaskell appears to avoid emphasising the political aspect of Elliott's reputation, her selections do focus attention upon his status as a symbol of working-class social and intellectual achievement. As Waithe observes, it is no coincidence that it is an Elliott quotation that 'is chosen to preface the novel's description of learned weavers who botanize and read Newton's *Principia*'.[135] The epigraph in question consists of four lines taken from Elliott's 'The Splendid Village', and it prefaces the chapter in which Gaskell first introduces the Bartons' scientifically knowledgeable friend Job Legh:

> Learned he was; nor bird, nor insect flew,
> But he its leafy home and history knew:
> Nor wild-flower decked the rock, nor moss the well,
> But he its name and qualities could tell.
> ELLIOTT.
> (*Mary Barton*, p. 38)[136]

The following prose text commences with a description of 'a class of men in Manchester [. . .] whose existence will probably be doubted by many, who yet may claim kindred with all the noble names that science recognises' (*Mary Barton*, p. 38). Gaskell is evidently sincerely concerned that the intellectual accomplishment she describes should not be regarded as implausible, since she provides a verifiable anecdote detailing how the acclaimed botanist Sir James Edward Smith had sought information concerning a rare plant species from 'a hand-loom weaver in Manchester' (*Mary Barton*, p. 38). Foster notes that the incident had previously been reported in various newspapers,[137] but by prefacing this chapter with a quotation composed by someone publicly considered to be a working-class poet such as Elliott, and in which he writes of the scientific knowledge of his peers, Gaskell underscores her point still further. Writing on Gaskell's early work, Elizabeth Ludlow obliquely identifies the function of the epigraphs in *Mary Barton* as one of 'instruct[ing] the reader how to feel'.[138] Yet the pragmatic rather than aesthetic character of Gaskell's epigraphs in this instance might make it more accurate to say that their main purpose is to instruct the reader how to think, and in particular how to think about the text in the manner in which she wants and intends them to.

In Gaskell's only other novel to feature epigraphic paratext, *North and South*, the prefatory quotations also appear to have been a late addition to an already basically completed narrative. The work was originally published under the editorship of Charles Dickens in his magazine *Household Words*, appearing between September 1854 and January 1855. In this version of the text, chapters are typically headed with only a descriptive, numerically based appellation, for example 'Chapter the First' and 'Chapter the Second'.[139] One prefatory quotation appears at the head of the first instalment, and preceding the first chapter heading, but this disappears completely in the subsequent two-volume edition:

> Ah, yet, though all the world forsake,
> Though fortune clip my wings,

I will not cramp my heart, nor take
   Half-views of men and things.
Let Whig and Tory stir their blood;
   There must be stormy weather;
But for some true result of good
   All parties work together.
             TENNYSON.[140]

In his short study of this novel's epigraphs, Jeffrey Jackson suggests 'that this difference demands a different reading', adding that 'the epigraphs of the 1855 two-volume edition suggest a different understanding of text and space, the relationship of *North and South*'s prose world to surrounding texts'.[141] The incorporation of epigraphs in the two-volume edition thus constitutes a crucial element in the novel's transition from episodic tale to cohesive narrative entity: Gaskell herself describes it as 'being republished as a whole' when she wrote to her friend Anna Jameson. Yet her subsequent speculation as to whether she 'shall [. . .] alter & enlarge what is already written' only refers to her frustration at having been 'compelled to desperate compression' in concluding the story within the confines of the serial format. She does not allude in any way to the paratextual additions that would be made.[142]

In her examination of the paratextual quotation of Felicia Hemans in *North and South*, Ada Sharpe notes that most of the novel's pre-chapter quotations are 'excerpted from the works of canonical and contemporaneous British poets'.[143] As with *Mary Barton*, all of Gaskell's epigraphs in *North and South* are presented in English, although they are drawn from a significantly wider range of sources. Whilst *Mary Barton* featured a range of around 21 writers across a total of 42 epigraphs, *North and South* features at least 35 different authorial sources throughout a total of 54 epigraphic quotations. Only 6 of these epigraphs remain unidentified and, as with the unidentified epigraphs in *Mary Barton*, it is quite possible that these were written by Gaskell or her husband (see Appendix, Figures 17 and 18). Once again, epigraphs are always taken from poetic or dramatic sources rather than prose, suggesting that Gaskell's approach to pre-chapter paratext is not drawn from contemporaries such as Gore, but from earlier users of the device such as Scott and Radcliffe. Unlike the majority of novels by these two authors, however, *North and South* also features chapter titles which appear before the epigraph in each new chapter.

In adding epigraphs, Gaskell gains an additional space in which to comment upon her narrative and to guide her readers' interpretations of the text; yet the addition of the chapter title acts as a boundary, limiting the quotation's potential for intertextual commentary by distancing it from the preceding narrative. Instead, the epigraph here becomes a means of transitioning between the chapter title and the chapter itself, as it typically expands upon a short appellative phrase to point proleptically towards forthcoming narrative developments. For example, volume 1 chapter 9 begins:

DRESSING FOR TEA

Let China's earth, enrich'd with colour'd stains,
Pencil'd with gold, and streak'd with azure veins,
The grateful flavour of the Indian leaf,
Or Mocho's sunburnt berry glad receive.
MRS. BARBAULD.
(North and South, p. 72)[144]

Here, the title itself refers directly to the main focal point of the chapter, which is the fact that the wealthy Manchester industrialist Mr Thornton has 'come home to dress' for tea with the genteel though impoverished Hale family, and his mother's concern that his attentiveness may be prompted by a romantic interest in the daughter of the family, Margaret Hale (*North and South*, p. 74). The epigraph then provides a richly descriptive portrayal of a tea-table scene, in which a sense of delicate luxury is conveyed through details of the crockery being 'enrich'd' with 'gold' and 'azure veins'. Yet this image is immediately undercut by Margaret Hale's more homely preparations involving homemade 'cocoa-nut cakes' and ironing her mother's caps (*North and South*, p. 73). The epigraph conveys a sense of the kind of luxurious scene Thornton is expecting from the tea-table of two sophisticated southern 'ladies' (*North and South*, p. 74), and that he is perhaps a little intimidated at the prospect of. The epigraph allows the reader to perceive the contrast between this erroneous perception and the reality before it is overtly presented in the narrative, thus enhancing the concept of social misunderstanding and miscommunication which Gaskell is attempting to convey. The original narrative of the poem is of little or no relevance here, since the lines are taken from a poem in which an anthropomorphised tankard bemoans its fate as a vessel used for water rather than the alcohol which filled it in former days. As part of this diatribe against non-alcoholic beverages, it disparagingly consigns the 'Indian leaf' of tea and 'Mocho's sunburnt berry' of coffee to 'China's earth', elegantly decorated. A derogative emphasis is placed upon the fragility of china that is only 'pencil'd' and 'streak'd' with 'veins', but it is the isolated image of this luxurious delicacy that Gaskell really seems to be using here.

This primarily proleptic application is a key characteristic of the epigraphs throughout *North and South*, and the effect is enhanced by the fact that chapter breaks almost invariably signal a shift in character focus or setting. Yet by constructing the majority of her narrative in this way, Gaskell also renders more striking those rare occasions when a scene is continued upon both sides of the chapter boundary. A good example of this occurs during an early scene in which the London lawyer Henry Lennox makes an unsuccessful offer of marriage to Margaret. Following the proposal, and after an awkward conclusion to his visit with Margaret's family, Lennox accompanies his departure with a request to Margaret not to 'despise' him and a confession that 'I believe I love you more than ever' (*North and South*, p. 33). The prose of the ensuing chapter follows on from this, beginning with the sentence '[h]e was gone' and continuing the narrative with Margaret's perspective upon the proposal, and her ensuing evening. Yet despite this apparent continuity, the chapter title and epigraph actually do little to interact with this moment of the narrative:

DOUBTS AND DIFFICULTIES.

Cast me upon some naked shore,
Where I may tracke
Only the print of some sad wracke,
If thou be there, though the seas roare,
I shall no gentler calm implore.
                    HABINGTON.
                              (*North and South*, p. 34)[145]

Superficially, the 'DOUBTS' alluded to in the title might seem to interact with the image of dependency upon companionship described in the quotation, thus potentially suggesting that Margaret is about to regret refusing Lennox's offer. Yet the certainty with which Margaret declared that she 'could never think of [him]' as anything other than a friend is almost immediately confirmed in the new chapter when she is described as 'thinking over the day, [. . .] and the uncomfortable, miserable walk in the garden' (*North and South*, pp. 32, 34). In fact, it quickly becomes apparent that the 'DOUBTS AND DIFFICULTIES' of the title actually refer to her father's determination to reject his religious vocation and move his family to the distant town of Milton-Northern. The remoteness and industrial unfamiliarity of this location is metaphorically characterised as the 'naked shore' of the epigraph. The sense of 'calm' afforded by companionship sets the emotional tenor of a chapter in which Margaret's sense of familial unity is the unspoken consolation that strengthens her to face the ordeal of breaking the news of the move to her mother. She speaks 'decidedly' as she tries to determine whether she and her parents could 'live on a hundred a year in some very cheap – very quiet part of England', and only assails her father with 'passionate entreaty' when she feels that his theological doubts will mean that he will be 'for ever separate from me, from mamma' (*North and South*, pp. 39, 41).

Yet it is also worth noting that the separation between forms of pre-chapter paratext does not remain constant throughout the novel, since five of the titles feature quotation marks. In one instance, this is not necessarily because the title itself is a quotation, but rather to indicate its proverbial status: 'THE MORE HASTE THE WORSE SPEED' (*North and South*, p. 26). However, in all four other instances the quotation marks are an indication that the chapter title is taken either from the title of another work – such as 'HASTE TO THE WEDDING' – or (more commonly) from a line within another work, for example 'SHOULD AULD ACQUAINTANCE BE FORGOT?' (*North and South*, pp. 11, 232). In a further sixth instance, editor Elisabeth Jay points out that the chapter title 'ALONE! ALONE!' could plausibly be a reference to Coleridge's *Rime of the Ancient Mariner*, even though it is presented without quotation marks (*North and South*, pp. 321, 431 n. 111). Despite the comparative rarity of quotation-based chapter titles in the novel, it does nonetheless constitute a decisive blurring of paratextual boundaries. Unlike Scott, whose use of quotation-based chapter titles in *Waverley* may have been presented as such because there was no consistent pattern of epigraphic paratext elsewhere in the novel, Gaskell uses both forms of paratext and then highlights their potential for interchangeability.

Within the lifetimes of Gore and Gaskell, the perceived function of the epigraph had undergone radical change. From a means through which Scott could indulge in self-reflexive narrative commentary, it had developed into a space in which fashionable novelists could appropriate texts to create humour and even incorporate verbal phrases and sayings from the society and culture to which the author belonged. Gore emphasised especially the prioritisation of a quotation's relevance to the text over monolingual conformity, whilst also exploiting the pragmatic potential of pre-chapter paratext to enhance the construction of a distinct narrative persona. Gaskell drew on the earlier tradition of epigraphic selection, focusing upon verse, and limiting the function to a proleptic dialogue with the ensuing narrative. Most importantly of all, by the mid-nineteenth century the epigraph had developed alongside the evolving novel to move away from its earlier representation as a characteristically Gothic or Romantic device.

CONCLUSION: A NEW UNDERSTANDING OF EPIGRAPHS

1st Gent.	How class your man? – as better than the most,
	Or, seeming better, worse beneath that cloak?
	As saint or knave, pilgrim or hypocrite?
2nd Gent.	Nay, tell me how you class your wealth of books,
	The drifted relics of all time. As well
	Sort them at once by size and livery:
	Vellum, tall copies, and the common calf
	Will hardly cover more diversity
	Than all your labels cunningly devised
	To class your unread authors.[1]

Appearing in George Eliot's masterpiece of Victorian realist fiction *Middlemarch* (1871–72), the above lines preface a comparatively early chapter of the narrative in which the character and worth of both ambitious young Dr Lydgate and middle-class scapegrace Fred Vincy are weighed by the influential banker Nicholas Bulstrode. As Michael Wheeler remarks in his study of allusion in Victorian literature, this epigraph is not unique in Eliot's novel in its capacity to 'radiate beyond the local area of reference', and the invitation to the reader to consider the difference between appearance and substance is a theme that remains relevant throughout the text.[2] As well as its immediate application to the appraisal of Lydgate and Vincy, it also carries a proleptic resonance since Bulstrode himself will later prove to have only *appeared* to be 'better than the most'. The idea of conflict between appearance and substance is far from being original, of course, but the manner in which Eliot signals it in her novel certainly is; for although the presence of *dramatis personae* labels implies that this is a quotation, these lines have never been identified elsewhere and are presumed to have been authored by Eliot herself. In fact, the novel features 6 such pseudo-dramatic epigraphs (*Middlemarch*, pp. 32, 67, 115, 256, 303, 608), each one framing a moral truism as a debate between one '*Gent.*' and another;

153

these represent a small but striking portion of the novel's 86 epigraphs, and a solid fifth of the 30 of these written solely by Eliot. Imitating Walter Scott's tendency to conceal self-authored epigraphs as faux extracts from a long-forgotten drama or '*Old Play*', Eliot likewise borrows his use of this paratextual space as an outlet through which a narrative voice or persona can comment upon the tale as it unfolds. Yet where Scott creates just one authoritative voice in his epigraphic commentary, Eliot develops the device by dividing the epigraphic persona into two everyman figures whose discussion does not so much provide answers as invite debate. In her own role of author, Eliot is naturally responsible for both sides of these conversations, yet this epigraphic dialogue nonetheless presents the quest for ethical truth and enlightenment not as an individual search, but as a collective human endeavour.

There has been a tendency within scholarship to credit Eliot with having 'revived'[3] the epigraph after a hiatus of just under forty years. Whilst examining Eliot's use of epigraphs in her final novel, Eike Kronshage identifies this assumed disappearance of the epigraph as a stylistic indication 'marking the difference between romantic fiction and [. . .] realist writing', citing as examples of realist writers 'Austen, Balzac, Dickens, the Brontë sisters, Thackeray, Trollope, Flaubert, and Zola'.[4] Yet, as has already been noted, labelling the epigraph as a paratextual element present solely in 'romantic fiction' overlooks the generic complexities of the works of writers such as Catherine Gore and Elizabeth Gaskell, both of whom frequently juxtapose elements typically associated with the Romantic and realist genres. By assessing a broader range of English fiction, I have compiled substantial statistical evidence demonstrating that the epigraph continued to recur within a significant proportion of English novels that received their first editions each year from the time of the epigraph's initial rise in popularity in the 1790s through to the mid-nineteenth century (see Appendix, Table 2 and Figures 1 and 2). In 1850, the last year included in the statistical survey, 39 first-published novels out of an assessed total of 121 were found to feature some form of pre-chapter epigraphic quotation (equivalent to just over 32%). Although the actual number of novels believed to have received their first edition that year is substantially higher (at least 175),[5] the size and essentially random nature of the sample of novels ensures that it is nonetheless broadly representative (see Appendix, Table 2). By surveying the works of lesser-known writers as well as canonically recognised authors, I have already established that the epigraph was far from being either out of use or 'out of fashion' during the 1830s and 1840s. Whilst a longer statistical survey would be required to establish whether or not pre-chapter epigraphs continue to be used during the 1850s and 1860s, there is likewise no evidence to indicate the extinction of a device that was still very much in use in 1850. This presumption of extinction is derived largely from the retrospectively selective nature of canonical status.

CONCLUSION

By following the development of the epigraph through the English novel in the long eighteenth and early nineteenth centuries, my investigation highlights the strongly interconnected nature of literary development. Canonical users of epigraphs such as Ann Radcliffe, Scott, Gaskell, and even Eliot appear no longer as lone innovators but as contributors to an evolving dialogue between text and paratext, as links within a chain of literary production, inspiration, and direct quotation. This sense of an evolving continuum is particularly evident through the often unexpected ways in which novels from disparate genres relate to or reflect each other's use of epigraphic paratext. Even if connections between Eliot's philosophising realism and the much earlier moral didacticism of William Chaigneau, and Sarah Fielding and Jane Collier might seem readily apparent, it is only through an appreciation of paratextual similarity that we can understand the extent to which the works of all four writers are also related to, for example, the Gothic novels of Radcliffe and Matthew Lewis, the socio-political fiction of Charlotte Smith, and the historical novels of Scott and Katherine Thomson. When the history of the novel includes only canonical authors, it tells only half the story; by placing these writers within a wider context of literary development, the narrative of the novel's history becomes much more complex and dynamic.

As a stylistic feature of prose fiction, the epigraph's potential for generic associations is not derived from simple presence or absence, but rather from the author's creative decisions regarding epigraphic content. For example, the educational intention of some of the earliest novels that feature epigraphs is reflected in the strong reliance upon epigraphic quotations drawn from classical writers, whilst Gothic authors such as Radcliffe and Lewis typically include a higher proportion of Shakespearean epigraphs. Scott exploits the fragile authenticity of historical fiction through his habit of inventing (and then attributing) many of his epigraphic quotations, whilst fashionable novelists such as Gore and Edward Bulwer-Lytton instead explore the device's comedic potential. When considered as stages of continuous development, it becomes clear that the epigraph does not determine genre, but is itself determined and influenced by the genre in which the author is working.

Considered as such, it becomes possible to see that the traditional view, derived from Gérard Genette, that an epigraph is primarily 'a password of intellectuality'[6] does not go far enough in encompassing the potential functionality of this form of paratext. As my analysis has demonstrated, the creative possibilities offered by the device are limited only by the ingenuity of the author using them. The debate in the Eliot quotation with which this chapter begins conveys the difficulties of categorising either people or books, and, as a component of the latter, epigraphs present precisely the same challenge. Epigraphs may be analeptic, proleptic, or transitional; they may agree with the text (whether seriously or ironically), or they may critique it; they may highlight a moral or other interpretive

155

meaning, or they may simply mock one or more of the novel's characters or even the narrative itself; they may be quotations, authorial compositions, or authorial compositions presented as quotations; when they are quotations, they may construct an intertextual link with elements of the work in which they originated, or they may constitute an appropriation of only that one excerpt in isolation. Indeed, the one unifying quality that all epigraphs seem to possess is that they represent a kind of intertextual riddle loaded with interpretative possibilities, the sense and truth of which must be unscrambled by the reader before they may understand its relevance to the text. The riddle of the epigraph may be as simple or as complicated as the author wishes, and its comprehension relies upon the ingenuity of the reader (or in some cases upon their knowledge of the text from previous readings). Most importantly, this proves that epigraphs are very far from being simplistic symbols or assertions of canonical parity; in fact, they are usually carefully crafted textual elements that are intended to be read and understood as part of a wider fictional whole. Reading pre-chapter epigraphs not only enriches our experience of a text, it also involves us as active participants in a vast literary tapestry of interconnection, interpretation, and inspiration.

APPENDIX

Table I Number of novels first-published with epigraphs 1770–1836 in figures

The numerical data for this table has been compiled using bibliographic data in conjunction with extensive surveying of individual books to determine epigraphic content. The bibliographies consulted were Peter Garside, James Raven, and Rainer Schöwerling (gen. eds.), *The English Novel* 1770–1829: *A Bibliographical Survey of Prose Fiction Published in the British Isles* (Oxford: Oxford University Press, 2000), and Verena Ebbes et al. (eds), 'The English Novel, 1830–1836: A Bibliographical Survey of Fiction Published in the British Isles', *Romantic Textualities* (Cardiff: Cardiff University Press, 2016) <http://www.romtext.org.uk/resources/english-novel-1830-36/> [accessed throughout 2017].

Year	Number of novels with epigraphs	Number of novels listed in the bibliographic references	Number of these novels that have had their epigraphic content assessed	Number of these novels that have not had their epigraphic content assessed	Percentage of novels with epigraphs as proportion of total number (%)	Percentage of novels with epigraphs as proportion of number of novels assessed (%)
1770	2	40	34	6	5	5.88
1771	0	60	42	18	0	0
1772	0	41	33	8	0	0
1773	0	39	30	9	0	0
1774	0	35	30	5	0	0

(continued)

Year	Number of novels with epigraphs	Number of novels listed in the bibliographic references	Number of these novels that have had their epigraphic content assessed	Number of these novels that have not had their epigraphic content assessed	Percentage of novels with epigraphs as proportion of total number (%)	Percentage of novels with epigraphs as proportion of number of novels assessed (%)
1775	0	31	22	9	0	0
1776	0	18	14	4	0	0
1777	0	18	11	7	0	0
1778	0	16	14	2	0	0
1779	0	18	16	2	0	0
1780	0	24	21	3	0	0
1781	0	22	17	5	0	0
1782	0	22	15	7	0	0
1783	0	24	22	2	0	0
1784	0	24	19	5	0	0
1785	0	47	41	6	0	0
1786	0	40	36	4	0	0
1787	0	51	48	3	0	0
1788	4	80	68	12	5.00	5.88
1789	2	71	65	6	2.82	3.08
1790	4	74	62	12	5.41	6.45
1791	3	74	68	6	4.05	4.41
1792	3	58	50	8	5.17	6.00
1793	4	45	44	1	8.89	9.09
1794	4	56	53	3	7.14	7.55
1795	8	50	49	1	16.00	16.33
1796	15	91	84	7	16.48	17.86
1797	14	79	67	12	17.72	20.90
1798	22	75	68	7	29.33	32.35

APPENDIX

Year	Number of novels with epigraphs	Number of novels listed in the bibliographic references	Number of these novels that have had their epigraphic content assessed	Number of these novels that have not had their epigraphic content assessed	Percentage of novels with epigraphs as proportion of total number (%)	Percentage of novels with epigraphs as proportion of number of novels assessed (%)
1799	22	99	87	12	22.22	25.29
1800	19	81	79	2	23.46	24.05
1801	19	72	67	5	26.39	28.36
1802	19	61	56	5	31.15	33.93
1803	14	79	71	8	17.72	19.72
1804	11	73	61	12	15.07	18.03
1805	20	75	68	7	26.67	29.41
1806	15	70	60	10	21.43	25.00
1807	12	70	60	10	17.14	20.00
1808	19	111	96	15	17.12	19.79
1809	20	79	64	15	25.32	31.25
1810	28	89	73	14	31.46	38.36
1811	17	80	67	13	21.25	25.37
1812	15	66	57	9	22.73	26.32
1813	25	63	56	7	39.68	44.64
1814	14	61	55	6	22.95	25.45
1815	16	54	52	2	29.63	30.77
1816	18	59	54	5	30.51	33.33
1817	15	55	54	1	27.27	27.78
1818	19	62	58	4	30.65	32.76
1819	23	73	70	3	31.51	32.86
1820	35	72	67	5	48.61	52.24
1821	34	76	71	5	44.74	47.89

(continued)

EPIGRAPHS IN THE ENGLISH NOVEL 1750–1850

Year	Number of novels with epigraphs	Number of novels listed in the bibliographic references	Number of these novels that have had their epigraphic content assessed	Number of these novels that have not had their epigraphic content assessed	Percentage of novels with epigraphs as proportion of total number (%)	Percentage of novels with epigraphs as proportion of number of novels assessed (%)
1822	35	82	80	2	42.68	43.75
1823	36	87	84	3	41.38	42.86
1824	36	101	96	5	35.64	37.50
1825	40	91	89	2	43.96	44.94
1826	33	77	75	2	42.86	44.00
1827	40	79	75	4	50.63	53.33
1828	35	83	82	1	42.17	42.68
1829	39	82	80	2	47.56	48.75
1830	48	108	94	14	44.44	51.06
1831	25	69	67	2	36.23	37.31
1832	32	88	80	8	36.36	40.00
1833	25	80	75	5	31.25	33.33
1834	30	77	73	4	38.96	41.10
1835	50	112	103	9	44.64	48.54
1836	25	78	71	7	32.05	35.21
Total	1063	4297	3870	425	24.74	27.47

APPENDIX

Table 2 Number of novels first-published with epigraphs 1837–50

The numerical data for this table has been compiled using bibliographic data in conjunction with extensive surveying of individual books to determine epigraphic content. The bibliography consulted was Andrew Block, *The English Novel, 1740–1850: A Catalogue Including Prose Romances, Short Stories, and Translations of Foreign Fiction*, with Introductions by John Crow and Ernest A. Baker, new and rev. edn (London: Dawson, 1961); publication years of some individual titles have been altered after being cross-checked for accuracy against Troy J. Bassett, *At the Circulating Library: A Database of Victorian Fiction, 1837–1850* <http://victorianresearch.org/atcl/index.php> [accessed March–August 2019], and against records held on WorldCat <https://www.worldcat.org/> [accessed March–August 2019], as well as on title pages of surveyed novels.

Year	Number of novels with epigraphs	Number of novels listed in Block's bibliography	Number of these novels that have had their epigraphic content assessed	Number of these novels that have not had their epigraphic content assessed	Percentage of novels with epigraphs as proportion of total number (%)	Percentage of novels with epigraphs as proportion of number of novels assessed (%)
1837	31	115	93	22	26.96	33.33
1838	39	111	89	22	35.14	43.82
1839	37	121	106	15	30.58	35.24
1840	44	155	118	37	28.39	37.29
1841	41	140	112	28	29.29	36.61
1842	34	143	108	35	23.78	31.48
1843	41	140	115	25	29.29	35.65
1844	54	201	170	31	26.87	31.76
1845	43	201	162	39	21.39	26.54
1846	39	186	141	43	20.97	27.66
1847	39	196	134	63	19.90	29.10
1848	41	234	164	70	17.52	25.00
1849	29	206	111	95	14.08	26.13
1850	39	175	121	54	22.29	32.23
Total	551	2324	1744	579	23.71	31.59

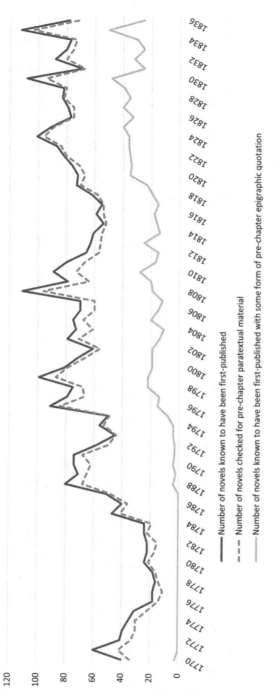

Figure 1 Number of novels first-published with epigraphs 1770–1836

The numerical data for this graph has been compiled using bibliographic data in conjunction with extensive surveying of individual books to determine epigraphic content. The bibliographies consulted were Peter Garside, James Raven, and Rainer Schöwerling (gen. eds), *The English Novel 1770–1829: A Bibliographical Survey of Prose Fiction Published in the British Isles*, 2 vols (Oxford: Oxford University Press, 2000), and Verena Ebbes, Peter Garside, Angela Koch, Anthony Mandal, and Rainer Schöwerling (eds), 'The English Novel, 1830–1836: A Bibliographical Survey of Fiction Published in the British Isles', *Romantic Textualities* (Cardiff: Cardiff University Press, 2016) <http://www.romtext.org.uk/resources/english-novel-1830-36/> [accessed throughout 2017].

APPENDIX

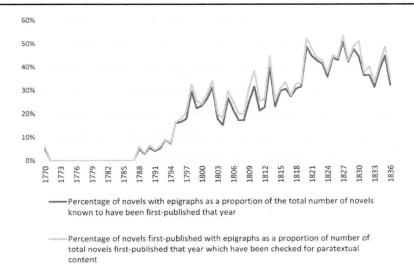

—— Percentage of novels with epigraphs as a proportion of the total number of novels known to have been first-published that year

----- Percentage of novels first-published with epigraphs as a proportion of number of total novels first-published that year which have been checked for paratextual content

Figure 2 Quantity of novels first-published with epigraphs 1770–1836 as a percentage of total number of novels known to have been published

The numerical data for this graph has been compiled using bibliographic data in conjunction with extensive surveying of individual books to determine epigraphic content. The bibliographies consulted were Garside, Raven, and Schöwerling (gen. eds), *The English Novel 1770–1829*, and Ebbes et al. (eds), 'The English Novel, 1830–1836'.

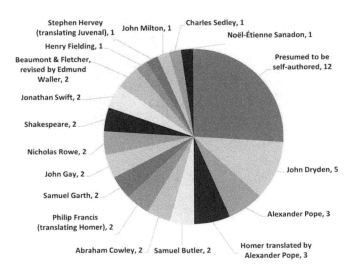

Figure 3 Sources of epigraphic quotation in William Chaigneau, *The History of Jack Connor*, ed. by Ian Campbell Ross (Dublin: Four Courts Press, 2013)

163

EPIGRAPHS IN THE ENGLISH NOVEL 1750–1850

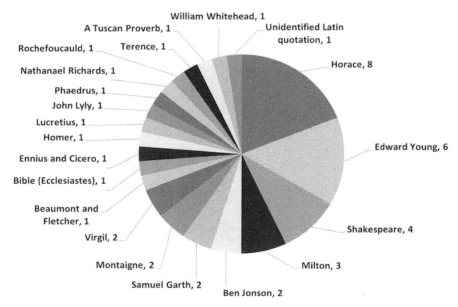

Figure 4 Sources of epigraphic quotation in Sarah Fielding and Jane Collier, *The Cry: A New Dramatic Fable*, 3 vols (London: R. and J. Dodsley, 1754)

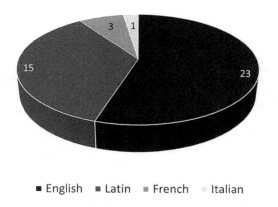

■ English ■ Latin ■ French ■ Italian

Figure 5 Languages of epigraphic quotation in Sarah Fielding and Jane Collier, *The Cry: A New Dramatic Fable*, 3 vols (London: R. and J. Dodsley, 1754)

APPENDIX

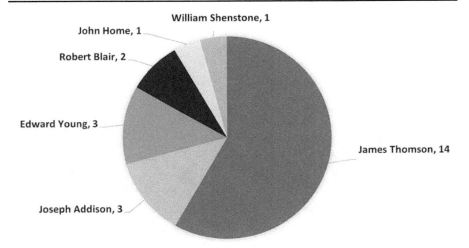

Figure 6 Sources of epigraphs in Elizabeth Helme, *Louisa; or, The Cottage on the Moor*, *The fourth edition, corrected*, 2 vols (London: G. Kearsley, 1787)

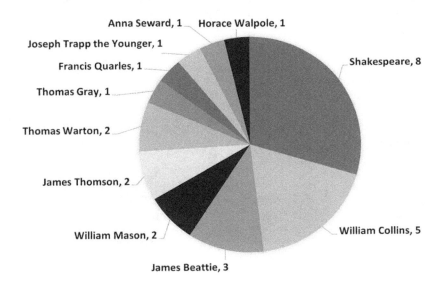

Figure 7 Sources of epigraphs in Ann Radcliffe, *The Romance of the Forest*, ed. by Chloe Chard (Oxford: Oxford University Press, 2009)

This chart also incorporates the correct sources of two epigraphs not attributed in this edition of the text, but which were identified as part of the present study.

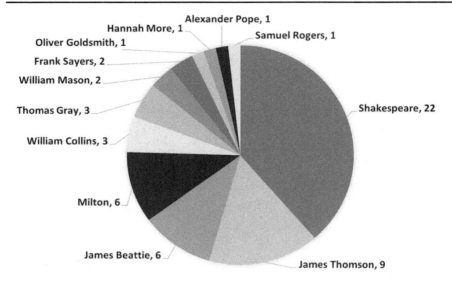

Figure 8 Sources of epigraphs in Ann Radcliffe, *The Mysteries of Udolpho*, ed. by Bonamy Dobrée (Oxford: Oxford University Press, 1998)

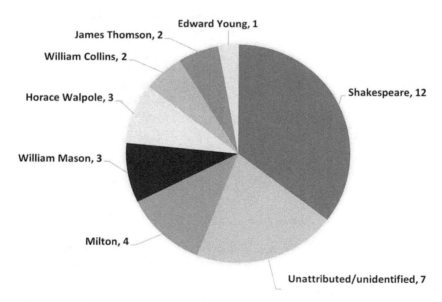

Figure 9 Sources of epigraphs in Ann Radcliffe, *The Italian*, ed. by Frederick Garber, rev. by Nick Groom (Oxford: Oxford University Press, 2017)

APPENDIX

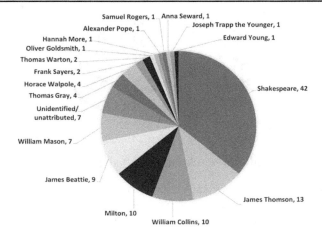

Figure 10 Sources of epigraphs in Ann Radcliffe, *The Romance of the Forest*, ed. by Chloe Chard (Oxford: Oxford University Press, 2009); *The Mysteries of Udolpho*, ed. by Bonamy Dobrée (Oxford: Oxford University Press, 1998); *The Italian*, ed. by Frederick Garber, rev. by Nick Groom (Oxford: Oxford University Press, 2017)

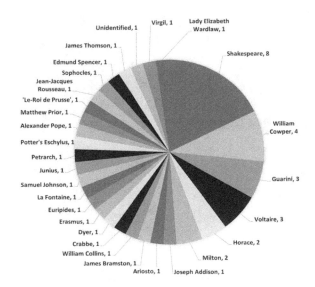

Figure 11 Sources of epigraphs in Charlotte Smith, *The Banished Man*, in *The Works of Charlotte Smith*, gen. ed. Stuart Curran, 14 vols (London: Pickering & Chatto, 2005–07), VII

This chart records genuine attributions only, thus overlooking occasional errors or omissions in Smith's attributions.

EPIGRAPHS IN THE ENGLISH NOVEL 1750–1850

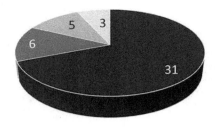

■ English   ■ French   ■ Italian   ■ Latin

Figure 12 Languages of epigraphic quotation in Charlotte Smith, *The Banished Man*, in *The Works of Charlotte Smith*, gen. ed. Stuart Curran, 14 vols (London: Pickering & Chatto, 2005–07), VII

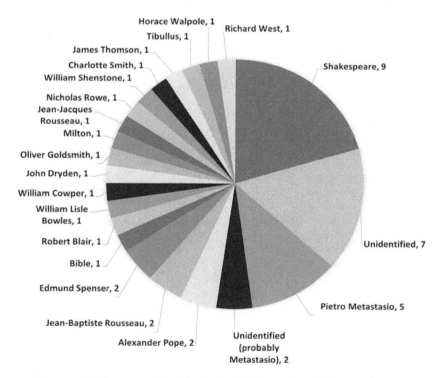

Figure 13 Sources of epigraphs in Charlotte Smith, *Marchmont*, in *The Works of Charlotte Smith*, IX

APPENDIX

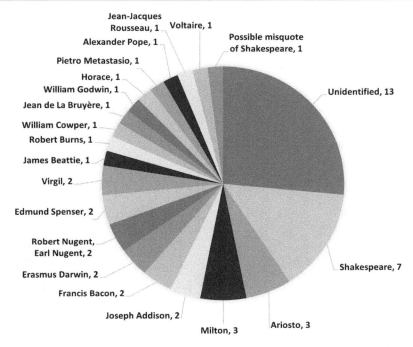

Figure 14 Sources of epigraphs in Charlotte Smith, *The Young Philosopher*, in *The Works of Charlotte Smith*, X

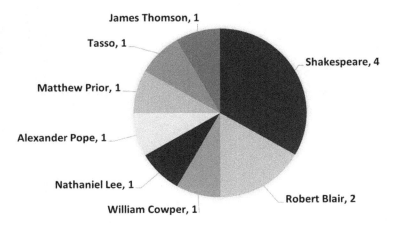

Figure 15 Sources of epigraphs in Matthew Lewis, *The Monk*, ed. by Howard Anderson, rev. with an Introduction and Notes by Nick Groom (Oxford: Oxford University Press, 2016)

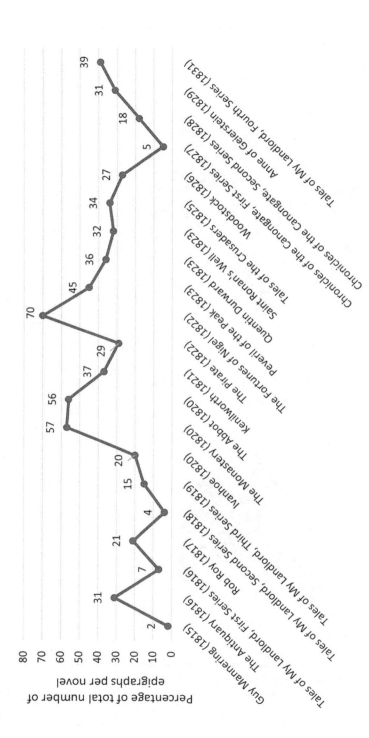

Figure 16 Graph to show the percentage of epigraphs in Scott's novels which are presumed to be, or definitely known to be, authored by Scott

The data upon which this graph is based was gathered from first editions of Scott's novels; attributions were cross-checked with the *Edinburgh Edition of the Waverley Novels*, gen. ed. David Hewitt, 30 vols (Edinburgh: Edinburgh University Press, 1993–2012).

APPENDIX

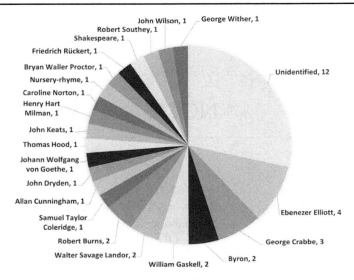

Figure 17 Sources of epigraphic quotations in Elizabeth Gaskell, *Mary Barton: A Tale of Manchester Life*, in *Works of Elizabeth Gaskell*, gen. ed. Joanne Shattock, 10 vols (London: Pickering & Chatto, 2005–06), V

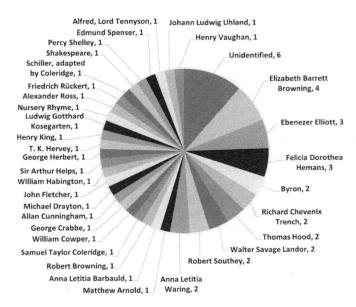

Figure 18 Sources of epigraphs in Elizabeth Gaskell, *North and South*, in *Works of Elizabeth Gaskell*, gen. ed. Joanne Shattock, 10 vols (London: Pickering & Chatto, 2005–06), VII

|171|

NOTES

INTRODUCTION

1. Walter Scott, *Rob Roy*, in *Edinburgh Edition of the Waverley Novels*, gen. ed. David Hewitt, 30 vols (Edinburgh: Edinburgh University Press, 1993–2012), V, 22.
2. Bonamy Dobrée, 'Introduction', in Ann Radcliffe, *The Mysteries of Udolpho*, ed. by Bonamy Dobrée (Oxford: Oxford University Press, 1998), p. xiii.
3. Gérard Genette, *Paratexts: Thresholds of Interpretation*, trans. by Jane E. Lewin (Cambridge: Cambridge University Press, 1997), p. 160.
4. When summarising typographic conventions for the epigraph Genette includes a cautious qualifier to his judgement that he 'do[es] not think a norm has been established for these matters, at least in France' (*Paratexts*, p. 152).
5. Michael Peled Ginsburg, 'Pseudonym, Epigraphs, and Narrative Voice: Middlemarch and the Problem of Authorship', *English Literary History*, 47: 3 (Autumn 1980), 542–58 (p. 547).
6. Rainier Grutman, 'Quoting Europe: Mottomania in the Romantic Age', in *Time Refigured: Myths, Foundation Texts and Imagined Communities*, ed. by Martin Procházka and Ondřej Pilný (Prague: Litteraria Pragensia, 2005), pp. 281–95 (p. 285).
7. Rainier Grutman, 'How to Do Things with Mottoes: Recipes from the Romantic Era (with Special Reference to Stendhal)', *Neohelicon*, 37: 1 (June 2010), 139–53 (p. 142).
8. Gary Kelly, *English Fiction of the Romantic Period 1789–1830* (London: Routledge, 1989), p. 54.
9. Edward Jacobs, 'Ann Radcliffe and Romantic Print Culture', in *Ann Radcliffe, Romanticism, and the Gothic*, ed. by Dale Townshend and Angela Wright (Cambridge: Cambridge University Press, 2014), pp. 49–66 (pp. 60–61).
10. Leah Price, *The Anthology and the Rise of the Novel: From Richardson to George Eliot* (Cambridge: Cambridge University Press, 2000, repr. 2004), pp. 91, 93.
11. Kate Rumbold, *Shakespeare and the Eighteenth-Century Novel: Cultures of Quotation from Samuel Richardson to Jane Austen* (Cambridge: Cambridge University Press, 2016), p. 133.
12. For examples of the use of the term 'mottos' or 'mottoes', see Elizabeth Helme, *Louisa; or, the Cottage on the Moor, The fourth edition, corrected*, 2 vols (London: G. Kearsley, 1787), I, vi; Walter Scott, 'Introduction', in *Chronicles of the Canongate*, in *Edinburgh Edition of the Waverley Novels*, gen. ed. Hewitt, XX, 9; Scott,

NOTES

Rob Roy, p. 3; Elizabeth Gaskell to Edward Chapman, 17 April 1848, in *The Letters of Mrs. Gaskell*, ed. by J. A. V. Chapple and Arthur Pollard (Manchester: Manchester University Press, 1997), p. 56. For use of 'chapter-tags', see Tom B. Haber, 'The Chapter-Tags in the Waverley Novels', *PMLA*, 45: 4 (December 1930), 1140–49 (p. 1140); Matthew Whiting Rosa, *The Silver-Fork School* (New York: Columbia University Press, 1936), p. 144.

13. Eike Kronshage, 'The Function of Poetic Epigraphs in George Eliot's *Daniel Deronda*', *Connotations*, 23: 2 (2013/14), 230–60 (p. 253); Janine Barchas, *Graphic Design, Print Culture, and the Eighteenth-Century Novel* (Cambridge: Cambridge University Press, 2003), p. 89.

14. Barchas, *Graphic Design*, p. 89.

15. Sudha Shastri, *Intertextuality and Victorian Studies* (Himayatnagar, Hyderabad: Orient Longman, 2001), p. 121.

16. For the identification of Radcliffe as the originator of epigraphs, see John Claiborne Isbell, 'Romantic Novel and Verse Romance, 1750–1850: Is There a Romance Continuum?', in *Romantic Prose Fiction*, ed. by Gerald Gillespie, Manfred Engel, and Bernard Dieterle (Amsterdam: John Benjamins, 2008), pp. 496–516 (p. 502); Jacobs, 'Ann Radcliffe and Romantic Print Culture', p. 63; Price, *The Anthology and the Rise of the Novel*, p. 92; see also Stuart Curran, 'Charlotte Smith: Intertextualities', in *Charlotte Smith in British Romanticism*, ed. by Jacqueline M. Labbe (London: Pickering & Chatto, 2008), pp. 175–88 (p. 176).

17. Jacobs, 'Ann Radcliffe and Romantic Print Culture', p. 62.

18. Kronshage, 'The Function of Poetic Epigraphs', p. 254; see also Grutman, 'Quoting Europe', p. 287.

19. Andrew Block, *The English Novel, 1740–1850: A Catalogue Including Prose Romances, Short Stories, and Translations of Foreign Fiction*, with Introductions by John Crow and Ernest A. Baker, new and rev. edn (London: Dawson, 1961); Peter Garside, James Raven, and Rainer Schöwerling (gen. eds), *The English Novel 1770–1829: A Bibliographical Survey of Prose Fiction Published in the British Isles*, 2 vols (Oxford: Oxford University Press, 2000); Verena Ebbes, Peter Garside, Angela Koch, Anthony Mandal, and Rainer Schöwerling (eds), 'The English Novel, 1830–1836: A Bibliographical Survey of Fiction Published in the British Isles', *Romantic Textualities* (Cardiff: Cardiff University Press, 2016) <http://www.romtext.org.uk/resources/english-novel-1830-36/> [accessed throughout 2017]; Troy J. Bassett, *At the Circulating Library: A Database of Victorian Fiction, 1837–1850* <http://victorianresearch.org/atcl/index.php> [accessed March–August 2019].

20. Garside, Raven, and Schöwerling, *The English Novel 1770–1829*, II, 695.

21. An example of this is Royall Tyler, *The Algerine Captive; or, The Life and Adventures of Doctor Updike Underhill, Six Years a Prisoner Among the Algerines*, 2 vols (London: G. and J. Robinson, 1802), for which the 1967 Scholars' Facsimiles & Reprints edition was consulted.

22. See Ian Campbell Ross, 'Introduction', in William Chaigneau, *The History of Jack Connor*, ed. by Ian Campbell Ross (Dublin: Four Courts Press, 2013), pp. 11–32 (p. 16); see also Steven Moore, *The Novel: An Alternative History 1600–1800* (London: Bloomsbury, 2013), p. 779.

EPIGRAPHS IN THE ENGLISH NOVEL 1750–1850

23. Rachel Sagner Buurma, 'Epigraphs', in Dennis Duncan and Adam Smyth (eds), *Book Parts* (Oxford: Oxford University Press, 2019), pp. 165–75 (pp 167, 168, 170–71).

24. Grutman, 'How to Do Things with Mottoes', p. 142.

25. Louis G. Locke, *Tillotson: A Study in Seventeenth-Century Literature* (Copenhagen: Rosenkilde and Bagger, 1954), p. 14.

26. Richard Steele, *Tatler*, 101 (1 December 1709), in *The Tatler*, ed. by Donald Bond, 3 vols (Oxford: Clarendon Press, 1987), II, 122; William Fraser Mitchell, *English Pulpit Oratory from Andrewes to Tillotson: A Study of its Literary Aspects* (New York: Russell & Russell, 1962), p. 349.

27. For a statistical examination of the popularity of sermons, based upon quantities of multiple editions published per year, see Jennifer Farooq, *Preaching in Eighteenth-Century London* (Woodbridge: Boydell Press, 2013), p. 95.

28. Ana Vogrinčič, 'The Novel-Reading Panic in 18th-Century in England: An Outline of an Early Moral Media Panic', *Medijska Istrazivanja/Media Research*, 14: 2 (2008), 103–24.

29. Grutman, 'How to Do Things with Mottoes', p. 142.

30. John Tillotson, *Sermons preach'd upon several occasions. The fourth volume* (London: Br. Aylmer and W. Rogers, 1695), p. 83.

31. *Spectator*, 221 (13 November 1711), in *The Spectator*, ed. by Donald Bond, 5 vols (Oxford: Clarendon Press, 1965), II, 358.

32. *Spectator*, 221 (13 November 1711), p. 358.

33. See, for example, John Tillotson, *Sermons preach'd upon several occasions*, 6th edn corrected, 2 vols (London: Brabazon Aylmer, 1685), I; John Tillotson, *Sermons and discourses: Some of which Never before Printed. The third volume* (London: B. Aylmer and W. Rogers, 1686).

34. See Tillotson, *Sermons preach'd upon several occasions. The fourth volume*, The Texts of each Sermon.

35. For a full discussion of the significance of prefatory mottos in the *Tatler–Female Tatler* rivalry, see Corrina Readioff, 'A Paratextual Battle: Mottos, Meaning and Conflict in Printed Journals 1709–1712', *The Review of English Studies*, 73: 309 (2022), 302–20.

36. The visual similarity between pre-chapter epigraphs and mottos in the anthologised *Spectator* was recently noted by Eirian Jade Yem, 'Forgetting Oneself: Epigraphs and Escapism in Ann Radcliffe's Novels', *Journal for Eighteenth-Century Studies*, 45: 3 (September 2022), 305–21. Prior to this the idea was a foundational concept in my own PhD thesis, begun in 2015 and submitted in 2018.

37. Kenneth Haynes, *English Literature and Ancient Languages* (Oxford: Oxford University Press, 2007), p. 34.

Chapter 1

1. Quotation of an epigraph from *The Histories of Some of the Penitents in the Magdalen House*, ed. by Jennie Batchelor and Megan Hiatt (London: Pickering & Chatto, 2007), p. 153.

NOTES

2. John Dryden, 'Palamon and Arcite: or, The Knight's Tale', in *Fables Ancient and Modern: Translated into Verse, from Homer, Ovid Boccace, and Chaucher: with original poems* (London: Jacob Tonson, 1713), pp. 1–114 (p. 98). The original line gives 'my' instead of 'our'.

3. Ian Campbell Ross, 'An Irish Picaresque Novel: William Chaigneau's *The History of Jack Connor*', *An Irish Quarterly Review*, 71: 283 (Autumn 1982), 270–79 (p. 270). See also Ian Campbell Ross, 'Introduction', in William Chaigneau, *The History of Jack Connor*, ed. by Ian Campbell Ross (Dublin: Four Courts Press, 2013), pp. 11–32 (p. 16); Steven Moore, *The Novel: An Alternative History 1600–1800* (London: Bloomsbury, 2013), p. 779.

4. Moore, *The Novel*, p. 779. For the similarities between Chaigneau's and Fielding's work, see also Aileen Douglas, 'The Novel before 1800', in *The Cambridge Companion to the Irish Novel*, ed. by John Wilson Foster (Cambridge: Cambridge University Press, 2006), pp. 22–38 (p. 28); Catherine Skeen, '*Gulliver's Travels, Jack Connor*, and *John Buncle*', *Modern Philology*, 100: 3 (February 2003), 330–59 (p. 348).

5. Clark Lawlor, 'The Grotesque, Reform and Sensibility in Dryden, Sarah Fielding and Jane Collier', *British Journal for Eighteenth-Century Studies*, 22 (1999), 187–205 (p. 204).

6. *Public Advertiser*, 4: 6059 (1 April 1754).

7. Timothy Dykstal, 'Provoking the Ancients: Classical Learning and Imitation in Fielding and Collier', *College Literature* 31: 3 (Summer 2004), 102–22 (p. 107).

8. Sarah Fielding and Jane Collier, *The Cry: A New Dramatic Fable*, ed. by Carolyne Woodward (Lexington, KY: University of Kentucky Press, 2017), p. 54. All quotations will be from this edition of the text.

9. Moore, *The Novel*, p. 779.

10. Chaigneau, *The History of Jack Connor*, pp. 41, 240 n.

11. Henry Fielding, *Tom Jones*, ed. by John Bender and Simon Stern, with an Introduction by John Bender (Oxford: Oxford University Press, 2008), p. 279.

12. Virgil, 'Aeneid Books 1–6', in *Eclogues. Georgics. Aeneid: Books 1–6*, trans. by H. Rushton Fairclough, rev. by G. P. Goold (Cambridge, MA: Harvard University Press, 1999), pp. 261–597 (pp. 262–63, l. 1).

13. Review of '*The History of Jack Connor*', *Monthly Review*, 6 (June 1752), 447–49 (p. 447); Skeen, '*Gulliver's Travels, Jack Connor*, and *John Buncle*', p. 351.

14. Campbell Ross, 'An Irish Picaresque Novel', p. 276.

15. Douglas, 'The Novel before 1800', p. 29.

16. Clive Probyn, 'Fielding, Sarah (1710–1768)', in *Oxford Dictionary of National Biography* (Oxford: Oxford University Press, 2004) <http://www.oxforddnb.com/view/article/9405> [accessed 8 March 2016].

17. Patrick C. Fleming, 'The Rise of the Moral Tale: Children's Literature, the Novel, and *The Governess*', *Eighteenth-Century Studies*, 46: 4 (Summer 2013), 463–77 (p. 475).

18. See, for example, *Whitehall Evening Post*, 550 (19 August 1749) and 793 (12 March 1751); *General Advertiser*, 5114 (13 March 1750).

19. Christine Perkell, 'Aeneid I: An Epic Program', in *Reading Vergil's Aeneid: An Interpretive Guide*, ed. by Christine Perkell (Norman: University of Oklahoma Press, 1999), pp. 29–49 (p. 29).

20. Edmund Spenser, *The Faerie Queene*, ed. by A. C. Hamilton, rev. 2nd edn (London: Routledge, 2013), pp. 29 n., 31 n.
21. Femke Molekamp, 'Genevan Legacies', in *The Oxford Handbook of the Bible in Early Modern England, c. 1530–1700*, ed. by Kevin Killeen, Helen Smith, and Rachel Judith Willie (Oxford: Oxford University Press, 2015), pp. 38–53 (p. 52); Femke Molekamp, *Women and the Bible in Early Modern England: Religious Reading and Writing* (Oxford: Oxford University Press, 2013), p. 31.
22. Kenneth Boris and Meredith Donaldson Clark, 'Hymnic Epic and *The Faerie Queene*'s Original Printed Format: Canto-Canticles and Psalmic Arguments', *Renaissance Quarterly*, 64 (2011), 1148–93 (pp. 1176, 1170, 1180, 1181).
23. Stephen Orgel and Jonathan Goldberg, 'Introduction', in John Milton, *Paradise Lost*, ed. by Stephen Orgel and Jonathan Goldberg (Oxford: Oxford University Press, 2004), pp. vii–xxxiv (p. xiv).
24. John M. Steadman, 'Una and the Clergy: The Ass Symbol in *The Faerie Queene*', *Journal of the Warburg and Courtauld Institutes*, 21: 1/2 (1958), 134–37 (p. 135).
25. Lesley Brill, 'Other Places, Other Times: The Sites of the Proems to *The Faerie Queene*', *Studies in English Literature, 1500–1900*, 34 (1994), 1–17 (pp. 2, 3).
26. Milton, *Paradise Lost*, p. 82 (III.686–89).
27. G. A. Starr, 'From Socrates to Sarah Fielding: Benevolence, Irony, and Conversation', in *Passionate Encounters in a Time of Sensibility*, ed. by Maximillian E. Novak and Anne Mellor (Newark: University of Delaware Press, 2000), pp. 106–26 (p. 111).
28. *The Cry*, ed. Woodward, p. 57; Horace, 'Epistles', in *Satires. Epistles. The Art of Poetry*, trans. by H. Rushton Fairclough (Cambridge, MA: Harvard University Press, 1929), pp. 247–441 (pp. 356–57, I.xvi.65).
29. *Latin Dictionary* (Glasgow: HarperCollins, 1997, repr. 2001), p. 133.
30. Dykstal, 'Provoking the Ancients', p. 108.
31. Carolyn Woodward, 'Who Wrote *The Cry*?: A Fable for Our Times', *Eighteenth-Century Fiction*, 9: 1 (October 1996), 91–97 (p. 92).
32. Mika Suzuki, '"Words I in Fancy say for you": Sarah Fielding's Letters and Epistolary Method', *The Yearbook of English Studies*, 28 (1998), 196–211 (p. 207).
33. *Spectator*, 10 (12 March 1711), in *The Spectator*, ed. by Donald Bond, 5 vols (Oxford: Clarendon Press, 1965), I, 44.
34. Elizabeth Kowaleski-Wallace, *Consuming Subjects: Women, Shopping, and Business in the Eighteenth Century* (New York: Columbia University Press, 1997), p. 21.
35. *Spectator*, 370 (5 May 1712), in *The Spectator*, III, 393.
36. George Justice, '*The Spectator* and Distance Education', in *The Spectator: Emerging Discourses*, ed. by Donald J. Newman (Newark: University of Delaware Press, 2005), pp. 265–99 (pp. 269, 270).
37. Dan Hooley, 'Roman Satire and Epigram: Horace, Juvenal, and Martial', in *The Oxford History of Classical Reception in English Literature*, ed. by David Hopkins and Charles Martindale, 5 vols (Oxford: Oxford University Press, 2012–2019), III, 217–54 (p. 217).
38. John R. Mulder, *The Temple of the Mind: Education and Literary Taste in Seventeenth-Century England* (New York: Pegasus, 1969), p. 25.

NOTES

39. Merry E. Wiesner, *Women and Gender in Early Modern Europe*, 2nd edn (Cambridge: Cambridge University Press, 2000), p. 144.

40. The first edition of the *Spectator* to feature simultaneous translations of mottos appears to have been the thirteenth Tonson duodecimo edition in eight volumes, published in 1744.

41. For a sample of the original advertising see *Public Advertiser*, 4: 6059 (1 April 1754); for the later, revised advertisement see *Public Advertiser*, 6273 (10 December 1754).

42. Linda Bree, *Sarah Fielding* (New York: Twayne Publishers, 1996), p. 99.

43. Bree, *Sarah Fielding*, p. 99.

44. Adam Smyth, *Autobiography in Early Modern England* (Cambridge: Cambridge University Press, 2010), pp. 4–5, 125.

45. Lucia Dacome, 'Noting the Mind: Commonplace Books and the Pursuit of the Self in Eighteenth-Century Britain', *Journal of the History of Ideas*, 65: 4 (October 2004), 603–25 (p. 611).

46. John Oldmixon, *A Complete History of Addresses, from their first original under Oliver Cromwell, to this present year 1710*, 2nd edn (London, 1710), p. 114.

47. Jonathan Swift, *A Tale of a Tub and Other Works*, ed. by Marcus Walsh (Cambridge: Cambridge University Press, 2010), pp. 66, 385 n. 38.

48. John Boswell, *A Method of Study: or an useful library*, 2 vols (London: Printed for the Author, 1738–43), I, 236. For biographical details of John Boswell, see Richard Sharp 'Boswell, John (1698–1757)', in *Oxford Dictionary of National Biography* (Oxford: Oxford University Press, 2004) <http://www.oxforddnb.com/view/article/2952> [accessed 6 April 2016].

49. John Mason, *Self-knowledge. A treatise, shewing the nature and benefit of that important science, and the way to attain it* (London: J. Waugh, 1745), p. 131.

50. Dacome, 'Noting the Mind', p. 619.

51. Boswell, *A Method of Study*, p. 236.

52. Stephen Jarrod Bernard, 'Edward Bysshe and *The Art of English Poetry*: Reading Writing in the Eighteenth Century', *Eighteenth-Century Studies*, 46: 1 (Fall 2012), 113–29 (pp. 117, 114).

53. Edward Bysshe, *The Art of English Poetry* (London: Robert Knaplock, Edward Castle, Benjamin Tooke, 1702), preface.

54. Elizabeth Knowles, *And I Quote . . . A History of Using Other People's Words* (Oxford: Oxford University Press, 2018), p. 15.

55. Edward Bysshe, *The British Parnassus: Or, A Compleat Common-Place-Book of English Poetry*, 2 vols (London: J. Nutt, 1714), I, title page and preface.

56. Anna Maria Mackenzie, 'To the Readers of Modern Romance', *Mysteries Elucidated, A Novel*, 3 vols (London: William Lane, 1795), I, i–xvi (pp. iii–iv).

CHAPTER 2

1. Ann Radcliffe, *The Italian*, ed. by Frederick Garber, rev. by Nick Groom (Oxford: Oxford University Press, 2017), p. 308. All references will be to this edition of the text. For Shakespeare's original, see William Shakespeare, *The Tragedy of King Richard III*, ed. by John Jowett (Oxford: Oxford University Press, 2008), p. 343, V.iv.159–61.

2. Heather McPherson, 'Theatrical Celebrity and the Commodification of the Actor', in *The Oxford Handbook of the Georgian Theatre 1737–1832*, ed. by Julia Swindells and David Francis Taylor (Oxford: Oxford University Press, 2014), pp. 192–212 (pp. 206–07).

3. Edward Jacobs, 'Ann Radcliffe and Romantic Print Culture', in *Ann Radcliffe, Romanticism, and the Gothic*, ed. by Dale Townshend and Angela Wright (Cambridge: Cambridge University Press, 2014), pp. 49–66 (p. 63); see also John Claiborne Isbell, 'Romantic Novel and Verse Romance, 1750–1850: Is There a Romance Continuum?', in *Romantic Prose Fiction*, ed. by Gerald Gillespie, Manfred Engel, and Bernard Dieterle (Amsterdam: John Benjamins, 2008), pp. 496–516 (p. 502).

4. Stuart Curran, 'Charlotte Smith: Intertextualities', in *Charlotte Smith in British Romanticism*, ed. by Jacqueline M. Labbe (London: Pickering & Chatto, 2008), pp. 175–88 (p. 176).

5. Helme's novel is included in the count of 21 here, but excluded from the Appendix survey (which focuses exclusively on first editions) because Helme's epigraphs were only added in the fourth edition. For a year-by-year statistical analysis, see Appendix, Table 1 and Figure 1, and the 'Chronology of Novels with Pre-chapter Epigraphs', available at https://edinburghuniversitypress.com/book-epigraphs-in-the-english-novel-1750-1850.html.

6. The figure of 1158 titles was derived from two sources: 795 novels were identified as first-published during the period 1770–90 in Peter Garside, James Raven, and Rainer Schöwerling (gen. eds), *The English Novel 1770–1829: A Bibliographical Survey of Prose Fiction Published in the British Isles*, 2 vols (Oxford: Oxford University Press, 2000), of which 660 (or 83%) were checked; the remaining 363 titles were drawn from Andrew Block, *The English Novel, 1740–1850: A Catalogue Including Prose Romances, Short Stories, and Translations of Foreign Fiction*, with Introductions by John Crow and Ernest A. Baker, new and rev. edn (London: Dawson, 1961), and of these 325 (89%) have been checked. Combined, this equates to 85% of titles checked.

7. Elizabeth Helme, *Louisa; or, The Cottage on the Moor, The fourth edition, corrected*, 2 vols (London: G. Kearsley, 1787); [Anon.], *The Adventures of a Watch!* (London: G. Kearsley, 1788); [Anon.], *The Amicable Quixote; or, the enthusiasm of friendship*, 4 vols (London: J. Walter, 1788); Henry Clarke, *The School Candidates, A Prosaic Burlesque: Occasioned by the Late Election of a Schoolmaster. At the Village of Boudinnoir* (Manchester, 1788); Anna Maria Mackenzie, *Retribution: A Novel*, 3 vols (London: Printed for G. G. J. and J. Robinson, Pater-Noster Row, 1788); Anna Maria Mackenzie, *Calista, a Novel*, 2 vols (London: William Lane, 1789); John Moore, *Zeluco. Various Views of Human Nature, Taken from Life and Manners, Foreign and Domestic*, 2 vols (London: A. Strahan and T. Cadell, 1789); [Anon.], *Lucretia; or, Virtue the Best Dowry*, 2 vols (London: Printed by L. Wayland, for T. Vernor, 1790); Rossetta Ballin, *The Statue Room: An Historical Tale*, 2 vols (London: H. D. Symonds, 1790); Jane Timbury, *The Philanthropic Rambler* (London: Printed for and sold by the Author, sold also by J. Southern and W. Nicoll, 1790); Jean Claude Gorjy, *Victorina, A Novel. Translated from the French* (London: Lane, Minerva, 1790).

NOTES

8. See, for example, Review of 'The Adventures of a Watch', The Critical Review, or Annals of Literature, 65 (June 1788), 569: 'All has been told before, in a better manner; and the reflections are trite, and tediously expanded'; also 'Art. 14. The Statue Room; an Historical Tale', English Review, or, An abstract of English and foreign literature, 16 (December 1790), 466: 'We have read through this miserable compilation [. . .] without being able to guess at the intention of the writer, except it might be to excruciate his readers.'

9. Garside, Raven, and Schöwerling (gen. eds), The English Novel 1770–1829, I, 40.

10. The other two novels are [Anon.], Persiana, The Nymph of the Sea. A Novel, 3 vols (London: William Lane, 1791) and Jane Timbury, A Sequel to the Philanthropic Rambler (London: Printed for the Author; and sold by G. G. J. and J. Robinson, R. Faulder, and J. Southern, 1791).

11. Helme, Louisa, I, title page and p. vi.

12. This numerical survey was conducted using the bibliography contained in Garside, Raven, and Schöwerling (gen. eds), The English Novel 1770–1829, I, 390–415. Where possible, first editions of novels published in 1787 have been consulted.

13. Review of 'Observations on the Land Revenue of the Crown', European Magazine and London Review, 12 (August 1787), 121–25 (p. 125).

14. Kim Ian Michasiw, 'Ann Radcliffe and the Terrors of Power', Eighteenth-Century Fiction, 6: 4 (July 1994), 327–46 (p. 344).

15. See, for example, Anne Williams, Art of Darkness: A Poetics of Gothic (Chicago: University of Chicago Press, 1995), p. 16; Coral Ann Howells, 'The Pleasure of the Woman's Text: Ann Radcliffe's Subtle Transgressions in The Mysteries of Udolpho and The Italian', in Gothic Fictions: Prohibition/Transgression, ed. by Kenneth W. Graham (New York: AMS, 1989), pp. 151–62 (p. 158).

16. David Punter, The Literature of Terror: A History of Gothic Fictions from 1765 to the Present Day, 2nd edn (London: Routledge, 2013), pp. 55–56.

17. Ann Radcliffe, The Romance of the Forest, ed. by Chloe Chard (Oxford: Oxford University Press, 2009), title page; Ann Radcliffe, The Mysteries of Udolpho, ed. by Bonamy Dobrée (Oxford: Oxford University Press, 1998), title page. All further quotations will be from these editions of the text unless stated otherwise. For instances where the phrase has been interpreted in this way, see Beatrice Battaglia, 'The "Pieces of Poetry" in Ann Radcliffe's The Mysteries of Udolpho', in Romantic Women Poets, ed. by Lilla Maria Crisafulli and Cecilia Pietropoli (Amsterdam: Rodopi, 2007), pp. 137–51 (p. 142); Eike Kronshage, 'The Function of Poetic Epigraphs in George Eliot's Daniel Deronda', Connotations, 23: 2 (2013/14), 230–60 (p. 253).

18. Gary Kelly, English Fiction of the Romantic Period 1789–1830 (London: Routledge, 1989), p. 54.

19. E., 'ART. XII. The Romance of the Forest: Interspersed with some Pieces of Poetry', Monthly Review, 8 (May 1792), 82–87 (p. 85).

20. A. Y., 'ART. IV. The Mysteries of Udolpho, a Romance; interspersed with some pieces of Poetry', Analytical Review, 19: 2 (June 1794), 140–45 (p. 144).

21. 'ART. II. The Mysteries of Udolpho, a Romance; Interspersed with some Pieces of Poetry', British Critic, 4 (August 1794), 110–21 (p. 120).

22. Helen Maria Williams, *Julia, a novel; interspersed with some poetical pieces*, 2 vols (London: T. Cadell, 1790), I, title page.
23. Jacobs, 'Ann Radcliffe and Romantic Print Culture', p. 49.
24. Nicholas Rowe, *The Tragedy of Jane Shore. Written in Imitation of Shakespear's Style* (London: Bernard Lintott, 1714), p. 36 (V.i).
25. Radcliffe, *The Romance of the Forest*, p. 173; Thomas Percy, 'Cynthia, An Elegiac Poem', in *A Collection of Poems in six volumes*, 6 vols (London: Printed by J. Hughs, for R. and J. Dodsley, 1758), VI, 234–39 (p. 237).
26. James Thomson, 'Summer', in *The Seasons*, ed. by James Sambrook (Oxford: Oxford University Press, 1981), pp. 58–142 (p. 92, ll. 673–75; p. 96, ll. 773–77). The word 'piney' has been replaced with the term 'spicy' in the Sambrook edition.
27. Isbell, 'Romantic Novel and Verse Romance, 1750–1850', p. 502.
28. JoEllen DeLucia, 'From the Female Gothic to a Feminist Theory of History: Ann Radcliffe and the Scottish Enlightenment', *The Eighteenth Century*, 50: 1 (Spring 2009), 101–15 (p. 101); JoEllen DeLucia, *A Feminine Enlightenment: British Women Writers and the Philosophy of Progress, 1759–1820* (Edinburgh: Edinburgh University Press, 2015), pp. 125–26.
29. Rictor Norton, 'Ann Radcliffe, "The Shakespeare of Romance Writers"', in *Shakespearean Gothic*, ed. by Christy Desmet and Anne Williams (Cardiff: University of Wales Press, 2009), pp. 37–59 (pp. 42, 46).
30. Norton, 'Ann Radcliffe', p. 46.
31. Joanna Kokot, 'Between Harmony and Chaos: Poetry and Music in Ann Radcliffe's *The Mysteries of Udolpho*', in *The Enchantress of Words, Sounds and Image: Anniversary Essays on Ann Radcliffe (1764–1823)*, ed. by Jakub Lipski and Jacek Mydla (Palo Alto, CA: Academica Press, 2015), pp. 53–70 (p. 67); Leah Price, *The Anthology and the Rise of the Novel: From Richardson to George Eliot* (Cambridge: Cambridge University Press, 2000, repr. 2004), p. 93.
32. Francesca Saggini, *The Gothic Novel and the Stage: Romantic Appropriations* (Abingdon: Routledge, 2016), p. 106.
33. Kelly, *English Fiction of the Romantic Period 1789–1830*, p. 54.
34. Jacobs, 'Ann Radcliffe and Romantic Print Culture', p. 60.
35. Henry Fielding, *Tom Jones*, ed. by John Bender and Simon Stern, with an Introduction by John Bender (Oxford: Oxford University Press, 2008), p. 36.
36. Ansgar Nunning, 'On Metanarrative: Towards a Definition, a Typology and an Outline of the Functions of Metanarrative Commentary', in *The Dynamics of Narrative Form: Studies in Anglo-American Narratology*, ed. by John Pier (Berlin; New York: Walter de Gruyter, 2005), pp. 11–58 (p. 23).
37. Oliver Goldsmith, *The Vicar of Wakefield*, ed. by Arthur Friedman, with an Introduction and Notes by Robert L. Mack (Oxford: Oxford University Press, 2008), p. 15.
38. Jacobs, 'Ann Radcliffe and Romantic Print Culture', pp. 60–61.
39. Kelly, *English Fiction of the Romantic Period*, p. 55.
40. Adapted quotation, see William Shakespeare, *Macbeth*, ed. by Nicholas Brooke (Oxford: Oxford University Press, 2008), p. 147 (III.i.111–14).

NOTES

41. [Anon.], *Modern characters for 1778. By Shakespear* (London: D. Brown, 1778), p. 33.

42. Kate Rumbold, *Shakespeare and the Eighteenth-Century Novel: Cultures of Quotation from Samuel Richardson to Jane Austen* (Cambridge: Cambridge University Press, 2016), pp. 156, 159.

43. David Durant, 'Ann Radcliffe and the Conservative Gothic', *Studies in English Literature, 1500–1900*, 22: 3 (Summer 1982), 519–30 (pp. 519, 526).

44. Horace Walpole, 'The Mysterious Mother', in *Five Romantic Plays 1768–1821*, ed. by Paul Baines and Edward Burns (Oxford: Oxford University Press, 2000), pp. 1–69 (p. 5, ll. 1–7). Radcliffe alters the line structure here to conceal the removal of the speech's opening hemi-stitch. The original reads:

> What an awful silence! How these antique towers
> And vacant courts chill the suspended soul,
> Till expectation wears the cast of fear;
> And fear, half-ready to become devotion,
> Mumbles a kind of mental orison,
> It knows not wherefore. What a kind of being
> Is circumstance!

45. Francis Quarles, *Emblemes, divine and moral* (London: Printed by G. M. and Sold at John Marriots shop, 1635), p. 169 (III.xii.16–18). All further quotations will be from this edition.

46. 'The General Epistle of James', in *The Bible: Authorized King James Version with Apocrypha*, ed. by Robert Carroll and Stephen Prickett (Oxford: Oxford University Press, 2008), New Testament, pp. 281–85 (p. 281, I.15).

47. Paul Miner, 'Francis Quarles's Influence on Europe 11', *Blake/An Illustrated Quarterly*, 47: 4 (2014) <https://blakequarterly.org/index.php/blake/article/view/miner474> [accessed 9 January 2023].

48. Sharp, 'Letter', *Gentleman's Magazine: and historical chronicle*, 56: 6 (December 1786), 1106.

49. 'ART. VI. Thirty Letters on various Subjects', *English Review, or, An abstract of English and foreign literature*, 2 (July 1783), 40–47 (p. 46).

50. For the original lines, see Thomson, 'Winter', in *The Seasons*, pp. 202–52 (p. 220, ll. 379–81).

51. Shakespeare, *Macbeth*, p. 107 (I.iii.138–39).

52. Thomson, 'Spring', in *The Seasons*, pp. 2–57 (p. 54, l. 1105).

53. For the first quotation, see Shakespeare, *Macbeth*, p. 199 (V.iii.22–23). Nicholas Brooke notes in the Oxford edition that this line was emended to 'May' by George Steevens and Samuel Johnson. However, other editors in the late eighteenth century, such as Edmund Malone, appear to have followed the Folio version of the text in printing 'Way'. For the second quotation, see Thomas Warton, 'Ode VI: The Suicide', in *Poems. A New Edition, With Additions* (London: T. Becket, 1777), pp. 42–47 (p. 43, ll. 25–29).

54. Warton, 'The Suicide', p. 43 (ll. 19–20). The full epigraph extends to line 24 of Warton's poem.

181

55. William Collins, 'Ode to Fear', in *The Poems of Thomas Gray, William Collins, Oliver Goldsmith*, ed. by Roger Lonsdale (London: Longmans, 1969), pp. 418–23 (p. 422, ll. 53–57). The epigraph features minor punctuational differences from the original poem.
56. Rumbold, *Shakespeare and the Eighteenth-Century Novel*, p. 137.
57. Marshall Brown, 'Romanticism and Enlightenment', in *The Cambridge Companion to British Romanticism*, ed. by Stuart Curran (Cambridge: Cambridge University Press, 1993), pp. 25–47 (p. 28).
58. Kenneth P. Winkler, 'Perception and Ideas, Judgement', in *The Cambridge Book of Eighteenth Century Philosophy*, ed. by Knud Haakonssen, 2 vols (Cambridge: Cambridge University Press, 2006), I, 234–85 (p. 259).
59. Robert Miles, *Gothic Writing 1750–1820: A Genealogy* (London: Routledge, 1993), p. 124.
60. John Milton, 'Comus', in *Selected Poems*, ed. by John Leonard (London: Penguin Books, 2007), pp. 32–61 (ll. 470–72).
61. Kristin M. Girten, '"Sublime Luxuries" of the Gothic Edifice: Immersive Aesthetics and Kantian Freedom in the Novels of Ann Radcliffe', *Eighteenth-Century Fiction*, 28: 4 (Summer 2016), 713–38 (p. 729).
62. Coral Ann Howells, *Love, Mystery and Misery: Feeling in Gothic Fiction* (London: Bloomsbury, 2013), p. 32.
63. Girten, '"Sublime Luxuries" of the Gothic Edifice', pp. 725, 726.
64. Andrew Smith, 'Radcliffe's Aesthetics: Or, the Problem with Burke and Lewis', *Women's Writing*, 22: 3 (2015), 317–30 (p. 317).
65. John Milton, *Paradise Lost*, ed. by Stephen Orgel and Jonathan Goldberg (Oxford: Oxford University Press, 2004), p. 23 (I.594–96); quoted in Edmund Burke, *A Philosophical Enquiry into the Sublime and Beautiful*, ed. by Paul Guyer (Oxford: Oxford University Press, 2015), p. 51.
66. Burke, *A Philosophical Enquiry*, p. 51.
67. Burke, *A Philosophical Enquiry*, p. 137.
68. Smith, 'Radcliffe's Aesthetics', p. 320.
69. Williams, *Art of Darkness*, p. 73.
70. Immanuel Kant, *The Critique of Judgement*, trans. James Meredith, rev. by Nicholas Walker (Oxford: Oxford University Press, 2008), p. 81.
71. Terrence Des Pres, 'Terror and the Sublime', *Human Rights Quarterly*, 5: 2 (May 1983), 135–46 (p. 141).
72. William Shakespeare, *Measure for Measure*, ed. by N. W. Bawcutt (Oxford: Oxford University Press, 2008), pp. 208–09 (V.i.116–19); Radcliffe appears to have introduced a misquotation as she gives 'in ripen'd time' rather than 'with ripened time'.
73. Girten, '"Sublime Luxuries" of the Gothic Edifice', p. 737.
74. Vartan P. Messier, 'The Conservative, the Transgressive, and the Reactionary: Ann Radcliffe's *The Italian* as a Response to Matthew Lewis' *The Monk*', *Atenea*, 25: 2 (2005), 37–48 (p. 46).
75. Markman Ellis, *The History of Gothic Fiction* (Edinburgh: Edinburgh University Press, 2005), p. 52.
76. William Shakespeare, *Julius Caesar*, ed. by Arthur Humphrys (Oxford: Oxford University Press, 2008), p. 148 (II.ii.14–16).

NOTES

77. Joseph Crawford, '"Every Night, The Same Routine": Recurring Nightmares and the Repetition Compulsion in Gothic Fiction', *Moveable Type*, 6 (2010), p. 8.

78. Rictor Norton, *Mistress of Udolpho: The Life of Ann Radcliffe* (London: Leicester University Press, 1998), p. 193; see also Frances Chiu, 'Introduction', in Ann Radcliffe, *Gaston de Blondeville*, ed. by Frances Chiu (Chicago: Valancourt Books, 2006), p. vii.

79. Jacobs, 'Ann Radcliffe and Romantic Print Culture', p. 58.

80. Syndy M. Conger, 'Sensibility Restored: Radcliffe's Answer to Lewis' *The Monk*', in *Gothic Fictions*, ed. Graham, pp. 113–49 (p. 113).

81. Smith, 'Radcliffe's Aesthetics', p. 327.

82. Norton, *Mistress of Udolpho*, p. 3.

83. Radcliffe, *The Italian*, p. 409 n. 3; see also Rebecca Ehlerd, 'S. Maria Del Pianto: Loss, Remembrance and Legacy in Seventeenth Century Naples', PhD thesis, Queen's University Kingston, Ontario, Canada (2007), p. 53.

84. Henry Swinburne, *Travels in the Two Sicilies. In the years 1777, 1778, 1779, and 1780*, 2 vols (London: P. Elmsly, 1783–85), I, 94–95.

85. Diego Saglia, 'Looking at the Other: Cultural Difference and the Traveller's Gaze in *The Italian*', *Studies in the Novel*, 28: 1 (Spring 1996), 12–37 (p. 15).

86. Walpole, 'The Mysterious Mother', p. 9 (I.i.161–62).

87. Paul Baines and Edward Burns, 'Introduction', in *Five Romantic Plays 1768–1821*, ed. by Baines and Burns, p. xiii.

88. Miles, *Gothic Writing 1750–1820*, p. 171.

89. Caroline Gonda, *Reading Daughters' Fictions 1709–1834: Novels and Society from Manley to Edgeworth* (Cambridge: Cambridge University Press, 1996), p. 149.

90. David Salter, '"This demon in the garb of a monk": Shakespeare, the Gothic and the Discourse of Anti-Catholicism', *Shakespeare*, 5: 1 (April 2009), 52–67 (p. 55).

91. William Shakespeare, *Romeo and Juliet*, ed. by Jill L. Levenson (Oxford: Oxford University Press, 2008), p. 314 (IV.iii.23–24).

92. Salter, '"This demon in the garb of a monk"', p. 55.

93. William Shakespeare, *Hamlet*, ed. by G. R. Hibbard (Oxford: Oxford University Press, 2008), p. 145 (I.i.39).

94. Shakespeare, *Macbeth*, p. 121 (I.vii.80–81).

95. Andrew Warren, 'Designing and Undrawing Veils: Anxiety and Authorship in Radcliffe's *The Italian*', *The Eighteenth Century*, 54: 4 (2013), 521–44 (pp. 523, 528).

96. 'ART. VI. *Gaston de Blondeville*', *Monthly Review*, 2: 8 (July 1826), 280–93 (p. 291).

97. Punter, *Literature of Terror*, p. 55

98. 'Novelists', *Supplement to La Belle Assemblée*, new series, 3 (July 1826), 303–07 (p. 303); 'ART. VI. *Gaston de Blondeville*', p. 281.

99. Cheryl Nixon, 'Ann Radcliffe's Commonplace Book: Assembling the Female Body and the Material Text', *Women's Writing*, 22: 3 (2015), 355–75 (p. 357).

100. Boston Public Library, MS Ch.K.1.10, Ann Radcliffe's Commonplace Book; for the original source, see Walter Scott, 'Life of John Dryden', in *The Works of John Dryden*, ed. by Walter Scott, 18 vols (London: William Miller; Edinburgh: James Ballantyne, 1808), I, 315.

101. Nixon, 'Ann Radcliffe's Commonplace Book', p. 358.

CHAPTER 3

1. [Anon.], *Argentum: or, Adventures of a Shilling* (London: Printed by J. Nichols and sold by J. Pridden, 1794); the translation, which does not appear in the original, is taken from Horace, 'Satires', in *Satires. Epistles. The Art of Poetry*, trans. by H. Rushton Fairclough (Cambridge, MA: Harvard University Press, 1929), pp. 1–245 (pp. 12–21, I.x.71).
2. *Argentum*, pp. 89–90.
3. See Appendix, Table 1 and Figures 1 and 2. Since these figures are intended only as a general guide rather than a definitive survey, all percentages have been rounded to the nearest 0.5%.
4. [Anon.], *Arville Castle. An Historical Romance*, 2 vols (London: B. Crosby, and T. White, 1795); Anna Maria Mackenzie, *Mysteries Elucidated, A Novel*, 3 vols (London: William Lane, 1795); Francis Lathom, *The Castle of Ollada. A Romance*, 2 vols (London: William Lane, 1795). For an example of inclusion of these texts in a bibliography of typically Gothic fiction, see Margarita Georgieva, *The Gothic Child* (Basingstoke: Palgrave Macmillan, 2013), pp. 202–06. The novels by Mackenzie and Lathom are both also referred to in Rictor Norton (ed.), *Gothic Readings: The First Wave, 1764–1840* (London: Leicester University Press, 2006), pp. 27, 129.
5. [Anon.], *The Amicable Quixote; or, the enthusiasm of friendship*, 4 vols (London: J. Walter, 1788).
6. See, for example, Margaret Mitchell, *Tales of Instruction and Amusement. Written for the Use of Young Persons*, 2 vols (London: E. Newbery, 1795), I, 9. This title is not one of the 7 novels of 1795 published with epigraphs referred to above, since it was listed in the appendices of Peter Garside, James Raven, and Rainer Schöwerling (gen. eds), *The English Novel 1770–1829: A Bibliographical Survey of Prose Fiction Published in the British Isles*, 2 vols (Oxford: Oxford University Press, 2000) (I, 812–13), which were not included in the statistical investigation.
7. Examples of the same motto adorning the title pages of each volume in a multi-volume novel are not difficult to come by, and include works such as Tobias Smollett, *The Adventures of Peregrine Pickle*, 4 vols (London: Printed for the Author, 1751); [Anon.], *The Histories of Some of the Penitents in the Magdalen House*, 2 vols (London: John Rivington and J. Dodsley, 1760); Oliver Goldsmith, *The Vicar of Wakefield: A Tale*, 2 vols (Salisbury: Printed by B. Collins, for F. Newbury, 1766); Eliza Parsons, *Errors of Education*, 3 vols (London: William Lane, 1791); as well as Radcliffe's *The Romance of the Forest* and *Udolpho*.
8. Judith Phillips Stanton, 'Introduction', in Charlotte Smith, *The Collected Letters of Charlotte Smith*, ed. by Judith Phillips Stanton (Bloomington: Indiana University Press, 2003), pp. xiii–xxxii (p. xv).
9. Smith to Thomas Cadell, Sr, 16 December 1793, in *The Collected Letters of Charlotte Smith*, p. 89.
10. Smith to Joseph Cooper Walker, [9 October 1793], in *The Collected Letters of Charlotte Smith*, p. 79.
11. Charlotte Smith, *The Banished Man*, in *The Works of Charlotte Smith*, gen. ed. Stuart Curran, 14 vols (London: Pickering & Chatto, 2005–07), VII, 195.

NOTES

12. Jillian Heydt-Stevenson and Charlotte Sussman, '"Launched upon the Sea of Moral and Political Inquiry": The Ethical Experiments of the Romantic Novel', in *Recognizing the Romantic Novel: New Histories of British Fiction, 1780–1830*, ed. by Jillian Heydt-Stevenson and Charlotte Sussman (Liverpool: Liverpool University Press, 2010), pp. 13–48 (p. 26).

13. Stuart Curran, 'Charlotte Smith: Intertextualities', in *Charlotte Smith in British Romanticism*, ed. by Jacqueline M. Labbe (London: Pickering & Chatto, 2008), pp. 175–88 (p. 177); Matthew Prior, 'Henry and Emma, A Poem, Upon the Model of The Nut-brown Maid', in *Poems on Several Occasions* (London, 1709), pp. 232–71 (p. 246).

14. Antje Blank, 'Things as They Were: The Gothic of Real Life in Charlotte Smith's *The Emigrants* and *The Banished Man*', *Women's Writing*, 16: 1 (May 2009), 78–93 (p. 87).

15. Heydt-Stevenson and Sussman, '"Launched upon the Sea of Moral and Political Inquiry"', p. 28.

16. A. A. Markley, 'Banished Men and the "New Order of Things": The French Émigré and the Complexities of Revolutionary Politics in Charlotte Smith and Mary Robinson', *Women's Writing*, 19: 4 (November 2012), 387–403 (p. 391).

17. Dani Napton and Stephanie Russo, 'Place in Charlotte Smith's *The Banished Man* and Walter Scott's *Woodstock*', *Studies in English Literature*, 52: 4 (Autumn 2012), 747–63 (p. 749). See also Blank, 'Things as They Were', p. 86; Markley, 'Banished Men and the "New Order of Things"', p. 390; Stephanie Russo, '"A people driven by terror": Charlotte Smith, *The Banished Man* and the Politics of Counter-Revolution', in *The French Revolution and the British Novel in the Romantic Period*, ed. by A. D. Cousins, Dani Napton, and Stephanie Russo (New York: Lang, 2011), pp. 37–54 (p. 39).

18. Napton and Russo, 'Place in Charlotte Smith's *The Banished Man* and Walter Scott's *Woodstock*', p. 754.

19. Napton and Russo, 'Place in Charlotte Smith's *The Banished Man* and Walter Scott's *Woodstock*', p. 750.

20. Blank, 'Things as They Were', p. 80; Stanton, 'Introduction', in *The Collected Letters of Charlotte Smith*, p. xxxi.

21. Melissa Sodeman, 'Charlotte Smith's Literary Exile', *English Literary History*, 76 (2009), 131–52 (p. 147).

22. Smith to James Upton Tripp, [4 May 1794], in *The Collected Letters of Charlotte Smith*, p. 115.

23. See Smith to Joseph Cooper Walker, [9 October 1793], in *The Collected Letters of Charlotte Smith*, p. 79.

24. *The Amicable Quixote*, II, 185.

25. *The Amicable Quixote*, II, 185.

26. Russo, '"A people driven by terror"', p. 40.

27. Loraine Fletcher, *Charlotte Smith: A Critical Biography* (Basingstoke: Macmillan, 1998), p. 216.

28. Smith to Joseph Cooper Walker, 20 February 1793, in *Collected Letters of Charlotte Smith*, p. 62.

EPIGRAPHS IN THE ENGLISH NOVEL 1750–1850

29. Sodeman, 'Charlotte Smith's Literary Exile', pp. 133, 145.
30. In the first edition of the text this was volume 4 chapter 2.
31. Sodeman, 'Charlotte Smith's Literary Exile', p. 144.
32. Smith to Thomas Cadell, Jr, 29 August 1794, in *Collected Letters of Charlotte Smith*, p. 149.
33. William Shakespeare, *Henry V*, ed. by Gary Taylor (Oxford: Oxford University Press, 2008), p. 267 (V.ii.41–46).
34. The translation is from the notes by Matthew Grenby in the *Complete Works* edition of the text, and was not included in the novel printed by Cadell and Davies. See Smith, *The Banished Man*, p. 487 n. 30.
35. Matthew Prior, 'Solomon: a Poem in Three Books', in *Poems on Several Occasions* (London: J. Tonson and J. Barber, 1725), pp. 147–250 (p. 249). All the pronouns have been altered here, since the original reads 'On either Side our thoughts incessant turn: / Forward We dread; and looking back We mourn.'
36. This translation almost exactly matches that given for the quotation prefacing number 67 of the *Rambler* in the accompanying 'Version of the Mottos' or 'Mottos and Quotations in the Second Volume Translated'; the English text is credited to Johnson, and replaced a shorter Greek epigram used in the first edition. See Samuel Johnson, *The Rambler*, 8 vols (Edinburgh: W. Gordon et al., 1750–52), III, 113; Samuel Johnson, *The Rambler*, 2nd edn, 8 vols (Edinburgh: W. Gordon et al., 1751–52); Samuel Johnson, *The Rambler*, 6 vols (London: J. Payne, 1752), II, n.p.; Samuel Johnson, *The Works of Samuel Johnson*, ed. by O. M. Brack, Jr. and Robert DeMaria, Jr., 23 vols (New Haven, CT; London: Yale University Press, 1958–2019), III, 353.
37. The attribution is given here as it was in later editions, despite being incorrect. The original may be found in Alexander Pope, *The Iliad of Homer Books X–XXIV*, in *The Poems of Alexander Pope*, gen. ed. John Butt, 11 vols (London: Methuen, 1967), VIII, 456 (ll. 84–86).
38. John Milton, *Paradise Lost*, ed. by Stephen Orgel and Jonathan Goldberg (Oxford: Oxford University Press, 2004), p. 254 (X.469–71, 474–76).
39. William Shakespeare, *Macbeth*, ed. by Nicholas Brooke (Oxford: Oxford University Press, 2008), p. 149 (III.ii.26–29).
40. Curran, 'Charlotte Smith: Intertextualities', p. 177.
41. Fletcher, *Charlotte Smith*, p. 244.
42. Smith, *Marchmont*, in *The Works of Charlotte Smith*, IX, 4.
43. Smith, *Marchmont*, p. 181.
44. Examples of this include: [Anon.], *Arville Castle. An Historical Romance*; Lathom, *The Castle of Ollada. A Romance*; Sarah Lansdell, *Manfredi, Baron St. Osmund. An Old English Romance*, 2 vols (London: William Lane, 1796); John Palmer, *The Mystery of the Black Tower, A Romance*, 2 vols (London: Printed for the Author, by William Lane, 1796); Joseph Fox, *Santa-Maria; or, the Mysterious Pregnancy. A Romance*, 3 vols (London: G. Kearsley, 1797); Agnes Musgrave, *Edmund of the Forest. An Historical Novel*, 4 vols (London: William Lane, 1797).
45. Smith to Thomas Cadell, Jr, and William Davies, 15 September 1794, in *Collected Letters of Charlotte Smith*, p. 160.
46. For discussion of Smith as Charlotte Denzil, see Fletcher, *Charlotte Smith*, p. 219.

186

NOTES

47. See Stanton, 'Introduction', in *The Collected Letters of Charlotte Smith*, pp. xlii–xliii.
48. Smith to Thomas Cadell, Jr, [5 September 1794], in *The Collected Letters of Charlotte Smith*, p. 151.
49. Charlotte Smith, *The Young Philosopher*, in *The Works of Charlotte Smith*, X, 140; the lines originate in Erasmus Darwin, *The Botanic Garden; A Poem In Two Parts* (London: J. Johnson, 1791), p. 122 (II.iii.399–404).
50. Matthew Lewis, *The Monk*, ed. by Howard Anderson, rev. with an Introduction and Notes by Nick Groom (Oxford: Oxford University Press, 2016), p. 7; original quotation from William Shakespeare, *Measure for Measure*, ed. by N. W. Bawcutt (Oxford: Oxford University Press, 2008), p. 108 (I.iii.50–53).
51. Coral Ann Howells, *Love, Mystery and Misery: Feeling in Gothic Fiction* (London: Bloomsbury, 2013), p. 18.
52. Robert Blair, 'from *The Grave*', in *The New Oxford Book of Eighteenth-Century Verse*, ed. by Roger Lonsdale (Oxford: Oxford University Press, 2009), pp. 368–69 (ll. 11–20).
53. See Shakespeare, *Macbeth*, p. 158 (III.iv.93–96, 106–07).
54. Kate Rumbold, *Shakespeare and the Eighteenth-Century Novel: Cultures of Quotation from Samuel Richardson to Jane Austen* (Cambridge: Cambridge University Press, 2016), p. 147.
55. Matthew Lewis to Frances Maria Lewis, 18 May 1794, in *The Life and Correspondence of M. G. Lewis*, 2 vols (London: Henry Colburn, 1839), I, 123.
56. David Lorne Macdonald, *Monk Lewis: A Critical Biography* (Toronto: University of Toronto Press, 2000), p. 110.
57. Review of 'The Monk: a Romance. By M. G. Lewis, Esq.', *The Critical Review, or Annals of Literature*, 19 (February 1797), 194–200 (p. 197).
58. Gary Kelly, *English Fiction of the Romantic Period 1789–1830* (London: Routledge, 1989), p. 54.
59. John Claiborne Isbell, 'Romantic Novel and Verse Romance, 1750–1850: Is There a Romance Continuum?', in *Romantic Prose Fiction*, ed. by Gerald Gillespie, Manfred Engel, and Bernard Dieterle (Amsterdam: John Benjamins, 2008), pp. 496–516 (p. 502).
60. Jessamyn Jackson, 'Why Novels Make Bad Mothers', *NOVEL: A Forum on Fiction*, 27: 2 (Winter 1994), 161–74 (p. 161).
61. Gary Kelly, 'Unbecoming a Heroine: Novel Reading, Romanticism, and Barrett's *The Heroine*', *Nineteenth-Century Literature*, 45: 2 (September 1990), 220–41 (p. 239).
62. William Shakespeare, *As You Like It*, ed. by Alan Brissenden (Oxford: Oxford University Press, 2008), p. 152 (II.vii.175); the original line gives 'winter' instead of 'wintry'. See also Thomas Moore, 'A Canadian Boat Song', in *Epistles, Odes, and Other Poems* (London: James Carpenter, 1806), pp. 305–07 (p. 307), where the quotation appears twice.
63. See, for example, *The Amicable Quixote* (1788); and Richard Sicklemore, *Rashleigh Abbey; or, The Ruin on the Rock. A Romance*, 3 vols (London: Lane, Newman, and Co., 1805).
64. There are numerous occurrences of these phrases in the works of each poet, rendering it impossible to identify the precise instances referenced here.

EPIGRAPHS IN THE ENGLISH NOVEL 1750–1850

65. Richard Brinsley Sheridan, 'The Duenna', in *The School for Scandal and other plays*, ed. by Michael Cordner (Oxford: Oxford University Press, 1998), pp. 87–143 (p. 113, II.ii.177–79).

66. Kelly, 'Unbecoming a Heroine', p. 228.

67. Katherine Sobba Green, 'The Heroine's Blazon and Hardwicke's Marriage Act: Commodification for a Novel Market', *Tulsa Studies in Women's Literature*, 9: 2 (Autumn 1990), 273–90 (p. 282).

68. Jane Austen to Cassandra Austen, 2 March 1814, in *Jane Austen's Letters*, ed. by Deirdre Le Faye, 3rd edn (Oxford: Oxford University Press, 1995), p. 256.

69. Jane Austen, *Northanger Abbey*, ed. by James Kinsley and John Davie, with an Introduction and Notes by Claudia L. Johnson (Oxford: Oxford University Press, 2003), p. 7.

70. Leah Price, *The Anthology and the Rise of the Novel: From Richardson to George Eliot* (Cambridge: Cambridge University Press, 2000, repr. 2004), p. 91.

71. Rachel Sagner Buurma, 'Epigraphs', in Dennis Duncan and Adam Smyth (eds), *Book Parts* (Oxford: Oxford University Press, 2019), pp. 165–75 (p. 172).

72. Bharat Tandon, 'The Literary Context', in *The Cambridge Companion to 'Emma'*, ed. by Peter Sabor (Cambridge: Cambridge University Press, 2015), pp. 17–35 (p. 31).

Chapter 4

1. Christian Isobel Johnstone, *Clan-Albin: A National Tale*, 4 vols (Edinburgh: Macredie, Skelly, and Muckersy; London: Longman and others, 1815), I, 52. The lines are from Walter Scott, 'Glenfinlas; or Lord Ronald's Coronach', first published in Matthew Lewis (ed.), *Tales of Wonder*, 2 vols (London: W. Bulmer, 1801), I, 122–36 (p. 136).

2. Scott, 'Glenfinlas', p. 131.

3. Claire Lamont, 'William Collins's "Ode on the Popular Superstitions of the Highlands of Scotland" – A Newly Recovered Manuscript', *The Review of English Studies*, 19: 74 (May 1968), 137–47 (p. 137). The first printed version of 'Glenfinlas' in Lewis's *Tales of Wonder* mistakenly states that the lines are 'ORIGINAL. – WALTER SCOTT'.

4. Scott, 'Glenfinlas', p. 131; although the poem was republished several times before 1815, the only alteration in the phrase was the inclusion of an apostrophe after 'rie', i.e. 'O hone a rie'!' See, for example, Walter Scott, *Minstrelsy of the Scottish Border: Consisting of Historical and Romantic Ballads*, 5th edn, 3 vols (Edinburgh: James Ballantyne and Co., 1812), II, 309–26 (pp. 322–23).

5. These percentages have been calculated as a proportion of novels surveyed rather than total number of novels known to have been first-published; though there is necessarily some variation between the two figures, the attempt to make the survey as extensive as possible means that this variation is typically small (see Appendix, Table 1 and Figures 1 and 2).

6. Walter Scott, 'Prefatory Memoir To Mrs Ann Radcliffe', in *The Novels of Ann Radcliffe* (London: Hurst, Robinson, and Co.; Edinburgh: James Ballantyne, 1824), pp. i–xxxix (p. iv).

7. Walter Scott, *Waverley*, in *Edinburgh Edition of the Waverley Novels*, gen. ed. David Hewitt, 30 vols (Edinburgh: Edinburgh University Press, 1993–2012), I, 3–4. All quotations will be from this edition of the text, unless stated otherwise.

188

NOTES

8. Isaac D'Israeli, *Flim-Flams! Or, the Life and Errors of My Uncle, and the Amours of my Aunt! With Illustrations and Obscurities, by Messieurs Tag, Rag, and Bobtail. With an Illuminating Index!*, 3 vols (London: John Murray, 1805), I, xvii.

9. Anthony Frederick Holstein [pseud.], *The Assassin of St. Glenroy; or, The Axis of Life. A Novel*, 4 vols (London: A. K. Newman and Co., 1810).

10. Henry Kett, *Emily, A Moral Tale, Including Letters from a Father to his Daughter, Upon the Most Important Subjects*, 2 vols (London: Messrs. Rivingtons and others, 1809/11).

11. [Anon.], *The Citizen's Daughter; or What Might Be* (London: Printed by N. Biggs for Vernor and Hood, 1804).

12. Rainier Grutman, 'How to Do Things with Mottoes: Recipes from the Romantic Era (with Special Reference to Stendhal)', *Neohelicon*, 37: 1 (June 2010), 139–53 (p. 141).

13. John Davis, *The Post-Captain; or, The Wooden Walls Well Manned; Comprehending a View of Naval Society and Manners* (London: Thomas Tegg, 1806); Sarah Green, *The Private History of the Court of England*, 2 vols (London: Printed for the Author, and sold by B. Crosby, 1808).

14. Robert Charles Dallas, *The Knights: Tales Illustrative of the Marvellous*, 3 vols (London: Longman, Hurst, Rees, and Orme, 1808).

15. Additional epigraphs derived from Scott's poetry also occur in Johnstone, *Clan-Albin* at III, 1; and IV, 1, 23, 206. See also [Anon.], *St. Clyde; A Novel*, 3 vols (London: Gale and Fenner, 1816), which features the same Scott quotation upon the title page of each volume as well as numerous epigraphic quotations derived from Scott, occurring in I, 132, 140, 152, 200; and III, 1, 37, 49.

16. Walter Scott, *The Journal of Walter Scott*, ed. by W. E. K. Anderson (Oxford: Clarendon Press, 1972), p. 119.

17. See J. H. Alexander, *Walter Scott's Books: Reading the Waverley Novels* (New York; Abingdon: Routledge, 2017), pp. 83–84.

18. This figure considers compound works such as *Tales of My Landlord* (First Series, 1816) as one complete work, rather than the two narratives (*The Black Dwarf* and *The Tale of Old Mortality*) of which it is comprised. Further references to numbers of Scott's prose works will be similarly calculated, unless explicitly stated otherwise.

19. Alexander, *Walter Scott's Books*, p. 84.

20. Thomas McCrie, Review of '*Tales of My Landlord*; Collected and Arranged by Jedediah Cleishbotham', *Edinburgh Christian Instructor*, 14 (January 1817), 41–73; (February 1817), 100–40 (101); (March 1817), 170–201.

21. McCrie, Review of '*Tales of My Landlord*' (February 1817), p. 101; (January 1817), p. 41.

22. McCrie, Review of '*Tales of My Landlord*' (February 1817), p. 100.

23. Walter Scott to Lady Louisa Stuart, 31 January 1817, in *The Letters of Sir Walter Scott*, ed. by H. J. C. Grierson, 12 vols (London: Constable, 1932–37), IV, 381.

24. Nicholas Mason, *Literary Advertising and the Shaping of British Romanticism* (Baltimore, MD: Johns Hopkins University Press, 2013), p. 133; Walter Scott, 'Art. VIII. Tales of My Landlord', *The Quarterly Review*, January 1817, 430–80 (p. 480).

25. McCrie, Review of '*Tales of My Landlord*' (January 1817), p. 41.
26. McCrie, Review of '*Tales of My Landlord*' (February 1817), p. 100.
27. McCrie, Review of '*Tales of My Landlord*' (February 1817), p. 100.
28. Scott to Miss Clephane, [October 1810], in *The Letters of Sir Walter Scott*, II, 379.
29. Scott to His Grace the Duke of Buccleuch, [January 1816], in *The Letters of Sir Walter Scott*, IV, 160–61.
30. Scott to D. Terry, 31 July 1822, in *The Letters of Sir Walter Scott*, VII, 214–15.
31. Scott to John Richardson, [9 February 1819], in *The Letters of Sir Walter Scott*, V, 305.
32. See, for example, the description of the shield of Ivanhoe's antithesis Brian de Bois-Guilbert, which 'bore a raven in full flight, holding in its claws a skull, and bearing the motto, *Gare le Corbeau*'; Walter Scott, *Ivanhoe*, in *Edinburgh Edition of the Waverley Novels*, gen. ed. Hewitt, VIII, 83.
33. *Ivanhoe*, p. 244.
34. A pun upon the motto of the Scottish Clan Hay, meaning 'Keep the yoke'; see Scott to Charles Kirkpatrick Sharpe, 9 July [1824], in *The Letters of Sir Walter Scott*, VIII, 324.
35. Scott to Lady Compton, [c. 21 December 1824], in *The Letters of Sir Walter Scott*, VIII, 463. Roughly translated this means 'better a kind stranger than a strange kinsman'; see 'kind, *n., adj., v., adv.*' and 'fremd, *adj. n., v.*', in *Dictionary of the Scots Language* (*Dictionar o the Scots Leid*) (Scottish Language Dictionaries, 2004) <http://www.dsl.ac.uk/entry/snd/kind> [accessed 26 August 2018].
36. For examples of this see Walter Scott, 'Introduction', in *Chronicles of the Canongate*, in *Edinburgh Edition of the Waverley Novels*, gen. ed. Hewitt, XX, 9; Walter Scott, *Rob Roy*, in *Edinburgh Edition of the Waverley Novels*, gen. ed. Hewitt, V, 3.
37. Ballantyne's note on the proofs, quoted in Alexander, *Walter Scott's Books*, p. 86.
38. Alexander, *Walter Scott's Books*, p. 86.
39. These figures have been compiled from first editions of Scott's novels, with attributions cross-checked against the *Edinburgh Edition of the Waverley Novels*, gen. ed. Hewitt.
40. 'Art I. 1. Ivanhoe.', *Edinburgh Review*, 33: 65 (January 1820), 1–54 (p. 54).
41. Tom B. Haber, 'The Chapter-Tags in the Waverley Novels', *PMLA*, 45: 4 (December 1930), 1140–49 (p. 1142).
42. The quotation in question is:

> Never to man shall Catherine give her hand.
> *Taming of a Shrew.*

See Walter Scott, *The Fair Maid of Perth*, in *Edinburgh Edition of the Waverley Novels*, gen. ed. Hewitt, XXI, 53; David Garrick, *The Taming of the Shrew; or, Catherine and Petruchio. A comedy. Altered from Shakespeare* (London: Bathurst and others, 1786), p. 14. In the original line 'Catherine' is written as '*Cath'rine*'.
43. John Gibson Lockhart, *Memoirs of the Life of Sir Walter Scott, Bart*, 7 vols (Edinburgh: Robert Cadell, 1837), IV, 13–14.
44. See Walter Scott, *Guy Mannering*, in *Edinburgh Edition of the Waverley Novels*, gen. ed. Hewitt, II, 91.

NOTES

45. Alexander, *Walter Scott's Books*, p. 94.

46. Walter Scott to Archibald Constable, 23 March 1822, in *The Letters of Sir Walter Scott*, VII, 104.

47. Walter Scott to James Ballantyne, [1814–15], in *The Letters of Sir Walter Scott*, IV, 1–2.

48. John George Cochrane, *Catalogue of the Library at Abbotsford* (Edinburgh: T. Constable, 1838), pp. 41–42.

49. Cochrane, *Catalogue*, p. 190.

50. Walter Scott, *A Legend of the Wars of Montrose*, in *Edinburgh Edition of the Waverley Novels*, gen. ed. Hewitt, VIIb, 144; Walter Scott, *The Abbot*, in *Edinburgh Edition of the Waverley Novels*, gen. ed. Hewitt, X, 5; Walter Scott, *Saint Ronan's Well*, in *Edinburgh Edition of the Waverley Novels*, gen. ed. Hewitt, XVI, 12; Scott, *Chronicles of the Canongate*, p. 13.

51. 'Introduction', in *Chronicles of the Canongate*, pp. 3, 9.

52. Margret Fetzer, 'Beyond Beginning: Walter Scott's (Para)textualisation of Scottishness', *Anglia*, 128 (2010), 273–97 (p. 285).

53. Angela Wright, 'Scottish Gothic', in *The Routledge Companion to Gothic*, ed. by Catherine Spooner and Emma McEvoy (London: Routledge, 2007), pp. 73–82 (p. 77).

54. Wright, 'Scottish Gothic', p. 77.

55. Michael Gamer, '*Waverley* and the Object of (Literary) History', *Modern Language Quarterly*, 70 (2009), 495–525 (p. 502).

56. See Walter Scott, *Waverley*, ed. by Claire Lamont, with an Introduction by Kathryn Sutherland, rev. edn (Oxford: Oxford University Press, 2015), p. 472 n. 363.

57. *The Psalms, hymns, prayers, graces, and dulce domum, used by the scholars of Winchester College. Revised and corrected* (Winchester: Printed for T. Burdon, 1760), pp. 9–11 (ll. 5–9).

58. Helen Maria Williams (trans.), 'Dulce Domum', in *Poems on various subjects: with introductory remarks on the present state of science and literature in France* (London: G. and W. B. Whittaker, 1823), pp. 219–21 (p. 219).

59. Alexander, *Walter Scott's Books*, p. 83.

60. This assessment is based on titles listed in Anne Stevens, *British Historical Fiction before Scott* (Basingstoke: Palgrave Macmillan, 2010), pp. 16–18. Of this list of 85 novels, three have not yet been assessed for chapter-based paratext.

61. Alexander, *Walter Scott's Books*, p. 83.

62. William Shakespeare, *Much Ado About Nothing*, ed. by Sheldon P. Zitner (Oxford: Oxford University Press, 2008), p. 132 (II.iii.66).

63. See Scott, *Waverley*, ed. by Lamont, p. 434 n. 44; Henry Fielding, *Tom Jones*, ed. by John Bender and Simon Stern, with an Introduction by John Bender (Oxford: Oxford University Press, 2008), p. 130.

64. William Shakespeare, *Measure for Measure*, ed. by N. W. Bawcutt (Oxford: Oxford University Press, 2008), p. 126 (II.ii.84).

65. Joan Garden Cooper, 'Scott's Critique of the English Treason Law in *Waverley*', *Scottish Studies Review*, 4: 2 (2003), 17–36 (p. 26).

66. Juliet Feibel, 'Highland Histories: Jacobitism and Second Sight', *CLIO*, 30: 1 (2000), 51–77 (p. 76).

67. Alan Freeman, 'Allegories of Ambivalence: Scottish Fiction, Britain and Empire', in *Readings of the Particular: The Postcolonial in the Postnational*, ed. by Anne Holden Ronning and Lene Johannessen (Amsterdam: Rodopi, 2007), pp. 39–56 (pp. 46–47).

68. Margaret Bruzelius, *Romancing the Novel: Adventure from Scott to Sebald* (Lewisburg, PA: Bucknell University Press, 2007), p. 79; Isabelle Bour, 'Sensibility as Epistemology in *Caleb Williams, Waverley,* and *Frankenstein*', *Studies in English Literature, 1500–1900*, 45 (2005), 813–27 (p. 817).

69. Thomas Campbell, 'Lochiel's Warning', in *The Complete Poetical Works of Thomas Campbell*, ed. by J. Logie Robertson (London: Oxford University Press, 1907), pp. 157–60 (p. 160, ll. 69–70). The original second line reads 'The war-drum is muffled, and black is the bier'.

70. Cathrine Frank, 'Wandering Narratives and Wavering Conclusions: Irreconciliation in Frances Burney's *The Wanderer* and Walter Scott's *Waverley*', *European Romantic Review*, 12 (2001), 429–56 (p. 435).

71. Gamer, '*Waverley* and the Object of (Literary) History', p. 516.

72. Scott to John Ballantyne, 17 October 1814, in *The Letters of Sir Walter Scott*, III, 506.

73. Alexander, *Walter Scott's Books*, p. 83.

74. William Shakespeare, *The Winter's Tale*, ed. by Stephen Orgel (Oxford: Oxford University Press, 2008), p. 159 (IV.i.1–7). The epigraph features minor punctuational differences from the original play.

75. [Anon.], 'The Heir of Linne', in *Reliques of Ancient Poetry*, ed. by Thomas Percy, 3 vols (London: J. Dodsley, 1765), II, 309–18 (pp. 310–11, ll. 29–36).

76. [Anon.], 'Johnie Armstrang', in Walter Scott (ed.), *Minstrelsy of the Scottish Border*, ed. by T. F. Henderson, 4 vols (Edinburgh: Blackwood and Sons, 1902), I, 352–58 (p. 352, stanza 3). Minor alterations to punctuation have been made in the second line.

77. Richard Brinsley Sheridan, 'The Critic', in *The School for Scandal and Other Plays*, ed. by Michael Cordner (Oxford: Oxford University Press, 1998), pp. 289–337 (III.i.53–54, 56–59).

78. Wright, 'Scottish Gothic', p. 78.

79. Robert P. Irvine, 'Enlightenment, Agency and Romance: The Case of Scott's *Guy Mannering*', *Journal of Narrative Theory*, 30: 1 (2000), 29–54 (pp. 40–41).

80. Fetzer, 'Beyond Beginning', p. 282.

81. Fetzer, 'Beyond Beginning', p. 277.

82. Andrew Lincoln, 'Scott and Empire: The Case of *Rob Roy*', *Studies in the Novel*, 34 (2002), 43–58 (p. 49).

83. Lincoln, 'Scott and Empire', p. 50.

84. Deborah D. Rogers, *The Matrophobic Gothic and its Legacy: Sacrificing Mothers in the Novel and in Popular Culture* (New York: Peter Lang, 2007), p. 102.

85. Isaac Gomez, *Selections of a father for the use of his children* (New York: Printed by Southwick and Pelsue, 1820), pp. 265–66; John F. Addington (ed.), *Poetical Quotations: Being a Complete Dictionary of the Most Elegant Moral, Sublime, and Humorous Passages in The British Poets*, 4 vols (Philadelphia: John Grigg, 1829), III, 288.

86. Alexander, *Walter Scott's Books*, p. 111.

NOTES

87. See Scott, *The Abbot*, pp. 314, 322, 332, 354; Walter Scott, *The Monastery*, in *Edinburgh Edition of the Waverley Novels*, gen. ed. Hewitt, IX, 57, 67; Walter Scott, *The Fortunes of Nigel*, in *Edinburgh Edition of the Waverley Novels*, gen. ed. Hewitt, XIII, 75, 85, 178; Scott, *Peveril of the Peak*, in *Edinburgh Edition of the Waverley Novels*, gen. ed. Hewitt, XIV, 249, 278.
88. Haber, 'The Chapter-Tags in the Waverley Novels', p. 1145.
89. Alexander, *Walter Scott's Books*, p. 85.
90. See Walter Scott, *Kenilworth: A Romance*, in *Edinburgh Edition of the Waverley Novels*, gen. ed. Hewitt, XI, 308; Scott, *The Abbot*, pp. 211, 218.
91. See Scott, *The Fortunes of Nigel*, p. 19; Scott, *The Monastery*, pp. 57, 67.
92. For example, see Charles Perrault, *Histories, or tales of past times* (London: J. Pote, 1729), title page; [Anon.], *A pretty book for children: or, an easy guide to the English tongue* (London: J. Newbery, 1761), pp. 74–86; [Anon.], *Cinderella; or, the history of the little glass slipper* (York: Wilson, Spence, & Mawman, [1795?]).
93. For more details of the death of the real Amy Robsart, see Carole Levin, *The Heart and Stomach of a King: Elizabeth I and the Politics of Sex and Power*, 2nd edn (Philadelphia: University of Pennsylvania Press, 2013), p. 46.
94. Haber, 'The Chapter-Tags in the Waverley Novels', p. 1149.
95. Walter Scott, quoted in 'Essay on the Text', in *The Betrothed*, in *Edinburgh Edition of the Waverley Novels*, gen. ed. Hewitt, XVIIIa, 279–321 (p. 303).
96. Scott, 3 February 1826, in *The Journal of Walter Scott*, p. 75.
97. 'Remarks on "Tales of the Crusaders"', *Edinburgh Magazine and literary miscellany*, 16 (June 1825), 641–46 (p. 644).
98. Once again, these figures have been calculated as a proportion of the number of novels surveyed rather than as a percentage of the total number of novels known to have been published. A full numerical comparison can be found in Appendix, Table 1 and Figures 1 and 2.
99. David Carey, *A Legend of Argyle; or 'Tis a Hundred Years Since*, 3 vols (London: G. and W. B. Whittaker, 1821); [Anon.], *Nice Distinctions: A Tale* (Dublin: J. Cumming, 1820), pp. v–vii.
100. Matthew Weld Hartstonge, *The Eve of All-Hallows; or, Adelaide or Tyrconnel; A Romance*, 3 vols (London: G. B. Whittaker, 1825), I, dedication.
101. Alexander Sutherland, *Tales of a Pilgrim* (Edinburgh: William Hunter; London: James Duncan, 1827), p. 3.
102. See, for example, William Chaigneau, *The History of Jack Connor*, ed. by Ian Campbell Ross (Dublin: Four Courts Press, 2013), pp. 41; Davies, *The Post-Captain*, p. 9.

CHAPTER 5

1. Anna Letitia Barbauld, 'Song I', in *Anna Letitia Barbauld: Selected Poetry and Prose*, ed. by William McCarthy and Elizabeth Kraft (Peterborough, ON: Broadview Press, 2002), pp. 75–77 (ll. 37–42). The text is presented here as it appeared in Katherine Thomson, *Widows and Widowers. A Romance of Real Life*, 3 vols (London: Richard Bentley, 1842), I, 335. In the original version lines 1, 2, 5, and 6 are all indented, and there are some minor variations in the distribution of punctuation.

2. *General Evening Post*, 7257 (2 September 1780); *Morning Post*, 2609 (31 March 1781).
3. See, for example, *London Chronicle*, 3719 (3 October 1780); *St. James's Chronicle, or British Evening Post*, 3066 (26 October 1780); *The Gazetteer and New Daily Advertiser*, 16278 (2 April 1781).
4. Barbauld, 'Song I', ll. 5–6.
5. For examples of this, see Gérard Genette, *Paratexts: Thresholds of Interpretation*, trans. by Jane E. Lewin (Cambridge: Cambridge University Press, 1997), p. 149; Leah Price, *The Anthology and the Rise of the Novel: From Richardson to George Eliot* (Cambridge: Cambridge University Press, 2000, repr. 2004), p. 115; Edward Jacobs, 'Ann Radcliffe and Romantic Print Culture', in *Ann Radcliffe, Romanticism, and the Gothic*, ed. by Dale Townshend and Angela Wright (Cambridge: Cambridge University Press, 2014), pp. 49–66 (p. 62).
6. Jacobs, 'Ann Radcliffe and Romantic Print Culture', p. 62.
7. Frederick Chamier, *Ben Bradshawe; The Man without a Head. A Novel*, 3 vols (London: T. C. Newby, 1843).
8. Examples include: William Henry De Merle, *Glenlonely; Or the Demon Friend*, 3 vols (London: Longman, Rees, Orme, Brown, Green, and Longman, 1837); William Henry De Merle, *Melton de Mowbray: Or, The Banker's Son. A Novel*, 3 vols (London: R. Bentley, 1838); Robert Plumer Ward, *Pictures of the World at Home and Abroad*, 3 vols (London: Henry Colburn, 1839); Elizabeth Stone, *William Langshawe, the Cotton Lord*, 2 vols (London: Richard Bentley, 1842); Louisa Stuart Costello, *The Queen's Poisoner; Or, France in the Sixteenth Century. A Romance*, 3 vols (London: Richard Bentley, 1841); Louisa Stuart Costello, *Gabrielle; Or, Pictures of a Reign. A Historical Novel*, 3 vols (London: T. C. Newby; and T. & W. Boone, 1843); Mrs C. D. Burdett, *Walter Hamilton. A Novel*, 3 vols (London: Thomas Cautley Newby, 1846); Erskine Neale, *Self-Sacrifice; or, the Chancellor's Chaplain* (London: Bogue, 1844); Erskine Neale, *Experiences of a Gaol Chaplain; Comprising Recollections of Ministerial Intercourse With Criminals of various classes, With their Confessions*, 3 vols (London: Richard Bentley, 1847).
9. The term 'novel' here encompasses not just the three-volume works that comprise the majority of Gore's prose output, but also a small number of shorter works that might more typically be categorised as 'novellas'. Since, very occasionally, these may be reprinted in an anthology of shorter fiction, the figures presented here should be used as a rough approximation rather than a definitive survey.
10. Molly Engelhardt, '"The Novelist of a New Era": Deepening the Sketch of Catherine Gore', *Victorian Review*, 42: 1 (Spring 2016), 65–84 (p. 65). See also Bonnie Anderson, 'The Writings of Catherine Gore', *Journal of Popular Culture*, 10: 2 (Fall 1976), 404–23 (p. 405); Matthew Whiting Rosa, *The Silver-Fork School* (New York: Columbia University Press, 1936), p. 143.
11. William Hazlitt, 'The Dandy School', *The Examiner*, 1033 (18 November 1827), 721–23 (pp. 721, 722).
12. April Kendra, 'Silver-Forks and Double Standards: Gore, Thackeray and the Problem of Parody', *Women's Writing*, 16: 2 (2009), 191–217 (p. 211); Cheryl Wilson, *Fashioning the Silver Fork Novel* (London: Pickering & Chatto, 2012), p. 69.

NOTES

13. Muireann O'Cinneide, *Aristocratic Women and the Literary Nation, 1832–1867* (London: Palgrave Macmillan, 2008), p. 48.

14. April Kendra, 'Gendering the Silver Fork: Catherine Gore and the Society Novel', *Women's Writing*, 11: 1 (2004), 25–38 (p. 28).

15. Catherine Gore to Edward Bulwer-Lytton [as editor of the *New Monthly*], 4 July 1832, quoted in Michael Sadleir, *Bulwer: A Panorama. Edward and Rosina 1803–1836* (London: Constable, 1931), pp. 301–02.

16. Ella Dzelzainis, 'Silver-Fork, Industrial, and Gothic Fiction', in *The Cambridge Companion to Victorian Women's Writing*, ed. by Linda H. Peterson (Cambridge: Cambridge University Press, 2015), pp. 105–18 (p. 107). See also Wilson, *Fashioning the Silver Fork Novel*, p. 15; April Kendra, 'Silver Forks, Stereotypes, and Regency Romance', *Studies in the Humanities*, 34: 2 (December 2007), 142–63 (p. 159).

17. Kendra, 'Silver-Forks and Double Standards', p. 201.

18. William Makepeace Thackeray, 'Novels by Eminent Hands', in *The Complete Works of William Makepeace Thackeray*, ed. by Micael Clarke, 27 vols (Newcastle upon Tyne: Cambridge Scholars Publishing, 2008), XXI, 112–20 (I, 112). Originally published as part of *Punch's Prize Novelists* (1847), but later reprinted as *Novels by Eminent Hands* (1856); see also Kendra, 'Silver-Forks and Double Standards', p. 201.

19. Whiting Rosa, *The Silver-Fork School*, p. 145; see also Anderson's agreement with this assessment, 'The Writings of Catherine Gore', p. 406.

20. Kendra, 'Silver-Forks and Double Standards', pp. 204, 207; see also William Makepeace Thackeray to Mrs. Gore, [1850], in *Letters and Private Papers of William Makepeace Thackeray*, ed. by Gordon N. Ray, 4 vols (London: Oxford University Press, 1945), II, 724–25 (p. 724).

21. See Anderson, 'The Writings of Catherine Gore', p. 406.

22. 'Mrs. Gore', *The London Review and weekly journal of politics, literature, art, and society* (23 February 1861), p. 208.

23. Whiting Rosa, *The Silver-Fork School*, p. 116.

24. Wilson, *Fashioning the Silver Fork Novel*, p. 13.

25. Catherine Grace Frances Gore, *Theresa Marchmont; or, The Maid of Honour. A Tale* (London: J. Andrews, 1824), pp. 3, 25, 31.

26. William Shakespeare, *Macbeth*, ed. by Nicholas Brooke (Oxford: Oxford University Press, 2008), p. 158 (III. iv.103–04, 107–08).

27. Matthew Lewis, *The Monk*, ed. by Howard Anderson, rev. with an Introduction and Notes by Nick Groom (Oxford: Oxford University Press, 2016), pp. 101, 110.

28. James Boaden, *Fontainville Forest, a play, in five acts* (London: Hookham and Carpenter, 1794), p. 41.

29. Francesca Saggini, *The Gothic Novel and the Stage: Romantic Appropriations* (Abingdon: Routledge, 2016), p. 128.

30. Catherine Grace Frances Gore, *The Lettre de Cachet; A Tale. The Reign of Terror; A Tale* (London: J. Andrews, 1827), p. 191. The epigraph reads:

> Who is it that comes thro the forest so fast,
> While night glooms around him, – while chill roars the blast?
> M. G. LEWIS.

It appears in Matthew Lewis, 'The Erl-King', in *Tales of Wonder* (London: W. Bulmer, 1801), I, 51–52 (ll. 1–2). The original features some minor variations, but as none of these materially affect the meaning of the quotation, it seems likely that these are errors possibly indicating that it was transcribed from memory, e.g. 'thro' is given for 'through', 'glooms' for 'frowns', and 'chill' for 'shrill'.

31. Catherine Grace Frances Gore, *Cecil: or, The Adventures of a Coxcomb*, in *Silver Fork Novels, 1826–1841*, gen. ed. Harriet Devine Jump, 6 vols (London: Pickering & Chatto, 2005), VI, 186. All further quotations from *Cecil* will be from this edition of the text.

32. William Shakespeare, *The Tragedy of King Richard III*, ed. by John Jowett (Oxford: Oxford University Press, 2008), p. 306 (IV.iv.143–44).

33. William Shakespeare, *Anthony and Cleopatra*, ed. by Michael Neill (Oxford: Oxford University Press, 2008), pp. 167–68 (I.iii.87–89). The phrases 'Sir, you and I have lov'd' and 'Sir, you and I must part' appear to have been swapped between lines.

34. 'Chit-Chat; Literary And Miscellaneous', *Literary magnet: or, monthly journal of the belles-lettres*, 3 (January 1827), 383–86 (p. 384).

35. Royce Mahawatte, '"Life that is not clad in the same coat-tails and flounces": The Silver-Fork Novel, George Eliot and the Fear of the Material', *Women's Writing*, 16: 2 (2009), 323–44 (p. 330).

36. Winifred Hughes, 'Gore [née Moody], Catherine Grace Frances (1799/1800–1861), Novelist and Playwright', in *Oxford Dictionary of National Biography* (Oxford: Oxford University Press, 2004) <http://www.oxforddnb.com/view/10.1093/ref:odnb/9780198614128.001.0001/odnb-9780198614128-e-11091> [accessed 27 April 2018].

37. British Library, Add MS 46611, letter from Catherine Gore to Richard Bentley, January 1830, ff. 92–93 (f. 92).

38. Catherine Grace Frances Gore, *Pin Money; A Novel*, 3 vols (London: Henry Colburn and Richard Bentley, 1831), I, preface.

39. This is an approximate figure that discounts prose lines derived from dramatic works.

40. Lady Caroline Lucy Scott, *A Marriage in High Life*, 2 vols (London: Henry Colburn, 1828), I, 21; see also William Shakespeare, *A Midsummer Night's Dream*, ed. by Peter Holland (Oxford: Oxford University Press, 2008), p. 166 (II.i.199–201).

41. William Sotheby, *Ellen; or, The Confession: A Tragedy. In Five Acts. Altered and Adapted for Representation* (London: Printed for John Murray, 1816), p. 30 (III.i). Minor grammatical differences occur between source and epigraph.

42. Lady Charlotte Susan Maria Bury, *The Divorced*, 2 vols (London: Henry Colburn, 1837), II; see also Shakespeare, A *Midsummer Night's Dream*, p. 140–41 (I.i.134–49).

43. William Shakespeare, *The Tempest*, ed. by Stephen Orgel (Oxford: Oxford University Press, 2008), p. 154 (III.i.44–45).

44. Catherine Grace Frances Gore, *Greville: or, A Season in Paris*, 3 vols (London: Henry Colburn, 1841), III, 38.

45. Samuel Warren, 'Ten Thousand A-Year: Part XII', *Blackwood's Edinburgh Magazine*, 48: 300 (October 1840), 431–61 (p. 432).

46. Catherine Gore to Edward Bulwer-Lytton, 4 July 1832, quoted in Sadleir, *Bulwer*, pp. 301–02 (p. 302).

NOTES

47. Edward Bulwer-Lytton, *Pelham; or, the Adventures of a Gentleman*, 3 vols (London: Henry Colburn, 1828), I, 58.
48. William Shakespeare, *Henry V*, ed. by Gary Taylor (Oxford: Oxford University Press, 2008), p. 113 (I.ii.213).
49. The original line reads 'Uneasy lies the head that wears a crown' and can be found in William Shakespeare, *Henry IV, Part Two*, ed. by René Weiss (Oxford: Oxford University Press, 2008), p. 191 (III.i.31).
50. Antoine Lilti, *The World of the Salons: Sociability and Worldliness in Eighteenth-Century Paris*, trans. by Lydia G. Cochrane (Oxford: Oxford University Press, 2005), p. 136.
51. [Anon.], *The Amicable Quixote; or, the enthusiasm of friendship*, 4 vols (London: J. Walter, 1788), II, 185; William Jerdan, *National Portrait Gallery of Illustrious and Eminent Personages of the Nineteenth Century; With Memoirs*, 5 vols (London: H. Fisher, R. Fisher, & P. Jackson, 1833), IV, 10–11.
52. Lilti, *The World of the Salons*, p. 136.
53. Lilti, *The World of the Salons*, p. 136.
54. Amy Prendergest, *Literary Salons Across Britain and Ireland in the Long Eighteenth Century* (Basingstoke: Palgrave Macmillan, 2015), p. 56.
55. Wilson, *Fashioning the Silver Fork Novel*, p. 32.
56. See O'Cinneide, *Aristocratic Women*, p. 53.
57. Elisabeth Jay, *British Writers and Paris 1830–1875* (Oxford: Oxford University Press, 2016), p. 113.
58. Coventry Patmore, quoted in D. Patmore, *The Life and Times of Coventry Patmore* (London: Constable, 1949), p. 37.
59. Catherine Grace Frances Gore, *Cecil, a Peer, A Sequel to Cecil, or the Adventures of a Coxcomb. By the same author*, 3 vols (London: T. and W. Boone, 1841), I, 112. This novel was renamed *Ormington, or Cecil, a Peer* for the second edition.
60. Kendra, 'Silver-Forks and Double Standards', p. 211.
61. Edward Copeland, *The Silver Fork Novel: Fashionable Fiction in the Age of Reform* (Cambridge: Cambridge University Press, 2012, p. 18.
62. Anna Maria Hall and Samuel Carter Hall, 'Memories of Authors. A Series of Portraits From Personal Acquaintance. Miss Landon', *Atlantic Monthly*, 65: 89 (March 1865), pp. 330–40 (p. 332); see also Cynthia Lawford, 'Turbans, Tea and Talk of Books: The Literary Parties of Elizabeth Spence and Elizabeth Benger', *Corvey Women Writers on the Web 1796–1834 CW³ Journal* <https://www2.shu.ac.uk/corvey/cw3journal/issues/lawford.html> [accessed 20 June 2018].
63. O'Cinneide, *Aristocratic Women*, p. 52.
64. Anna Maria Hall records that on one occasion her husband had been invited to one of Spence's gatherings; Hall herself was not asked to attend since at that point in time she was not yet a published writer (Hall and Hall, 'Memories of Authors', p. 332).
65. Oliver Goldsmith, *Letters from a Citizen of the World*, 2 vols (London: J. Newbery, 1762), II, 196. Some editing is present in Gore's quotation, as the original reads '[. . .] when a couple are now to be married, mutual love or an union of minds is the last and most trifling consideration. If their goods and chattels can be brought to unite [. . .]'.

197

66. Walter Scott, *The Bride of Lammermoor*, in *Edinburgh Edition of the Waverley Novels*, gen. ed. David Hewitt, 30 vols (Edinburgh: Edinburgh University Press, 1993–2012), VIIa, 177.

67. Catherine Grace Frances Gore, *Mothers and Daughters; A Tale of the Year 1830*, 3 vols (London: Henry Colburn and Richard Bentley, 1831), I, 44; misattributed to Shakespeare, this line was originally '[w]hen Greeks joyn'd Greeks, then was the tug of War' and can be found in Nathaniel Lee, *The Rival Queens, or the Death of Alexander the Great* (London: James Magnes and Richard Bentley, 1677), p. 48. The misidentification may have been a popular misconception, since it is later attributed to 'the immortal bard', a reference unlikely to allude to Nathaniel Lee. See Walter Donaldson, *Theatrical Portraits: Or, The Days of Shakespeare, Betterton, Garrick, and Kemble* (London: Varnham, 1870), p. 91.

68. See Josephine Richstad, 'Genre in Amber: Preserving the Fashionable Novel for a Victorian Decade, Catherine Gore's *Hamiltons* (1834 and 1850)', *Modern Philology*, 111: 3 (February 2014), 549–65 (p. 558).

69. Thomas Henry Lister, 'ART. VI. *Women as they Are; or, the Manners of the Day*', *Edinburgh Review*, 51: 102 (July 1830), 444–62 (p. 452).

70. Yale, Beinecke Rare Book and Manuscript Library, GEN MSS 1126 Box 1 Folio; Oxford, Bodleian Library, Dep Hughenden 129-2, ff. 102–03 (f. 103ʳ).

71. Oxford, Bodleian Library, MS. Beckford d. 17, p. i; d. 15, f. 36; d. 21, f. 15.

72. Jay, *British Writers and Paris 1830–1875*, p. 248.

73. Whiting Rosa, *The Silver-Fork School*, p. 144. As has been previously noted, Tom Haber used the term 'chapter-tags' to refer to pre-chapter epigraphs in his survey of Scott's use of the device, published (contemporaneously with Whiting Rosa's work) in 1930. See Tom B. Haber, 'The Chapter-Tags in the Waverley Novels', *PMLA*, 45: 4 (December 1930), 1140–49.

74. Whiting Rosa, *The Silver-Fork School*, p. 144.

75. Whiting Rosa, *The Silver-Fork School*, p. 144.

76. Catherine Grace Frances Gore, *The Heir of Selwood: Or, Three Epochs of A Life*, 3 vols (London: Henry Colburn, 1838), I, 64.

77. 'The Lounger: No. 65. Saturday, April 29, 1786', in *The British Essayists: Containing the Spectator, Tatler, Guardian, Rambler, Idler, Adventurer, Connoisseur, Mirror, Lounger, World, Observer, Knox's Essays, Olla Podrida, And Microcosm. University Edition*, 5 vols (London: Jones, 1828), IV, 133–35 (p. 135).

78. *Lounger*, 65 (29 April 1786), p. 257.

79. Catherine Grace Frances Gore, *Stokeshill Place; Or The Man of Business*, 3 vols (London: Henry Colburn, 1837), II, 18.

80. 'The Spectator: No. 508. Monday, October 13, 1712', in *The British Essayists*, I, 728–30 (p. 728).

81. Cornelius Nepos, 'The Book on the Great Generals of Foreign Nations. Militiades', in *Cornelius Nepos*, trans. by John Carew Rolfe (Cambridge, MA; London: Harvard University Press; W. Heinemann, 2015), pp. 6–23 (p. 20); see also 'The Spectator: No. 508. Monday, October 13, 1712', in *The British Essayists*, I, 728–30 (p. 728). Here, the variation 'habentur et dicuntur' is used, but otherwise the quotations are substantially the same. The translation given in Rolfe's edition reads '[b]ut all men

NOTES

are called tyrants, and regarded as such, who hold permanent rule in a city which has enjoyed a democratic form of government' (p. 21).

82. 'Art. II.-1. Cecil; or, The Adventures of a Coxcomb', *Edinburgh Review*, 73: 148 (July 1841), 366–88 (p. 382).

83. R. H. Horne, *A New Spirit of the Age*, 2 vols (London: Smith, Elder and Co., 1844), I, 234.

84. Lewis Melville, *The Life and Letters of William Beckford of Fonthill. By Lewis Melville* (London: Heinemann, 1910), p. 351.

85. MS. Beckford c. 14, ff. 94–95 (f. 95^r).

86. MS. Beckford d. 17, p. i; d. 15, f. 36; d. 21, f. 15.

87. Yale, Beinecke Rare Book and Manuscript Library, OSB MSS 135 Box 28, f. 1043.

88. See Gore, *Cecil*, pp. 110, 280. Both of the Beckford quotations used as epigraphs to these chapters feature in William Beckford, *Italy, Spain, and Portugal, with an excursion to the monasteries of Alcobaça and Batalha*, A New Edition (London: Richard Bentley, 1840). Some light editing has been performed on each, and some phrases omitted from the original context.

89. British Library Add MS 46611, ff. 92–93 (f. 92^r).

90. British Library Add MS 46650, ff. 171–72 (f. 171^r); Dep Hughenden 129-2, ff. 112–13 (f. 113^v). For samples of Gore's customary signature, see Dep Hughenden 129-2, ff. 102–03 (f. 103^r) and Dep Hughenden 129-2, ff. 104–05 (f. 104^v).

91. Wilson, *Fashioning the Silver Fork Novel*, p. 30.

92. Byron to Thomas Moore, 28 January 1817, in George Gordon Byron, *Byron's Letters and Journals*, ed. by Leslie A. Marchand, 12 vols (Cambridge, MA: Harvard University Press, 1973–82), V, 165.

93. Edgar Allan Poe, *Edgar Allan Poe's Annotated Short Stories*, ed. by Andrew Barger ([S.I.]: Bottletree Books, 2008), p. 554.

94. 'Mrs. Gore', *La Belle Assemblée, or, Bell's Court and Fashionable Magazine Addressed Particularly to the Ladies*, 10: 3 (1 March 1837), 124–28.

95. British Library Add MS 46611, ff. 92–93 (f. 92^v). The underlining is transcribed here from the original.

96. Catherine Gore to Edward Bulwer-Lytton [as editor of the *New Monthly*], 4 July 1832, quoted in Sadleir, *Bulwer*, pp. 301–02 (p. 302).

97. 'Literary Notices', *Bradford Observer*, 10: 492 (10 August 1843), p. 7.

98. 'AINSWORTH'S', *Satirist; or Censor of the Times*, 609 (17 December 1843), p. 410.

99. Catherine Grace Frances Gore, *Modern Chivalry, Or a New Orlando Furioso*, 2 vols (London: Mortimer, 1843), I, 3, 27, 69, 155; II, 27, 107, 157.

100. Étienne de Jouy, 'N° XLII,— 25 *avril* 1815. Le Déménagement', in *Guillaume le Franc-Parleur, ou Observations Sur Les Mœurs Et Les Usages Français Au Commencement Du XIXe Siècle*, 4th edn, 2 vols (Paris: Chez Pillet, Imprimeur-Libraire, 1817), II, 207–20 (p. 208). In Gore's novel the quotation has been slightly edited since the original uses the plural of 'vive' and gives 'des situations de la vie que vous avez prévues', 'au sortir de son lit', and 'tout le long du jour'. The two-volume edition mistakenly gives 'violà' instead of 'voilà' but this error is not present in the serialised version. Jouy's text also includes a semi-colon instead of a full-stop after 'charme'.

101. A proverb still very much in use in modern-day Turkey. The translations to modern Turkish and English, along with other notes regarding the context and use of the phrase, were kindly provided by Nazan Osman.

102. Alphonse Royer, 'Le Peau du Renard', *Revue de Paris*, 36 (February 1832), pp. 23–46 (p. 23).

103. Catherine Grace Frances Gore, *The Tuileries. A Tale*, 3 vols (London: Henry Colburn and Richard Bentley, 1831), II, 194; see also Walter Scott, *Guy Mannering*, in *Edinburgh Edition of the Waverley Novels*, gen. ed. Hewitt, II, 262.

104. Michael Fry, *Edinburgh: A History of the City* (Basingstoke: Macmillan, 2009), p. 78.

105. 'Miscellaneous Literature. Traditionary Notices of the Old Tolbooth and its Tenants. *By the Author of the "Histories of the Scottish Rebellions"'*, *Edinburgh Literary Journal; or, Weekly Register of Criticism and Belles Lettres*, 39 (8 August 1829), 138–40 (p. 138).

106. Whiting Rosa, *The Silver-Fork School*, p. 144.

107. Hughes, 'Gore [née Moody], Catherine Grace Frances (1799/1800–1861)'.

108. Dep Hughenden 129-2, ff. 119–20 (f. 119^r).

109. Jenny Uglow, *Elizabeth Gaskell: A Habit of Stories* (London: Faber & Faber, 1993, repr. 1999), p. 41; Anna Unsworth, 'Elizabeth Gaskell and German Romanticism', *Gaskell Society Journal*, 8 (1994), 1–14 (pp. 8–9); Elizabeth Gaskell, *Mary Barton: A Tale of Manchester Life*, in *Works of Elizabeth Gaskell*, gen. ed. Joanne Shattock, 10 vols (London: Pickering & Chatto, 2005–06), V, 195, 235. All further references will be from this edition of the text, unless otherwise stated.

110. Muriel Smith, 'Lines from Ludwig Uhland: A Note', *Notes and Commentary: The Gaskell Society Journal*, 11 (1 January 1997), 103–04 (p. 103).

111. Uglow, *Elizabeth Gaskell*, p. 40; see also Elizabeth Gaskell to Catherine Winkworth, 29 November 1848, in *The Letters of Mrs. Gaskell*, ed. by J. A. V. Chapple and Arthur Pollard (Manchester: Manchester University Press, 1997), p. 64.

112. Marion Shaw, '*Sylvia's Lovers* and Other Historical Fiction', in *The Cambridge Companion to Elizabeth Gaskell*, ed. by Jill L. Matus (Cambridge: Cambridge University Press, 2007), pp. 75–89 (p. 77); Shirley Foster, 'Elizabeth Gaskell's Shorter Pieces', in *The Cambridge Companion to Elizabeth Gaskell*, ed. by Matus, pp. 108–30 (p. 122).

113. Gaskell to Louis Hachette, [c. 17 March 1855], in *Further Letters of Mrs. Gaskell*, ed. by John Chapple and Alan Shelston (Manchester: Manchester University Press, 2003), p. 127.

114. Uglow, *Elizabeth Gaskell*, p. 21.

115. Elizabeth Barrett Browning to Mary Russell Mitford, 13 December 1850, in *The Brownings' Correspondence*, ed. by Philip Kelley et al., 29 vols to date (Winfield, KS: Wedgestone, 1984–date), XVI, 245.

116. Gaskell to Edward Chapman, 21 March [1848], in *The Letters of Mrs. Gaskell*, p. 54.

117. Gaskell to Edward Chapman, 2 April [1848], in *The Letters of Mrs. Gaskell*, p. 56.

118. *Douglas Jerrold's Weekly Newspaper*, 81 (9 January 1848), p. 160; *Douglas Jerrold's Weekly Newspaper*, 85 (26 February 1848), p. 288.

NOTES

119. Gaskell to Edward Chapman, 21 March [1848], in *The Letters of Mrs. Gaskell*, p. 54.
120. Gaskell to Edward Chapman, 17 April 1848, in *The Letters of Mrs. Gaskell*, p. 56.
121. Joanne Wilkes, 'Introduction', in *Works of Elizabeth Gaskell*, V, xi; Uglow, *Elizabeth Gaskell*, p. 185.
122. Shirley Foster notes that there was discussion upon this point, but resists a judgement as to who first suggested including mottos. See Shirley Forster, 'Note on the Text', in Elizabeth Gaskell, *Mary Barton*, ed. by Shirley Foster (Oxford: Oxford University Press, 2008), pp. xxvii–xxviii (p. xxvii).
123. Gaskell to Edward Chapman, 10 July [1848], in *The Letters of Mrs. Gaskell*, p. 58.
124. Gaskell to Edward Chapman, 26 May [1848], in *Further Letters of Mrs. Gaskell*, p. 39.
125. See Appendix, Figure 17.
126. To date, none of Gaskell's editors have been able to discover these quotations within the manuscripts and/or published works of Elizabeth or William Gaskell. Yet it is worth noting that it is not unknown for new sources to be suddenly uncovered, for example the recent identification of the previously unidentified lines with which Gaskell concludes the preface to the first edition of *North and South* (1854–55):

    Beseking hym lowly, or mercy and pite,
    Of its rude making to have compassion.

    See Elizabeth Gaskell, *North and South*, in *Works of Elizabeth Gaskell*, VII, 9. All further references will be to this edition of the text. For more information regarding the attribution of this quotation, see A. S. G. Edwards, 'Gaskell's *North and South* and John Lydgate', *Notes and Queries*, 56: 3 (September 2009), 399.
127. Barbara Brill, *William Gaskell 1805–1884: A Portrait* (Manchester: Manchester Literary and Philosophical Publications, 1984), pp. 54–55.
128. Henry Fothergill Chorley, Review of '*North and South*', *Athenaeum*, 1432 (7 April 1855), p. 403.
129. James Eli Adams, *A History of Victorian Literature* (Chichester: Wiley-Blackwell, 2009), pp. 104–05.
130. Uglow, *Elizabeth Gaskell*, p. 201.
131. Marcus Waithe, 'The Pen and the Hammer: Thomas Carlyle, Ebenezer Elliott, and the "active poet"', in *Class and the Canon: Constructing Labouring-Class Poetry and Poetics, 1780–1900*, ed. by Kirstie Blair and Mina Gorji (Basingstoke: Palgrave Macmillan, 2013), pp. 116–35 (p. 126).
132. Uglow, *Elizabeth Gaskell*, p. 201.
133. Jayne Hildebrand, 'The Ranter and the Lyric: Reform and Genre Heterogeneity in Ebenezer Elliott's *Corn Law Rhymes*', *Victorian Review*, 39: 1 (2013), 101–24 (p. 102).
134. Gaskell, *Mary Barton*, ed. by Foster, p. 418 n. 27.
135. Waithe, 'The Pen and the Hammer', p. 125.

136. Ebenezer Elliott, 'The Splendid Village', in *The Splendid Village: Corn Law Rhymes; and Other Poems* (London: Benjamin Steill, Paternoster Row. J. Pearce, Sheffield, 1833), pp. 17–44 (p. 25).

137. Gaskell, *Mary Barton*, ed. by Foster, p. 420 n. 38.

138. Elizabeth Ludlow, 'Elizabeth Gaskell's Early Contributions to *Household Words*: The Use of Parable and the Transformation of Communities through "Kinder Understanding"', *Victorian Review*, 42: 1 (Spring 2016), 107–25 (p. 118).

139. Elizabeth Gaskell, 'North and South', *Household Words*, 10: 232 (2 September 1854), 61–68 (pp. 61, 65).

140. Gaskell, 'North and South', p. 61; see also Alfred Tennyson, 'Will Waterproof's Lyrical Monologue', in *The Poems of Tennyson*, ed. by Christopher Rick, 2nd edn, 3 vols (Harlow: Longman, 1987), II, 96–104 (p. 98, ll. 49–56).

141. Jeffrey E. Jackson, 'Elizabeth Gaskell and the Dangerous Edge of Things: Epigraphs in *North and South* and Victorian Publishing Practices', *Pacific Coast Philology*, 40: 2 (2005), 56–72 (pp. 57, 62).

142. Gaskell to Anna Jameson, [January 1855], in *The Letters of Mrs. Gaskell*, p. 328.

143. Ada Sharpe, 'Margaret Hale's Books and Flowers: *North and South*'s Paratextual Dialogues with Felicia Hemans', *Victorian Review*, 40: 1 (Spring 2014), 197–209, p. 197.

144. Anna Letitia Barbauld, 'The Groans of the Tankard', in *Selected Poetry and Prose*, pp. 83–86 (ll. 47–50).

145. William Habington '*Vias tuas Domine demonstra mihi*', in *The Poems of William Habington*, ed. by Kenneth Allott (Liverpool: Liverpool University Press, 1948), pp. 140–41 (p. 141, ll. 46–50).

CONCLUSION

1. George Eliot, *Middlemarch*, ed. by David Caroll (Oxford: Oxford University Press, 1996, reissued 2008), p. 115.

2. Michael Wheeler, *The Art of Allusion in Victorian Fiction* (London; Basingstoke: Macmillan, 1979), p. 82.

3. Eike Kronshage, 'The Function of Poetic Epigraphs in George Eliot's *Daniel Deronda*', *Connotations*, 23: 2 (2013/14), 230–60 (p. 254); see also the brief discussion of epigraphs in Daniel Pollack-Pelzner, 'Quoting Shakespeare in the British Novel', in *Shakespeare and Quotation*, ed. by Julie Maxwell and Kate Rumbold (Cambridge: Cambridge University Press, 2018), pp. 136–55 (p. 143).

4. Kronshage, 'The Function of Poetic Epigraphs', p. 254.

5. This figure was calculated from publication years of titles listed in Andrew Block, *The English Novel, 1740–1850: A Catalogue Including Prose Romances, Short Stories, and Translations of Foreign Fiction*, with Introductions by John Crow and Ernest A. Baker, new and rev. edn (London: Dawson, 1961).

6. Gérard Genette, *Paratexts: Thresholds of Interpretation*, trans. by Jane E. Lewin (Cambridge: Cambridge University Press, 1997), p. 160.

BIBLIOGRAPHY

Manuscripts

Boston Public Library, MS Ch.K.1.10, Ann Radcliffe's Commonplace Book
British Library, Add MS 46611, Bentley Papers, ff. 92–93
Oxford, Bodleian Library, Dep Hughenden 129-2, Papers of Benjamin Disraeli,
    1st Earl of Beaconsfield (1804–1881) and of his family
—— MS. Beckford, The Papers of William Beckford, 1772–1857
Yale, Beinecke Rare Book and Manuscript Library, OSB MSS 135, Edward G.
    and Hortense R. Levy autograph collection, part one (1718–1955), Box
    28, f. 1043
—— GEN MSS 1126, James Osborn collection of Lady Sydney Morgan
    (1803–1859), Box 1 Folio

Primary Sources

All anonymously authored works have been listed alphabetically by title.

Addington, John F. (ed.), *Poetical Quotations: Being a Complete Dictionary of
    the Most Elegant Moral, Sublime, and Humorous Passages in The British
    Poets*, 4 vols (Philadelphia: John Grigg, 1829)
The Adventures of a Watch! (London: G. Kearsley, 1788)
'AINSWORTH'S', *Satirist; or Censor of the Times*, 609 (17 December 1843)
The Amicable Quixote; or, the enthusiasm of friendship, 4 vols (London:
    J. Walter, 1788)
Argentum: or, Adventures of a Shilling (London: Printed by J. Nichols and sold
    by J. Pridden, 1794)
'Art I. 1. Ivanhoe.', *Edinburgh Review*, 33: 65 (January 1820), 1–54
'Art. II.-1. Cecil; or, The Adventures of a Coxcomb', *Edinburgh Review*, 73:
    148 (July 1841), 366–88
'ART. II. *The Mysteries of Udolpho, a Romance; Interspersed with some Pieces
    of Poetry*', *British Critic*, 4 (August 1794), 110–21
'ART. VI. *Gaston de Blondeville*', *Monthly Review*, 2: 8 (July 1826), 280–93
'ART. VI. Thirty Letters on various Subjects', *English Review, or, An abstract
    of English and foreign literature*, 2 (July 1783), 40–47

'Art. 14. *The Statue Room; an Historical Tale*', *English Review, or, An abstract of English and foreign literature*, 16 (December 1790), 466

Arville Castle. An Historical Romance, 2 vols (London: B. Crosby, and T. White, 1795)

Austen, Jane, *Jane Austen's Letters*, ed. by Deirdre Le Faye, 3rd edn (Oxford: Oxford University Press, 1995)

—— *Northanger Abbey*, ed. by James Kinsley and John Davie, with an Introduction and Notes by Claudia L. Johnson (Oxford: Oxford University Press, 2003)

A. Y., 'ART. IV. *The Mysteries of Udolpho, a Romance; interspersed with some pieces of Poetry*', *Analytical Review*, 19: 2 (June 1794), 140–45

Baines, Paul, and Edward Burns (eds), *Five Romantic Plays 1768–1821* (Oxford: Oxford University Press, 2000)

Ballin, Rossetta, *The Statue Room: An Historical Tale*, 2 vols (London: H. D. Symonds, 1790)

Barbauld, Anna Letitia, *Anna Letitia Barbauld: Selected Poetry and Prose*, ed. by William McCarthy and Elizabeth Kraft (Peterborough, ON: Broadview Press, 2002)

Beckford, William, *Italy, Spain, and Portugal, with an excursion to the monasteries of Alcobaça and Batalha*, A New Edition (London: Richard Bentley, 1840)

The Bible: Authorized King James Version with Apocrypha, ed. by Robert Carroll and Stephen Prickett (Oxford: Oxford University Press, 2008)

Blagdon, F. W., *A New Dictionary of Classical Quotations, on an Improved Plan: Accompanied by Corresponding Paraphrases, or Translations, from the Works of Celebrated British Poets* (London: Robert Stodart; Edinburgh: Bell and Bradfute, 1819)

Blair, Robert, 'from *The Grave*', in *The New Oxford Book of Eighteenth-Century Verse*, ed. by Roger Lonsdale (Oxford: Oxford University Press, 2009), pp. 368–69

Boaden, James, *Fontainville Forest, a play, in five acts* (London: Hookham and Carpenter, 1794)

Boswell, John, *A Method of Study: or an useful library*, 2 vols (London: Printed for the Author, 1738–43)

The British Essayists: Containing the Spectator, Tatler, Guardian, Rambler, Idler, Adventurer, Connoisseur, Mirror, Lounger, World, Observer, Knox's Essays, Olla Podrida, And Microcosm. University Edition, 5 vols (London: Jones, 1828)

Browning, Elizabeth Barrett, and Robert Browning, *The Brownings' Correspondence*, ed. by Philip Kelley et al., 29 vols to date (Winfield, KS: Wedgestone, 1984–date)

Bulwer-Lytton, Edward, *Pelham; or, the Adventures of a Gentleman*, 3 vols (London: Henry Colburn, 1828)

BIBLIOGRAPHY

Burdett, Mrs C. D., *Walter Hamilton. A Novel*, 3 vols (London: Thomas Cautley Newby, 1846)

Burke, Edmund, *A Philosophical Enquiry into the Sublime and Beautiful*, ed. by Paul Guyer (Oxford: Oxford University Press, 2015)

Bury, Lady Charlotte Susan Maria, *The Divorced*, 2 vols (London: Henry Colburn, 1837)

Byron, George Gordon, *Byron's Letters and Journals*, ed. by Leslie A. Marchand, 12 vols (Cambridge, MA: Harvard University Press, 1973–82)

Bysshe, Edward, *The Art of English Poetry* (London: Robert Knaplock, Edward Castle, Benjamin Tooke, 1702)

—— *The British Parnassus: Or, A Compleat Common-Place-Book of English Poetry*, 2 vols (London: J. Nutt, 1714)

Campbell, Thomas, 'Lochiel's Warning', in *The Complete Poetical Works of Thomas Campbell*, ed. by J. Logie Robertson (London: Oxford University Press, 1907), pp. 157–60

Carey, David, *A Legend of Argyle; or 'Tis a Hundred Years Since*, 3 vols (London: G. and W. B. Whittaker, 1821)

Chaigneau, William, *The History of Jack Connor*, ed. by Ian Campbell Ross (Dublin: Four Courts Press, 2013)

Chamier, Frederick, *Ben Bradshawe; The Man without a Head. A Novel*, 3 vols (London: T. C. Newby, 1843)

'Chit-Chat; Literary And Miscellaneous', *Literary magnet: or, monthly journal of the belles-lettres*, 3 (January 1827), 383–86

Chorley, Henry Fothergill, Review of '*North and South*', *Athenaeum*, 1432 (7 April 1855), p. 403

Cinderella; or, the history of the little glass slipper (York: Wilson, Spence, & Mawman, [1795?])

The Citizen's Daughter; or What Might Be (London: Printed by N. Biggs for Vernor and Hood, 1804)

Clarke, Henry, *The School Candidates, A Prosaic Burlesque: Occasioned by the Late Election of a Schoolmaster. At the Village of Boudinnoir* (Manchester, 1788)

Cochrane, John George, *Catalogue of the Library at Abbotsford* (Edinburgh: T. Constable, 1838)

Collins, William, 'Ode to Fear', in *The Poems of Thomas Gray, William Collins, Oliver Goldsmith*, ed. by Roger Lonsdale (London: Longmans, 1969), pp. 418–23

Cornelius Nepos, trans. by John Carew Rolfe (Cambridge, MA; London: Harvard University Press; W. Heinemann, 2015)

Costello, Louisa Stuart, *Gabrielle; Or, Pictures of a Reign. A Historical Novel*, 3 vols (London: T. C. Newby; and T. & W. Boone, 1843)

—— *The Queen's Poisoner; Or, France in the Sixteenth Century. A Romance*, 3 vols (London: Richard Bentley, 1841)

Dallas, Robert Charles, *The Knights: Tales Illustrative of the Marvellous*, 3 vols (London: Longman, Hurst, Rees, and Orme, 1808)

Darwin, Erasmus, *The Botanic Garden; A Poem In Two Parts* (London: J. Johnson, 1791)

Davis, John, *The Post-Captain; or, The Wooden Walls Well Manned; Comprehending a View of Naval Society and Manners* (London: Thomas Tegg, 1806)

De Merle, William Henry, *Glenlonely; Or the Demon Friend*, 3 vols (London: Longman, Rees, Orme, Brown, Green, and Longman, 1837)

—— *Melton de Mowbray: Or, The Banker's Son. A Novel*, 3 vols (London: R. Bentley, 1838)

Devine Jump, Harriet (gen. ed.), *Silver Fork Novels, 1826–1841*, 6 vols (London: Pickering & Chatto, 2005)

Dictionary of the Scots Language (*Dictionar o the Scots Leid*) (Scottish Language Dictionaries, 2004) <http://www.dsl.ac.uk/entry/snd/kind> [accessed 26 August 2018]

D'Israeli, Isaac, *Flim-Flams! Or, the Life and Errors of My Uncle, and the Amours of my Aunt! With Illustrations and Obscurities, by Messieurs Tag, Rag, and Bobtail. With an Illuminating Index!*, 3 vols (London: John Murray, 1805)

Donaldson, Walter, *Theatrical Portraits: Or, The Days of Shakespeare, Betterton, Garrick, and Kemble* (London: Varnham, 1870)

Douglas Jerrold's Weekly Newspaper, 81 (9 January 1848)

—— 85 (26 February 1848)

Dryden, John, *Fables Ancient and Modern: Translated into Verse, from Homer, Ovid Boccace, and Chaucher: with original poems* (London: Jacob Tonson, 1713)

E., 'ART. XII. *The Romance of the Forest: Interspersed with some Pieces of Poetry*', *Monthly Review*, 8 (May 1792), 82–87

Eliot, George, *Middlemarch*, ed. by David Caroll (Oxford: Oxford University Press, 1996, reissued 2008)

Elliott, Ebenezer, *The Splendid Village: Corn Law Rhymes; and Other Poems* (London: Benjamin Steill, Paternoster Row. J. Pearce, Sheffield, 1833)

Fielding, Henry, *Tom Jones*, ed. by John Bender and Simon Stern, with an Introduction by John Bender (Oxford: Oxford University Press, 2008)

Fielding, Sarah, and Jane Collier, *The Cry: A New Dramatic Fable*, 3 vols (London: R. and J. Dodsley, 1754)

—— *The Cry: A New Dramatic Fable*, ed. by Carolyne Woodward (Lexington, KY: University of Kentucky Press, 2017)

Fox, Joseph, *Santa-Maria; or, the Mysterious Pregnancy. A Romance*, 3 vols (London: G. Kearsley, 1797)

Garrick, David, *The Taming of the Shrew; or, Catherine and Petruchio. A comedy. Altered from Shakespeare* (London: Bathurst and others, 1786)

Gaskell, Elizabeth Cleghorn, *Further Letters of Mrs. Gaskell*, ed. by John Chapple and Alan Shelston (Manchester: Manchester University Press, 2003)

—— *The Letters of Mrs. Gaskell*, ed. by J. A. V. Chapple and Arthur Pollard (Manchester: Manchester University Press, 1997)

—— *Mary Barton*, ed. by Shirley Foster (Oxford: Oxford University Press, 2006)

—— 'North and South', *Household Words*, 10: 232 (2 September 1854), 61–68

—— *Works of Elizabeth Gaskell*, gen. ed. Joanne Shattock (London: Pickering & Chatto, 2005–06)

The Gazetteer and New Daily Advertiser, 16278 (2 April 1781)

General Advertiser, 5114 (13 March 1750)

General Evening Post, 7257 (2 September 1780)

Goldsmith, Oliver, *Letters from a Citizen of the World*, 2 vols (London: J. Newbery, 1762)

—— *The Vicar of Wakefield: A Tale*, 2 vols (Salisbury: Printed by B. Collins, for F. Newbury, 1766)

—— *The Vicar of Wakefield*, ed. by Arthur Friedman, with an Introduction and Notes by Robert L. Mack (Oxford: Oxford University Press, 2008)

Gomez, Isaac, *Selections of a father for the use of his children* (New York: Printed by Southwick and Pelsue, 1820)

Gore, Catherine Grace Frances, *Cecil, a Peer, A Sequel to Cecil, or the Adventures of a Coxcomb. By the same author*, 3 vols (London: T. and W. Boone, 1841)

—— *Greville: or, A Season in Paris*, 3 vols (London: Henry Colburn, 1841)

—— *The Heir of Selwood: Or, Three Epochs of A Life*, 3 vols (London: Henry Colburn, 1838)

—— *The Lettre de Cachet; A Tale. The Reign of Terror; A Tale* (London: J. Andrews, 1827)

—— *Modern Chivalry, Or a New Orlando Furioso*, 2 vols (London: Mortimer, 1843)

—— *Mothers and Daughters; A Tale of the Year 1830*, 3 vols (London: Henry Colburn and Richard Bentley, 1831)

—— *Pin Money; A Novel*, 3 vols (London: Henry Colburn and Richard Bentley, 1831)

—— *Stokeshill Place; Or The Man of Business*, 3 vols (London: Henry Colburn, 1837)

—— *The Story of a Royal Favourite*, 3 vols (London: Henry Colburn, 1845)

—— *Theresa Marchmont; or, The Maid of Honour. A Tale* (London: J. Andrews, 1824)

—— *The Tuileries. A Tale*, 3 vols (London: Henry Colburn and Richard Bentley, 1831)

Gorjy, Jean Claude, *Victorina, A Novel. Translated from the French* (London: Lane, Minerva, 1790)

Green, Sarah, *The Private History of the Court of England*, 2 vols (London: Printed for the Author, and sold by B. Crosby and Co., 1808)

Habington, William, *The Poems of William Habington*, ed. by Kenneth Allott (Liverpool: Liverpool University Press, 1948)

Hall, Anna Maria, and Samuel Carter Hall, 'Memories of Authors. A Series of Portraits From Personal Acquaintance. Miss Landon', *Atlantic Monthly*, 65: 89 (March 1865), pp. 330–40

Hartstonge, Matthew Weld, *The Eve of All-Hallows; or, Adelaide or Tyrconnel; A Romance*, 3 vols (London: G. B. Whittaker, 1825)

Hazlitt, William, 'The Dandy School', *The Examiner*, 1033 (18 November 1827), 721–23

Headley, Henry, *Select Beauties of Ancient English Poetry*, 2 vols (London: T. Cadell, 1787)

'The Heir of Linne', in *Reliques of Ancient Poetry*, ed. by Thomas Percy, 3 vols (London: J. Dodsley, 1765), II, 309–18

Helme, Elizabeth, *Louisa; or, The Cottage on the Moor, The fourth edition, corrected*, 2 vols (London: G. Kearsley, 1787)

The Histories Of Some of the Penitents in the Magdalen-House, As supposed to be related by Themselves, 2 vols (London: John Rivington and J. Dodsley, 1760)

The Histories of Some of the Penitents in the Magdalen House, ed. by Jennie Batchelor and Megan Hiatt (London: Pickering & Chatto, 2007)

Hodgson, Solomon (ed.), *The Hive of Ancient & Modern Literature: A Collection of Essays, Narratives, Allegories and instructive Compositions*, 4th edn (Newcastle: Printed by and for S. Hodgson, 1812)

Holstein, Anthony Frederick [pseud.], *The Assassin of St. Glenroy; or, The Axis of Life. A Novel*, 4 vols (London: A. K. Newman and Co., 1810)

—— *Isadora of Milan*, 5 vols (London: Henry Colburn, 1811)

Horace, *Satires. Epistles. The Art of Poetry*, trans. by H. Rushton Fairclough (Cambridge, MA: Harvard University Press, 1929)

Horne, R. H., *A New Spirit of the Age*, 2 vols (London: Smith, Elder and Co., 1844)

Jerdan, William, *National Portrait Gallery of Illustrious and Eminent Personages of the Nineteenth Century; With Memoirs*, 5 vols (London: H. Fisher, R. Fisher, & P. Jackson, 1833)

BIBLIOGRAPHY

Johnson, Samuel, *The Rambler*, 8 vols (Edinburgh: W. Gordon et al., 1750–52)

—— *The Rambler*, 2nd edn, 8 vols (Edinburgh: W. Gordon et al., 1751–52)

—— *The Rambler*, 6 vols (London: J. Payne, 1752)

—— *The Works of Samuel Johnson*, ed. by O. M. Brack, Jr. and Robert DeMaria, Jr., 23 vols (New Haven, CT; London: Yale University Press, 1958–2019)

Johnstone, Christian Isobel, *Clan-Albin: A National Tale*, 4 vols (Edinburgh: Macredie, Skelly, and Muckersy; London: Longman and others, 1815)

Jouy, Étienne de, 'Nº XLII,— 25 *avril* 1815. Le Déménagement', in *Guillaume le Franc-Parleur, ou Observations Sur Les Mœurs Et Les Usages Français Au Commencement Du XIXᵉ Siècle*, 4th edn, 2 vols (Paris: Chez Pillet, Imprimeur-Libraire, 1817), II, 207–20

Kant, Immanuel, *The Critique of Judgement*, trans. James Meredith, rev. by Nicholas Walker (Oxford: Oxford University Press, 2008)

Kett, Henry, *Emily, A Moral Tale, Including Letters from a Father to his Daughter, Upon the Most Important Subjects*, 2 vols (London: Messrs. Rivingtons and others, 1809/11)

Lansdell, Sarah, *Manfredi, Baron St. Osmund. An Old English Romance*, 2 vols (London: William Lane, 1796)

Lathom, Francis, *The Castle of Ollada. A Romance*, 2 vols (London: William Lane, 1795)

Lee, Nathaniel, *The Rival Queens, or the Death of Alexander the Great* (London: James Magnes and Richard Bentley, 1677)

Lewis, Matthew, *The Life and Correspondence of M. G. Lewis*, 2 vols (London: Henry Colburn, 1839)

—— *The Monk*, ed. by Howard Anderson, rev. with an Introduction and Notes by Nick Groom (Oxford: Oxford University Press, 2016)

—— (ed.), *Tales of Wonder*, 2 vols (London: W. Bulmer, 1801)

Lister, Thomas Henry, 'ART. VI. *Women as they Are; or, the Manners of the Day*', *Edinburgh Review*, 51: 102 (July 1830), 444–62

'Literary Notices', *Bradford Observer*, 10: 492 (10 August 1843)

Lockhart, John Gibson, *Memoirs of the Life of Sir Walter Scott, Bart*, 7 vols (Edinburgh: Robert Cadell, 1837)

London Chronicle, 3719 (3 October 1780)

The Lounger, 65 (29 April 1786)

Lucretia; or, Virtue the Best Dowry, 2 vols (London: Printed by L. Wayland, for T. Vernor, 1790)

McCrie, Thomas, Review of '*Tales of My Landlord*; Collected and Arranged by Jedediah Cleishbotham', *Edinburgh Christian Instructor*, 14 (January 1817), 41–73; (February 1817), 100–40; (March 1817), 170–201

Mackenzie, Anna Maria, *Calista, a Novel*, 2 vols (London: William Lane, 1789)

—— *Mysteries Elucidated, A Novel*, 3 vols (London: William Lane, 1795)

—— *Retribution: A Novel*, 3 vols (London: Printed for G. G. J. and J. Robinson, Pater-Noster Row, 1788)

Mason, John, *Self-knowledge. A treatise, shewing the nature and benefit of that important science, and the way to attain it* (London: J. Waugh, 1745)

Meditations and contemplations on various subjects. To which are added Divine Poems, 2nd edn (London: G. Keith, 1761)

Melville, Lewis, *The Life and Letters of William Beckford of Fonthill. By Lewis Melville* (London: Heinemann, 1910)

Milton, John, *Paradise Lost*, ed. by Stephen Orgel and Jonathan Goldberg (Oxford: Oxford University Press, 2004)

—— *Selected Poems*, ed. by John Leonard (London: Penguin Books, 2007)

'Miscellaneous Literature. Traditionary Notices of the Old Tolbooth and its Tenants. *By the Author of the "Histories of the Scottish Rebellions"'*, *Edinburgh Literary Journal; or, Weekly Register of Criticism and Belles Lettres*, 39 (8 August 1829), 138–40

Mitchell, Margaret, *Tales of Instruction and Amusement. Written for the Use of Young Persons*, 2 vols (London: E. Newbery, 1795)

Modern characters for 1778. By Shakespear (London: D. Brown, 1778)

Moore, John, *Zeluco. Various Views of Human Nature, Taken from Life and Manners, Foreign and Domestic*, 2 vols (London: A. Strahan and T. Cadell, 1789)

Moore, Thomas, 'A Canadian Boat Song', in *Epistles, Odes, and Other Poems* (London: James Carpenter, 1806), pp. 305–07

Morning Post, 2609 (31 March 1781)

'Mrs. Gore', *La Belle Assemblée, or, Bell's Court and Fashionable Magazine Addressed Particularly to the Ladies*, 10: 3 (1 March 1837), 124–28

'Mrs. Gore', *The London Review and weekly journal of politics, literature, art, and society* (23 February 1861), p. 208

Musgrave, Agnes, *Edmund of the Forest. An Historical Novel*, 4 vols (London: William Lane, 1797)

Neale, Erskine, *Experiences of a Gaol Chaplain; Comprising Recollections of Ministerial Intercourse With Criminals of various classes, With their Confessions*, 3 vols (London: Richard Bentley, 1847)

—— *Self-Sacrifice; or, the Chancellor's Chaplain* (London: Bogue, 1844)

Nice Distinctions: A Tale (Dublin: J. Cumming, 1820)

'Novelists', *Supplement to La Belle Assemblée*, new series, 3 (July 1826), 303–07

Oldmixon, John, *A Complete History of Addresses, from their first original under Oliver Cromwell, to this present year 1710*, 2nd edn (London, 1710)

Palmer, John, *The Mystery of the Black Tower, A Romance*, 2 vols (London: Printed for the Author, by William Lane, 1796)

Parsons, Eliza, *Errors of Education*, 3 vols (London: William Lane, 1791)

Percy, Thomas, 'Cynthia, An Elegiac Poem', in *A Collection of Poems in six volumes*, 6 vols (London: Printed by J. Hughs, for R. and J. Dodsley, 1758), VI, 234–39

Perrault, Charles, *Histories, or tales of past times* (London: J. Pote, 1729)

Persiana, The Nymph of the Sea. A Novel, 3 vols (London: William Lane, 1791)

Poe, Edgar Allan, *Edgar Allan Poe's Annotated Short Stories*, ed. by Andrew Barger ([S.I.]: Bottletree Books, 2008)

Pope, Alexander, *The Poems of Alexander Pope*, gen. ed. John Butt, 11 vols (London: Methuen, 1967)

A pretty book for children: or, an easy guide to the English tongue (London: J. Newbery, 1761)

Prior, Matthew, 'Henry and Emma, A Poem, Upon the Model of The Nut-brown Maid', in *Poems on Several Occasions* (London, 1709), pp. 232–71

—— 'Solomon: a Poem in Three Books', in *Poems on Several Occasions* (London: J. Tonson and J. Barber, 1725), pp. 147–250

The Psalms, hymns, prayers, graces, and dulce domum, used by the scholars of Winchester College. Revised and corrected (Winchester: Printed for T. Burdon, 1760)

Public Advertiser, 4: 6059 (1 April 1754)

—— 6273 (10 December 1754)

Quarles, Francis, *Emblemes, divine and moral* (London: Printed by G. M. and Sold at John Marriots shop, 1635)

Radcliffe, Ann, *Gaston de Blondeville*, ed. by Frances Chiu (Chicago: Valancourt Books, 2006)

—— *The Italian*, ed. by Frederick Garber, rev. by Nick Groom (Oxford: Oxford University Press, 2017)

—— *The Mysteries of Udolpho*, ed. by Bonamy Dobrée (Oxford: Oxford University Press, 1998)

—— *The Romance of the Forest*, ed. by Chloe Chard (Oxford: Oxford University Press, 2009)

—— *The Romance of the Forest: Interspersed with Some Pieces of Poetry*, 3 vols (London: T. Hookham and J. Carpenter, 1791)

'Remarks on "Tales of the Crusaders"', *Edinburgh Magazine and literary miscellany*, 16 (June 1825), 641–46

Review of '*The Adventures of a Watch*', *The Critical Review, or Annals of Literature*, 65 (June 1788), 569

Review of '*The History of Jack Connor*', *Monthly Review*, 6 (June 1752), 447–49

Review of 'The Monk: a Romance. By M. G. Lewis, Esq.', *The Critical Review, or Annals of Literature*, 19 (February 1797), 194–200

Review of 'Observations on the Land Revenue of the Crown', *European Magazine and London Review*, 12 (August 1787), 121–25

Rowe, Nicholas, *The Tragedy of Jane Shore. Written in Imitation of Shakespear's Style* (London: Bernard Lintott, 1714)

Royer, Alphonse, 'Le Peau du Renard', *Revue de Paris*, 36 (February 1832), pp. 23–46

St. Clyde; A Novel, 3 vols (London: Gale and Fenner, 1816)

St. James's Chronicle, or British Evening Post, 3066 (26 October 1780)

Scott, Lady Caroline Lucy, *A Marriage in High Life*, 2 vols (London: Henry Colburn, 1828)

Scott, Walter, 'Art. VIII. Tales of My Landlord', *The Quarterly Review*, January 1817, 430–80

—— *Edinburgh Edition of the Waverley Novels*, gen. ed. David Hewitt, 30 vols (Edinburgh: Edinburgh University Press, 1993–2012)

—— *The Journal of Walter Scott*, ed. by W. E. K. Anderson (Oxford: Clarendon Press, 1972)

—— *The Letters of Sir Walter Scott*, ed. by H. J. C. Grierson, 12 vols (London: Constable, 1932–37)

—— 'Life of John Dryden', in *The Works of John Dryden*, ed. by Walter Scott, 18 vols (London: William Miller; Edinburgh: James Ballantyne, 1808), I

—— *Minstrelsy of the Scottish Border*, ed. by T. F. Henderson, 4 vols (Edinburgh: Blackwood and Sons, 1902)

—— *Minstrelsy of the Scottish Border: Consisting of Historical and Romantic Ballads*, 5th edn, 3 vols (Edinburgh: James Ballantyne and Co., 1812)

—— 'Prefatory Memoir To Mrs Ann Radcliffe', in *The Novels of Ann Radcliffe* (London: Hurst, Robinson, and Co.; Edinburgh: James Ballantyne, 1824), pp. i–xxxix

—— *Waverley*, ed. by Claire Lamont, with an Introduction by Kathryn Sutherland, rev. edn (Oxford: Oxford University Press, 2015)

Shakespeare, William, *Anthony and Cleopatra*, ed. by Michael Neill (Oxford: Oxford University Press, 2008)

—— *As You Like It*, ed. by Alan Brissenden (Oxford: Oxford University Press, 2008)

—— *Hamlet*, ed. by G. R. Hibbard (Oxford: Oxford University Press, 2008)

—— *Henry IV, Part Two*, ed. by René Weiss (Oxford: Oxford University Press, 2008)

—— *Henry V*, ed. by Gary Taylor (Oxford: Oxford University Press, 2008)

—— *Julius Caesar*, ed. by Arthur Humphrys (Oxford: Oxford University Press, 2008)

—— *Macbeth*, ed. by Nicholas Brooke (Oxford: Oxford University Press, 2008)

BIBLIOGRAPHY

—— *Measure for Measure*, ed. by N. W. Bawcutt (Oxford: Oxford University Press, 2008)

—— *A Midsummer Night's Dream*, ed. by Peter Holland (Oxford: Oxford University Press, 2008)

—— *Much Ado About Nothing*, ed. by Sheldon P. Zitner (Oxford: Oxford University Press, 2008)

—— *Romeo and Juliet*, ed. by Jill L. Levenson (Oxford: Oxford University Press, 2008)

—— *The Tempest*, ed. by Stephen Orgel (Oxford: Oxford University Press, 2008)

—— *The Tragedy of King Richard III*, ed. by John Jowett (Oxford: Oxford University Press, 2008)

—— *The Winter's Tale*, ed. by Stephen Orgel (Oxford: Oxford University Press, 2008)

Sharp, 'Letter', *Gentleman's Magazine: and historical chronicle*, 56: 6 (December 1786)

Sheridan, Richard Brinsley, *The School for Scandal and other plays*, ed. by Michael Cordner (Oxford: Oxford University Press, 1998)

Sicklemore, Richard, *Rashleigh Abbey; or, The Ruin on the Rock. A Romance*, 3 vols (London: Lane, Newman, and Co., 1805)

Smith, Charlotte, *The Collected Letters of Charlotte Smith*, ed. by Judith Phillips Stanton (Bloomington: Indiana University Press, 2003)

—— *The Works of Charlotte Smith*, gen. ed. Stuart Curran, 14 vols (London: Pickering & Chatto, 2005–07)

Smollett, Tobias, *The Adventures of Peregrine Pickle*, 4 vols (London: Printed for the Author, 1751)

Sotheby, William, *Ellen; or, The Confession: A Tragedy. In Five Acts. Altered and Adapted for Representation* (London: Printed for John Murray, 1816)

The Spectator, ed. by Donald Bond, 5 vols (Oxford: Clarendon Press, 1965)

Spenser, Edmund, *The Faerie Queene*, ed. by A. C. Hamilton, rev. 2nd edn (London: Routledge, 2013)

Stone, Elizabeth, *William Langshawe, the Cotton Lord*, 2 vols (London: Richard Bentley, 1842)

Sutherland, Alexander, *Tales of a Pilgrim* (Edinburgh: William Hunter; London: James Duncan, 1827)

Swift, Jonathan, *A Tale of a Tub and Other Works*, ed. by Marcus Walsh (Cambridge: Cambridge University Press, 2010)

Swinburne, Henry, *Travels in the Two Sicilies. In the years 1777, 1778, 1779, and 1780*, 2 vols (London: P. Elmsly, 1783–85)

The Tatler, ed. by Donald Bond, 3 vols (Oxford: Clarendon Press, 1987)

Tennyson, Alfred, 'Will Waterproof's Lyrical Monologue', in *The Poems of Tennyson*, ed. by Christopher Rick, 2nd edn, 3 vols (Harlow: Longman, 1987), II, 96–104

213

Thackeray, William Makepeace, *Letters and Private Papers of William Makepeace Thackeray*, ed. by Gordon N. Ray, 4 vols (London: Oxford University Press, 1945)

—— 'Novels by Eminent Hands', in *The Complete Works of William Makepeace Thackeray*, ed. by Micael Clarke, 27 vols (Newcastle upon Tyne: Cambridge Scholars Publishing, 2008), XXI, 112–20

Thomson, James, *The Seasons*, ed. by James Sambrook (Oxford: Oxford University Press, 1981)

Thomson, Katherine, *Widows and Widowers. A Romance of Real Life*, 3 vols (London: Richard Bentley, 1842)

Tillotson, John, *Sermons and discourses: Some of which Never before Printed. The third volume* (London: B. Aylmer and W. Rogers, 1686)

—— *Sermons preach'd upon several occasions*, 6th edn corrected, 2 vols (London: Brabazon Aylmer, 1685)

—— *Sermons preach'd upon several occasions. The fourth volume* (London: Br. Aylmer and W. Rogers, 1695)

Timbury, Jane, *The Philanthropic Rambler* (London: Printed for and sold by the Author, sold also by J. Southern and W. Nicoll, 1790)

—— *A Sequel to the Philanthropic Rambler* (London: Printed for the Author; and sold by G. G. J. and J. Robinson, R. Faulder, and J. Southern, 1791)

Tyler, Royall, *The Algerine Captive; or, The Life and Adventures of Doctor Updike Underhill, Six Years a Prisoner Among the Algerines*, 2 vols (London: G. and J. Robinson, 1802)

Virgil, 'Aeneid Books 1–6', in *Eclogues. Georgics. Aeneid: Books 1–6*, trans. by H. Rushton Fairclough, rev. by G. P. Goold (Cambridge, MA: Harvard University Press, 1999), pp. 261–597

Ward, Robert Plumer, *Pictures of the World at Home and Abroad*, 3 vols (London: Henry Colburn, 1839)

Warren, Samuel, 'Ten Thousand A-Year: Part XII', *Blackwood's Edinburgh Magazine*, 48: 300 (October 1840), 431–61

Warton, Thomas, *Poems. A new edition, with additions* (London: T. Becket, 1777)

Whitehall Evening Post, 550 (19 August 1749)

—— 793 (12 March 1751)

Williams, Helen Maria, *Julia, a novel; interspersed with some poetical pieces*, 2 vols (London: T. Cadell, 1790)

—— *Poems on various subjects: with introductory remarks on the present state of science and literature in France* (London: G. and W. B. Whittaker, 1823)

Secondary Sources

Adams, James Eli, *A History of Victorian Literature* (Chichester: Wiley-Blackwell, 2009)

Alexander, J. H., *Walter Scott's Books: Reading the Waverley Novels* (New York; Abingdon: Routledge, 2017)

BIBLIOGRAPHY

Anderson, Bonnie, 'The Writings of Catherine Gore', *Journal of Popular Culture*, 10: 2 (Fall 1976), 404–23

Barchas, Janine, *Graphic Design, Print Culture, and the Eighteenth-Century Novel* (Cambridge: Cambridge University Press, 2003)

Bassett, Troy J., *At the Circulating Library: A Database of Victorian Fiction, 1837–1850* <http://victorianresearch.org/atcl/index.php> [accessed March–August 2019]

Battaglia, Beatrice, 'The "Pieces of Poetry" in Ann Radcliffe's *The Mysteries of Udolpho*', in *Romantic Women Poets*, ed. by Lilla Maria Crisafulli and Cecilia Pietropoli (Amsterdam: Rodopi, 2007), pp. 137–51

Bernard, Stephen Jarrod, 'Edward Bysshe and *The Art of English Poetry*: Reading Writing in the Eighteenth Century', *Eighteenth-Century Studies*, 46: 1 (Fall 2012), 113–29

Blank, Antje, 'Things as They Were: The Gothic of Real Life in Charlotte Smith's *The Emigrants* and *The Banished Man*', *Women's Writing*, 16: 1 (May 2009), 78–93

Block, Andrew, *The English Novel, 1740–1850: A Catalogue Including Prose Romances, Short Stories, and Translations of Foreign Fiction*, with Introductions by John Crow and Ernest A. Baker, new and rev. edn (London: Dawson, 1961)

Boris, Kenneth, and Meredith Donaldson Clark, 'Hymnic Epic and *The Faerie Queene*'s Original Printed Format: Canto-Canticles and Psalmic Arguments', *Renaissance Quarterly*, 64 (2011), 1148–93

Bour, Isabelle, 'Sensibility as Epistemology in *Caleb Williams*, *Waverley*, and *Frankenstein*', *Studies in English Literature, 1500–1900*, 45 (2005), 813–27

Bree, Linda, *Sarah Fielding* (New York: Twayne Publishers, 1996)

Brill, Barbara, *William Gaskell 1805–1884: A Portrait* (Manchester: Manchester Literary and Philosophical Publications, 1984)

Brill, Lesley, 'Other Places, Other Times: The Sites of the Proems to *The Faerie Queene*', *Studies in English Literature, 1500–1900*, 34 (1994), 1–17

Brown, Marshall, 'Romanticism and Enlightenment', in *The Cambridge Companion to British Romanticism*, ed. by Stuart Curran (Cambridge: Cambridge University Press, 1993), pp. 25–47

Bruzelius, Margaret, *Romancing the Novel: Adventure from Scott to Sebald* (Lewisburg, PA: Bucknell University Press, 2007)

Campbell Ross, Ian, 'An Irish Picaresque Novel: William Chaigneau's *The History of Jack Connor*', *An Irish Quarterly Review*, 71: 283 (Autumn 1982), 270–79

Clery, E. J., *Women's Gothic: From Clara Reeve to Mary Shelley*, 2nd edn (Tavistock: Northcote House, 2004)

Conger, Syndy M., 'Sensibility Restored: Radcliffe's Answer to Lewis's *The Monk*', in *Gothic Fictions: Prohibition/Transgression*, ed. by Kenneth W. Graham (New York: AMS, 1989), pp. 113–49

Cooper, Joan Garden, 'Scott's Critique of the English Treason Law in *Waverley*', *Scottish Studies Review*, 4: 2 (2003), 17–36

Copeland, Edward, *The Silver Fork Novel: Fashionable Fiction in the Age of Reform* (Cambridge: Cambridge University Press, 2012)

Crawford, Joseph, '"Every Night, The Same Routine": Recurring Nightmares and the Repetition Compulsion in Gothic Fiction', *Moveable Type*, 6 (2010)

Dacome, Lucia, 'Noting the Mind: Commonplace Books and the Pursuit of the Self in Eighteenth-Century Britain', *Journal of the History of Ideas*, 65: 4 (October 2004), 603–25

DeLucia, JoEllen, *A Feminine Enlightenment: British Women Writers and the Philosophy of Progress, 1759–1820* (Edinburgh: Edinburgh University Press, 2015)

—— 'From the Female Gothic to a Feminist Theory of History: Ann Radcliffe and the Scottish Enlightenment', *The Eighteenth Century*, 50: 1 (Spring 2009), 101–15

Des Pres, Terrence, 'Terror and the Sublime', *Human Rights Quarterly*, 5: 2 (May 1983), 135–46

Douglas, Aileen, 'The Novel before 1800', in *The Cambridge Companion to the Irish Novel*, ed. by John Wilson Foster (Cambridge: Cambridge University Press, 2006), pp. 22–38

Duncan, Dennis, and Adam Smyth (eds), *Book Parts* (Oxford: Oxford University Press, 2019)

Durant, David, 'Ann Radcliffe and the Conservative Gothic', *Studies in English Literature, 1500–1900*, 22: 3 (Summer 1982), 519–30

Dykstal, Timothy, 'Provoking the Ancients: Classical Learning and Imitation in Fielding and Collier', *College Literature* 31: 3 (Summer 2004), 102–22

Dzelzainis, Ella, 'Silver-Fork, Industrial, and Gothic Fiction', in *The Cambridge Companion to Victorian Women's Writing*, ed. by Linda H. Peterson (Cambridge: Cambridge University Press, 2015), pp. 105–18

Ebbes, Verena, Peter Garside, Angela Koch, Anthony Mandal, and Rainer Schöwerling (eds), 'The English Novel, 1830–1836: A Bibliographical Survey of Fiction Published in the British Isles', *Romantic Textualities* (Cardiff: Cardiff University Press, 2016) <http://www.romtext.org.uk/resources/english-novel-1830-36/> [accessed throughout 2017]

Edwards, A. S. G., 'Gaskell's *North and South* and John Lydgate', *Notes and Queries*, 56: 3 (September 2009), 399

Ehlerd, Rebecca, 'S. Maria Del Pianto: Loss, Remembrance and Legacy in Seventeenth Century Naples', PhD thesis, Queen's University Kingston, Ontario, Canada (2007)

Ellis, Markman, *The History of Gothic Fiction* (Edinburgh: Edinburgh University Press, 2005)

BIBLIOGRAPHY

Engelhardt, Molly, '"The Novelist of a New Era": Deepening the Sketch of Catherine Gore', *Victorian Review*, 42: 1 (Spring 2016), 65–84

Farooq, Jennifer, *Preaching in Eighteenth-Century London* (Woodbridge: Boydell Press, 2013)

Feibel, Juliet, 'Highland Histories: Jacobitism and Second Sight', *CLIO*, 30: 1 (2000), 51–77

Fetzer, Margret, 'Beyond Beginning: Walter Scott's (Para)textualisation of Scottishness', *Anglia*, 128 (2010), 273–97

Fleming, Patrick C., 'The Rise of the Moral Tale: Children's Literature, the Novel, and *The Governess*', *Eighteenth-Century Studies*, 46: 4 (Summer 2013), 463–77

Fletcher, Loraine, *Charlotte Smith: A Critical Biography* (Basingstoke: Macmillan, 1998)

Frank, Cathrine, 'Wandering Narratives and Wavering Conclusions: Irreconciliation in Frances Burney's *The Wanderer* and Walter Scott's *Waverley*', *European Romantic Review*, 12 (2001), 429–56

Freeman, Alan, 'Allegories of Ambivalence: Scottish Fiction, Britain and Empire', in *Readings of the Particular: The Postcolonial in the Postnational*, ed. by Anne Holden Ronning and Lene Johannessen (Amsterdam: Rodopi, 2007), pp. 39–56

Fry, Michael, *Edinburgh: A History of the City* (Basingstoke: Macmillan, 2009)

Gamer, Michael, '*Waverley* and the Object of (Literary) History', *Modern Language Quarterly*, 70 (2009), 495–525

Garside, Peter, James Raven, and Rainer Shöwerling (gen. eds), *The English Novel 1770–1829: A Bibliographical Survey of Prose Fiction Published in the British Isles*, 2 vols (Oxford: Oxford University Press, 2000)

Genette, Gérard, *Paratexts: Thresholds of Interpretation*, trans. by Jane E. Lewin (Cambridge: Cambridge University Press, 1997)

Georgieva, Margarita, *The Gothic Child* (Basingstoke: Palgrave Macmillan, 2013)

Ginsburg, Michael Peled, 'Pseudonym, Epigraphs, and Narrative Voice: Middlemarch and the Problem of Authorship', *English Literary History*, 47: 3 (Autumn 1980), 542–58

Girten, Kristin M., '"Sublime Luxuries" of the Gothic Edifice: Immersive Aesthetics and Kantian Freedom in the Novels of Ann Radcliffe', *Eighteenth-Century Fiction*, 28: 4 (Summer 2016), 713–38

Gonda, Caroline, *Reading Daughters' Fictions 1709–1834: Novels and Society from Manley to Edgeworth* (Cambridge: Cambridge University Press, 1996)

Grutman, Rainier, 'How to Do Things with Mottoes: Recipes from the Romantic Era (with Special Reference to Stendhal)', *Neohelicon*, 37: 1 (June 2010), 139–53

—— 'Quoting Europe: Mottomania in the Romantic Age', in *Time Refigured: Myths, Foundation Texts and Imagined Communities*, ed. by Martin Procházka and Ondřej Pilný (Prague: Litteraria Pragensia, 2005), pp. 281–95

Haber, Tom B., 'The Chapter-Tags in the Waverley Novels', *PMLA*, 45: 4 (December 1930), 1140–49

Haynes, Kenneth, *English Literature and Ancient Languages* (Oxford: Oxford University Press, 2007)

Heydt-Stevenson, Jillian, and Charlotte Sussman, '"Launched upon the Sea of Moral and Political Inquiry": The Ethical Experiments of the Romantic Novel', in *Recognizing the Romantic Novel: New Histories of British Fiction, 1780–1830*, ed. by Jillian Heydt-Stevenson and Charlotte Sussman (Liverpool: Liverpool University Press, 2010), pp. 13–48

Hildebrand, Jayne, 'The Ranter and the Lyric: Reform and Genre Heterogeneity in Ebenezer Elliott's *Corn Law Rhymes*', *Victorian Review*, 39: 1 (2013), 101–24

Hooley, Dan, 'Roman Satire and Epigram: Horace, Juvenal, and Martial', in *The Oxford History of Classical Reception in English Literature*, ed. by David Hopkins and Charles Martindale, 5 vols (Oxford: Oxford University Press, 2012–2019), III, 217–54

Howells, Coral Ann, *Love, Mystery and Misery: Feeling in Gothic Fiction* (London: Bloomsbury, 2013)

—— 'The Pleasure of the Woman's Text: Ann Radcliffe's Subtle Transgressions in *The Mysteries of Udolpho* and *The Italian*', in *Gothic Fictions: Prohibition/Transgression*, ed. by Kenneth W. Graham (New York: AMS, 1989), pp. 151–62

Hughes, Winifred, 'Gore [née Moody], Catherine Grace Frances (1799/1800–1861), Novelist and Playwright', in *Oxford Dictionary of National Biography* (Oxford: Oxford University Press, 2004) <http://www.oxforddnb.com/view/10.1093/ref:odnb/9780198614128.001.0001/odnb-9780198614128-e-11091> [accessed 27 April 2018]

Hunter, J. Paul, *Before Novels: The Cultural Contexts of Eighteenth-Century English Fiction* (New York: W. W. Norton, 1990)

Irvine, Robert P., 'Enlightenment, Agency and Romance: The Case of Scott's *Guy Mannering*', *Journal of Narrative Theory*, 30: 1 (2000), 29–54

Isbell, John Claiborne, 'Romantic Novel and Verse Romance, 1750–1850: Is There a Romance Continuum?', in *Romantic Prose Fiction*, ed. by Gerald Gillespie, Manfred Engel, and Bernard Dieterle (Amsterdam: John Benjamins, 2008), pp. 496–516

Jackson, Jeffrey E., 'Elizabeth Gaskell and the Dangerous Edge of Things: Epigraphs in *North and South* and Victorian Publishing Practices', *Pacific Coast Philology*, 40: 2 (2005), 56–72

Jackson, Jessamyn, 'Why Novels Make Bad Mothers', *NOVEL: A Forum on Fiction*, 27: 2 (Winter 1994), 161–74

Jacobs, Edward, 'Ann Radcliffe and Romantic Print Culture', in *Ann Radcliffe, Romanticism, and the Gothic*, ed. by Dale Townshend and Angela Wright (Cambridge: Cambridge University Press, 2014), pp. 49–66

Jay, Elisabeth, *British Writers and Paris 1830–1875* (Oxford: Oxford University Press, 2016)

Kelly, Gary, *English Fiction of the Romantic Period 1789–1830* (London: Routledge, 1989)

—— 'Unbecoming a Heroine: Novel Reading, Romanticism, and Barrett's *The Heroine*', *Nineteenth-Century Literature*, 45: 2 (September 1990), 220–41

Kendra, April, 'Gendering the Silver Fork: Catherine Gore and the Society Novel', *Women's Writing*, 11: 1 (2004), 25–38

—— 'Silver-Forks and Double Standards: Gore, Thackeray and the Problem of Parody', *Women's Writing*, 16: 2 (2009), 191–217

—— 'Silver Forks, Stereotypes, and Regency Romance', *Studies in the Humanities*, 34: 2 (December 2007), 142–63

Knowles, Elizabeth, *And I Quote . . . A History of Using Other People's Words* (Oxford: Oxford University Press, 2018)

Kokot, Joanna, 'Between Harmony and Chaos: Poetry and Music in Ann Radcliffe's *The Mysteries of Udolpho*', in *The Enchantress of Words, Sounds and Image: Anniversary Essays on Ann Radcliffe (1764–1823)*, ed. by Jakub Lipski and Jacek Mydla (Palo Alto, CA: Academica Press, 2015), pp. 53–70

Kowaleski-Wallace, Elizabeth, *Consuming Subjects: Women, Shopping, and Business in the Eighteenth Century* (New York: Columbia University Press, 1997)

Kronshage, Eike, 'The Function of Poetic Epigraphs in George Eliot's *Daniel Deronda*', *Connotations*, 23: 2 (2013/14), 230–60

Labbe, Jacqueline M. (ed.), *Charlotte Smith in British Romanticism* (London: Pickering & Chatto, 2008)

Lamont, Claire, 'William Collins's "Ode on the Popular Superstitions of the Highlands of Scotland" – A Newly Recovered Manuscript', *The Review of English Studies*, 19: 74 (May 1968), 137–47 (p. 137)

Latin Dictionary (Glasgow: HarperCollins, 1997, repr. 2001)

Lawford, Cynthia, 'Turbans, Tea and Talk of Books: The Literary Parties of Elizabeth Spence and Elizabeth Benger', *Corvey Women Writers on the Web 1796–1834 CW³ Journal* <https://www2.shu.ac.uk/corvey/cw3journal/issues/lawford.html> [accessed 20 June 2018]

Lawlor, Clark, 'The Grotesque, Reform and Sensibility in Dryden, Sarah Fielding and Jane Collier', *British Journal for Eighteenth-Century Studies*, 22 (1999), 187–205

Levin, Carole, *The Heart and Stomach of a King: Elizabeth I and the Politics of Sex and Power*, 2nd edn (Philadelphia: University of Pennsylvania Press, 2013)

Lilti, Antoine, *The World of the Salons: Sociability and Worldliness in Eighteenth-Century Paris*, trans. by Lydia G. Cochrane (Oxford: Oxford University Press, 2005)

Lincoln, Andrew, 'Scott and Empire: The Case of *Rob Roy*', *Studies in the Novel*, 34 (2002), 43–58

Locke, Louis G., *Tillotson: A Study in Seventeenth-Century Literature* (Copenhagen: Rosenkilde and Bagger, 1954)

Ludlow, Elizabeth, 'Elizabeth Gaskell's Early Contributions to *Household Words*: The Use of Parable and the Transformation of Communities through "Kinder Understanding"', *Victorian Review*, 42: 1 (Spring 2016), 107–25

Macdonald, David Lorne, *Monk Lewis: A Critical Biography* (Toronto: University of Toronto Press, 2000)

McPherson, Heather, 'Theatrical Celebrity and the Commodification of the Actor', in *The Oxford Handbook of the Georgian Theatre 1737–1832*, ed. by Julia Swindells and David Francis Taylor (Oxford: Oxford University Press, 2014), pp. 192–212

Mahawatte, Royce, '"Life that is not clad in the same coat-tails and flounces": The Silver-Fork Novel, George Eliot and the Fear of the Material', *Women's Writing*, 16: 2 (2009), 323–44

Markley, A. A., 'Banished Men and the "New Order of Things": The French Émigré and the Complexities of Revolutionary Politics in Charlotte Smith and Mary Robinson', *Women's Writing*, 19: 4 (November 2012), 387–403

Mason, Nicholas, *Literary Advertising and the Shaping of British Romanticism* (Baltimore, MD: Johns Hopkins University Press, 2013)

Matus, Jill L. (ed.), *The Cambridge Companion to Elizabeth Gaskell* (Cambridge: Cambridge University Press, 2007)

Messier, Vartan P., 'The Conservative, the Transgressive, and the Reactionary: Ann Radcliffe's *The Italian* as a Response to Matthew Lewis' *The Monk*', *Atenea*, 25: 2 (2005), 37–48

Michasiw, Kim Ian, 'Ann Radcliffe and the Terrors of Power', *Eighteenth-Century Fiction*, 6: 4 (July 1994), 327–46

Miles, Robert, *Gothic Writing 1750–1820: A Genealogy* (London: Routledge, 1993)

Miner, Paul, 'Francis Quarles's Influence on Europe 11', *Blake: An Illustrated Quarterly*, 47: 4 (2014) <https://blakequarterly.org/index.php/blake/article/view/miner474> [accessed 9 January 2023]

Mitchell, William Fraser, *English Pulpit Oratory from Andrewes to Tillotson: A Study of its Literary Aspects* (New York: Russell & Russell, 1962)

Molekamp, Femke, 'Genevan Legacies', in *The Oxford Handbook of the Bible in Early Modern England, c. 1530–1700*, ed. by Kevin Killeen, Helen Smith, and Rachel Judith Willie (Oxford: Oxford University Press, 2015), pp. 38–53

—— *Women and the Bible in Early Modern England: Religious Reading and Writing* (Oxford: Oxford University Press, 2013)

Moore, Steven, *The Novel: An Alternative History 1600–1800* (London: Bloomsbury, 2013)

Mulder, John R., *The Temple of the Mind: Education and Literary Taste in Seventeenth-Century England* (New York: Pegasus, 1969)

Napton, Dani, and Stephanie Russo, 'Place in Charlotte Smith's *The Banished Man* and Walter Scott's *Woodstock*', *Studies in English Literature*, 52: 4 (Autumn 2012), 747–63

Newman, Donald J. (ed.), *The Spectator: Emerging Discourses* (Newark: University of Delaware Press, 2005)

Nixon, Cheryl, 'Ann Radcliffe's Commonplace Book: Assembling the Female Body and the Material Text', *Women's Writing*, 22: 3 (2015), 355–75

Norton, Rictor, 'Ann Radcliffe, "The Shakespeare of Romance Writers"', in *Shakespearean Gothic*, ed. by Christy Desmet and Anne Williams (Cardiff: University of Wales Press, 2009), pp. 37–59

—— (ed.), *Gothic Readings: The First Wave, 1764–1840* (London: Leicester University Press, 2006)

—— *Mistress of Udolpho: The Life of Ann Radcliffe* (London: Leicester University Press, 1998)

Nunning, Ansgar, 'On Metanarrative: Towards a Definition, a Typology and an Outline of the Functions of Metanarrative Commentary', in *The Dynamics of Narrative Form: Studies in Anglo-American Narratology*, ed. by John Pier (Berlin; New York: Walter de Gruyter, 2005), pp. 11–58

O'Cinneide, Muireann, *Aristocratic Women and the Literary Nation, 1832–1867* (London: Palgrave Macmillan, 2008)

Patmore, D., *The Life and Times of Coventry Patmore* (London: Constable, 1949)

Perkell, Christine, 'Aeneid I: An Epic Program', in *Reading Vergil's Aeneid: An Interpretive Guide*, ed. by Christine Perkell (Norman: University of Oklahoma Press, 1999), pp. 29–49

Pollack-Pelzner, Daniel, 'Quoting Shakespeare in the British Novel', in *Shakespeare and Quotation*, ed. by Julie Maxwell and Kate Rumbold (Cambridge: Cambridge University Press, 2018), pp. 136–55

Prendergest, Amy, *Literary Salons Across Britain and Ireland in the Long Eighteenth Century* (Basingstoke: Palgrave Macmillan, 2015)

Price, Leah, *The Anthology and the Rise of the Novel: From Richardson to George Eliot* (Cambridge: Cambridge University Press, 2000, repr. 2004)

Probyn, Clive, 'Fielding, Sarah (1710–1768)', in *Oxford Dictionary of National Biography* (Oxford: Oxford University Press, 2004) <http://www.oxforddnb.com/view/article/9405> [accessed 8 March 2016]

Punter, David, *The Literature of Terror: A History of Gothic Fictions from 1765 to the Present Day*, 2nd edn (London: Routledge, 2013)

Readioff, Corrina, 'A Paratextual Battle: Mottos, Meaning and Conflict in Printed Journals 1709–1712', *The Review of English Studies*, 73: 309 (2022), 302–20

Richstad, Josephine, 'Genre in Amber: Preserving the Fashionable Novel for a Victorian Decade, Catherine Gore's *Hamiltons* (1834 and 1850)', *Modern Philology*, 111: 3 (February 2014), 549–65

Rogers, Deborah D., *The Matrophobic Gothic and its Legacy: Sacrificing Mothers in the Novel and in Popular Culture* (New York: Peter Lang, 2007)

Rumbold, Kate, *Shakespeare and the Eighteenth-Century Novel: Cultures of Quotation from Samuel Richardson to Jane Austen* (Cambridge: Cambridge University Press, 2016)

Russo, Stephanie, '"A people driven by terror": Charlotte Smith, *The Banished Man* and the Politics of Counter-Revolution', in *The French Revolution and the British Novel in the Romantic Period*, ed. by A. D. Cousins, Dani Napton, and Stephanie Russo (New York: Lang, 2011), pp. 37–54

Sadleir, Michael, *Bulwer: A Panorama. Edward and Rosina 1803–1836* (London: Constable, 1931)

Saggini, Francesca, *The Gothic Novel and the Stage: Romantic Appropriations* (Abingdon: Routledge, 2016)

Saglia, Diego, 'Looking at the Other: Cultural Difference and the Traveller's Gaze in *The Italian*', *Studies in the Novel*, 28: 1 (Spring 1996), 12–37

Salter, David, '"This demon in the garb of a monk": Shakespeare, the Gothic and the Discourse of Anti-Catholicism', *Shakespeare*, 5: 1 (April 2009), 52–67

Sharp, Richard, 'Boswell, John (1698–1757)', in *Oxford Dictionary of National Biography* (Oxford: Oxford University Press, 2004) <http://www.oxforddnb.com/view/article/2952> [accessed 6 April 2016]

Sharpe, Ada, 'Margaret Hale's Books and Flowers: *North and South*'s Paratextual Dialogues with Felicia Hemans', *Victorian Review*, 40: 1 (Spring 2014), 197–209

Shastri, Sudha, *Intertextuality and Victorian Studies* (Himayatnagar, Hyderabad: Orient Longman, 2001)

Skeen, Catherine, '*Gulliver's Travels*, *Jack Connor*, and *John Buncle*', *Modern Philology*, 100: 3 (February 2003), 330–59

Smith, Andrew, 'Radcliffe's Aesthetics: Or, the Problem with Burke and Lewis', *Women's Writing*, 22: 3 (2015), 317–30

BIBLIOGRAPHY

Smith, Muriel, 'Lines from Ludwig Uhland: A Note', *Notes and Commentary: The Gaskell Society Journal*, 11 (1 January 1997), 103–04

Smyth, Adam, *Autobiography in Early Modern England* (Cambridge: Cambridge University Press, 2010)

Sobba Green, Katherine, 'The Heroine's Blazon and Hardwicke's Marriage Act: Commodification for a Novel Market', *Tulsa Studies in Women's Literature*, 9: 2 (Autumn 1990), 273–90

Sodeman, Melissa, 'Charlotte Smith's Literary Exile', *English Literary History*, 76 (2009), 131–52

Starr, G. A., 'From Socrates to Sarah Fielding: Benevolence, Irony, and Conversation', in *Passionate Encounters in a Time of Sensibility*, ed. by Maximillian E. Novak and Anne Mellor (Newark: University of Delaware Press, 2000), pp. 106–26

Steadman, John M., 'Una and the Clergy: The Ass Symbol in *The Faerie Queene*', *Journal of the Warburg and Courtauld Institutes*, 21: 1/2 (1958), 134–37

Stevens, Anne, *British Historical Fiction before Scott* (Basingstoke: Palgrave Macmillan, 2010)

Suzuki, Mika, '"Words I in Fancy say for you": Sarah Fielding's Letters and Epistolary Method', *The Yearbook of English Studies*, 28 (1998), 196–211

Tandon, Bharat, 'The Literary Context', in *The Cambridge Companion to 'Emma'*, ed. by Peter Sabor (Cambridge: Cambridge University Press, 2015), pp. 17–35

Uglow, Jenny, *Elizabeth Gaskell: A Habit of Stories* (London: Faber & Faber, 1993, repr. 1999)

Unsworth, Anna, 'Elizabeth Gaskell and German Romanticism', *Gaskell Society Journal*, 8 (1994), 1–14

Vogrinčič, Ana, 'The Novel-Reading Panic in 18th-Century in England: An Outline of an Early Moral Media Panic', *Medijska Istrazivanja/Media Research*, 14: 2 (2008), 103–24

Waithe, Marcus, 'The Pen and the Hammer: Thomas Carlyle, Ebenezer Elliott, and the "active poet"', in *Class and the Canon: Constructing Labouring-Class Poetry and Poetics, 1780–1900*, ed. by Kirstie Blair and Mina Gorji (Basingstoke: Palgrave Macmillan, 2013), pp. 116–35

Warren, Andrew, 'Designing and Undrawing Veils: Anxiety and Authorship in Radcliffe's *The Italian*', *The Eighteenth Century*, 54: 4 (2013), 521–44

Wheeler, Michael, *The Art of Allusion in Victorian Fiction* (London; Basingstoke: Macmillan, 1979)

Whiting Rosa, Matthew, *The Silver-Fork School* (New York: Columbia University Press, 1936)

Wiesner, Merry E., *Women and Gender in Early Modern Europe*, 2nd edn (Cambridge: Cambridge University Press, 2000)

Williams, Anne, *Art of Darkness: A Poetics of Gothic* (Chicago: University of Chicago Press, 1995)

Wilson, Cheryl, *Fashioning the Silver Fork Novel* (London: Pickering & Chatto, 2012)

Winkler, Kenneth P., 'Perception and Ideas, Judgement', in *The Cambridge Book of Eighteenth Century Philosophy*, ed. by Knud Haakonssen, 2 vols (Cambridge: Cambridge University Press, 2006), I, 234–85

Woodward, Carolyn, 'Who Wrote *The Cry*?: A Fable for Our Times', *Eighteenth-Century Fiction*, 9: 1 (October 1996), 91–97

WorldCat, <https://www.worldcat.org/> [accessed March–August 2019]

Wright, Angela, 'Scottish Gothic', in *The Routledge Companion to Gothic*, ed. by Catherine Spooner and Emma McEvoy (London: Routledge, 2007), pp. 73–82

Yem, Eirian Jade, 'Forgetting Oneself: Epigraphs and Escapism in Ann Radcliffe's Novels', *Journal for Eighteenth-Century Studies*, 45: 3 (September 2022), 305–21

INDEX

Literary works are listed under individual authors' names.

Addington, John, *Poetical Quotations*, 111
Addison, Joseph, 8, 9, 26, 27
advertisements, 15, 28, 92, 109, 123, 138, 144
allegory, 15, 21, 22–3
Amicable Quixote, The, 65, 71, 86n63, 127
anthologies, 141
    of periodicals, 9, 10, 25, 27, 133
    of prose, 6, 118, 119, 123, 124, 135, 136
    of poetry, 69, 98, 100, 101
    of sermons, 9
Argentum: or Adventures of a Shilling, 64, 65
arguments (prefatory, in verse), 20–1, 22, 24, 61
Ariosto, 20
    Orlando Furioso, 1, 111
Austen, Jane, 5, 91, 119, 124, 154
    Emma, 88
    Northanger Abbey, 12, 66, 87–8, 89

Bacon, Francis, 126
Baillie, Joanna, 109
Ballantyne, James, 91, 94, 97, 98, 100, 105, 113
Barbauld, Anna Letitia, 116, 150
Barchas, Janine, 4
Barrett, Eaton Stannard, 88, 91
    The Heroine: or, Adventures of a Fair Romance Reader, 12, 66, 85–7, 91, 92
    The Miss-led General; A Serio-Comic, Satiric, Mock-Heroic Romance, 87
Barrett Browning, Elizabeth, 143
Bassett, Troy J., 5, 117
Beattie, James, 39, 71, 84

Beaumont and Fletcher, 30, 98
Beckford, William, 126, 132, 134–5
    Vathek, 36
Bell, Joseph, 67
Bentley, Richard, 124, 136, 138
Bible, 7, 8, 9, 18, 20, 30, 45–6
Blackwood's Magazine, 126
Blair, Robert, 82, 84
Blake, William, 46
Block, Andrew, 5, 117
Boaden, James, *Fontainville Forest*, 121
bons mots, 120, 127, 128
British Critic, 37
British Essayists, The, 133–4
Brontë sisters, 5, 118, 154
Bulwer-Lytton, Edward, 118, 120, 126, 129, 130, 131, 138, 155
    Pelham, 12, 124, 127–8, 129, 132
Burke, Edmund, 50–1, 62
    Philosophical Enquiry into the Sublime and Beautiful, 51
Burney, Frances, 34, 138
Bury, Lady Charlotte Susan Maria, 118, 124
    The Divorced, 125, 133
    The Exclusives, 138
    Flirtation, 124
    The Separation, 124
Butler, Samuel, *Hudibras*, 100
Byron, Lord, 126, 136, 137
Bysshe, Edmund, 31

Cadell, Thomas, 70
Cadell, Thomas Jr, 72, 79
Campbell, Thomas, 'Lochiel's Warning', 105

canonicity, 3, 5, 10, 27, 39, 40, 41, 73, 86, 115, 118, 143, 149, 154, 155, 156
Cervantes, Miguel de, 10, 16, 32, 40
Chaigneau, William, 32, 91, 103, 114, 115, 155
The History of Jack Connor, 7, 10, 15, 16–19, 31, 34, 43, 66, 85, 163
self-authored epigraphs, 17, 115
Chapman, Edward, 144–5
chapter descriptors/summaries, 5, 6, 16,17, 40, 85–6, 92–3, 118
chapter-tags, 4, 5, 98, 118, 133; *see also* chapter titles; epigraphs
chapter titles, 4, 5, 6, 41, 86, 92, 94, 102–3
absence of, 56, 124, 142
definition of, 5
humorous, 10, 16, 40–1, 102–3
interchangeability with epigraphs, 40, 41, 89, 92–3, 102, 113, 118
frequency of use, 35, 91, 102, 118
quotation-based, 9, 12, 94, 102–3, 104, 152
used alongside epigraphs, 1, 35, 92–3, 118, 149–50, 151–2
Chaucer, Geoffrey, 'The Knight's Tale', 14
Colburn, Henry, 135, 142
Coleridge, Samuel Taylor, *Rime of the Ancient Mariner*, 152
Collier, Jane, 10, 37, 91, 103, 114, 155
The Cry: A New Dramatic Fable, 10, 11, 15, 16, 19–32, 34, 36, 71, 72, 85, 165
see also Fielding, Sarah
Collins, William, 39, 48, 60, 71, 84, 90
commonplace book, 30–1, 79, 88, 137, 142
Ann Radcliffe's, 62–3
contents lists, 9, 93

Dacre, Charlotte, 65
Davis, John, *The Post-Captain*, 93, 115
dedications, 92, 114, 142
Defoe, Daniel, 10, 109
Dickens, Charles, 5, 118, 148, 154
didactic fiction, 10, 14, 15, 28, 32, 36–7, 73, 89, 155
Disraeli, Benjamin, 120, 136, 138, 142
Vivian Grey, 119
Dodsley, John, *A Collection of Poems*, 38
Dryden, John, 14; *see also* Scott, Sir Walter, *Life of Dryden*

Edgeworth, Maria, 119, 138, 147
education, 10–11, 16, 18, 19, 27, 28–9, 30, 31, 32, 53, 56, 65, 71, 87, 89, 133, 141, 143, 155
Eliot, George, 4, 117, 119, 123, 154, 155, 156
Middlemarch, 2, 13, 117, 153–4
Elliott, Ebenezer, 147–8
epigraphs
and drama/theatricality, 33, 40, 42, 44, 58, 83, 99, 101, 106, 108, 111–2, 121–2, 124, 125, 126, 149, 153–4
anonymously authored, 16, 97–8, 126
as morals, 14–15, 16, 17, 19, 23, 24–5, 31, 43, 153–4, 155
as summary, 24, 42
attributions, 16, 42–3, 44, 46–7, 48, 54, 58, 63, 74, 75, 78–9, 80, 93, 97–8, 102, 110–3, 115, 126, 127, 131, 139, 140, 141, 146–7, 155
definition of, 4–5
from canonical literature, 3, 39, 41, 73, 86, 115, 149; *see also* canonicity
functionality of, 2–5, 10, 11, 23, 25, 29, 39–40, 45, 46, 57–8, 63, 64, 74, 76, 80, 88–9, 93, 95, 97, 111, 113, 120, 121–2, 125, 127, 130–1, 146, 148, 152, 155–6
humorous/comedic, 17, 64, 66, 76, 87, 94, 103, 120, 127, 129–32, 137, 152, 155
in French, 71, 72, 132, 133, 136, 138, 139–40, 142
in Gaelic, 90–1, 100
in German, 132, 133, 136, 142
in Greek, 132, 133, 134, 135–6
in Italian, 71, 72, 132, 133, 136
in Latin, 27, 28, 30, 35–6, 71, 72, 100–1, 102, 132, 133–4, 135, 136
in prose, 5, 6, 124–5, 126, 127, 130, 131, 137, 139–40, 142, 149; *see also* arguments (prefatory, in verse)
in Spanish, 132
in Turkish, 140
multiple, 47, 69–70, 85–6, 111, 118, 137, 142
number of novels featuring, 7, 11, 12, 15, 34, 65, 91, 95, 102, 106, 114, 117–18, 154
self-authored/invented, 1, 4, 11, 13, 17, 54–5, 66, 94, 99–100, 111–12, 113, 115, 126, 142, 146, 153–4

INDEX

terminology, 2, 4–5, 97, 133, 144
and translation 16, 27, 35, 54, 71, 100–1, 133–4, 139–40, 142
epilogue, 25
epistolary fiction, 10, 35, 36, 85
Euripides, 75
European Magazine, 35

Female Tatler, 9
Fielding, Henry, 10, 15, 16, 32, 40, 102
Tom Jones, 15, 40, 103
Fielding, Sarah, 10, 37, 91, 103, 114, 155
The Cry: A Dramatick Fable, 10, 11, 15, 16, 19–32, 34, 36, 71–2, 85, 164
Familiar Letters, 26
The Governess, 19
frame narratives, 55–8, 62, 110
French Revolution, 66, 68, 69

Garrick, David, 33, 98
Garside, Peter, James Raven and Rainer Schöwerling (gen. eds), *The English Novel 1770–1829*, 5–6, 65, 117
Garth, Samuel, 30
Gaskell, Elizabeth, 4, 12, 119, 120, 142, 143, 154, 155
Mary Barton, 12, 120, 142, 143, 144–8, 149, 171
North and South, 1–2, 12, 120, 145, 147, 148–52, 171
Wives and Daughters, 143
Gaskell, William, 145, 146, 149
Genette, Gérard, 2, 3, 4, 155
Gentleman's Magazine, 46
ghosts, 33, 50, 53, 59, 62, 78, 81, 83, 105, 121–2
Goëthe, 137
Goldsmith, Oliver, 126
The Deserted Village, 72
Letters from a Citizen of the World, 130
The Vicar of Wakefield, 40, 41
Gore, Catherine Grace Frances, 12, 118–21, 124, 128, 129, 130, 132–3, 136, 138, 142, 143, 149, 152, 154, 155
and languages of epigraphs, 132–6, 138, 139–41, 142
and self-authored epigraphs, 126, 127
and translated epigraphs, 134–5, 139–41

Cecil, a Peer, 128, 133, 134–5, 138, 139, 141
Cecil: Or, The Adventures of a Coxcomb, 122, 123, 126, 133, 134–8, 139, 141
The Courtier of the Days of Charles the Second, and other Tales, 135
The Dean's Daughter, 142
friendship with William Beckford, 132, 134–5
The Heir of Selwood, 133
The Manners of the Day, 123, 124, 132, 136
Mothers and Daughters, 131, 133, 143
Modern Chivalry, 139–41
Pin Money, 124, 130–1
The Reign of Terror, 122
Romances of Real Life, 123
Self, 135, 138
The Story of a Royal Favourite, 135
Theresa Marchmont, 120–1, 122–3, 126
Gothic fiction, 3, 4, 11, 13, 32, 36, 37, 40, 43, 50, 55, 56, 57, 62, 65, 66, 67, 68, 71, 77, 78, 80, 85–6, 87, 88, 101, 103, 108, 114, 119, 120, 121, 122, 123, 126, 143, 152, 155
Grand Tour, 56, 57
Gray, Thomas, 39, 84, 88
'Elegy Written in a Country Churchyard', 88

Hall, Anna Maria, 129
Hartley, David, *Observations on Man*, 49
Hazlitt, William, 119
Helme, Elizabeth, 35
Louisa; or, The Cottage on the Moor, 4n12, 34–5, 166
Hemans, Felicia Dorothea, 149
heraldry, 7, 9, 96–7
historical fiction, 4, 62, 78, 102, 121, 143, 155
The Histories of Some of the Penitents in the Magdalen House, 14–15, 32
Hogarth, William, 33
Homer, 16, 20, 28, 30, 101
Hook, Theodore, *Sayings and Doings*, 119
Horace, 24, 26, 27, 28, 30, 64, 70
Hugo, Victor, 93

immorality, 23, 25, 28, 58, 138
introductions (of books), 2, 20, 91–2, 99, 100, 101

227

Jacobites, 104, 105
Jacobs, Edward, 3, 5, 33, 37, 40, 41, 55, 118
Jerdan, William, 128
Jewsbury, Geraldine, *The Half-Sisters*, 144
Johnson, Samuel, 47n53, 70
   The Rambler, 16, 75n36
Johnstone, Christian Isobel, *Clan-Albin: A National Tale*, 90–1, 94
Jonson, Ben, 30, 126
Jouy, Étienne de, 139
Juvenal, 16, 18

Kant, Immanuel, 50, 51, 52
Kearsley, George, 35
Kelly, Gary, 3, 37, 40, 41, 84, 85, 87
Kelly, Isabella, 65
Kemble, John Philip, 121
Kotzebue, 137

Lane, William, 35
Lathom, Francis, 65
Lee, Nathaniel, 84
   Rival Queens, 132
Lee, Sophia, *The Recess*, 36
Lewis, Matthew, 4, 34, 80, 85, 86, 122, 124, 155
   quoted in an epigraph, 122
   Tales of Wonder, 90, 122n30
   The Monk, 4, 11, 55, 66, 81–4, 89, 121, 169
Lister, Thomas, *Granby*, 124
Locke, John, 30, 31
Louis XVI, 77
Lounger, 133
Lucretius, 30

Mackenzie, Anna Maria, 32, 34, 65
Mackenzie, Henry, *The Man of Feeling* 109
Macpherson, James, 39
Mason, John, *Self-Knowledge*, 30–1
Mason, William, 84
Milton, John, 20, 21, 30, 60, 70, 77, 84, 86, 126
   Comus, 50
   'On the Morning of Christ's Nativity', 60
   Paradise Lost, 20, 21, 23, 24, 51, 76
miscellanies *see* anthologies
Molière, 126
Moore, John, *Zeluco*, 34

Moore, Thomas, 86
Montagu, Elizabeth, 126
Monthly Review, 18
morality, 8, 9, 10, 14, 15, 16, 17–19, 23, 24–5, 26, 27, 28–9, 31, 32, 37, 43–4, 52–3, 65, 68, 69, 77, 81, 84, 121, 123, 125, 153, 155; *see also* didactic fiction; immorality
mottos, 3, 4, 7, 96–7, 128, 133
   Tatler and *Spectator*, 8–9, 10, 12, 16, 29
   see also epigraphs; title-page mottos

novel of manners, 119

object/'it' narratives, 64, 105
Oldmixon, John, *A Complete History of Addresses*, 30

parody, 55, 85, 87, 88, 92, 108, 120, 127
Parsons, Eliza
   Castle of Wolfenbach, 65
   Errors of Education, 66n7
periodicals, 4, 7, 8–10, 16, 25–8, 29, 133, 141
Plato, 28, 29
politics, 1, 7, 66, 68, 69, 71, 73, 75, 89, 103, 104, 105, 128, 131, 138, 147, 155
Pope, Alexander, 16, 70, 78, 84, 86, 88
   translations by, 74, 75, 101
prefaces, 16, 28, 31n55, 34, 68, 78, 79, 92, 104, 116, 145; *see also* introductions
Prior, Matthew, 68, 70, 74, 84
proems, 20, 22
prologue, 20, 21, 25, 56

Quarles, Francis, *Emblemes*, 45–6
quotation, in-text, 37–9, 109; *see also* epigraphs

Radcliffe, Ann, 3, 4, 5, 11, 33–4, 36, 37, 39, 40, 43, 49, 50, 54, 55, 60, 62, 63, 65, 66, 70, 71, 73, 78, 79, 83, 85, 86, 87, 88, 91, 92, 98, 100, 103, 113, 115, 117, 118, 124, 143, 149, 155
   and sleep, 48, 49, 50, 51, 52, 54, 58, 59, 60, 84
   commonplace-book, 62–3
   A Sicilian Romance, 36, 54
   The Castles of Athlin and Dunbayne, 36, 54

INDEX

Gaston de Blondeville, 11, 36, 54–5, 61, 62, 63, 109
influence on Catherine Gore, 121, 122, 123, 126
influence on Charlotte Smith, 69–71
influence on Matthew Lewis, 83–4, 85
influence on Sir Walter Scott, 113, 115
The Italian, 33, 36, 39, 54, 55–60, 63, 83, 109, 126, 166, 167
The Mysteries of Udolpho, 2, 4, 11, 16, 36, 37, 38, 39, 48–50, 51, 52, 53–4, 55, 56, 60, 62, 63, 64, 65, 69, 71, 83, 84, 88, 92, 166, 167
The Romance of the Forest, 16, 34, 36, 37, 38, 39, 40, 41–5, 46–8, 54, 55, 56, 57, 63, 65, 69, 70, 71, 84, 87, 121, 165, 167
self-authored epigraphs, 4, 11, 54–5, 115
Reeve, Clara, *The Old English Baron*, 36
refugees, 71–2
reviews, 18, 34, 35–6, 37, 46, 60, 61, 62, 84, 94–6, 98, 114, 126, 132, 133, 138, 139, 147
and misogyny, 120, 134–5, 138
Richardson, Samuel, 32, 37, 119, 126, 138
Romantic fiction, 3, 5, 11, 12–13, 32, 33, 37, 39, 63, 65, 68, 85, 86, 87, 88, 91, 108, 114, 119, 120, 121, 152, 154
Romanticism, 3, 33, 49, 147
Rowe, Nicholas, *The Tragedy of Jane Shore*, 38
Rumbold, Kate, 3, 42, 49, 83, 88

St. John, John, *Observations on the Land Revenue of the Crown*, 35
satire, 11, 27, 66, 85, 86, 87, 88, 89, 91, 108, 122
Scott, Caroline, *A Marriage in High Life*, 125
Scott, Sir Walter, 4, 5, 6, 12, 62, 92, 94, 95, 98, 99, 100, 103, 109, 111, 115, 117, 124, 126, 130, 131, 137, 138, 141, 143, 146, 147, 149, 152, 155, 170
The Abbot, 100, 111, 112
The Antiquary, 98, 100
The Bride of Lammermoor, 6, 130
Chronicles of the Canongate (First Series), 99, 100, 101
dedications to, 114

enthusiasm for quotations and mottos, 90–1, 94, 96–7, 113
The Fair Maid of Perth, 98
The Fortunes of Nigel, 111, 112
'Glenfinlas', 90, 91
Guy Mannering, 91, 95, 98, 100, 105–8, 114, 141
The Heart of Midlothian, 99
Ivanhoe, 96, 100, 114
Kenilworth, 112–13, 114, 143
Life of Dryden, 63
The Monastery, 100, 111, 112
Peveril of the Peak, 112
politics 101, 104, 105
quoted in epigraphs, 90–1, 93–4, 130–1, 141
Redgauntlet, 94
Rob Roy, 1, 12, 109–11, 112, 115
self-authored/invented epigraphs, 1, 4, 93, 94, 99–100, 111–12, 113, 115, 126, 146–7, 154
Tales of the Crusaders, 94, 113, 114
Tales of My Landlord series, 6, 93, 94–5, 100
theatricality, 99, 101, 106, 108
Waverley, 12, 91–2, 94, 95, 100, 101–5, 106, 108, 109, 114, 152
Woodstock, 94, 113
sermons, 7–8, 9
Seward, Anna, 109
Shakespeare, William, 3, 30, 39, 42, 44, 70, 71, 84, 85, 88, 97, 102, 121, 122, 126, 131–2, 155
A Midsummer Night's Dream, 125
Anthony and Cleopatra, 122–3
As You Like It, 86
David Garrick's adaptation of, 98
Hamlet, 53, 59, 61, 72
Henry IV Part Two, 127
Henry V, 73, 127, 129
Julius Caesar, 53
Macbeth, 41, 42, 43, 47, 59–60, 77, 83, 121, 122
Measure for Measure, 52, 81, 99, 104
Much Ado About Nothing, 103, 108
Richard III, 33, 122
Romeo and Juliet, 58–9, 103
Twelfth Night (Malvolio), 95
The Winter's Tale, 106, 108

229

Sheridan, Richard Brinsley
  Critic, The, 108–9
  Duenna, The, 87
silver-fork novels, 119, 120, 121, 123, 124, 133
Smith, Charlotte, 5, 11, 12, 34, 66, 67, 68, 69, 70, 71, 77, 78, 79, 80, 86, 88, 91, 100, 155
  The Banished Man, 11, 66, 67–71, 72–7, 79, 80, 81, 85, 89, 167
  Marchmont, 72, 78–9, 80, 89, 168
  Montalbert, 77, 78, 79
  The Old Manor House, 66
  Rural Walks, 78, 79
  politics, 66, 68–9, 71, 73, 75, 76, 89, 155
  The Young Philosopher, 72, 78, 80, 89, 169
Smith, Sir James Edward, 148
Socrates, 29
Spectator, 8–9, 10, 16, 25–7, 29, 31, 126, 133
Spence, Elizabeth Isabella, 129
Spenser, Edmund, 25, 28, 31, 32
  The Faerie Queene, 10, 16, 20, 21–2, 24
Staël, Madame de, 128
Steele, Richard, 8, 9
Sterne, Laurence, *The Life and Opinions of Tristram Shandy, Gentleman*, 66
sublime, the, 37, 50–3, 61, 62
subtitles, 31, 78, 112, 114, 116, 144, 147

Swift, Jonathan, 16, 30, 92
Swinburne, Henry, *Travels in the Two Sicilies*, 56

Tatler, 8, 9, 16
Tennyson, Alfred Lord, 149
terror, 36, 50, 51–3, 54, 60, 62, 81
Thackeray, William, 5, 118, 120, 154
Thomson, James, 39, 84, 88
  The Seasons, 35, 38–9, 47
Thomson, Katherine, 118, 143, 155
  Widows and Widowers, 116–17
Tillotson, Rev. John, 8, 9
title pages, 4, 34, 37, 49, 57, 67, 80, 81, 85, 95
title-page mottos, 4, 66, 67, 80, 82, 94

Virgil, 17, 20, 28, 30, 100
Voltaire, 70
  Amélie ou le Duc de Foix, 74

Walpole, Horace
  The Castle of Otranto, 36
  The Mysterious Mother, 44, 58
Warton, Thomas, 'The Suicide', 47, 48
Whole Duty of Man, The, 18
Williams, Helen Maria
  Julia, A Novel, 37
  Poems on Various Subjects, 102
Wordsworth, William, 109, 145

Young, Edward, 30

www.ingramcontent.com/pod-product-compliance
Lightning Source LLC
LaVergne TN
LVHW021603060925
820435LV00004B/60